T0215651

Undergraduate Topics in Computer Science

'Undergraduate Topics in Computer Science' (UTiCS) delivers high-quality instructional content for undergraduates studying in all areas of computing and information science. From core foundational and theoretical material to final-year topics and applications, UTiCS books take a fresh, concise, and modern approach and are ideal for self-study or for a one- or two-semester course. The texts are all authored by established experts in their fields, reviewed by an international advisory board, and contain numerous examples and problems, many of which include fully worked solutions.

More information about this series at http://www.springer.com/series/7592

Max Bramer

Principles of Data Mining

Fourth Edition

 Springer

Prof. Max Bramer
School of Computing
University of Portsmouth
Portsmouth, Hampshire, UK

ISSN 1863-7310   ISSN 2197-1781 (electronic)
Undergraduate Topics in Computer Science
ISBN 978-1-4471-7492-9   ISBN 978-1-4471-7493-6 (eBook)
DOI 10.1007/978-1-4471-7493-6

About This Book

This book is designed to be suitable for an introductory course at either undergraduate or masters level. It can be used as a textbook for a taught unit in a degree programme on potentially any of a wide range of subjects including Computer Science, Business Studies, Marketing, Artificial Intelligence, Bioinformatics and Forensic Science. It is also suitable for use as a self-study book for those in technical or management positions who wish to gain an understanding of the subject that goes beyond the superficial. It goes well beyond the generalities of many introductory books on Data Mining but — unlike many other books — you will not need a degree and/or considerable fluency in Mathematics to understand it.

Mathematics is a language in which it is possible to express very complex and sophisticated ideas. Unfortunately it is a language in which 99% of the human race is not fluent, although many people have some basic knowledge of it from early experiences (not always pleasant ones) at school. The author is a former Mathematician who now prefers to communicate in plain English wherever possible and believes that a good example is worth a hundred mathematical symbols.

One of the author's aims in writing this book has been to eliminate mathematical formalism in the interests of clarity wherever possible. Unfortunately it has not been possible to bury mathematical notation entirely. A 'refresher' of everything you need to know to begin studying the book is given in Appendix A. It should be quite familiar to anyone who has studied Mathematics at school level. Everything else will be explained as we come to it. If you have difficulty following the notation in some places, you can usually safely ignore it, just concentrating on the results and the detailed examples given. For those who would like to pursue the mathematical underpinnings of Data Mining in greater depth, a number of additional texts are listed in Appendix C.

No introductory book on Data Mining can take you to research level in the subject — the days for that have long passed. This book will give you a good grounding in the principal techniques without attempting to show you this year's latest fashions, which in most cases will have been superseded by the time the book gets into your hands. Once you know the basic methods, there are many sources you can use to find the latest developments in the field. Some of these are listed in Appendix C. The other appendices include information about the main datasets used in the examples in the book, many of which are of interest in their own right and are readily available for use in your own projects if you wish, and a glossary of the technical terms used in the book.

Self-assessment Exercises are included for each chapter to enable you to check your understanding. Specimen solutions are given in Appendix E.

Note on the Fourth Edition

Since the first edition there has been a vast and ever-accelerating increase in the volume of data available for data mining. According to IBM (in 2016) 2.5 billion billion bytes of data is produced every day from sensors, mobile devices, online transactions and social networks, with 90 percent of the data in the world having been created in the last two years alone. Today the amount of healthcare data available in the world is estimated as over 2 trillion gigabytes. To reflect the growing popularity of 'deep learning' a new final chapter has been added which gives a detailed introduction to one of the most important types of neural net and shows how it can be applied to classification tasks.

Acknowledgements

I would like to thank my daughter Bryony for drawing many of the more complex diagrams and for general advice on design, Dr. Frederic Stahl for advice on Chapters 21 and 22 and my wife Dawn for her very valuable comments on draft chapters and for preparing the index. The responsibility for any errors that may have crept into the final version remains with me.

Max Bramer
Emeritus Professor of Information Technology
University of Portsmouth, UK
May 2020

Contents

1
Introduction to Data Mining

1.1 The Data Explosion

Modern computer systems are accumulating data at an almost unimaginable rate and from a very wide variety of sources: from point-of-sale machines in the high street to machines logging every bank cash withdrawal and credit card transaction, to Earth observation satellites in space, and with an ever-growing volume of information available from social media and the Internet.

Some examples will serve to give an indication of the volumes of data involved (by the time you read this, some of the numbers will have increased considerably):

- The current NASA Earth observation satellites generate a terabyte (i.e. 10^{12} bytes) of data *every day*. This is more than the total amount of data ever transmitted by all previous observation satellites.

- Biologists are generating around 15 million gigabytes of gene sequence data every year.

- Many companies maintain large Data Warehouses of customer transactions. A fairly small data warehouse might contain more than a hundred million transactions.

- There are vast amounts of data recorded every day on automatic recording devices, such as credit card transaction files and web logs, as well as non-symbolic data such as CCTV recordings.

- There are estimated to be over 1.5 billion websites, some extremely large.

- There are over 2.4 billion active users of Facebook, with an estimated 350 million photographs uploaded every day.

© Springer-Verlag London Ltd., part of Springer Nature 2020
M. Bramer, *Principles of Data Mining*, Undergraduate Topics
in Computer Science, DOI 10.1007/978-1-4471-7493-6_1

Alongside advances in storage technology, which increasingly make it possible to store such vast amounts of data at relatively low cost whether in commercial data warehouses, scientific research laboratories or elsewhere, has come a growing realisation that such data contains buried within it knowledge that can be critical to a company's growth or decline, knowledge that could lead to important discoveries in science, knowledge that could enable us accurately to predict the weather and natural disasters, knowledge that could enable us to identify the causes of and possible cures for lethal illnesses, knowledge that could literally mean the difference between life and death. Yet the huge volumes involved mean that most of this data is merely stored — never to be examined in more than the most superficial way, if at all. It has rightly been said that the world is becoming 'data rich but knowledge poor'.

As well as all the stored data, data streams of over a million records a day, potentially continuing forever, are now commonplace.

Machine learning technology, some of it very long established, has the potential to solve the problem of the tidal wave of data that is flooding around organisations, governments and individuals.

1.2 Knowledge Discovery

Knowledge Discovery has been defined as the 'non-trivial extraction of implicit, previously unknown and potentially useful information from data'. It is a process of which data mining forms just one part, albeit a central one.

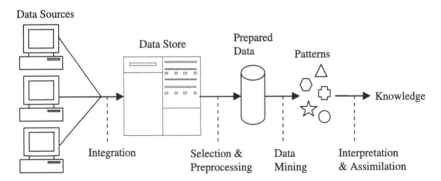

Figure 1.1 The Knowledge Discovery Process

Figure 1.1 shows a slightly idealised version of the complete knowledge discovery process.

Data comes in, possibly from many sources. It is integrated and placed in some common data store. Part of it is then taken and pre-processed into a standard format. This 'prepared data' is then passed to a data mining algorithm which produces an output in the form of rules or some other kind of 'patterns'. These are then interpreted to give—and this is the Holy Grail for knowledge discovery—new and potentially useful knowledge.

This brief description makes it clear that although the data mining algorithms, which are the principal subject of this book, are central to knowledge discovery they are not the whole story. The pre-processing of the data and the interpretation (as opposed to the blind use) of the results are both of great importance. They are skilled tasks that are far more of an art (or a skill learnt from experience) than an exact science. Although they will both be touched on in this book, the algorithms of the data mining stage of knowledge discovery will be its prime concern.

1.3 Applications of Data Mining

There is a rapidly growing body of successful applications in a wide range of areas as diverse as:

- analysing satellite imagery
- analysis of organic compounds
- automatic abstracting
- bioinformatics
- credit card fraud detection
- criminal investigation
- customer relationship management
- electric load prediction
- financial forecasting
- fraud detection
- healthcare
- market basket analysis
- medical diagnosis
- predicting share of television audiences
- product design
- real estate valuation
- targeted marketing
- text summarisation
- thermal power plant optimisation
- toxic hazard analysis
- weather forecasting

and many more.

Some examples of applications (potential or actual) are:

- a supermarket chain mines its customer transactions data to optimise targeting of high value customers

- a credit card company can use its data warehouse of customer transactions for fraud detection

- a major hotel chain can use survey databases to identify attributes of a 'high-value' prospect

- predicting the probability of default for consumer loan applications by improving the ability to predict bad loans

- reducing fabrication flaws in VLSI chips

- data mining systems can sift through vast quantities of data collected during the semiconductor fabrication process to identify conditions that are causing yield problems

- predicting audience share for television programmes, allowing television executives to arrange show schedules to maximise market share and increase advertising revenues

- predicting the probability that a cancer patient will respond to chemotherapy, thus reducing health-care costs without affecting quality of care

- analysing motion-capture data for elderly people

- trend mining and visualisation in social networks

- analysing data from a face recognition system to locate a suspected criminal in a crowd

- analysing information about a range of drugs and natural compounds to identify significant candidates for new antibiotics

- analysing MRI images to identify possible brain tumours.

Applications can be divided into four main types: classification, numerical prediction, association and clustering. Each of these is explained briefly below. However first we need to distinguish between two types of data.

1.4 Labelled and Unlabelled Data

In general we have a dataset of examples (called *instances*), each of which comprises the values of a number of variables, which in data mining are often called *attributes*. There are two types of data, which are treated in radically different ways.

For the first type there is a specially designated attribute and the aim is to use the data given to predict the value of that attribute for instances that have not yet been seen. Data of this kind is called *labelled*. Data mining using labelled data is known as *supervised learning*. If the designated attribute is *categorical*, i.e. it must take one of a number of distinct values such as 'very good', 'good' or 'poor', or (in an object recognition application) 'car', 'bicycle', 'person', 'bus' or 'taxi' the task is called *classification*. If the designated attribute is numerical, e.g. the expected sale price of a house or the opening price of a share on tomorrow's stock market, the task is called *regression*.

Data that does not have any specially designated attribute is called *unlabelled*. Data mining of unlabelled data is known as *unsupervised learning*. Here the aim is simply to extract the most information we can from the data available.

1.5 Supervised Learning: Classification

Classification is one of the most common applications for data mining. It corresponds to a task that occurs frequently in everyday life. For example, a hospital may want to classify medical patients into those who are at high, medium or low risk of acquiring a certain illness, an opinion polling company may wish to classify people interviewed into those who are likely to vote for each of a number of political parties or are undecided, or we may wish to classify a student project as distinction, merit, pass or fail.

This example shows a typical situation (Figure 1.2). We have a dataset in the form of a table containing students' grades on five subjects (the values of attributes SoftEng, ARIN, HCI, CSA and Project) and their overall degree classifications. The row of dots indicates that a number of rows have been omitted in the interests of simplicity. We want to find some way of predicting the classification for other students given only their grade 'profiles'.

There are several ways we can do this, including the following.

Nearest Neighbour Matching. This method relies on identifying (say) the five examples that are 'closest' in some sense to an unclassified one. If the five 'nearest neighbours' have grades Second, First, Second, Second and Second we might reasonably conclude that the new instance should be classified as 'Second'.

Classification Rules. We look for rules that we can use to predict the classification of an unseen instance, for example:

SoftEng	ARIN	HCI	CSA	Project	Class
A	B	A	B	B	Second
A	B	B	B	B	Second
B	A	A	B	A	Second
A	A	A	A	B	First
A	A	B	B	A	First
B	A	A	B	B	Second
....	....	....	....	....	....
A	A	B	A	B	First

Figure 1.2   Degree Classification Data

IF SoftEng = A AND Project = A THEN Class = First
IF SoftEng = A AND Project = B AND ARIN = B THEN Class = Second
IF SoftEng = B THEN Class = Second

Classification Tree.   One way of generating classification rules is via an intermediate tree-like structure called a *classification tree* or a *decision tree.*

Figure 1.3 shows a possible decision tree corresponding to the degree classification data.

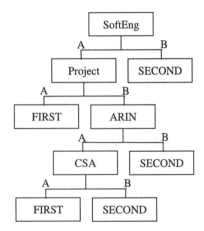

Figure 1.3   Decision Tree for Degree Classification Data

1.6 Supervised Learning: Numerical Prediction

Classification is one form of prediction, where the value to be predicted is a label. Numerical prediction (often called *regression*) is another. In this case we wish to predict a numerical value, such as a company's profits or a share price.

A very popular way of doing this is to use a *Neural Network* as shown in Figure 1.4 (often called by the simplified name *Neural Net*).

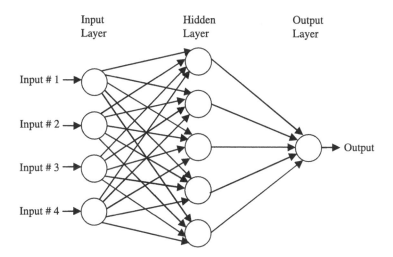

Figure 1.4 A Neural Network

This is a complex modelling technique based on a model of a human neuron. A neural net is given a set of inputs and is used to predict one or more outputs.

One of the most widely used types of neural network is discussed in Chapter 23. However the focus is primarily on classification rather than numerical prediction.

1.7 Unsupervised Learning: Association Rules

Sometimes we wish to use a training set to find any relationship that exists amongst the values of variables, generally in the form of rules known as *association rules*. There are many possible association rules derivable from any given dataset, most of them of little or no value, so it is usual for association rules to be stated with some additional information indicating how reliable they are, for example:

IF variable_1 > 85 and switch_6 = open
THEN variable_23 < 47.5 and switch_8 = closed (probability = 0.8)

A common form of this type of application is called 'market basket analysis'. If we know the purchases made by all the customers at a store for say a week, we may be able to find relationships that will help the store market its products more effectively in the future. For example, the rule

IF cheese AND milk THEN bread (probability = 0.7)

indicates that 70% of the customers who buy cheese and milk also buy bread, so it would be sensible to move the bread closer to the cheese and milk counter, if customer convenience were the prime concern, or to separate them to encourage impulse buying of other products if profit were more important.

1.8 Unsupervised Learning: Clustering

Clustering algorithms examine data to find groups of items that are similar. For example, an insurance company might group customers according to income, age, types of policy purchased or prior claims experience. In a fault diagnosis application, electrical faults might be grouped according to the values of certain key variables (Figure 1.5).

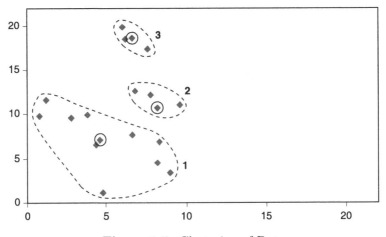

Figure 1.5 Clustering of Data

2
Data for Data Mining

Data for data mining comes in many forms: from computer files typed in by human operators, business information in SQL or some other standard database format, information recorded automatically by equipment such as fault logging devices, to streams of binary data transmitted from satellites. For purposes of data mining (and for the remainder of this book) we will assume that the data takes a particular standard form which is described in the next section. We will look at some of the practical problems of data preparation in Section 2.3.

2.1 Standard Formulation

We will assume that for any data mining application we have a *universe of objects* that are of interest. This rather grandiose term often refers to a collection of people, perhaps all human beings alive or dead, or possibly all the patients at a hospital, but may also be applied to, say, all dogs in England, or to inanimate objects such as all train journeys from London to Birmingham, all the rocks on the moon or all the pages stored in the World Wide Web.

The universe of objects is normally very large and we have only a small part of it. Usually we want to extract information from the data available to us that we hope is applicable to the large volume of data that we have not yet seen.

Each object is described by a number of *variables* that correspond to its properties. In data mining variables are often called *attributes*. We will use both terms in this book.

© Springer-Verlag London Ltd., part of Springer Nature 2020
M. Bramer, *Principles of Data Mining*, Undergraduate Topics
in Computer Science, DOI 10.1007/978-1-4471-7493-6_2

The set of variable values corresponding to each of the objects is called a *record* or (more commonly) an *instance*. The complete set of data available to us for an application is called a *dataset*. A dataset is often depicted as a table, with each row representing an instance. Each column contains the value of one of the variables (attributes) for each of the instances. A typical example of a dataset is the 'degrees' data given in the Introduction (Figure 2.1).

SoftEng	ARIN	HCI	CSA	Project	Class
A	B	A	B	B	Second
A	B	B	B	B	Second
B	A	A	B	A	Second
A	A	A	A	B	First
A	A	B	B	A	First
B	A	A	B	B	Second
....	....	....	....	....	....
A	A	B	A	B	First

Figure 2.1   The Degrees Dataset

This dataset is an example of *labelled* data, where one attribute is given special significance and the aim is to predict its value. In this book we will give this attribute the standard name 'class'. When there is no such significant attribute we call the data *unlabelled*.

2.2 Types of Variable

In general there are many types of variable that can be used to measure the properties of an object. A lack of understanding of the differences between the various types can lead to problems with any form of data analysis. At least six main types of variable can be distinguished.

Nominal Variables

A variable used to put objects into categories, e.g. the name or colour of an object. A nominal variable may be numerical in form, but the numerical values have no mathematical interpretation. For example we might label 10 people as numbers $1, 2, 3, \ldots, 10$, but any arithmetic with such values, e.g. $1 + 2 = 3$

would be meaningless. They are simply labels. A **classification** can be viewed as a nominal variable which has been designated as of particular importance.

Binary Variables

A binary variable is a special case of a nominal variable that takes only two possible values: true or false, 1 or 0 etc.

Ordinal Variables

Ordinal variables are similar to nominal variables, except that an ordinal variable has values that can be arranged in a meaningful order, e.g. small, medium, large.

Integer Variables

Integer variables are ones that take values that are genuine integers, for example 'number of children'. Unlike nominal variables that are numerical in form, arithmetic with integer variables is meaningful (1 child + 2 children = 3 children etc.).

Interval-scaled Variables

Interval-scaled variables are variables that take numerical values which are measured at equal intervals from a zero point or origin. However the origin does not imply a true absence of the measured characteristic. Two well-known examples of interval-scaled variables are the Fahrenheit and Celsius temperature scales. To say that one temperature measured in degrees Celsius is greater than another or greater than a constant value such as 25 is clearly meaningful, but to say that one temperature measured in degrees Celsius is twice another is meaningless. It is true that a temperature of 20 degrees is twice as far from the zero value as 10 degrees, but the zero value has been selected arbitrarily and does not imply 'absence of temperature'. If the temperatures are converted to an equivalent scale, say degrees Fahrenheit, the 'twice' relationship will no longer apply.

Ratio-scaled Variables

Ratio-scaled variables are similar to interval-scaled variables except that the zero point does reflect the absence of the measured characteristic, for example Kelvin temperature and molecular weight. In the former case the zero value corresponds to the lowest possible temperature 'absolute zero', so a temperature of 20 degrees Kelvin is twice one of 10 degrees Kelvin. A weight of 10 kg is twice one of 5 kg, a price of 100 dollars is twice a price of 50 dollars etc.

2.2.1 Categorical and Continuous Attributes

Although the distinction between different categories of variable can be important in some cases, many practical data mining systems divide attributes into just two types:

- **categorical** corresponding to nominal, binary and ordinal variables

- **continuous** corresponding to integer, interval-scaled and ratio-scaled variables.

This convention will be followed in this book. For many applications it is helpful to have a third category of attribute, the 'ignore' attribute, corresponding to variables that are of no significance for the application, for example the name of a patient in a hospital or the serial number of an instance, but which we do not wish to (or are unable to) delete from the dataset.

It is important to choose methods that are appropriate to the types of variable stored for a particular application. The methods described in this book are applicable to categorical and continuous attributes as defined above. There are other types of variable to which they would not be applicable without modification, for example any variable that is measured on a logarithmic scale. Two examples of logarithmic scales are the Richter scale for measuring earthquakes (an earthquake of magnitude 6 is 10 times more severe than one of magnitude 5, 100 times more severe than one of magnitude 4 etc.) and the Stellar Magnitude Scale for measuring the brightness of stars viewed by an observer on Earth.

2.3 Data Preparation

Although this book is about data mining not data preparation, some general comments about the latter may be helpful.

For many applications the data can simply be extracted from a database in the form described in Section 2.1, perhaps using a standard access method such as ODBC. However, for some applications the hardest task may be to get the data into a standard form in which it can be analysed. For example data values may have to be extracted from textual output generated by a fault logging system or (in a crime analysis application) extracted from transcripts of interviews with witnesses. The amount of effort required to do this may be considerable.

2.3.1 Data Cleaning

Even when the data is in the standard form it cannot be assumed that it is error free. In real-world datasets erroneous values can be recorded for a variety of reasons, including measurement errors, subjective judgements and malfunctioning or misuse of automatic recording equipment.

Erroneous values can be divided into those which are possible values of the attribute and those which are not. Although usage of the term *noise* varies, in this book we will take a *noisy* value to mean one that is valid for the dataset, but is incorrectly recorded. For example the number 69.72 may accidentally be entered as 6.972, or a categorical attribute value such as *brown* may accidentally be recorded as another of the possible values, such as *blue*. Noise of this kind is a perpetual problem with real-world data.

A far smaller problem arises with noisy values that are invalid for the dataset, such as 69.7X for 6.972 or *bbrown* for *brown*. We will consider these to be *invalid values*, not noise. An invalid value can easily be detected and either corrected or rejected.

It is hard to see even very 'obvious' errors in the values of a variable when they are 'buried' amongst say 100,000 other values. In attempting to 'clean up' data it is helpful to have a range of software tools available, especially to give an overall visual impression of the data, when some anomalous values or unexpected concentrations of values may stand out. However, in the absence of special software, even some very basic analysis of the values of variables may be helpful. Simply sorting the values into ascending order (which for fairly small datasets can be accomplished using just a standard spreadsheet) may reveal unexpected results. For example:

– A numerical variable may only take six different values, all widely separated. It would probably be best to treat this as a categorical variable rather than a continuous one.

– All the values of a variable may be identical. The variable should be treated as an 'ignore' attribute.

– All the values of a variable except one may be identical. It is then necessary to decide whether the one different value is an error or a significantly different value. In the latter case the variable should be treated as a categorical attribute with just two values.

– There may be some values that are outside the normal range of the variable. For example, the values of a continuous attribute may all be in the range 200 to 5000 except for the highest three values which are 22654.8, 38597 and 44625.7. If the data values were entered by hand a reasonable guess is that the first and third of these abnormal values resulted from pressing the initial key twice by accident and the second one is the result of leaving out the decimal point. If the data were recorded automatically it may be that the equipment malfunctioned. This may not be the case but the values should certainly be investigated.

– We may observe that some values occur an abnormally large number of times. For example if we were analysing data about users who registered for a web-based service by filling in an online form we might notice that the 'country' part of their addresses took the value 'Albania' in 10% of cases. It may be that we have found a service that is particularly attractive to inhabitants of that country. Another possibility is that users who registered either failed to choose from the choices in the country field, causing a (not very sensible) default value to be taken, or did not wish to supply their country details and simply selected the first value in a list of options. In either case it seems likely that the rest of the address data provided for those users may be suspect too.

– If we are analysing the results of an online survey collected in 2002, we may notice that the age recorded for a high proportion of the respondents was 72. This seems unlikely, especially if the survey was of student satisfaction, say. A possible interpretation for this is that the survey had a 'date of birth' field, with subfields for day, month and year and that many of the respondents did not bother to override the default values of 01 (day), 01 (month) and 1930 (year). A poorly designed program then converted the date of birth to an age of 72 before storing it in the database.

It is important to issue a word of caution at this point. Care is needed when dealing with anomalous values such as 22654.8, 38597 and 44625.7 in one of the examples above. They may simply be errors as suggested. Alternatively they may be *outliers*, i.e. genuine values that are significantly different from the others. The recognition of outliers and their significance may be the key to major discoveries, especially in fields such as medicine and physics, so we need to be careful before simply discarding them or adjusting them back to 'normal' values.

2.4 Missing Values

In many real-world datasets data values are not recorded for all attributes. This can happen simply because there are some attributes that are not applicable for some instances (e.g. certain medical data may only be meaningful for female patients or patients over a certain age). The best approach here may be to divide the dataset into two (or more) parts, e.g. treating male and female patients separately.

It can also happen that there are attribute values that should be recorded that are missing. This can occur for several reasons, for example

– a malfunction of the equipment used to record the data

– a data collection form to which additional fields were added after some data had been collected

– information that could not be obtained, e.g. about a hospital patient.

There are several possible strategies for dealing with missing values. Two of the most commonly used are as follows.

2.4.1 Discard Instances

This is the simplest strategy: delete all instances where there is at least one missing value and use the remainder.

This strategy is a very conservative one, which has the advantage of avoiding introducing any data errors. Its disadvantage is that discarding data may damage the reliability of the results derived from the data. Although it may be worth trying when the proportion of missing values is small, it is not recommended in general. It is clearly not usable when all or a high proportion of all the instances have missing values.

2.4.2 Replace by Most Frequent/Average Value

A less cautious strategy is to estimate each of the missing values using the values that are present in the dataset.

A straightforward but effective way of doing this for a categorical attribute is to use its most frequently occurring (non-missing) value. This is easy to justify if the attribute values are very unbalanced. For example if attribute X has possible values a, b and c which occur in proportions 80%, 15% and 5% respectively, it seems reasonable to estimate any missing values of attribute X by the value a. If the values are more evenly distributed, say in proportions 40%, 30% and 30%, the validity of this approach is much less clear.

In the case of continuous attributes it is likely that no specific numerical value will occur more than a small number of times. In this case the estimate used is generally the *average* value.

Replacing a missing value by an estimate of its true value may of course introduce noise into the data, but if the proportion of missing values for a variable is small, this is not likely to have more than a small effect on the results derived from the data. However, it is important to stress that if a variable value is not meaningful for a given instance or set of instances any attempt to replace the 'missing' values by an estimate is likely to lead to invalid results. Like many of the methods in this book the 'replace by most frequent/average value' strategy has to be used with care.

There are other approaches to dealing with missing values, for example using the 'association rule' methods described in Chapter 16 to make a more reliable estimate of each missing value. However, as is generally the case in this field, there is no one method that is more reliable than all the others for all possible datasets and in practice there is little alternative to experimenting with a range of alternative strategies to find the one that gives the best results for a dataset under consideration.

2.5 Reducing the Number of Attributes

In some data mining application areas the availability of ever-larger storage capacity at a steadily reducing unit price has led to large numbers of attribute values being stored for every instance, e.g. information about all the purchases made by a supermarket customer for three months or a large amount of detailed information about every patient in a hospital. For some datasets there can be substantially more attributes than there are instances, perhaps as many as 10 or even 100 to one.

Although it is tempting to store more and more information about each instance (especially as it avoids making hard decisions about what information is really needed) it risks being self-defeating. Suppose we have 10,000 pieces of information about each supermarket customer and want to predict which customers will buy a new brand of dog food. The number of attributes of any relevance to this is probably very small. At best the many irrelevant attributes will place an unnecessary computational overhead on any data mining algorithm. At worst, they may cause the algorithm to give poor results.

Of course, supermarkets, hospitals and other data collectors will reply that they do not necessarily know what is relevant or will come to be recognised as relevant in the future. It is safer for them to record everything than risk throwing away important information.

Although faster processing speeds and larger memories may make it possible to process ever larger numbers of attributes, this is inevitably a losing struggle in the long term. Even if it were not, when the number of attributes becomes large, there is always a risk that the results obtained will have only superficial accuracy and will actually be less reliable than if only a small proportion of the attributes were used — a case of 'more means less'.

There are several ways in which the number of attributes (or 'features') can be reduced before a dataset is processed. The term *feature reduction* or *dimension reduction* is generally used for this process. We will return to this topic in Chapter 10.

2.6 The UCI Repository of Datasets

Most of the commercial datasets used by companies for data mining are — unsurprisingly — not available for others to use. However there are a number of 'libraries' of datasets that are readily available for downloading from the World Wide Web free of charge by anyone.

The best known of these is the 'Repository' of datasets maintained by the University of California at Irvine, generally known as the 'UCI Repository' [1]. The URL for the Repository is `https://archive.ics.uci.edu/ml/`. It contains over 350 datasets on topics as diverse as predicting the age of abalone from physical measurements, predicting good and bad credit risks, classifying patients with a variety of medical conditions and learning concepts from the sensor data of a mobile robot. Some datasets are complete, i.e. include all possible instances, but most are relatively small samples from a much larger number of possible instances. Datasets with missing values and noise are included.

The UCI site also has links to other repositories of both datasets and programs, maintained by a variety of organisations such as the (US) National Space Science Center, the US Bureau of Census and the University of Toronto.

The datasets in the UCI Repository were collected principally to enable data mining algorithms to be compared on a standard range of datasets. There are many new algorithms published each year and it is standard practice to state their performance on some of the better-known datasets in the UCI Repository. Several of these datasets will be described later in this book.

The availability of standard datasets is also very helpful for new users of data mining packages who can gain familiarisation using datasets with published performance results before applying the facilities to their own datasets.

In recent years a potential weakness of establishing such a widely used set of standard datasets has become apparent. In the great majority of cases the datasets in the UCI Repository give good results when processed by standard algorithms of the kind described in this book. Datasets that lead to poor results tend to be associated with unsuccessful projects and so may not be added to the Repository. The achievement of good results with selected datasets from the Repository is no guarantee of the success of a method with new data, but experimentation with such datasets can be a valuable step in the development of new methods.

A welcome relatively recent development is the creation of the UCI 'Knowledge Discovery in Databases Archive' at `http://kdd.ics.uci.edu`. This contains a range of large and complex datasets as a challenge to the data mining research community to scale up its algorithms as the size of stored datasets, especially commercial ones, inexorably rises.

2.7 Chapter Summary

This chapter introduces the standard formulation for the data input to data mining algorithms that will be assumed throughout this book. It goes on to distinguish between different types of variable and to consider issues relating to the preparation of data prior to use, particularly the presence of missing data values and noise. The UCI Repository of datasets is introduced.

2.8 Self-assessment Exercises for Chapter 2

Specimen solutions to self-assessment exercises are given in Appendix E.

1. What is the difference between labelled and unlabelled data?

2. The following information is held in an employee database.

Name, Date of Birth, Sex, Weight, Height, Marital Status, Number of Children

What is the type of each variable?

3. Give two ways of dealing with missing data values.

Reference

[1] Dua, D., & Graff, C. (2019). UCI Machine Learning Repository. Irvine: University of California, School of Information and Computer Science. https://archive.ics.uci.edu/ml/.

3

Introduction to Classification: Naïve Bayes and Nearest Neighbour

3.1 What Is Classification?

Classification is a task that occurs very frequently in everyday life. Essentially it involves dividing up objects so that each is assigned to one of a number of mutually exhaustive and exclusive categories known as *classes*. The term 'mutually exhaustive and exclusive' simply means that each object must be assigned to precisely one class, i.e. never to more than one and never to no class at all.

Many practical decision-making tasks can be formulated as classification problems, i.e. assigning people or objects to one of a number of categories, for example

- customers who are likely to buy or not buy a particular product in a super-market

- people who are at high, medium or low risk of acquiring a certain illness

- student projects worthy of a distinction, merit, pass or fail grade

- objects on a radar display which correspond to vehicles, people, buildings or trees

- people who closely resemble, slightly resemble or do not resemble someone seen committing a crime

© Springer-Verlag London Ltd., part of Springer Nature 2020
M. Bramer, *Principles of Data Mining*, Undergraduate Topics
in Computer Science, DOI 10.1007/978-1-4471-7493-6_3

– houses that are likely to rise in value, fall in value or have an unchanged value in 12 months' time

– people who are at high, medium or low risk of a car accident in the next 12 months

– people who are likely to vote for each of a number of political parties (or none)

– the likelihood of rain the next day for a weather forecast (very likely, likely, unlikely, very unlikely).

We have already seen an example of a (fictitious) classification task, the 'degree classification' example, in the Introduction.

In this chapter we introduce two classification algorithms: one that can be used when all the attributes are categorical, the other when all the attributes are continuous. In the following chapters we come on to algorithms for generating classification trees and rules (also illustrated in the Introduction).

3.2 Naïve Bayes Classifiers

In this section we look at a method of classification that does not use rules, a decision tree or any other explicit representation of the classifier. Rather, it uses the branch of Mathematics known as *probability theory* to find the most likely of the possible classifications.

The significance of the first word of the title of this section will be explained later. The second word refers to the Reverend Thomas Bayes (1702–1761), an English Presbyterian minister and Mathematician whose publications included "Divine Benevolence, or an Attempt to Prove That the Principal End of the Divine Providence and Government is the Happiness of His Creatures" as well as pioneering work on probability. He is credited as the first Mathematician to use probability in an inductive fashion.

A detailed discussion of probability theory would be substantially outside the scope of this book. However the mathematical notion of probability corresponds fairly closely to the meaning of the word in everyday life.

The *probability* of an *event*, e.g. that the 6.30 p.m. train from London to your local station arrives on time, is a number from 0 to 1 inclusive, with 0 indicating 'impossible' and 1 indicating 'certain'. A probability of 0.7 implies that if we conducted a long series of *trials*, e.g. if we recorded the arrival time of the 6.30 p.m. train day by day for N days, we would expect the train to be on time on $0.7 \times N$ days. The longer the series of trials the more reliable this estimate is likely to be.

Usually we are not interested in just one event but in a set of alternative possible events, which are *mutually exclusive* and *exhaustive*, meaning that one and only one must always occur.

In the train example, we might define four mutually exclusive and exhaustive events

$E1$ – train cancelled
$E2$ – train ten minutes or more late
$E3$ – train less than ten minutes late
$E4$ – train on time or early.

The probability of an event is usually indicated by a capital letter P, so we might have

$P(E1) = 0.05$
$P(E2) = 0.1$
$P(E3) = 0.15$
$P(E4) = 0.7$

(Read as 'the probability of event $E1$ is 0.05' etc.)

Each of these probabilities is between 0 and 1 inclusive, as it has to be to qualify as a probability. They also satisfy a second important condition: the sum of the four probabilities has to be 1, because precisely one of the events must always occur. In this case

$$P(E1) + P(E2) + P(E3) + P(E4) = 1$$

In general, the sum of the probabilities of a set of mutually exclusive and exhaustive events must always be 1.

Generally we are not in a position to know the true probability of an event occurring. To do so for the train example we would have to record the train's arrival time for all possible days on which it is scheduled to run, then count the number of times events $E1$, $E2$, $E3$ and $E4$ occur and divide by the total number of days, to give the probabilities of the four events. In practice this is often prohibitively difficult or impossible to do, especially (as in this example) if the trials may potentially go on forever. Instead we keep records for a *sample* of say 100 days, count the number of times $E1$, $E2$, $E3$ and $E4$ occur, divide by 100 (the number of days) to give the frequency of the four events and use these as estimates of the four probabilities.

For the purposes of the classification problems discussed in this book, the 'events' are that an instance has a particular classification. Note that classifications satisfy the 'mutually exclusive and exhaustive' requirement.

The outcome of each trial is recorded in one row of a table. Each row must have one and only one classification.

For classification tasks, the usual terminology is to call a table (dataset) such as Figure 3.1 a *training set*. Each row of the training set is called an *instance*. An instance comprises the values of a number of attributes and the corresponding classification.

The training set constitutes the results of a sample of trials that we can use to predict the classification of other (unclassified) instances.

Suppose that our training set consists of 20 instances, each recording the value of four attributes as well as the classification. We will use classifications: *cancelled, very late, late* and *on time* to correspond to the events $E1$, $E2$, $E3$ and $E4$ described previously.

day	season	wind	rain	class
weekday	spring	none	none	on time
weekday	winter	none	slight	on time
weekday	winter	none	slight	on time
weekday	winter	high	heavy	late
saturday	summer	normal	none	on time
weekday	autumn	normal	none	very late
holiday	summer	high	slight	on time
sunday	summer	normal	none	on time
weekday	winter	high	heavy	very late
weekday	summer	none	slight	on time
saturday	spring	high	heavy	cancelled
weekday	summer	high	slight	on time
saturday	winter	normal	none	late
weekday	summer	high	none	on time
weekday	winter	normal	heavy	very late
saturday	autumn	high	slight	on time
weekday	autumn	none	heavy	on time
holiday	spring	normal	slight	on time
weekday	spring	normal	none	on time
weekday	spring	normal	slight	on time

Figure 3.1 The *train* Dataset

How should we use probabilities to find the most likely classification for an unseen instance such as the one below?

weekday	winter	high	heavy	????

One straightforward (but flawed) way is just to look at the frequency of each of the classifications in the training set and choose the most common one. In this case the most common classification is *on time*, so we would choose that.

The flaw in this approach is, of course, that all unseen instances will be classified in the same way, in this case as *on time*. Such a method of classification is not necessarily bad: if the probability of *on time* is 0.7 and we guess that every unseen instance should be classified as *on time*, we could expect to be right about 70% of the time. However, the aim is to make correct predictions as often as possible, which requires a more sophisticated approach.

The instances in the training set record not only the classification but also the values of four attributes: *day*, *season*, *wind* and *rain*. Presumably they are recorded because we believe that in some way the values of the four attributes affect the outcome. (This may not necessarily be the case, but for the purpose of this chapter we will assume it is true.) To make effective use of the additional information represented by the attribute values we first need to introduce the notion of *conditional probability*.

The probability of the train being on time, calculated using the frequency of *on time* in the training set divided by the total number of instances is known as the *prior probability*. In this case $P(\text{class} = \text{on time}) = 14/20 = 0.7$. If we have no other information this is the best we can do. If we have other (relevant) information, the position is different.

What is the probability of the train being on time if we know that the season is winter? We can calculate this as the number of times class = on time and season = winter (in the same instance), divided by the number of times the season is winter, which comes to $2/6 = 0.33$. This is considerably less than the prior probability of 0.7 and seems intuitively reasonable. Trains are less likely to be on time in winter.

The probability of an event occurring if we know that an attribute has a particular value (or that several variables have particular values) is called the *conditional probability* of the event occurring and is written as, e.g.

$P(\text{class} = \text{on time} \mid \text{season} = \text{winter})$.

The vertical bar can be read as 'given that', so the whole term can be read as 'the probability that the class is *on time* given that the season is *winter*'.

$P(\text{class} = \text{on time} \mid \text{season} = \text{winter})$ is also called a *posterior probability*. It is the probability that we can calculate for the classification *after* we have obtained the information that the season is winter. By contrast, the prior probability is that estimated *before* any other information is available.

To calculate the most likely classification for the 'unseen' instance given previously we could calculate the probability of

$$P(\text{class} = \text{on time} \quad | \quad \text{day} = \text{weekday and season} = \text{winter}$$
$$\text{and wind} = \text{high and rain} = \text{heavy})$$

and do similarly for the other three possible classifications. However there are only two instances in the training set with that combination of attribute values and basing any estimates of probability on these is unlikely to be helpful.

To obtain a reliable estimate of the four classifications a more indirect approach is needed. We could start by using conditional probabilities based on a single attribute.

For the *train* dataset

$P(\text{class} = \text{on time} \mid \text{rain} = \text{heavy}) = 1/5 = 0.2$
$P(\text{class} = \text{late} \mid \text{rain} = \text{heavy}) = 1/5 = 0.2$
$P(\text{class} = \text{very late} \mid \text{rain} = \text{heavy}) = 2/5 = 0.4$
$P(\text{class} = \text{cancelled} \mid \text{rain} = \text{heavy}) = 1/5 = 0.2$

The third of these has the largest value, so we could conclude that the most likely classification is very late, a different result from using the prior probability as before.

We could do a similar calculation with attributes day, season and wind. This might result in other classifications having the largest value. Which is the best one to take?

The **Naïve Bayes** algorithm gives us a way of combining the prior probability and conditional probabilities in a single formula, which we can use to calculate the probability of each of the possible classifications in turn. Having done this we choose the classification with the largest value.

Incidentally the first word in the rather derogatory sounding name Naïve Bayes refers to the assumption that the method makes, that the effect of the value of one attribute on the probability of a given classification is independent of the values of the other attributes. In practice, that may not be the case. Despite this theoretical weakness, the Naïve Bayes method often gives good results in practical use.

The method uses conditional probabilities, but the other way round from before. (This may seem a strange approach but is justified by the method that follows, which is based on a well-known Mathematical result known as Bayes Rule.)

Instead of (say) the probability that the class is very late given that the season is winter, $P(\text{class} = \text{very late} \mid \text{season} = \text{winter})$, we use the conditional probability that the season is winter given that the class is very late, i.e. $P(\text{season} = \text{winter} \mid \text{class} = \text{very late})$. We can calculate this as the number of times that season = winter and class = very late occur in the same instance, divided by the number of instances for which the class is *very late*.

In a similar way we can calculate other conditional probabilities, for example $P(\text{rain} = \text{none} \mid \text{class} = \text{very late})$.

For the *train* data we can tabulate all the conditional and prior probabilities as shown in Figure 3.2.

	class = on time	class = late	class = very late	class = cancelled
day = weekday	9/14 = 0.64	1/2 = 0.5	3/3 = 1	0/1 = 0
day = saturday	2/14 = 0.14	1/2 = 0.5	0/3 = 0	1/1 = 1
day = sunday	1/14 = 0.07	0/2 = 0	0/3 = 0	0/1 = 0
day = holiday	2/14 = 0.14	0/2 = 0	0/3 = 0	0/1 = 0
season = spring	4/14 = 0.29	0/2 = 0	0/3 = 0	1/1 = 1
season = summer	6/14 = 0.43	0/2 = 0	0/3 = 0	0/1 = 0
season = autumn	2/14 = 0.14	0/2 = 0	1/3 = 0.33	0/1 = 0
season = winter	**2/14 = 0.14**	**2/2 = 1**	**2/3 = 0.67**	**0/1 = 0**
wind = none	5/14 = 0.36	0/2 = 0	0/3 = 0	0/1 = 0
wind = high	**4/14 = 0.29**	**1/2 = 0.5**	**1/3 = 0.33**	**1/1 = 1**
wind = normal	5/14 = 0.36	1/2 = 0.5	2/3 = 0.67	0/1 = 0
rain = none	5/14 = 0.36	1/2 =0.5	1/3 = 0.33	0/1 = 0
rain = slight	8/14 = 0.57	0/2 = 0	0/3 = 0	0/1 = 0
rain = heavy	**1/14 = 0.07**	**1/2 = 0.5**	**2/3 = 0.67**	**1/1 = 1**
Prior Probability	**14/20 = 0.70**	**2/20 = 0.10**	**3/20 = 0.15**	**1/20 = 0.05**

Figure 3.2 Conditional and Prior Probabilities: *train* Dataset

For example, the conditional probability $P(\text{day} = \text{weekday} \mid \text{class} = \text{on time})$ is the number of instances in the *train* dataset for which day = weekday and class = on time, divided by the total number of instances for which class = on time. These numbers can be counted from Figure 3.1 as 9 and 14, respectively. So the conditional probability is 9/14 = 0.64.

The prior probability of class = very late is the number of instances in Figure 3.1 for which class = very late divided by the total number of instances, i.e. 3/20 = 0.15.

We can now use these values to calculate the probabilities of real interest to us. These are the posterior probabilities of each possible class occurring for a specified instance, i.e. for known values of all the attributes. We can calculate these posterior probabilities using the method given in Figure 3.3.

Naïve Bayes Classification

Given a set of k mutually exclusive and exhaustive classifications $c_1, c_2, \ldots,$ c_k, which have prior probabilities $P(c_1), P(c_2), \ldots, P(c_k)$, respectively, and n attributes $a_1, a_2, \ldots, a_n$ which for a given instance have values $v_1, v_2,$ $\ldots, v_n$ respectively, the posterior probability of class c_i occurring for the specified instance can be shown to be proportional to

$$P(c_i) \times P(a_1 = v_1 \text{ and } a_2 = v_2 \ldots \text{ and } a_n = v_n \mid c_i)$$

Making the assumption that the attributes are independent, the value of this expression can be calculated using the product

$$\boldsymbol{P(c_i) \times P(a_1 = v_1 \mid c_i) \times P(a_2 = v_2 \mid c_i) \times \ldots \times P(a_n = v_n \mid c_i)}$$

We calculate this product for each value of i from 1 to k and choose the classification that has the largest value.

Figure 3.3 The Naïve Bayes Classification Algorithm

The formula shown in bold in Figure 3.3 combines the prior probability of c_i with the values of the n possible conditional probabilities involving a test on the value of a single attribute.

It is often written as $P(c_i) \times \prod\limits_{j=1}^{n} P(a_j = v_j \mid class = c_i)$.

Note that the Greek letter $\prod$ (pronounced pi) in the above formula is not connected with the mathematical constant 3.14159.... It indicates the product obtained by multiplying together the n values $P(a_1 = v_1 \mid c_i)$, $P(a_2 = v_2 \mid c_i)$ etc.

($\prod$ is the capital form of 'pi'. The lower case form is π. The equivalents in the Roman alphabet are P and p. P is the first letter of 'Product'.)

When using the Naïve Bayes method to classify a series of unseen instances the most efficient way to start is by calculating all the prior probabilities and also all the conditional probabilities involving one attribute, though not all of them may be required for classifying any particular instance.

Using the values in each of the columns of Figure 3.2 in turn, we obtain the following posterior probabilities for each possible classification for the unseen instance:

weekday	winter	high	heavy	????

class = on time

$0.70 \times 0.64 \times 0.14 \times 0.29 \times 0.07 = 0.0013$

class = late

$0.10 \times 0.50 \times 1.00 \times 0.50 \times 0.50 = 0.0125$

class = very late

$0.15 \times 1.00 \times 0.67 \times 0.33 \times 0.67 = 0.0222$

class = cancelled

$0.05 \times 0.00 \times 0.00 \times 1.00 \times 1.00 = 0.0000$

The largest value is for class = very late.

Note that the four values calculated are not themselves probabilities, as they do not sum to 1. This is the significance of the phrasing 'the posterior probability ... can be shown to be proportional to' in Figure 3.3. Each value can be 'normalised' to a valid posterior probability simply by dividing it by the sum of all four values. In practice, we are interested only in finding the largest value so the normalisation step is not necessary.

The Naïve Bayes approach is a very popular one, which often works well. However it has a number of potential problems, the most obvious one being that it relies on all attributes being categorical. In practice, many datasets have a combination of categorical and continuous attributes, or even only continuous attributes. This problem can be overcome by converting the continuous attributes to categorical ones, using a method such as those described in Chapter 8 or otherwise.

A second problem is that estimating probabilities by relative frequencies can give a poor estimate if the number of instances with a given attribute/value combination is small. In the extreme case where it is zero, the posterior probability will inevitably be calculated as zero. This happened for class = cancelled in the above example. This problem can be overcome by using a more complicated formula for estimating probabilities, but this will not be discussed further here.

3.3 Nearest Neighbour Classification

Nearest Neighbour classification is mainly used when all attribute values are continuous, although it can be modified to deal with categorical attributes.

The idea is to estimate the classification of an unseen instance using the classification of the instance or instances that are *closest* to it, in some sense that we need to define.

Supposing we have a training set with just two instances such as the following

a	b	c	d	e	f	Class
yes	no	no	6.4	8.3	low	negative
yes	yes	yes	18.2	4.7	high	positive

There are six attribute values, followed by a classification (positive or negative).

We are then given a third instance

yes	no	no	6.6	8.0	low	????

What should its classification be?

Even without knowing what the six attributes represent, it seems intuitively obvious that the unseen instance is *nearer* to the first instance than to the second. In the absence of any other information, we could reasonably predict its classification using that of the first instance, i.e. as 'negative'.

In practice there are likely to be many more instances in the training set but the same principle applies. It is usual to base the classification on those of the k nearest neighbours (where k is a small integer such as 3 or 5), not just the nearest one. The method is then known as *k-Nearest Neighbour* or just *k-NN classification* (Figure 3.4).

Basic k-Nearest Neighbour Classification Algorithm

− Find the k training instances that are closest to the unseen instance.

− Take the most commonly occurring classification for these k instances.

Figure 3.4 The Basic k-Nearest Neighbour Classification Algorithm

We can illustrate *k-NN* classification diagrammatically when the *dimension* (i.e. the number of attributes) is small. The following example illustrates the case where the dimension is just 2. In real-world data mining applications it can of course be considerably larger.

Figure 3.5 shows a training set with 20 instances, each giving the values of two attributes and an associated classification.

How can we estimate the classification for an 'unseen' instance where the first and second attributes are 9.1 and 11.0, respectively?

For this small number of attributes we can represent the training set as 20 points on a two-dimensional graph with values of the first and second attributes measured along the horizontal and vertical axes, respectively. Each point is labelled with a + or − symbol to indicate that the classification is positive or negative, respectively. The result is shown in Figure 3.6.

Attribute 1	Attribute 2	Class
0.8	6.3	−
1.4	8.1	−
2.1	7.4	−
2.6	14.3	+
6.8	12.6	−
8.8	9.8	+
9.2	11.6	−
10.8	9.6	+
11.8	9.9	+
12.4	6.5	+
12.8	1.1	−
14.0	19.9	−
14.2	18.5	−
15.6	17.4	−
15.8	12.2	−
16.6	6.7	+
17.4	4.5	+
18.2	6.9	+
19.0	3.4	−
19.6	11.1	+

Figure 3.5 Training Set for k-Nearest Neighbour Example

A circle has been added to enclose the five nearest neighbours of the unseen instance, which is shown as a small circle close to the centre of the larger one.

The five nearest neighbours are labelled with three + signs and two − signs, so a basic 5-NN classifier would classify the unseen instance as 'positive' by a form of majority voting. There are other possibilities, for example the 'votes' of each of the k nearest neighbours can be weighted, so that the classifications of closer neighbours are given greater weight than the classifications of more distant ones. We will not pursue this here.

We can represent two points in two dimensions ('in two-dimensional space' is the usual term) as (a_1, a_2) and (b_1, b_2) and visualise them as points in a plane.

When there are three attributes we can represent the points by (a_1, a_2, a_3) and (b_1, b_2, b_3) and think of them as points in a room with three axes at right angles. As the number of dimensions (attributes) increases it rapidly becomes impossible to visualise them, at least for anyone who is not a physicist (and most of those who are).

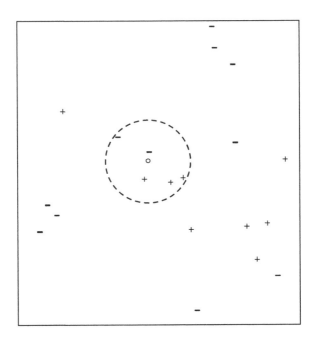

Figure 3.6 Two-dimensional Representation of Training Data in Figure 3.5

When there are n attributes, we can represent the instances by the points $(a_1, a_2, \ldots, a_n)$ and $(b_1, b_2, \ldots, b_n)$ in 'n-dimensional space'.

3.3.1 Distance Measures

There are many possible ways of measuring the distance between two instances with n attribute values, or equivalently between two points in n-dimensional space. We usually impose three requirements on any distance measure we use. We will use the notation $\mathbf{dist}(X, Y)$ to denote the distance between two points X and Y.

1. The distance of any point A from itself is zero, i.e. $\mathbf{dist}(A, A) = 0$.

2. The distance from A to B is the same as the distance from B to A, i.e. $\mathbf{dist}(A, B) = \mathbf{dist}(B, A)$ (the *symmetry condition*).

The third condition is called the *triangle inequality* (Figure 3.7). It corresponds to the intuitive idea that 'the shortest distance between any two points is a straight line'. The condition says that for any points A, B and Z: $\mathbf{dist}(A, B) \leq \mathbf{dist}(A, Z) + \mathbf{dist}(Z, B)$.

As usual, it is easiest to visualise this in two dimensions.

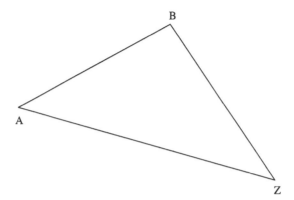

Figure 3.7 The Triangle Inequality

The equality only occurs if Z is the same point as A or B or is on the direct route between them.

There are many possible distance measures, but the most popular is almost certainly the *Euclidean Distance* (Figure 3.8). This measure is named after the Greek Mathematician Euclid of Alexandria, who lived around 300 BC and is celebrated as the founder of geometry. It is the measure of distance assumed in Figure 3.6.

We will start by illustrating the formula for Euclidean distance in two dimensions. If we denote an instance in the training set by (a_1, a_2) and the unseen instance by (b_1, b_2) the length of the straight line joining the points is

$$\sqrt{(a_1 - b_1)^2 + (a_2 - b_2)^2}$$

by Pythagoras' Theorem.

If there are two points (a_1, a_2, a_3) and (b_1, b_2, b_3) in a three-dimensional space the corresponding formula is

$$\sqrt{(a_1 - b_1)^2 + (a_2 - b_2)^2 + (a_3 - b_3)^2}$$

The formula for Euclidean distance between points $(a_1, a_2, \ldots, a_n)$ and $(b_1, b_2, \ldots, b_n)$ in n-dimensional space is a generalisation of these two results. The Euclidean distance is given by the formula

$$\sqrt{(a_1 - b_1)^2 + (a_2 - b_2)^2 + \ldots + (a_n - b_n)^2}$$

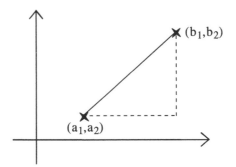

Figure 3.8 Example of Euclidean Distance

Another measure sometimes used is called *Manhattan Distance* or *City Block Distance*. The analogy is with travelling around a city such as Manhattan, where you cannot (usually) go straight from one place to another but only by moving along streets aligned horizontally and vertically.

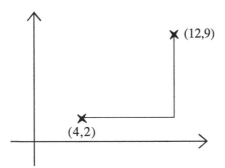

Figure 3.9 Example of City Block Distance

The City Block distance between the points $(4, 2)$ and $(12, 9)$ in Figure 3.9 is $(12 - 4) + (9 - 2) = 8 + 7 = 15$.

A third possibility is the *maximum dimension distance*. This is the largest absolute difference between any pair of corresponding attribute values. (The absolute difference is the difference converted to a positive number if it is negative.) For example the maximum dimension distance between instances

| 6.2 | −7.1 | −5.0 | 18.3 | −3.1 | 8.9 |

and

| 8.3 | 12.4 | −4.1 | 19.7 | −6.2 | 12.4 |

is $12.4 - (-7.1) = 19.5$.

For many applications, Euclidean distance seems the most natural way of measuring the distance between two instances.

3.3.2 Normalisation

A major problem when using the Euclidean distance formula (and many other distance measures) is that the large values frequently swamp the small ones.

Suppose that two instances are as follows for some classification problem associated with cars (the classifications themselves are omitted).

Mileage (miles)	Number of doors	Age (years)	Number of owners
18,457	2	12	8
26,292	4	3	1

When the distance of these instances from an unseen one is calculated, the *mileage* attribute will almost certainly contribute a value of several thousands squared, i.e. several millions, to the sum of squares total. The number of doors will probably contribute a value less than 10. It is clear that in practice the only attribute that will matter when deciding which neighbours are the nearest using the Euclidean distance formula is the mileage. This is unreasonable as the unit of measurement, here the mile, is entirely arbitrary. We could have chosen an alternative measure of distance travelled such as millimetres or perhaps light years. Similarly we might have measured age in some other unit such as milliseconds or millennia. The units chosen should not affect the decision on which are the nearest neighbours.

To overcome this problem we generally *normalise* the values of continuous attributes. The idea is to make the values of each attribute run from 0 to 1. Suppose that for some attribute A the smallest value found in the training data is -8.1 and the largest is 94.3. First we adjust each value of A by adding 8.1 to it, so the values now run from 0 to $94.3+8.1 = 102.4$. The spread of values from highest to lowest is now 102.4 units, so we divide all values by that number to make the spread of values from 0 to 1.

In general if the lowest value of attribute A is *min* and the highest value is *max*, we convert each value of A, say a, to $(a - min)/(max - min)$.

Using this approach all continuous attributes are converted to small numbers from 0 to 1, so the effect of the choice of unit of measurement on the outcome is greatly reduced.

Note that it is possible that an unseen instance may have a value of A that is less than *min* or greater than *max*. If we want to keep the adjusted numbers in the range from 0 to 1 we can just convert any values of A that are less than *min* or greater than *max* to 0 or 1, respectively.

Another issue that occurs with measuring the distance between two points is the *weighting* of the contributions of the different attributes. We may believe that the mileage of a car is more important than the number of doors it has (although no doubt not a thousand times more important, as with the unnormalised values). To achieve this we can adjust the formula for Euclidean distance to

$$\sqrt{w_1(a_1 - b_1)^2 + w_2(a_2 - b_2)^2 + \ldots + w_n(a_n - b_n)^2}$$

where $w_1, w_2, \ldots, w_n$ are the weights. It is customary to scale the weight values so that the sum of all the weights is one.

3.3.3 Dealing with Categorical Attributes

One of the weaknesses of the nearest neighbour approach to classification is that there is no entirely satisfactory way of dealing with categorical attributes. One possibility is to say that the difference between any two identical values of the attribute is zero and that the difference between any two different values is 1. Effectively this amounts to saying (for a colour attribute) red − red = 0, red − blue = 1, blue − green = 1, etc.

Sometimes there is an ordering (or a partial ordering) of the values of an attribute, for example we might have values *good, average* and *bad*. We could treat the difference between *good* and *average* or between *average* and *bad* as 0.5 and the difference between *good* and *bad* as 1. This still does not seem completely right, but may be the best we can do in practice.

3.4 Eager and Lazy Learning

The Naïve Bayes and Nearest Neighbour algorithms described in Sections 3.2 and 3.3 illustrate two alternative approaches to automatic classification, known by the slightly cryptic names of *eager learning* and *lazy learning*, respectively.

In eager learning systems the training data is 'eagerly' generalised into some representation or model such as a table of probabilities, a decision tree or a neural net without waiting for a new (unseen) instance to be presented for classification.

In lazy learning systems the training data is 'lazily' left unchanged until an unseen instance is presented for classification. When it is, only those calculations that are necessary to classify that single instance are performed.

The lazy learning approach has some enthusiastic advocates, but if there are a large number of unseen instances, it can be computationally very expensive to carry out compared with eager learning methods such as Naïve Bayes and the other methods of classification that are described in later chapters.

A more fundamental weakness of the lazy learning approach is that it does not give any idea of the underlying causality of the task domain. This is also true of the probability-based Naïve Bayes eager learning algorithm, but to a lesser extent. X is the classification for no reason deeper than that if you do the calculations X turns out to be the answer. We now turn to methods that give an explicit way of classifying any unseen instance that can be used (and critiqued) independently from the training data used to generate it. We call such methods *model-based*.

3.5 Chapter Summary

This chapter introduces classification, one of the most common data mining tasks. Two classification algorithms are described in detail: the Naïve Bayes algorithm, which uses probability theory to find the most likely of the possible classifications, and Nearest Neighbour classification, which estimates the classification of an unseen instance using the classification of the instances 'closest' to it. These two methods generally assume that all the attributes are categorical and continuous, respectively.

3.6 Self-assessment Exercises for Chapter 3

1. Using the Naïve Bayes classification algorithm with the *train* dataset, calculate the most likely classification for the following unseen instances.

weekday	summer	high	heavy	????

sunday	summer	normal	slight	????

2. Using the training set shown in Figure 3.5 and the Euclidean distance measure, calculate the 5-nearest neighbours of the instance with first and second attributes 9.1 and 11.0, respectively.

4
Using Decision Trees for Classification

In this chapter we look at a widely-used method of constructing a model from a dataset in the form of a decision tree or (equivalently) a set of decision rules. It is often claimed that this representation of the data has the advantage compared with other approaches of being meaningful and easy to interpret.

4.1 Decision Rules and Decision Trees

In many fields, large collections of examples, possibly collected for other purposes, are readily available. Automatically generating classification rules (often called *decision rules*) for such tasks has proved to be a realistic alternative to the standard Expert System approach of eliciting the rules from experts. The British academic Donald Michie [1] reported two large applications of 2,800 and 30,000+ rules, developed using automatic techniques in only one and 9 man-years, respectively, compared with the estimated 100 and 180 man-years needed to develop the celebrated 'conventional' Expert Systems MYCIN and XCON.

In many (but not all) cases decision rules can conveniently be fitted together to form a tree structure of the kind shown in the following example.

© Springer-Verlag London Ltd., part of Springer Nature 2020
M. Bramer, *Principles of Data Mining*, Undergraduate Topics
in Computer Science, DOI 10.1007/978-1-4471-7493-6_4

4.1.1 Decision Trees: The Golf Example

A fictitious example which has been used for illustration by many authors, notably Quinlan [2], is that of a golfer who decides whether or not to play each day on the basis of the weather.

Figure 4.1 shows the results of two weeks (14 days) of observations of weather conditions and the decision on whether or not to play.

Outlook	Temp (°F)	Humidity (%)	Windy	Class
sunny	75	70	true	play
sunny	80	90	true	don't play
sunny	85	85	false	don't play
sunny	72	95	false	don't play
sunny	69	70	false	play
overcast	72	90	true	play
overcast	83	78	false	play
overcast	64	65	true	play
overcast	81	75	false	play
rain	71	80	true	don't play
rain	65	70	true	don't play
rain	75	80	false	play
rain	68	80	false	play
rain	70	96	false	play

Classes
play, don't play
Outlook
sunny, overcast, rain
Temperature
numerical value
Humidity
numerical value
Windy
true, false

Figure 4.1 Data for the Golf Example

Assuming the golfer is acting consistently, what are the rules that determine the decision whether or not to play each day? If tomorrow the values of *Outlook*, *Temperature*, *Humidity* and *Windy* were sunny, 74°F, 77% and false respectively, what would the decision be?

One way of answering this is to construct a *decision tree* such as the one shown in Figure 4.2. This is a typical example of a decision tree, which will form the topic of several chapters of this book.

In order to determine the decision (classification) for a given set of weather conditions from the decision tree, first look at the value of *Outlook*. There are three possibilities.

1. If the value of *Outlook* is sunny, next consider the value of *Humidity*. If the value is less than or equal to 75 the decision is *play*. Otherwise the decision is *don't play*.

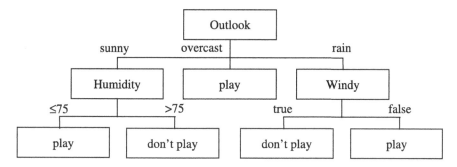

Figure 4.2 Decision Tree for the Golf Example

2. If the value of *Outlook* is overcast, the decision is *play*.

3. If the value of *Outlook* is rain, next consider the value of *Windy*. If the value is true the decision is *don't play*, otherwise the decision is *play*.

Note that the value of *Temperature* is never used.

4.1.2 Terminology

We will assume that the 'standard formulation' of the data given in Chapter 2 applies. There is a universe of *objects* (people, houses etc.), each of which can be described by the values of a collection of its *attributes*. Attributes with a finite (and generally fairly small) set of values, such as sunny, overcast and rain, are called *categorical*. Attributes with numerical values, such as *Temperature* and *Humidity*, are generally known as *continuous*. We will distinguish between a specially-designated categorical attribute called the *classification* and the other attribute values and will generally use the term 'attributes' to refer only to the latter.

Descriptions of a number of objects are held in tabular form in a *training set*. Each row of the figure comprises an *instance*, i.e. the (non-classifying) attribute values and the classification corresponding to one object.

The aim is to develop *classification rules* from the data in the training set. This is often done in the implicit form of a *decision tree*.

A decision tree is created by a process known as *splitting on the value of attributes* (or just *splitting on attributes*), i.e. testing the value of an attribute such as *Outlook* and then creating a branch for each of its possible values. In the case of continuous attributes the test is normally whether the value is 'less than or equal to' or 'greater than' a given value known as the *split value*.

The splitting process continues until each branch can be labelled with just one classification.

Decision trees have two different functions: *data compression* and *prediction*. Figure 4.2 can be regarded simply as a more compact way of representing the data in Figure 4.1. The two representations are equivalent in the sense that for each of the 14 instances the given values of the four attributes will lead to identical classifications.

However, the decision tree is more than an equivalent representation to the training set. It can be used to predict the values of other instances not in the training set, for example the one given previously where the values of the four attributes are sunny, 74, 77 and false respectively. It is easy to see from the decision tree that in this case the decision would be *don't play*. It is important to stress that this 'decision' is only a prediction, which may or may not turn out to be correct. There is no infallible way to predict the future!

So the decision tree can be viewed as not merely equivalent to the original training set but as a generalisation of it which can be used to predict the classification of other instances. These are often called *unseen instances* and a collection of them is generally known as a *test set* or an *unseen test set*, by contrast with the original training set.

4.1.3 The *degrees* Dataset

The training set shown in Figure 4.3 (taken from a fictitious university) shows the results of students for five subjects coded as SoftEng, ARIN, HCI, CSA and Project and their corresponding degree classifications, which in this simplified example are either FIRST or SECOND. There are 26 instances. What determines who is classified as FIRST or SECOND?

Figure 4.4 shows a possible decision tree corresponding to this training set. It consists of a number of *branches*, each ending with a *leaf node* labelled with one of the valid classifications, i.e. FIRST or SECOND. Each branch comprises the route from the root node (i.e. the top of the tree) to a leaf node. A node that is neither the root nor a leaf node is called an *internal node*.

We can think of the root node as corresponding to the original training set. All other nodes correspond to a subset of the training set.

At the leaf nodes each instance in the subset has the same classification. There are five leaf nodes and hence five branches.

Each branch corresponds to a *classification rule*. The five classification rules can be written in full as:

IF SoftEng = A AND Project = A THEN Class = FIRST
IF SoftEng = A AND Project = B AND ARIN = A AND CSA = A

SoftEng	ARIN	HCI	CSA	Project	Class
A	B	A	B	B	SECOND
A	B	B	B	A	FIRST
A	A	A	B	B	SECOND
B	A	A	B	B	SECOND
A	A	B	B	A	FIRST
B	A	A	B	B	SECOND
A	B	B	B	B	SECOND
A	B	B	B	B	SECOND
A	A	A	A	A	FIRST
B	A	A	B	B	SECOND
B	A	A	B	B	SECOND
A	B	B	A	B	SECOND
B	B	B	B	A	SECOND
A	A	B	A	B	FIRST
B	B	B	B	A	SECOND
A	A	B	B	B	SECOND
B	B	B	B	B	SECOND
A	A	B	A	A	FIRST
B	B	B	A	A	SECOND
B	B	A	A	B	SECOND
B	B	B	B	A	SECOND
B	A	B	A	B	SECOND
A	B	B	B	A	FIRST
A	B	A	B	B	SECOND
B	A	B	B	B	SECOND
A	B	B	B	B	SECOND

Classes
FIRST, SECOND
SoftEng
A,B
ARIN
A,B
HCI
A,B
CSA
A,B
Project
A,B

Figure 4.3 The *degrees* Dataset

THEN Class = FIRST
IF SoftEng = A AND Project = B AND ARIN = A AND CSA = B
THEN Class = SECOND
IF SoftEng = A AND Project = B AND ARIN = B
THEN Class = SECOND
IF SoftEng = B THEN Class = SECOND

The left-hand side of each rule (known as the *antecedent*) comprises a number of *terms* joined by the logical AND operator. Each term is a simple test on the value of a categorical attribute (e.g. SoftEng = A) or a continuous attribute (e.g. in Figure 4.2, Humidity > 75).

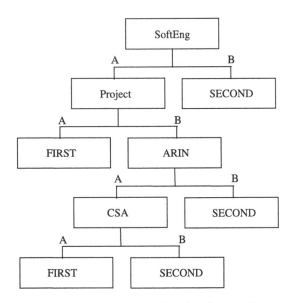

Figure 4.4 Decision Tree for the *degrees* Dataset

A set of rules of this kind is said to be in *Disjunctive Normal Form* (DNF). The individual rules are sometimes known as *disjuncts*.

Looking at this example in terms of data compression, the decision tree can be written as five decision rules with a total of 14 terms, an average of 2.8 terms per rule. Each instance in the original *degrees* training set could also be viewed as a rule, for example

IF SoftEng = A AND ARIN = B AND HCI = A AND CSA = B
AND Project = B THEN Class = SECOND

There are 26 such rules, one per instance, each with five terms, making a total of 130 terms. Even for this very small training set, the reduction in the number of terms requiring to be stored from the training set (130 terms) to the decision tree (14 terms) is almost 90%.

The order in which we write the rules generated from a decision tree is arbitrary, so the five rules given above could be rearranged to (say)

IF SoftEng = A AND Project = B AND ARIN = A AND CSA = B
THEN Class = SECOND
IF SoftEng = B THEN Class = SECOND
IF SoftEng = A AND Project = A THEN Class = FIRST
IF SoftEng = A AND Project = B AND ARIN = B
THEN Class = SECOND

IF SoftEng = A AND Project = B AND ARIN = A AND CSA = A
THEN Class = FIRST

without any change to the predictions the ruleset will make on unseen instances.

For practical use, the rules can easily be simplified to an equivalent nested set of IF ... THEN ... ELSE rules, with even more compression, e.g. (for the original set of rules)

```
if (SoftEng = A) {
    if (Project = A) Class = FIRST
    else {
        if (ARIN = A) {
            if (CSA = A) Class = FIRST
            else Class = SECOND
        }
        else Class = SECOND
    }
}
else Class = SECOND
```

4.2 The TDIDT Algorithm

Decision trees are widely used as a means of generating classification rules because of the existence of a simple but very powerful algorithm called **TDIDT**, which stands for *Top-Down Induction of Decision Trees*. This has been known since the mid-1960s and has formed the basis for many classification systems, two of the best-known being ID3 [3] and C4.5 [2], as well as being used in many commercial data mining packages.

The method produces decision rules in the implicit form of a decision tree. Decision trees are generated by repeatedly splitting on the values of attributes. This process is known as *recursive partitioning*.

In the standard formulation of the TDIDT algorithm there is a training set of instances. Each instance corresponds to a member of a universe of objects, which is described by the values of a set of categorical attributes. (The algorithm can be adapted to deal with continuous attributes, as will be discussed in Chapter 8.)

The basic algorithm can be given in just a few lines as shown in Figure 4.5.

At each non-leaf node an attribute is chosen for splitting. This can potentially be any attribute, except that the same attribute must not be chosen twice in the same branch. This restriction is entirely innocuous, e.g. in the branch

TDIDT: BASIC ALGORITHM

IF all the instances in the training set belong to the same class
THEN return the value of the class
ELSE (a) Select an attribute A to split on[+]
          (b) Sort the instances in the training set into subsets, one
                for each value of attribute A
          (c) Return a tree with one branch for each *non-empty* subset,
                each branch having a descendant subtree or a class
                value produced by applying the algorithm recursively

[+] Never select an attribute twice in the same branch

Figure 4.5 The TDIDT Algorithm

corresponding to the incomplete rule

IF SoftEng = A AND Project = B ......

it is not permitted to choose *SoftEng* or *Project* as the next attribute to split
on, but as their values are already known there would be no point in doing so.

However this harmless restriction has a very valuable effect. Each split on
the value of an attribute extends the length of the corresponding branch by one
term, but the maximum possible length for a branch is M terms where there
are M attributes. Hence the algorithm is guaranteed to terminate.

There is one important condition which must hold before the TDIDT algorithm can be applied. This is the *Adequacy Condition*: no two instances with
the same values of all the attributes may belong to different classes. This is simply a way of ensuring that the training set is consistent. Dealing with training
sets that are not consistent is the subject of Section 9.1.

A major problem with the TDIDT algorithm, which is not apparent at first
sight, is that it is *underspecified*. The algorithm specifies 'Select an attribute A
to split on' but no method is given for doing this.

Provided the adequacy condition is satisfied the algorithm is guaranteed to
terminate and any selection of attributes (even random selection) will produce
a decision tree, provided that an attribute is never selected twice in the same
branch.

This under-specification may seem desirable, but many of the resulting decision trees (and the corresponding decision rules) will be of little, if any, value
for predicting the classification of unseen instances.

Thus some methods of selecting attributes may be *much* more useful than
others. Making a good choice of attributes to split on at each stage is crucial to
the success of the TDIDT approach. This will be the main topic of Chapters 5
and 6.

4.3 Types of Reasoning

The automatic generation of decision rules from examples is known as *rule induction* or *automatic rule induction*.

Generating decision rules in the implicit form of a decision tree is also often called rule induction, but the terms *tree induction* or *decision tree induction* are sometimes preferred. We will end this chapter with a digression to explain the significance of the word 'induction' in these phrases and will return to the topic of attribute selection in Chapter 5.

Logicians distinguish between different types of reasoning. The most familiar is *deduction*, where the conclusion is shown to follow necessarily from the truth of the premises, for example

> All Men Are Mortal
> John is a Man
> _____
> Therefore John is Mortal

If the first two statements (the *premises*) are true, then the conclusion must be true.

This type of reasoning is entirely reliable but in practice rules that are 100% certain (such as 'all men are mortal') are often not available.

A second type of reasoning is called *abduction*. An example of this is

> All Dogs Chase Cats
> Fido Chases Cats
> _____
> Therefore Fido is a Dog

Here the conclusion is consistent with the truth of the premises, but it may not necessarily be correct. Fido may be some other type of animal that chases cats, or perhaps not an animal at all. Reasoning of this kind is often very successful in practice but can sometimes lead to incorrect conclusions.

A third type of reasoning is called *induction*. This is a process of generalisation based on repeated observations.

> After many observations of x and y occurring together, learn the rule
> **if x then y**

For example, if I see 1,000 dogs with four legs I might reasonably conclude that "if x is a dog then x has 4 legs" (or more simply "all dogs have four legs"). This is *induction*. The decision trees derived from the *golf* and *degrees* datasets are of this kind. They are generalised from repeated observations (the instances in the training sets) and we would expect them to be good enough to use for predicting the classification of unseen instances in most cases, but they may not be infallible.

4.4 Chapter Summary

This chapter introduces the TDIDT (Top-Down Induction of Decision Trees) algorithm for inducing classification rules via the intermediate representation of a decision tree. The algorithm can always be applied provided the 'adequacy condition' holds for the instances in the training set. The chapter ends by distinguishing three types of reasoning: deduction, abduction and induction.

4.5 Self-assessment Exercises for Chapter 4

1. What is the adequacy condition on the instances in a training set?

2. What are the most likely reasons for the condition not to be met for a given dataset?

3. What is the significance of the adequacy condition to automatic rule generation using the TDIDT algorithm?

4. What happens if the basic TDIDT algorithm is applied to a dataset for which the adequacy condition does not apply?

References

[1] Michie, D. (1990). Machine executable skills from 'silent' brains. In *Research and development in expert systems VII*. Cambridge: Cambridge University Press.

[2] Quinlan, J. R. (1993). *C4.5: programs for machine learning*. San Mateo: Morgan Kaufmann.

[3] Quinlan, J. R. (1986). Induction of decision trees. *Machine Learning, 1*, 81–106.

Decision Tree Induction: Using Entropy for Attribute Selection

5.1 Attribute Selection: An Experiment

In Chapter 4 it was shown that the TDIDT algorithm is guaranteed to terminate and to give a decision tree that correctly corresponds to the data, provided that the adequacy condition is satisfied. This condition is that no two instances with identical attribute values have different classifications.

However, it was also pointed out that the TDIDT algorithm is *underspecified*. Provided that the adequacy condition is satisfied, any method of choosing attributes will produce a decision tree. We will begin this chapter by considering the decision trees obtained from using some poorly chosen strategies for attribute selection and then go on to describe one of the most widely used approaches and look at how the results compare.

First we look at the decision trees produced by using the three attribute selection strategies listed below.

- *takefirst* – for each branch take the attributes in the order in which they appear in the training set, working from left to right, e.g. for the *degrees* training set in the order *SoftEng, ARIN, HCI, CSA* and *Project*.

- *takelast* – as for *takefirst*, but working from right to left, e.g. for the *degrees* training set in the order *Project, CSA, HCI, ARIN* and *SoftEng*.

- *random* – make a random selection (with equal probability of each attribute being selected).

© Springer-Verlag London Ltd., part of Springer Nature 2020   49
M. Bramer, *Principles of Data Mining*, Undergraduate Topics
in Computer Science, DOI 10.1007/978-1-4471-7493-6_5

As always no attribute may be selected twice in the same branch.

Warning: these three strategies are given here for purposes of illustration only. They are not intended for serious practical use but provide a basis for comparison with other methods introduced later.

Figure 5.1 shows the results of running the TDIDT algorithm with attribute selection strategies *takefirst*, *takelast* and *random* in turn to generate decision trees for the seven datasets *contact_lenses*, *lens24*, *chess*, *vote*, *monk1*, *monk2* and *monk3*. These datasets will be mentioned frequently as this book progresses. Information about all of them is given in Appendix B. The random strategy was used five times for each dataset. In each case the value given in the table is the number of branches in the decision tree generated.

The last two columns record the number of branches in the largest and the smallest of the trees generated for each of the datasets. In all cases there is a considerable difference. This suggests that although in principle the attributes can be chosen in any arbitrary way, the difference between a good choice and a bad one may be considerable. The next section looks at this issue from a different point of view.

Dataset	take first	take last	random					most	least
			1	2	3	4	5		
contact_lenses	42	27	34	38	32	26	35	42	26
lens24	21	9	15	11	15	13	11	21	9
chess	155	56	94	52	107	90	112	155	52
vote	40	79	96	78	116	110	96	116	40
monk1	60	75	82	53	87	89	80	89	53
monk2	142	112	122	127	109	123	121	142	109
monk3	69	69	43	46	62	55	77	77	43

Figure 5.1 Number of Branches Generated by TDIDT with Three Attribute Selection Methods

5.2 Alternative Decision Trees

Although (as was illustrated in the last section) any method of choosing attributes will produce a decision tree that does not mean that the method chosen is irrelevant. Some choices of attribute may be considerably more useful than others.

5.2.1 The Football/Netball Example

A fictitious university requires its students to enrol in one of its sports clubs, either the Football Club or the Netball Club. It is forbidden to join both clubs. Any student joining no club at all will be awarded an automatic failure in their degree (this being considered an important disciplinary offence).

Figure 5.2 gives a training set of data collected about 12 students, tabulating four items of data about each one (eye colour, marital status, sex and hair length) against the club joined.

eyecolour	married	sex	hairlength	class
brown	yes	male	long	football
blue	yes	male	short	football
brown	yes	male	long	football
brown	no	female	long	netball
brown	no	female	long	netball
blue	no	male	long	football
brown	no	female	long	netball
brown	no	male	short	football
brown	yes	female	short	netball
brown	no	female	long	netball
blue	no	male	long	football
blue	no	male	short	football

Figure 5.2 Training Set for the Football/Netball Example

What determines who joins which club?

It is possible to generate many different trees from this data using the TDIDT algorithm. One possible decision tree is Figure 5.3. (The numbers in parentheses indicate the number of instances corresponding to each of the leaf nodes.)

This is a remarkable result. All the blue-eyed students play football. For the brown-eyed students, the critical factor is whether or not they are married. If they are, then the long-haired ones all play football and the short-haired ones all play netball. If they are not married, it is the other way round: the short-haired ones play football and the long-haired ones play netball.

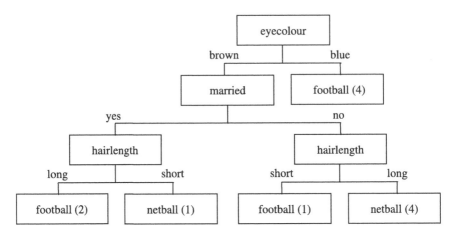

Figure 5.3 Football/Netball Example: Decision Tree 1

This would be an astonishing discovery, likely to attract worldwide attention, if it were correct — but is it?

Another decision tree that can be generated from the training set is Figure 5.4. This one looks more believable but is it correct?

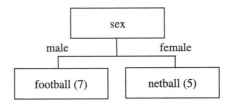

Figure 5.4 Football/Netball Example: Decision Tree 2

Although it is tempting to say that it is, it is best to avoid using terms such as 'correct' and 'incorrect' in this context. All we can say is that both decision trees are compatible with the data from which they were generated. The only way to know which one gives better results for unseen data is to use them both and compare the results.

Despite this, it is hard to avoid the belief that Figure 5.4 is right and Figure 5.3 is wrong. We will return to this point.

5.2.2 The *anonymous* Dataset

Now consider the different example in Figure 5.5.

a1	a2	a3	a4	class
a11	a21	a31	a41	c1
a12	a21	a31	a42	c1
a11	a21	a31	a41	c1
a11	a22	a32	a41	c2
a11	a22	a32	a41	c2
a12	a22	a31	a41	c1
a11	a22	a32	a41	c2
a11	a22	a31	a42	c1
a11	a21	a32	a42	c2
a11	a22	a32	a41	c2
a12	a22	a31	a41	c1
a12	a22	a31	a42	c1

Figure 5.5 The *anonymous* Dataset

Here we have a training set of 12 instances. There are four attributes, a1, a2, a3 and a4, with values a11, a12 etc., and two classes c1 and c2.

One possible decision tree we can generate from this data is Figure 5.6.

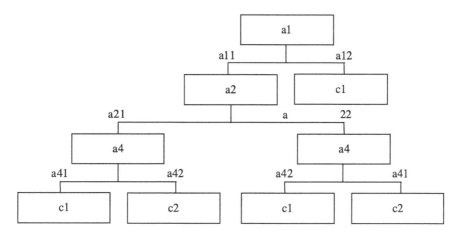

Figure 5.6 Anonymous Data: Decision Tree 1

Another possible tree is Figure 5.7.

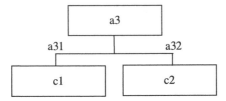

Figure 5.7 Anonymous Data: Decision Tree 2

Which tree is better?

This is the football/netball example in anonymised form, of course.

The effect of replacing meaningful attribute names such as *eyecolour* and *sex* with meaningless names such as *a1* and *a3* is considerable. Although we might say that we prefer Figure 5.7 because it is smaller, there seems no reason why Figure 5.6 should not be acceptable.

Data mining algorithms generally do not allow the use of any background knowledge the user has about the domain from which the data is drawn, such as the 'meaning' and relative importance of attributes, or which attributes are most or least likely, to determine the classification of an instance.

It is easy to see that a decision tree involving tests on *eyecolour, hairlength* etc. is meaningless when it is given in isolation, but if those attributes were part of a much larger number (possibly many thousands) in a practical application what would there be to prevent meaningless decision rules from being generated?

Apart from vigilance and a good choice of algorithm, the answer to this is 'nothing at all'. The quality of the strategy used to select the attribute to split on at each stage is clearly of vital importance. This is the topic to which we now turn.

5.3 Choosing Attributes to Split On: Using Entropy

The attribute selection techniques described in Section 5.1 (*takefirst, takelast* and *random*) were included for illustrative purposes only. For practical use several much superior methods are available. One commonly used method is to select the attribute that minimises the value of *entropy*, thus maximising the *information gain.* This method will be explained later in this chapter. Other commonly used methods will be discussed in Chapter 6.

Figure 5.8 is based on Figure 5.1, which gave the size of the tree with most and least branches produced by the *takefirst, takelast* and *random* attribute selection strategies for a number of datasets. The final column shows the number of branches generated by the 'entropy' attribute selection method (which has not yet been described). In almost all cases the number of branches is substantially reduced. The smallest number of branches, i.e. rules for each dataset, is in bold and underlined.

Dataset	excluding entropy		entropy
	most	least	
contact lenses	42	26	**<u>16</u>**
lens24	21	<u>9</u>	<u>9</u>
chess	155	52	**<u>20</u>**
vote	116	40	**<u>34</u>**
monk1	89	53	**<u>52</u>**
monk2	142	109	**<u>95</u>**
monk3	77	43	**<u>28</u>**

Figure 5.8 Most and Least Figures from Figure 5.1 Augmented by Information about Entropy Attribute Selection

In all cases the number of rules in the decision tree generated using the 'entropy' method is less than or equal to the smallest number generated using any of the other attribute selection criteria introduced so far. In some cases, such as for the *chess* dataset, it is considerably fewer.

There is no guarantee that using entropy will always lead to a small decision tree, but experience shows that it generally produces trees with fewer branches than other attribute selection criteria (not just the basic ones used in Section 5.1). Experience also shows that small trees tend to give more accurate predictions than large ones, although there is certainly no guarantee of infallibility.

5.3.1 The *lens24* Dataset

Before explaining the method of attribute selection using entropy, it will be helpful to say more about one of the small datasets used in Figures 5.1 and 5.8. The *lens24* dataset is ophthalmological data about contact lenses. It comprises

24 instances linking the values of four attributes *age* (i.e. age group), *specRx* (spectacle prescription), *astig* (whether astigmatic) and *tears* (tear production rate) with one of three classes 1, 2 and 3 (signifying respectively that the patient should be fitted with hard contact lenses, soft contact lenses or none at all). The complete training set is given as Figure 5.9.

Value of attribute				Class
age	specRx	astig	tears	
1	1	1	1	3
1	1	1	2	2
1	1	2	1	3
1	1	2	2	1
1	2	1	1	3
1	2	1	2	2
1	2	2	1	3
1	2	2	2	1
2	1	1	1	3
2	1	1	2	2
2	1	2	1	3
2	1	2	2	1
2	2	1	1	3
2	2	1	2	2
2	2	2	1	3
2	2	2	2	3
3	1	1	1	3
3	1	1	2	3
3	1	2	1	3
3	1	2	2	1
3	2	1	1	3
3	2	1	2	2
3	2	2	1	3
3	2	2	2	3

classes
1: hard contact lenses
2: soft contact lenses
3: no contact lenses

age
1: young
2: pre-presbyopic
3: presbyopic

specRx
(spectacle prescription)
1: myopia
2: high hypermetropia

astig
(whether astigmatic)
1: no
2: yes

tears
(tear production rate)
1: reduced
2: normal

Figure 5.9 Training Set for *lens24* Data

5.3.2 Entropy

> **Note: This description relies on an understanding of the mathematical function $\log_2 X$. If you are unfamiliar with this function, a brief summary of the essential points is given in Appendix A.3.**

Entropy is an information-theoretic measure of the 'uncertainty' contained in a training set, due to the presence of more than one possible classification.

If there are K classes, we can denote the proportion of instances with classification i by p_i for $i = 1$ to K. The value of p_i is the number of occurrences of class i divided by the total number of instances, which is a number between 0 and 1 inclusive.

The entropy of the training set is denoted by E. It is measured in 'bits' of information and is defined by the formula

$$E = - \sum_{i=1}^{K} p_i \log_2 p_i$$

summed over the non-empty classes only, i.e. classes for which $p_i \neq 0$.

An explanation of this formula will be given in Chapter 10. At present it is simplest to accept the formula as given and concentrate on its properties.

As is shown in Appendix A the value of $-p_i \log_2 p_i$ is positive for values of p_i greater than zero and less than 1. When $p_i = 1$ the value of $-p_i \log_2 p_i$ is zero. This implies that E is positive or zero for all training sets. It takes its minimum value (zero) if and only if all the instances have the same classification, in which case there is only one non-empty class, for which the probability is 1.

Entropy takes its maximum value when the instances are equally distributed amongst the K possible classes.

In this case the value of each p_i is $1/K$, which is independent of i, so

$$\begin{aligned} E &= - \sum_{i=1}^{K} (1/K) \log_2(1/K) \\ &= -K(1/K) \log_2(1/K) \\ &= - \log_2(1/K) = \log_2 K \end{aligned}$$

If there are 2, 3 or 4 classes this maximum value is 1, 1.5850 or 2, respectively.

For the initial *lens24* training set of 24 instances, there are 3 classes. There are 4 instances with classification 1, 5 instances with classification 2 and 15 instances with classification 3. So $p_1 = 4/24$, $p_2 = 5/24$ and $p_3 = 15/24$.

We will call the entropy E_{start}. It is given by
$E_{start} = -(4/24) \log_2(4/24) - (5/24) \log_2(5/24) - (15/24) \log_2(15/24)$
$= 0.4308 + 0.4715 + 0.4238$

= 1.3261 bits (these and subsequent figures in this chapter are given to four decimal places).

5.3.3 Using Entropy for Attribute Selection

The process of decision tree generation by repeatedly splitting on attributes is equivalent to partitioning the initial training set into smaller training sets repeatedly, until the entropy of each of these subsets is zero (i.e. each one has instances drawn from only a single class).

At any stage of this process, splitting on *any* attribute has the property that **the average entropy of the resulting subsets will be less than (or occasionally equal to) that of the previous training set**. This is an important result that we will state here without proof. We will come back to it in Chapter 10.

For the *lens24* training set, splitting on attribute *age* would give three subsets as shown in Figures 5.10(a), 5.10(b) and 5.10(c).

Training set 1 (age = 1)

Value of attribute				Class
age	specRx	astig	tears	
1	1	1	1	3
1	1	1	2	2
1	1	2	1	3
1	1	2	2	1
1	2	1	1	3
1	2	1	2	2
1	2	2	1	3
1	2	2	2	1

Figure 5.10(a)   Training Set 1 for *lens24* Example

Entropy $E_1 = -(2/8)\log_2(2/8) - (2/8)\log_2(2/8) - (4/8)\log_2(4/8)$
$= 0.5 + 0.5 + 0.5 = 1.5$

Training set 2 (age = 2)

Entropy $E_2 = -(1/8)\log_2(1/8) - (2/8)\log_2(2/8) - (5/8)\log_2(5/8)$
$= 0.375 + 0.5 + 0.4238 = 1.2988$

Training Set 3 (age = 3)

Entropy $E_3 = -(1/8)\log_2(1/8) - (1/8)\log_2(1/8) - (6/8)\log_2(6/8)$
$= 0.375 + 0.375 + 0.3113 = 1.0613$

Value of attribute				Class
age	specRx	astig	tears	
2	1	1	1	3
2	1	1	2	2
2	1	2	1	3
2	1	2	2	1
2	2	1	1	3
2	2	1	2	2
2	2	2	1	3
2	2	2	2	3

Figure 5.10(b) Training Set 2 for *lens24* Example

Value of attribute				Class
age	specRx	astig	tears	
3	1	1	1	3
3	1	1	2	3
3	1	2	1	3
3	1	2	2	1
3	2	1	1	3
3	2	1	2	2
3	2	2	1	3
3	2	2	2	3

Figure 5.10(c) Training Set 3 for *lens24* Example

Although the entropy of the first of these three training sets (E_1) is greater than E_{start}, the weighted average will be less. The values E_1, E_2 and E_3 need to be weighted by the proportion of the original instances in each of the three subsets. In this case all the weights are the same, i.e. 8/24.

If the average entropy of the three training sets produced by splitting on attribute age is denoted by E_{new}, then $E_{new} = (8/24)E_1 + (8/24)E_2 + (8/24)E_3 = 1.2867$ bits (to 4 decimal places).

If we define Information Gain $= E_{start} - E_{new}$ then the information gain from splitting on attribute *age* is $1.3261 - 1.2867 = 0.0394$ bits (see Figure 5.11).

The 'entropy method' of attribute selection is to choose to split on the attribute that gives the greatest reduction in (average) entropy, i.e. the one that maximises the value of Information Gain. This is equivalent to minimising the value of E_{new} as E_{start} is fixed.

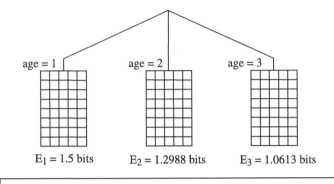

Figure 5.11   Information Gain for Splitting on Attribute age

5.3.4 Maximising Information Gain

The values of E_{new} and Information Gain for splitting on each of the four attributes *age, specRx, astig* and *tears* are as follows:

attribute *age*
$E_{new} = 1.2867$
Information Gain $= 1.3261 - 1.2867 = 0.0394$ bits

attribute *specRx*
$E_{new} = 1.2866$
Information Gain $= 1.3261 - 1.2866 = 0.0395$ bits

attribute *astig*
$E_{new} = 0.9491$
Information Gain $= 1.3261 - 0.9491 = 0.3770$ bits

attribute *tears*
$E_{new} = 0.7773$
Information Gain $= 1.3261 - 0.7773 = 0.5488$ bits

Thus, the largest value of Information Gain (and the smallest value of the new entropy E_{new}) is obtained by splitting on attribute *tears* (see Figure 5.12).

The process of splitting on nodes is repeated for each branch of the evolving decision tree, terminating when the subset at every leaf node has entropy zero.

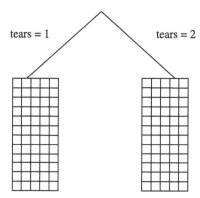

Figure 5.12   Splitting on Attribute *tears*

5.4 Chapter Summary

This chapter examines some alternative strategies for selecting attributes at each stage of the TDIDT decision tree generation algorithm and compares the size of the resulting trees for a number of datasets. The risk of obtaining decision trees that are entirely meaningless is highlighted, pointing to the importance of a good choice of attribute selection strategy. One of the most widely used strategies is based on minimising *entropy* (or equivalently maximising *information gain*) and this approach is illustrated in detail.

5.5 Self-assessment Exercises for Chapter 5

1. By constructing a spreadsheet or otherwise, calculate the following for the *degrees* dataset given in Section 4.1.3, Figure 4.3:

    a) the initial entropy E_{start}

    b) the weighted average entropy E_{new} of the training (sub)sets resulting from splitting on each of the attributes SoftEng, Arin, HCI, CSA and Project in turn and the corresponding value of Information Gain in each case.

    Using these results, verify that the attribute that will be chosen by the TDIDT algorithm for the first split on the data using the entropy selection criterion is SoftEng.

2. Suggest reasons why entropy (or information gain) is one of the most effective methods of attribute selection when using the TDIDT tree generation
   algorithm.

Decision Tree Induction: Using Frequency Tables for Attribute Selection

6.1 Calculating Entropy in Practice

The detailed calculations needed to choose an attribute to split on at a node in the evolving decision tree were illustrated in Section 5.3.3. At each node a table of values such as Figure 5.10(a), reproduced here as Figure 6.1, needs to be calculated for every possible value of every categorical attribute.

Value of attribute				Class
age	specRx	astig	tears	
1	1	1	1	3
1	1	1	2	2
1	1	2	1	3
1	1	2	2	1
1	2	1	1	3
1	2	1	2	2
1	2	2	1	3
1	2	2	2	1

Figure 6.1   Training Set 1 (age = 1) for *lens24* Example

For practical use a more efficient method is available which requires only a

© Springer-Verlag London Ltd., part of Springer Nature 2020
M. Bramer, *Principles of Data Mining*, Undergraduate Topics
in Computer Science, DOI 10.1007/978-1-4471-7493-6_6

single table to be constructed for each categorical attribute at each node. This method, which can be shown to be equivalent to the one given previously (see Section 6.1.1), uses a *frequency table*. The cells of this table show the number of occurrences of each combination of class and attribute value in the training set. For the *lens24* dataset the frequency table corresponding to splitting on attribute *age* is shown in Figure 6.2.

	age = 1	age = 2	age = 3
Class 1	2	1	1
Class 2	2	2	1
Class 3	4	5	6
Column sum	8	8	8

Figure 6.2 Frequency Table for Attribute age for *lens24* Example

We will denote the total number of instances by N, so $N = 24$.

The value of E_{new}, the average entropy of the training sets resulting from splitting on a specified attribute, can now be calculated by forming a sum as follows.

(a) For every non-zero value V in the main body of the table (i.e. the part above the 'column sum' row), subtract $V \times \log_2 V$.

(b) For every non-zero value S in the column sum row, add $S \times \log_2 S$.

Finally, divide the total by N.

Figure 6.3 gives the value of $\log_2 x$ for small integer values of x for reference.

Using the frequency table given as Figure 6.2, splitting on attribute *age* gives an E_{new} value of

$$-2 \log_2 2 - 1 \log_2 1 - 1 \log_2 1 - 2 \log_2 2 - 2 \log_2 2 - 1 \log_2 1$$
$$-4 \log_2 4 - 5 \log_2 5 - 6 \log_2 6 + 8 \log_2 8 + 8 \log_2 8 + 8 \log_2 8$$

divided by 24. This can be rearranged as

$$(-3 \times 2 \log_2 2 - 3 \log_2 1 - 4 \log_2 4 - 5 \log_2 5 - 6 \log_2 6 + 3 \times 8 \log_2 8)/24$$

$= 1.2867$ bits (to 4 decimal places), which agrees with the value calculated previously.

6.1.1 Proof of Equivalence

It remains to be proved that this method always gives the same value of E_{new} as the basic method described in Chapter 5.

x	$\log_2 x$
1	0
2	1
3	1.5850
4	2
5	2.3219
6	2.5850
7	2.8074
8	3
9	3.1699
10	3.3219
11	3.4594
12	3.5850

Figure 6.3 Some values of $\log_2 x$ (to 4 decimal places)

Assume that there are N instances, each relating the value of a number of categorical attributes to one of K possible classifications. (For the *lens24* dataset used previously, $N = 24$ and $K = 3$.)

Splitting on a categorical attribute with V possible values produces V subsets of the training set. The jth subset contains all the instances for which the attribute takes its jth value. Let N_j denote the number of instances in that subset. Then

$$\sum_{j=1}^{V} N_j = N$$

(For the frequency table shown in Figure 6.2, for attribute *age*, there are three values of the attribute, so $V = 3$. The three column sums are N_1, N_2 and N_3, which all have the same value (8). The value of N is $N_1 + N_2 + N_3 = 24$.)

Let f_{ij} denote the number of instances for which the classification is the ith one and the attribute takes its jth value (e.g. for Figure 6.2, $f_{32} = 5$). Then

$$\sum_{i=1}^{K} f_{ij} = N_j$$

The frequency table method of forming the sum for E_{new} given above amounts to using the formula

$$E_{new} = -\sum_{j=1}^{V}\sum_{i=1}^{K}(f_{ij}/N).\log_2 f_{ij} + \sum_{j=1}^{V}(N_j/N).\log_2 N_j$$

The basic method of calculating E_{new} using the entropies of the j subsets resulting from splitting on the specified attribute was described in Chapter 5.

The entropy of the jth subset is E_j where

$$E_j = -\sum_{i=1}^{K} (f_{ij}/N_j).\log_2(f_{ij}/N_j)$$

The value of E_{new} is the weighted sum of the entropies of these V subsets. The weighting is the proportion of the original N instances that the subset contains, i.e. N_j/N for the jth subset. So

$$
\begin{aligned}
E_{new} &= \sum_{j=1}^{V} N_j E_j/N \\
&= -\sum_{j=1}^{V}\sum_{i=1}^{K} (N_j/N).(f_{ij}/N_j).\log_2(f_{ij}/N_j) \\
&= -\sum_{j=1}^{V}\sum_{i=1}^{K} (f_{ij}/N).\log_2(f_{ij}/N_j) \\
&= -\sum_{j=1}^{V}\sum_{i=1}^{K} (f_{ij}/N).\log_2 f_{ij} + \sum_{j=1}^{V}\sum_{i=1}^{K} (f_{ij}/N).\log_2 N_j \\
&= -\sum_{j=1}^{V}\sum_{i=1}^{K} (f_{ij}/N).\log_2 f_{ij} + \sum_{j=1}^{V} (N_j/N).\log_2 N_j \quad [\text{as } \sum_{i=1}^{K} f_{ij} = N_j]
\end{aligned}
$$

This proves the result.

6.1.2 A Note on Zeros

The formula for entropy given in Section 5.3.2 excludes empty classes from the summation. They correspond to zero entries in the body of the frequency table, which are also excluded from the calculation.

If a complete column of the frequency table is zero it means that the categorical attribute never takes one of its possible values at the node under consideration. Any such columns are ignored. (This corresponds to ignoring empty subsets whilst generating a decision tree, as described in Section 4.2, Figure 4.5.)

6.2 Other Attribute Selection Criteria: Gini Index of Diversity

As well as entropy (or information gain) many other methods have been proposed for selecting the attribute to split on at each stage of the TDIDT algorithm. There is a useful review of several methods by Mingers [1].

One measure that is commonly used is the *Gini Index of Diversity*. If there are K classes, with the probability of the ith class being p_i, the Gini Index is defined as $1 - \sum_{i=1}^{K} p_i^2$.

This is a measure of the 'impurity' of a dataset. Its smallest value is zero, which it takes when all the classifications are the same. It takes its largest value $1 - 1/K$ when the classes are evenly distributed between the instances, i.e. the frequency of each class is $1/K$.

Splitting on a chosen attribute gives a reduction in the average Gini Index of the resulting subsets (as it does for entropy). The new average value Gini_{new} can be calculated using the same frequency table used to calculate the new entropy value in Section 6.1.

Using the notation introduced in that section, the value of the Gini Index for the jth subset resulting from splitting on a specified attribute is G_j, where

$$G_j = 1 - \sum_{i=1}^{K} (f_{ij}/N_j)^2$$

The weighted average value of the Gini Index for the subsets resulting from splitting on the attribute is

$$
\begin{aligned}
\text{Gini}_{new} &= \sum_{j=1}^{V} N_j . G_j / N \\
&= \sum_{j=1}^{V} (N_j/N) - \sum_{j=1}^{V} \sum_{i=1}^{K} (N_j/N).(f_{ij}/N_j)^2 \\
&= 1 - \sum_{j=1}^{V} \sum_{i=1}^{K} f_{ij}^2/(N.N_j) \\
&= 1 - (1/N) \sum_{j=1}^{V} (1/N_j) \sum_{i=1}^{K} f_{ij}^2
\end{aligned}
$$

At each stage of the attribute selection process the attribute is selected which maximises the reduction in the value of the Gini Index, i.e. $\text{Gini}_{start} - \text{Gini}_{new}$.

Again taking the example of the *lens24* dataset, the initial probabilities of the three classes as given in Chapter 5 are $p_1 = 4/24$, $p_2 = 5/24$ and $p_3 = 15/24$. Hence the initial value of the Gini Index is $G_{start} = 0.5382$.

For splitting on attribute *age* the frequency table, as before, is shown in Figure 6.4.

We can now calculate the new value of the Gini Index as follows.

1. For each non-empty column, form the sum of the squares of the values in the body of the table and divide by the column sum.

2. Add the values obtained for all the columns and divide by N (the number of instances).

	age = 1	age = 2	age = 3
Class 1	2	1	1
Class 2	2	2	1
Class 3	4	5	6
Column sum	8	8	8

Figure 6.4 Frequency Table for Attribute age for *lens24* Example

3. Subtract the total from 1.

For Figure 6.4 we have

$$\textbf{age = 1:} \ (2^2 + 2^2 + 4^2)/8 = 3$$
$$\textbf{age = 2:} \ (1^2 + 2^2 + 5^2)/8 = 3.75$$
$$\textbf{age = 3:} \ (1^2 + 1^2 + 6^2)/8 = 4.75$$

$G_{new} = 1 - (3 + 3.75 + 4.75)/24 = 0.5208$.

Thus the reduction in the value of the Gini Index corresponding to splitting on attribute *age* is $0.5382 - 0.5208 = 0.0174$.

For the other three attributes, the corresponding values are

specRx: $G_{new} = 0.5278$, so the reduction is $0.5382 - 0.5278 = 0.0104$
astig: $G_{new} = 0.4653$, so the reduction is $0.5382 - 0.4653 = 0.0729$
tears: $G_{new} = 0.3264$, so the reduction is $0.5382 - 0.3264 = 0.2118$

The attribute selected would be the one which gives the largest reduction in the value of the Gini Index, i.e. *tears*. This is the same attribute that was selected using entropy.

6.3 The χ^2 Attribute Selection Criterion

Another useful attribute selection measure that can be calculated using a frequency table is the χ^2 value. χ is the Greek letter often rendered in the Roman alphabet as chi (pronounced 'sky' without the initial 's'). The term χ^2 is pronounced 'chi-square' or 'chi-squared'. It is commonly used in statistics. Its relevance to attribute selection will soon become apparent.

The method will be described in more detail and in a fuller form in a later chapter on discretisation of continuous attributes, so only a fairly brief description will be given here.

Suppose that for some dataset with three possible classifications $c1$, $c2$ and $c3$ we have an attribute A with four values $a1$, $a2$, $a3$ and $a4$, and the frequency table given in Figure 6.5.

	a1	a2	a3	a4	Total
c1	27	64	93	124	308
c2	31	54	82	105	272
c3	42	82	125	171	420
Total	100	200	300	400	1000

Figure 6.5 Frequency Table for Attribute A

We start by making the assumption that the value of A has no effect whatsoever on the classification and look for evidence that this assumption (which statisticians call the *null hypothesis*) is false.

It is quite easy to imagine four-valued attributes that are certain or almost certain to be irrelevant to a classification. For example the values in each row might correspond to the number of patients achieving a large benefit, a little benefit or no benefit (classifications $c1$, $c2$ and $c3$) from a certain medical treatment, with attribute values $a1$ to $a4$ denoting a division of patients into four groups depending on the number of siblings they have (say zero, one, two, three or more). Such a division would appear (to this layman) highly unlikely to be relevant. Other four-valued attributes far more likely to be relevant include age and weight, each converted into four ranges in this case.

The example may be made more controversial by saying that $c1$, $c2$ and $c3$ are levels achieved in some kind of intelligence test and $a1$, $a2$, $a3$ and $a4$ denote people who are married and male, married and female, unmarried and male or unmarried and female, not necessarily in that order. Does the test score obtained depend on which category you are in? Please note that we are not trying to settle such sensitive questions in this book, especially not with invented data, just (as far as this chapter is concerned) deciding which attribute should be selected when constructing a decision tree.

From now on we will treat the data as test results but to avoid controversy will not say anything about the kind of people who fall into the four categories $a1$ to $a4$.

The first point to note is that from examining the *Total* row we can see that the people who took the test had attribute values $a1$ to $a4$ in the ratio 1:2:3:4. This is simply a fact about the data we happen to have obtained and in itself implies nothing about the null hypothesis, that the division of test subjects into four groups is irrelevant.

Next consider the $c1$ row. We can see that a total of 308 people obtained classification $c1$. If the value of attribute A were irrelevant we would expect the 308 values in the cells to split in the ratio 1:2:3:4.

In cell $c1/a1$ we would expect a value of $308 * 100/1000 = 30.8$.

In $c1/a2$ we would expect twice this, i.e. $308 * 200/1000 = 61.6$.

In $c1/a3$ we would expect $308 * 300/1000 = 92.4$.

In $c1/a4$ we would expect $308 * 400/1000 = 123.2$.

(Note that the total of the four values comes to 308, as it must.)

We call the four calculated values above the *expected* values for each class/attribute value combination. The actual values in the $c1$ row: 27, 64, 93 and 124 are not far away from these. Do they and the expected values for the $c2$ and $c3$ rows support or undermine the null hypothesis, that attribute A is irrelevant?

Although the 'ideal' situation is that all the expected values are identical to the corresponding actual values, known as the *observed* values, this needs a strong caveat. If you ever read a published research paper, newspaper article etc. where for some data the expected values all turn out to be exact integers that are exactly the same as the observed values for all classification/attribute value combinations, by far the most likely explanation is that the published data is an exceptionally incompetent fraud. In the real world, such perfect accuracy is never achieved. In this example, as with most real data it is in any case impossible for the expected values to be entirely identical to the observed ones, as the former are not usually integers and the latter must be.

Figure 6.6 is an updated version of the frequency table given previously, with the observed value in each of the cells from $c1/a1$ to $c3/a4$ followed by its expected value in parentheses.

	a1	a2	a3	a4	Total
c1	27 (30.8)	64 (61.6)	93 (92.4)	124 (123.2)	308
c2	31 (27.2)	54 (54.4)	82 (81.6)	105 (108.8)	272
c3	42 (42.0)	82 (84.0)	125 (126.0)	171 (168.0)	420
Total	100	200	300	400	1000

Figure 6.6 Frequency Table for Attribute A Augmented by Expected Values

The notation normally used is to represent the observed value for each cell by O and the expected value by E. The value of E for each cell is just the product of the corresponding column sum and row sum divided by the grand total number of instances given in the bottom right-hand corner of the table. For example the E value for cell $c3/a2$ is $200 * 420/1000 = 84.0$.

We can use the values of O and E for each cell to calculate a measure of how far the frequency table varies from what we would expect if the null hypothesis (that attribute A is irrelevant) were correct. We would like the measure to be zero in the case that the E values in every cell are always identical to the corresponding O values.

The measure generally used is the χ^2 value, which is defined as the sum of the values of $(O - E)^2/E$ over all the cells.

Calculating the χ^2 value for the updated frequency table above, we have $\chi^2 = (27 - 30.8)^2/30.8 + \ldots + (171 - 168.0)^2/168.0 = 1.35$ (to two decimal places).

Is this χ^2 value small enough to give support for the null hypothesis that attribute A is irrelevant to the classification? Or is it large enough to suggest that the null hypothesis is false?

This question will be important when the same method is used later in connection with the discretisation of continuous attributes, but as far as this chapter is concerned we will ignore the question of the validity of the null hypothesis and simply record the value of χ^2. We then repeat the process with all the attributes under consideration as the attribute to split on in our decision tree and choose the one with the largest χ^2 value as the one likely to have the greatest power of discrimination amongst the three classifications.

6.4 Inductive Bias

Before going on to describe a further method of attribute selection we will introduce the idea of *inductive bias*, which will help to explain why other methods are needed.

Consider the following question, which is typical of those that used to be (and probably still are) set for school children to answer as part of a so-called 'intelligence test'.

> Find the next term in the sequence
> 1, 4, 9, 16, ...

Pause and decide on your answer before going on.

Most readers will probably have chosen the answer 25, but this is misguided. The correct answer is 20. As should be obvious, the nth term of the series is calculated from the formula:

nth term $= (-5n^4 + 50n^3 - 151n^2 + 250n - 120)/24$

By choosing 25, you display a most regrettable bias towards perfect squares.

This is not serious of course, but it *is* trying to make a serious point. Mathematically it is possible to find some formula that will justify any further development of the sequence, for example

$$1, 4, 9, 16, 20, 187, -63, 947$$

It is not even necessary for a term in a sequence to be a number. The sequence

$$1, 4, 9, 16, dog, 36, 49$$

is perfectly valid mathematically. (A restriction to numerical values shows a bias towards numbers rather than the names of types of animal.)

Despite this, there is little doubt that anyone answering the original question with 20 will be marked as wrong. (Answering with 'dog' is definitely not to be recommended.)

In practice we have a strong preference for hypothesising certain kinds of solution rather than others. A sequence such as

	$1, 4, 9, 16, 25$	(perfect squares)
or	$1, 8, 27, 64, 125, 216$	(perfect cubes)
or	$5, 8, 11, 14, 17, 20, 23, 26$	(values differ by 3)

seems reasonable, whereas one such as

$$1, 4, 9, 16, 20, 187, -63, 947$$

does not.

Whether this is right or wrong is impossible to say absolutely — it depends on the situation. It illustrates an *inductive bias*, i.e. a preference for one choice rather than another, which is not determined by the data itself (in this case, previous values in the sequence) but by external factors, such as our preferences for simplicity or familiarity with perfect squares. In school we rapidly learn that the question-setter has a strong bias in favour of sequences such as perfect squares and we give our answers to match this bias if we can.

Turning back to the task of attribute selection, any formula we use for it, however principled we believe it to be, introduces an inductive bias that is not justified purely by the data. Such bias can be helpful or harmful, depending on the dataset. We can choose a method that has a bias that we favour, but we cannot eliminate inductive bias altogether. There is no neutral, unbiased method.

Clearly it is important to be able to say what bias is introduced by any particular method of selecting attributes. For many methods this is not easy to do, but for one of the best-known methods we can. Using entropy can be shown to have a bias towards selecting attributes with a large number of values.

For many datasets this does no harm, but for some it can be undesirable. For example we may have a dataset about people that includes an attribute 'place of birth' and classifies them as responding to some medical treatment 'well', 'badly' or 'not at all'. Although the place of birth may have some effect on the classification it is probably only a minor one. Unfortunately, the information gain selection method will almost certainly choose it as the first attribute to split on in the decision tree, generating one branch for each possible place of birth. The decision tree will be very large, with many branches (rules) with very low value for classification.

6.5 Using Gain Ratio for Attribute Selection

In order to reduce the effect of the bias resulting from the use of information gain, a variant known as Gain Ratio was introduced by the Australian academic Ross Quinlan in his influential system C4.5 [2]. Gain Ratio adjusts the information gain for each attribute to allow for the breadth and uniformity of the attribute values.

The method will be illustrated using the frequency table given in Section 6.1. The value of E_{new}, the average entropy of the training sets resulting from splitting on attribute age, has previously been shown to be 1.2867 and the entropy of the original training set E_{start} has been shown to be 1.3261. It follows that

$$\text{Information Gain} = E_{start} - E_{new} = 1.3261 - 1.2867 = 0.0394.$$

Gain Ratio is defined by the formula

Gain Ratio = Information Gain/Split Information

where Split Information is a value based on the column sums.

Each non-zero column sum s contributes $-(s/N)\log_2(s/N)$ to the Split Information. Thus for Figure 6.2 the value of Split Information is

$$-(8/24)\log_2(8/24) - (8/24)\log_2(8/24) - (8/24)\log_2(8/24) = 1.5850$$

Hence Gain Ratio = 0.0394/1.5850 = 0.0249 for splitting on attribute age.

For the other three attributes, the value of *Split Information* is 1.0 in each case. Hence the values of Gain Ratio for splitting on attributes *specRx*, *astig* and *tears* are 0.0395, 0.3770 and 0.5488 respectively.

The largest value of Gain Ratio is for attribute *tears*, so in this case Gain Ratio selects the same attribute as entropy.

6.5.1 Properties of Split Information

Split Information forms the denominator in the Gain Ratio formula. Hence the higher the value of Split Information, the lower the Gain Ratio.

The value of Split Information depends on the number of values a categorical attribute has and how uniformly those values are distributed (hence the name 'Split Information').

To illustrate this we will examine the case where there are 32 instances and we are considering splitting on an attribute a, which has values 1, 2, 3 and 4.

The 'Frequency' row in the tables below is the same as the column sum row in the frequency tables used previously in this chapter.

The following examples illustrate a number of possibilities.

1. Single Attribute Value

	$a = 1$	$a = 2$	$a = 3$	$a = 4$
Frequency	32	0	0	0

Split Information $= -(32/32) \times \log_2(32/32) = -\log_2 1 = 0$

2. Different Distributions of a Given Total Frequency

	$a = 1$	$a = 2$	$a = 3$	$a = 4$
Frequency	16	16	0	0

Split Information $= -(16/32) \times \log_2(16/32) - (16/32) \times \log_2(16/32) = -\log_2(1/2) = 1$

	$a = 1$	$a = 2$	$a = 3$	$a = 4$
Frequency	16	8	8	0

Split Information $= -(16/32) \times \log_2(16/32) - 2 \times (8/32) \times \log_2(8/32) = -(1/2)\log_2(1/2) - (1/2)\log_2(1/4) = 0.5 + 1 = 1.5$

	$a = 1$	$a = 2$	$a = 3$	$a = 4$
Frequency	16	8	4	4

Split Information $= -(16/32) \times \log_2(16/32) - (8/32) \times \log_2(8/32) - 2 \times (4/32) \times \log_2(4/32) = 0.5 + 0.5 + 0.75 = 1.75$

3. Uniform Distribution of Attribute Frequencies

	$a = 1$	$a = 2$	$a = 3$	$a = 4$
Frequency	8	8	8	8

Split Information $= -4 \times (8/32) \times \log_2(8/32) = -\log_2(1/4) = \log_2 4 = 2$

In general, if there are M attribute values, each occurring equally frequently, the Split Information is $\log_2 M$ (irrespective of the frequency value).

6.5.2 Summary

Split Information is zero when there is a single attribute value.

For a given number of attribute values, the largest value of Split Information occurs when there is a uniform distribution of attribute frequencies.

For a given number of instances that are uniformly distributed, Split Information increases when the number of different attribute values increases.

The largest values of Split Information occur when there are many possible attribute values, all equally frequent.

Information Gain is generally largest when there are many possible attribute values. Dividing this value by Split Information to give Gain Ratio substantially reduces the bias towards selecting attributes with a large number of values.

6.6 Number of Rules Generated by Different Attribute Selection Criteria

Figure 6.7 repeats the results given in Figure 5.8, augmented by the results for Gain Ratio. The largest value for each dataset is given in bold and underlined.

Dataset	Excluding Entropy and Gain Ratio		Entropy	Gain Ratio
	most	least		
contact_lenses	42	26	**16**	17
lens24	21	**9**	**9**	**9**
chess	155	52	**20**	**20**
vote	116	40	34	**33**
monk1	89	53	**52**	**52**
monk2	142	109	**95**	96
monk3	77	43	28	**25**

Figure 6.7 TDIDT with Various Attribute Selection Methods

For many datasets Information Gain (i.e. entropy reduction) and Gain Ratio give the same results. For others using Gain Ratio can give a significantly smaller decision tree. However, Figure 6.7 shows that neither Information Gain nor Gain Ratio invariably gives the smallest decision tree. This is in accord with the general result that no method of attribute selection is best for all possible datasets. In practice Information Gain is probably the most commonly used method, although the popularity of C4.5 makes Gain Ratio a strong contender.

6.7 Missing Branches

The phenomenon of missing branches can occur at any stage of decision tree generation but is more likely to occur lower down in the tree where the number of instances under consideration is smaller.

As an example, suppose that tree construction has reached the following stage (only some of the nodes and branches are labelled).

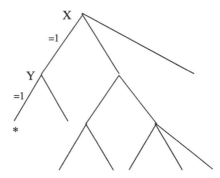

The left-most node (marked as ∗) corresponds to an incomplete rule
IF X =1 AND Y = 1 ...

Suppose that at ∗ it is decided to split on categorical attribute Z, which has four possible values a, b, c and d. Normally this would lead to four branches being created at that node, one for each of the possible categorical values. However it may be that for the instances being considered there (which may be only a small subset of the original training set) there are no cases where attribute Z has the value d. In that case only three branches would be generated, giving the following.

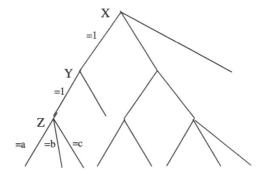

There is no branch for $Z = d$. This corresponds to an empty subset of instances where Z has that value. (The TDIDT algorithm states 'divide the instances into non-empty subsets'.)

This *missing branch* phenomenon occurs quite frequently but generally has little impact. Its drawback (if it is one) occurs when the tree is used to classify an unseen instance for which attributes X, Y and Z have the values 1, 1 and d respectively. In this case there will be no branches of the tree corresponding to the unseen instance and so none of the corresponding rules will fire and the instance will remain unclassified. This is not usually a significant problem as it may well be considered preferable to leave an unseen instance unclassified rather than to classify it wrongly. However it would be easy for a practical rule induction system to provide a facility for any unclassified instances to be given a default classification, say the largest class.

6.8 Chapter Summary

This chapter describes an alternative method of calculating the average entropy of the training (sub)sets resulting from splitting on an attribute, which uses frequency tables. It is shown to be equivalent to the method used in Chapter 5 but requires less computation. Two alternative attribute selection criteria, the Gini Index of Diversity and the χ^2 statistic, are illustrated and it is shown how they can also be calculated using a frequency table.

The important issue of inductive bias is introduced. This leads to a description of a further attribute selection criterion, Gain Ratio, which was introduced as a way of overcoming the bias of the entropy minimisation method, which is undesirable for some datasets.

6.9 Self-assessment Exercises for Chapter 6

1. Repeat Exercise 1 from Chapter 5 using the frequency table method of calculating entropy. Verify that the two methods give the same results.

2. When using the TDIDT algorithm, with the *degrees* dataset, find the attribute that will be chosen for the first split on the data using the Gain Ratio and Gini Index attribute selection strategies.

3. Suggest two datasets for which the Gain Ratio attribute selection strategy may be preferable to using entropy minimisation.

References

[1] Mingers, J. (1989). An empirical comparison of pruning methods for decision tree induction. *Machine Learning*, *4*, 227–243.

[2] Quinlan, J. R. (1993). *C4.5: programs for machine learning.* San Mateo: Morgan Kaufmann.

7

Estimating the Predictive Accuracy of a Classifier

7.1 Introduction

Any algorithm which assigns a classification to unseen instances is called a *classifier*. A decision tree of the kind described in earlier chapters is one very popular type of classifier, but there are several others, some of which are described elsewhere in this book.

This chapter is concerned with estimating the performance of a classifier of *any* kind but will be illustrated using decision trees generated with attribute selection using information gain, as described in Chapter 5.

Although the data compression referred to in Chapter 4 can sometimes be important, in practice the principal reason for generating a classifier is to enable unseen instances to be classified. However we have already seen that many different classifiers can be generated from a given dataset. Each one is likely to perform differently on a set of unseen instances.

The most obvious criterion to use for estimating the performance of a classifier is *predictive accuracy*, i.e. the proportion of a set of unseen instances that it correctly classifies. This is often seen as the most important criterion but other criteria are also important, for example algorithmic complexity, efficient use of machine resources and comprehensibility.

For most domains of interest the number of possible unseen instances is potentially very large (e.g. all those who might develop an illness, the weather for every possible day in the future or all the possible objects that might appear

© Springer-Verlag London Ltd., part of Springer Nature 2020
M. Bramer, *Principles of Data Mining*, Undergraduate Topics
in Computer Science, DOI 10.1007/978-1-4471-7493-6_7

on a radar display), so it is not possible ever to establish the predictive accuracy beyond dispute. Instead, it is usual to *estimate* the predictive accuracy of a classifier by measuring its accuracy for a sample of data not used when it was generated. There are three main strategies commonly used for this: dividing the data into a training set and a test set, *k-fold cross-validation* and *N-fold* (or *leave-one-out*) *cross-validation*.

7.2 Method 1: Separate Training and Test Sets

For the 'train and test' method the available data is split into two parts called a *training set* and a *test set* (Figure 7.1). First, the training set is used to construct a classifier (decision tree, neural net etc.). The classifier is then used to predict the classification for the instances in the test set. If the test set contains N instances of which C are correctly classified the *predictive accuracy* of the classifier for the test set is $p = C/N$. This can be used as an estimate of its performance on any unseen dataset.

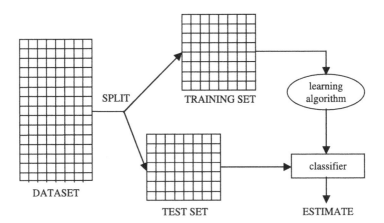

Figure 7.1 Train and Test

NOTE. For some datasets in the UCI Repository (and elsewhere) the data is provided as two separate files, designated as the training set and the test set. In such cases we will consider the two files together as comprising the 'dataset' for that application. In cases where the dataset is only a single file we need to divide it into a training set and a test set before using Method 1. This may be done in many ways, but a random division into two parts in proportions such as 1:1, 2:1, 70:30 or 60:40 would be customary.

7.2.1 Standard Error

It is important to bear in mind that the overall aim is not (just) to classify the instances in the test set but to estimate the predictive accuracy of the classifier for all possible unseen instances, which will generally be many times the number of instances contained in the test set.

If the predictive accuracy calculated for the test set is p and we go on to use the classifier to classify the instances in a different test set, it is very likely that a different value for predictive accuracy would be obtained. All that we can say is that p is an *estimate* of the true predictive accuracy of the classifier for all possible unseen instances.

We cannot determine the true value without collecting all the instances and running the classifier on them, which is usually an impossible task. Instead, we can use statistical methods to find a range of values within which the true value of the predictive accuracy lies, with a given probability or 'confidence level'.

To do this we use the *standard error* associated with the estimated value p. If p is calculated using a test set of N instances the value of its standard error is $\sqrt{p(1-p)/N}$. (The proof of this is outside the scope of this book, but can readily be found in many statistics textbooks.)

The significance of standard error is that it enables us to say that with a specified probability (which we can choose) the true predictive accuracy of the classifier is within so many standard errors above or below the estimated value p. The more certain we wish to be, the greater the number of standard errors. The probability is called the *confidence level*, denoted by CL and the number of standard errors is usually written as Z_{CL}.

Figure 7.2 shows the relationship between commonly used values of CL and Z_{CL}.

Confidence Level (CL)	0.9	0.95	0.99
Z_{CL}	1.64	1.96	2.58

Figure 7.2 Values of Z_{CL} for Certain Confidence Levels

If the predictive accuracy for a test set is p, with standard error S, then using this table we can say that with probability CL (or with a confidence level CL) the true predictive accuracy lies in the interval $p \pm Z_{CL} \times S$.

Example

If the classifications of 80 instances out of a test set of 100 instances were predicted accurately, the predictive accuracy on the test set would be $80/100 = 0.8$. The standard error would be $\sqrt{0.8 \times 0.2/100} = \sqrt{0.0016} = 0.04$. We can say that with probability 0.95 the true predictive accuracy lies in the interval $0.8 \pm 1.96 \times 0.04$, i.e. between 0.7216 and 0.8784 (to four decimal places).

Instead of a predictive accuracy of 0.8 (or 80%) we often refer to an *error rate* of 0.2 (or 20%). The standard error for the error rate is the same as that for predictive accuracy.

The value of CL to use when estimating predictive accuracy is a matter of choice, although it is usual to choose a value of at least 0.9. The predictive accuracy of a classifier is often quoted in technical papers as just $p \pm \sqrt{p(1-p)/N}$ without any multiplier Z_{CL}.

7.2.2 Repeated Train and Test

Here the classifier is used to classify k test sets, not just one. If all the test sets are of the same size, N, the predictive accuracy values obtained for the k test sets are then averaged to produce an overall estimate p.

As the total number of instances in the test sets is kN, the standard error of the estimate p is $\sqrt{p(1-p)/kN}$.

If the test sets are not all of the same size the calculations are slightly more complicated.

If there are N_i instances in the ith test set ($1 \le i \le k$) and the predictive accuracy calculated for the ith test set is p_i the overall predictive accuracy p is $\sum_{i=1}^{i=k} p_i N_i / T$ where $\sum_{i=1}^{i=k} N_i = T$, i.e. p is the weighted average of the p_i values. The standard error is $\sqrt{p(1-p)/T}$.

7.3 Method 2: k-fold Cross-validation

An alternative approach to 'train and test' that is often adopted when the number of instances is small (and which many prefer to use regardless of size) is known as *k-fold cross-validation* (Figure 7.3).

If the dataset comprises N instances, these are divided into k equal parts, k typically being a small number such as 5 or 10. (If N is not exactly divisible by k, the final part will have fewer instances than the other $k-1$ parts.) A series of k runs is now carried out. Each of the k parts in turn is used as a test set and the other $k - 1$ parts are used as a training set.

The total number of instances correctly classified (in all k runs combined) is divided by the total number of instances N to give an overall level of predictive accuracy p, with standard error $\sqrt{p(1-p)/N}$.

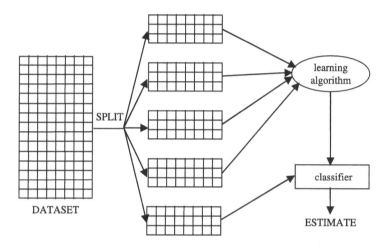

Figure 7.3 k-fold Cross-validation

7.4 Method 3: N-fold Cross-validation

N-fold cross-validation is an extreme case of k-fold cross-validation, often known as 'leave-one-out' cross-validation or jack-knifing, where the dataset is divided into as many parts as there are instances, each instance effectively forming a test set of one.

N classifiers are generated, each from $N - 1$ instances, and each is used to classify a single test instance. The predictive accuracy p is the total number correctly classified divided by the total number of instances. The standard error is $\sqrt{p(1-p)/N}$.

The large amount of computation involved makes N-fold cross-validation unsuitable for use with large datasets. For other datasets, it is not clear whether any gain in the accuracy of the estimates produced by using N-fold cross-validation justifies the additional computation involved. In practice, the method is most likely to be of benefit with very small datasets where as much data as possible needs to be used to train the classifier.

7.5 Experimental Results I

In this section we look at experiments to estimate the predictive accuracy of classifiers generated for four datasets.

All the results in this section were obtained using the TDIDT tree induction algorithm, with information gain used for attribute selection.

Basic information about the datasets is given in Figure 7.4 below. Further information about these and most of the other datasets mentioned in this book is given in Appendix B.

Dataset	Description	classes	attributes+		instances	
			categ	cts	training set	test set
vote	Voting in US Congress in 1984	2	16		300	135
pima-indians	Prevalence of Diabetes in Pima Indian Women	2		8	768	
chess	Chess Endgame	2	7		647	
glass	Glass Identification	7		9*	214	

+ categ: categorical; cts: continuous
* plus one 'ignore' attribute

Figure 7.4 Four Datasets

The *vote*, *pima-indians* and *glass* datasets are all taken from the UCI Repository. The *chess* dataset was constructed for a well-known series of machine learning experiments [1].

The *vote* dataset has separate training and test sets. The other three datasets were first divided into two parts, with every third instance placed in the test set and the other two placed in the training set in both cases.

The result for the *vote* dataset illustrates the point that TDIDT (along with some but not all other classification algorithms) is sometimes unable to classify an unseen instance (Figure 7.5). The reason for this was discussed in Section 6.7.

Dataset	Test set (instances)	Correctly classified	Incorrectly classified	Unclassified
vote	135	126 (93% ± 2%)	7	2
pima-indians	256	191 (75% ± 3%)	65	
chess	215	214 (99.5% ± 0.5%)	1	
glass	71	50 (70% ± 5%)	21	

Figure 7.5 Train and Test Results for Four Datasets

Unclassified instances can be dealt with by giving the classifier a 'default strategy', such as always allocating them to the largest class, and that will be the approach followed for the remainder of this chapter. It could be argued that it might be better to leave unclassified instances as they are, rather than risk introducing errors by assigning them to a specific class or classes. In practice the number of unclassified instances is generally small and how they are handled makes little difference to the overall predictive accuracy.

Figure 7.6 gives the 'train and test' result for the *vote* dataset modified to incorporate the 'default to largest class' strategy. The difference is slight.

Dataset	Test set (instances)	Correctly classified	Incorrectly classified
vote	135	127 (94% ± 2%)	8

Figure 7.6 Train and Test Results for vote Dataset (Modified)

Figures 7.7 and 7.8 show the results obtained using 10-fold and N-fold Cross-validation for the four datasets.

For the *vote* dataset the 300 instances in the training set are used. For the other two datasets all the available instances are used.

Dataset	Instances	Correctly classified	Incorrectly classified
vote	300	275 (92% ± 2%)	25
pima-indians	768	536 (70% ± 2%)	232
chess	647	645 (99.7% ± 0.2%)	2
glass	214	149 (70% ± 3%)	65

Figure 7.7 10-fold Cross-validation Results for Four Datasets

All the figures given in this section are estimates. The 10-fold cross-validation and N-fold cross-validation results for all four datasets are based

Dataset	Instances	Correctly classified	Incorrectly classified
vote	300	278 (93% ± 2%)	22
pima-indians	768	517 (67% ± 2%)	251
chess	647	646 (99.8% ± 0.2%)	1
glass	214	144 (67% ± 3%)	70

Figure 7.8 *N*-fold Cross-validation Results for Four Datasets

on considerably more instances than those in the corresponding test sets for the 'train and test' experiments and so are more likely to be reliable.

7.6 Experimental Results II: Datasets with Missing Values

We now look at experiments to estimate the predictive accuracy of a classifier in the case of datasets with missing values. As before we will generate all the classifiers using the TDIDT algorithm, with Information Gain for attribute selection.

Three datasets were used in these experiments, all from the UCI Repository. Basic information about each one is given in Figure 7.9 below.

Dataset	Description	classes	attributes[+]		instances	
			categ	cts	training set	test set
crx	Credit Card Applications	2	9	6	690 (37)	200 (12)
hypo	Hypothyroid Disorders	5	22	7	2514 (2514)	1258 (371)
labor-ne	Labor Negotiations	2	8	8	40 (39)	17 (17)

+ categ: categorical; cts: continuous

Figure 7.9 Three Datasets with Missing Values

Each dataset has both a training set and a separate test set. In each case, there are missing values in both the training set and the test set. The values in parentheses in the 'training set' and 'test set' columns show the number of instances that have at least one missing value.

The 'train and test' method was used for estimating predictive accuracy.

Two strategies for dealing with missing attribute values were described in Section 2.4. We give results for each of these in turn.

7.6.1 Strategy 1: Discard Instances

This is the simplest strategy: delete all instances where there is at least one missing value and use the remainder. This strategy has the advantage of avoiding introducing any data errors. Its main disadvantage is that discarding data may damage the reliability of the resulting classifier.

A second disadvantage is that the method cannot be used when a high proportion of the instances in the training set have missing values, as is the case for example with both the *hypo* and the *labor-ne* datasets. A final disadvantage is that it is not possible with this strategy to classify any instances in the test set that have missing values.

Together these weaknesses are quite substantial. Although the 'discard instances' strategy may be worth trying when the proportion of missing values is small, it is not recommended in general.

Of the three datasets listed in Figure 7.9, the 'discard instances' strategy can only be applied to *crx*. Doing so gives the possibly surprising result in Figure 7.10.

Dataset	MV strategy	Rules	Test set	
			Correct	Incorrect
crx	Discard Instances	118	188	0

Figure 7.10 Discard Instances Strategy with *crx* Dataset

Clearly discarding the 37 instances with at least one missing value from the training set (5.4%) does not prevent the algorithm constructing a decision tree capable of classifying the 188 instances in the test set that do not have missing values correctly in every case.

7.6.2 Strategy 2: Replace by Most Frequent/Average Value

With this strategy any missing values of a categorical attribute are replaced by its most commonly occurring value in the training set. Any missing values of a continuous attribute are replaced by its average value in the training set.

Figure 7.11 shows the result of applying the 'Most Frequent/Average Value' strategy to the *crx* dataset. As for the 'Discard Instances' strategy all instances in the test set are correctly classified, but this time all 200 instances in the test set are classified, not just the 188 instances in the test set that do not have missing values.

Dataset	MV strategy	Rules	Test set	
			Correct	Incorrect
crx	Discard Instances	118	188	0
crx	Most Frequent/Average Value	139	200	0

Figure 7.11 Comparison of Strategies with *crx* Dataset

With this strategy we can also construct classifiers from the *hypo* and *crx* datasets.

In the case of the *hypo* dataset, we get a decision tree with just 15 rules. The average number of terms per rule is 4.8. When applied to the test data this tree is able to classify correctly 1251 of the 1258 instances in the test set (99%; Figure 7.12). This is a remarkable result with so few rules, especially as there are missing values in every instance in the training set. It gives considerable credence to the belief that using entropy for constructing a decision tree is an effective approach.

Dataset	MV strategy	Rules	Test set	
			Correct	Incorrect
hypo	Most Frequent/Average Value	15	1251	7

Figure 7.12 Most Frequent Value/Average Strategy with *hypo* Dataset

In the case of the *labor-ne* dataset, we obtain a classifier with five rules, which correctly classifies 14 out of the 17 instances in the test set (Figure 7.13).

Dataset	MV strategy	Rules	Test set	
			Correct	Incorrect
labor-ne	Most Frequent/Average Value	5	14	3

Figure 7.13 Most Frequent Value/Average Strategy with *labor-ne* Dataset

7.6.3 Missing Classifications

It is worth noting that for each dataset given in Figure 7.9 the missing values are those of attributes, not classifications. Missing classifications in the training set are a far larger problem than missing attribute values. One possible approach would be to replace them all by the most frequently occurring classification but this is unlikely to prove successful in most cases. The best approach is probably to discard any instances with missing classifications.

7.7 Confusion Matrix

As well as the overall predictive accuracy on unseen instances it is often helpful to see a breakdown of the classifier's performance, i.e. how frequently instances of class X were correctly classified as class X or misclassified as some other class. This information is given in a *confusion matrix*.

The confusion matrix in Figure 7.14 gives the results obtained in 'train and test' mode from the TDIDT algorithm (using information gain for attribute selection) for the *vote* test set, which has two possible classifications: 'republican' and 'democrat'.

Correct	Classified as	
classification	democrat	republican
democrat	81 (97.6%)	2 (2.4%)
republican	6 (11.5%)	46 (88.5%)

Figure 7.14 Example of a Confusion Matrix

The body of the table has one row and column for each possible classification. The rows correspond to the correct classifications. The columns correspond to the predicted classifications.

The value in the ith row and jth column gives the number of instances for which the correct classification is the ith class which are classified as belonging to the jth class. If all the instances were correctly classified, the only non-zero entries would be on the 'leading diagonal' running from top left (i.e. row 1, column 1) down to bottom right.

To demonstrate that the use of a confusion matrix is not restricted to datasets with two classifications, Figure 7.15 shows the results obtained using 10-fold cross-validation with the TDIDT algorithm (using information gain for attribute section) for the *glass* dataset, which has six classifications: 1, 2, 3, 5, 6 and 7 (there is also a class 4 but it is not used for the training data).

Correct	Classified as					
classification	1	2	3	5	6	7
1	52	10	7	0	0	1
2	15	50	6	2	1	2
3	5	6	6	0	0	0
5	0	2	0	10	0	1
6	0	1	0	0	7	1
7	1	3	0	1	0	24

Figure 7.15   Confusion Matrix for *glass* Dataset

7.7.1 True and False Positives

When a dataset has only two classes, one is often regarded as 'positive' (i.e. the class of principal interest) and the other as 'negative'. In this case the entries in the two rows and columns of the confusion matrix are referred to as *true and false positives* and *true and false negatives* (Figure 7.16).

Correct classification	Classified as	
	+	−
+	true positives	false negatives
−	false positives	true negatives

Figure 7.16   True and False Positives and Negatives

When there are more than two classes, one class is sometimes important enough to be regarded as positive, with all the other classes combined treated as negative. For example we might consider class 1 for the *glass* dataset as the 'positive' class and classes 2, 3, 5, 6 and 7 combined as 'negative'. The confusion matrix given as Figure 7.15 can then be rewritten as shown in Figure 7.17.

Of the 73 instances classified as positive, 52 genuinely are positive (true positives) and the other 21 are really negative (false positives). Of the 141 instances classified as negative, 18 are really positive (false negatives) and the other 123 are genuinely negative (true negatives). With a perfect classifier there would be no false positives or false negatives.

Correct classification	Classified as	
	+	−
+	52	18
−	21	123

Figure 7.17 Revised Confusion Matrix for *glass* Dataset

False positives and false negatives may not be of equal importance, e.g. we may be willing to accept some false positives as long as there are no false negatives or vice versa. We will return to this topic in Chapter 12.

7.8 Chapter Summary

This chapter is concerned with estimating the performance of a classifier (of any kind). Three methods are described for estimating a classifier's predictive accuracy. The first of these is to divide the data available into a training set used for generating the classifier and a test set used for evaluating its performance. The other methods are k-fold cross-validation and its extreme form N-fold (or leave-one-out) cross-validation.

A statistical measure of the accuracy of an estimate formed using any of these methods, known as *standard error* is introduced. Experiments to estimate the predictive accuracy of the classifiers generated for various datasets are described, including datasets with missing attribute values. Finally a tabular way of presenting classifier performance information called a *confusion matrix* is introduced, together with the notion of true and false positive and negative classifications.

7.9 Self-assessment Exercises for Chapter 7

1. Calculate the predictive accuracy and standard error corresponding to the confusion matrices given in Figures 7.14 and 7.15. For each dataset, state the range in which the true value of the predictive accuracy can be expected to lie with probability 0.9, 0.95 and 0.99.

2. Suggest some classification tasks for which either false positive or false negative classifications (or both) would be undesirable. For these tasks, what

proportion of false negative (positive) classifications would you be willing to accept in order to reduce the proportion of false positives (negatives) to zero?

Reference

[1] Quinlan, J. R. (1979). Discovering rules by induction from large collections of examples. In D. Michie (Ed.), *Expert systems in the micro-electronic age* (pp. 168–201). Edinburgh: Edinburgh University Press.

Continuous Attributes

8.1 Introduction

Many data mining algorithms, including the TDIDT tree generation algorithm, require all attributes to take categorical values. However, in the real world many attributes are naturally *continuous*, e.g. height, weight, length, temperature and speed. It is essential for a practical data mining system to be able to handle such attributes. In some cases the algorithms can be adapted for use with continuous attributes. In other cases, this is hard or impossible to do.

Although it would be possible to treat a continuous attribute as a categorical one with values 6.3, 7.2, 8.3, 9.2 etc., say, this is very unlikely to prove satisfactory in general. If the continuous attribute has a large number of different values in the training set, it is likely that any particular value will only occur a small number of times, perhaps only once, and rules that include tests for specific values such as $X = 7.2$ will probably be of very little value for prediction.

The standard approach is to split the values of a continuous attribute into a number of non-overlapping ranges. For example a continuous attribute X might be divided into the four ranges $X < 7$, $7 \leq X < 12$, $12 \leq X < 20$ and $X \geq 20$. This allows it to be treated as a categorical attribute with four possible values. In the figure below, the values 7, 12 and 20 are called *cut values* or *cut points*.

$X < 7$	$7 \leq X < 12$	$12 \leq X < 20$	$X \geq 20$
	7	12	20

© Springer-Verlag London Ltd., part of Springer Nature 2020
M. Bramer, *Principles of Data Mining*, Undergraduate Topics
in Computer Science, DOI 10.1007/978-1-4471-7493-6_8

As further examples, an *age* attribute might be converted from a continuous numerical value into six ranges, corresponding to infant, child, young adult, adult, middle-aged and old, or a continuous attribute *height* might be replaced by a categorical one with values such as very short, short, medium, tall, very tall.

Converting a continuous attribute to one with a discrete set of values, i.e. a categorical attribute, is known as *discretisation*.

There are a number of possible approaches to discretising continuous attributes. Ideally the boundary points chosen for the ranges (the cut points) should reflect real properties of the domain being investigated, e.g. constant values in a physical or mathematical law. In practice it is very rarely possible to give principled reasons for choosing one set of ranges over another (for example where should the boundary be between tall and very tall or between medium and tall?) and the choice of ranges will generally have to be made pragmatically.

Suppose that we have a continuous attribute *length*, with values in the range from 0.3 to 6.6 inclusive. One possibility would be to divide these into three ranges of equal size, i.e.

$0.3 \leq length < 2.4$

$2.4 \leq length < 4.5$

$4.5 \leq length \leq 6.6$

This is known as the *equal width intervals* method. However there are obvious problems. Why choose three ranges, not four or two (or twelve)? More fundamentally it may be that some, or perhaps even many, of the values are in a narrow range such as 2.35 to 2.45. In this case any rule involving a test on *length* < 2.4 would include instances where *length* is say 2.39999 and exclude those where *length* is 2.40001. It is highly unlikely that there is any real difference between those values, especially if they were all measured imprecisely by different people at different times. On the other hand, if there were no values between say 2.3 and 2.5, a test such as *length* < 2.4 would probably be far more reasonable.

Another possibility would be to divide *length* into three ranges, this time so that there are the same number of instances in each of the three ranges. This might lead to a split such as

$0.3 \leq length < 2.385$

$2.385 \leq length < 3.0$

$3.0 \leq length \leq 6.6$

This is known as the *equal frequency intervals* method. It would seem to be preferable to the equal width intervals method given above but is still prone to the same problem at cut points, e.g. why is a length of 2.99999 treated differently from one of 3.00001?

The problem with any method of discretising continuous attributes is that of over-sensitivity. Whichever cut points are chosen there will always be a potential problem with values that fall just below a cut point being treated differently from those that fall just above for no principled reason.

Ideally we would like to find 'gaps' in the range of values. If in the *length* example there were many values from 0.3 to 0.4 with the next smallest value being 2.2, a test such as *length* < 1.0 would avoid problems around the cut point, as there are no instances (in the training set) with values close to 1.0. The value 1.0 is obviously arbitrary and a different cut point, e.g. 1.5 could just as well have been chosen. Unfortunately the same gaps may not occur in unseen test data. If there were values such as 0.99, 1.05, 1.49 and 1.51 in the test data, whether the arbitrary choice of cut point was 1.0 or 1.5 could be of critical importance.

Although both the equal width intervals and the equal frequency intervals methods are reasonably effective, they both suffer from the fundamental weakness, as far as classification problems are concerned, that they take no account of the classifications when determining where to place the cut points, and other methods which do make use of the classifications are generally preferred. Two of these are described in Sections 8.3 and 8.4.

8.2 Local versus Global Discretisation

Some data mining algorithms, such as the TDIDT rule generation algorithm, can be adapted so that each continuous attribute is converted to a categorical attribute at each stage of the process (e.g. at each node of the decision tree). This is known as *local discretisation*.

An alternative approach is to use a *global discretisation* algorithm to convert each continuous attribute to a categorical one once and for all independently of any data mining algorithm that may subsequently be applied to the converted training set. For example, continuous attribute *Age* might be converted to categorical attribute *Age2*, with four values *A*, *B*, *C* and *D*, corresponding to ages in the intervals 0 to under 16, 16 to under 30, 30 to under 60 and 60 and over, respectively, with the three 'split values' 16, 30 and 60 determined *globally* from consideration of the training set as a whole. Although attractive in principle, finding an appropriate global discretisation is not necessarily easy to achieve in practice.

8.3 Adding Local Discretisation to TDIDT

The TDIDT algorithm is a widely used method of generating classification rules via the intermediate representation of a decision tree. (For definiteness in the description that follows we shall assume that the information gain attribute selection criterion is used, but this is not essential.) TDIDT can be extended to deal with continuous attributes in a number of ways. For example, at each node in the decision tree each continuous attribute can be converted to a categorical attribute with several values, by one of the methods described in Section 8.1 or otherwise.

An alternative approach is at each node to convert each continuous attribute to a number of alternative categorical attributes. For example if continuous attribute A has values -12.4, -2.4, 3.5, 6.7 and 8.5 (each possibly occurring several times) a test such as $A < 3.5$ splits the training data into two parts, those instances for which $A < 3.5$ and those for which $A \geq 3.5$. A test such as $A < 3.5$ can be considered as equivalent to a kind of categorical attribute with the two possible values true and false. We will use the phrase *pseudo-attribute* to describe it.

If a continuous attribute A has n distinct values $v_1, v_2, \ldots, v_n$ (in ascending numerical order) there are $n-1$ possible corresponding pseudo-attributes (all binary), i.e. $A < v_2$, $A < v_3$, $\ldots$, $A < v_n$ (we omit $A < v_1$ as no values of A can be less than v_1, the smallest value).

We can imagine that for the part of the training set under consideration at each node all the continuous attribute columns are replaced by new columns for each pseudo-attribute derived from each continuous attribute. They would then be in competition for selection with each other and with any genuine categorical attributes. This imaginary replacement table will probably have far more columns than before but as all the attributes/pseudo-attributes are categorical it can be processed by the standard TDIDT algorithm to find the one with the largest corresponding information gain (or other measure).

If it turns out that one of the pseudo-attributes, say $Age < 27.3$, is selected at a given node, we can consider the continuous attribute Age as having been discretised into two intervals with cut point 27.3.

This is a local discretisation which does not (in the standard form of this method) lead to the continuous attribute itself being discarded. Hence there may be a further test such as $Age < 14.1$ at a lower level in the 'yes' branch descending from the test $Age < 27.3$.

The process described above may seem resource intensive but it is not as bad as it would first appear. We will come back to this point in Section 8.3.2, but leaving it aside at the moment, we have an algorithm for incorporating local discretisation into TDIDT as follows.

At each node:

1. For each continuous attribute A

   a) Sort the instances into ascending numerical order.

   b) If there are n distinct values $v_1, v_2, \ldots, v_n$, calculate the values of information gain (or other measure) for each of the $n-1$ corresponding pseudo-attributes $A < v_2, A < v_3, \ldots, A < v_n$.

   c) Find which of the $n-1$ attribute values gives the largest value of information gain (or optimises some other measure). If this is v_i return the pseudo-attribute $A < v_i$, and the value of the corresponding measure.

2. Calculate the value of information gain (or other measure) for any categorical attributes.

3. Select the attribute or pseudo-attribute with the largest value of information gain (or which optimises some other measure).

8.3.1 Calculating the Information Gain of a Set of Pseudo-attributes

At any node of the evolving decision tree the entropy values (and hence the information gain values) of all the pseudo-attributes derived from a given continuous attribute can be calculated with a single pass through the training data. The same applies to any other measure that can be calculated using the frequency table method described in Chapter 6. There are three stages.

Stage 1
Before processing any continuous attributes at a node we first need to count the number of instances with each of the possible classifications in the part of the training set under consideration at the node. (These are the sums of the values in each row of a frequency table such as Figure 6.2.) These values do not depend on which attribute is subsequently processed and so only have to be counted once at each node of the tree.

Stage 2
We next work through the continuous attributes one by one. We will assume that a particular continuous attribute under consideration is named *Var* and that the aim is to find the largest value of a specified measure for all possible pseudo-attributes *Var* < *X* where *X* is one of the values of *Var* in the part of the training set under consideration at the given node. We will call the values of attribute *Var candidate cut points*. We will call the largest value of measure *maxmeasure* and the value of *X* that gives that largest value the *cut point* for attribute *Var*.

Stage 3
Having found the value of *maxmeasure* (and the corresponding cut points) for all the continuous attributes, we next need to find the largest and then compare it with the values of the measure obtained for any categorical attributes to determine which attribute or pseudo-attribute to split on at the node.

To illustrate this process we will use the *golf* training set introduced in Chapter 4. For simplicity we will assume that we are at the root node of the decision tree but the same method can be applied (with a reduced training set of course) at any node of the tree.

We start by counting the number of instances with each of the possible classifications. Here there are 9 *play* and 5 *don't play*, making a total of 14.

We now need to process each of the continuous attributes in turn (Stage 2). There are two: *temperature* and *humidity*. We will illustrate the processing involved at Stage 2 using attribute *temperature*.

The first step is to sort the values of the attribute into ascending numerical order and create a table containing just two columns: one for the sorted attribute values and the other for the corresponding classification. We will call this the *sorted instances table*.

Figure 8.1 shows the result of this for our example. Note that temperature values 72 and 75 both occur twice. There are 12 distinct values 64, 65, ..., 85.

Temperature	Class
64	play
65	don't play
68	play
69	play
70	play
71	don't play
72	play
72	don't play
75	play
75	play
80	don't play
81	play
83	play
85	don't play

Figure 8.1 Sorted Instances Table for *golf* Dataset

The algorithm for processing the sorted instances table for continuous attribute *Var* is given in Figure 8.2. It is assumed that there are n instances and the rows in the sorted instances table are numbered from 1 to n. The attribute value corresponding to row i is denoted by value(i) and the corresponding class is denoted by class(i).

Essentially, we work through the table row by row from top to bottom, accumulating a count of the number of instances with each classification. As each row is processed its attribute value is compared with the value for the row below. If the latter value is larger it is treated as a candidate cut point and the value of the measure is computed using the frequency table method (the example that follows will show how this is done). Otherwise the attribute values must be the same and processing continues to the next row. After the last but one row has been processed, processing stops (the final row has nothing below it with which to compare).

The algorithm returns two values: *maxmeasure* and *cutvalue*, which are respectively the largest value of the measure that can be obtained for a pseudo-attribute derived from attribute *Var* and the corresponding cut value.

Algorithm for Processing a Sorted Instances Table
Set count of all classes to zero

Set maxmeasure to a value less than the smallest
possible value of the measure used

for $i = 1$ to $n - 1$ {
  increase count of class(i) by 1
  if value(i) < value($i + 1$){
    (a) Construct a frequency table for pseudo-attribute
       Var < value($i + 1$)
    (b) Calculate the value of *measure*
    (c) If measure > maxmeasure {
        maxmeasure = measure
        cutvalue = value($i + 1$)
    }
  }
}

Figure 8.2 Algorithm for Processing a Sorted Instances Table

Returning to the *golf* training set and continuous attribute temperature, we start with the first instance, which has temperature 64 and class *play*. We increase the count for class *play* to 1. The count for class *don't play* is zero. The value of temperature is less than that for the next instance so we construct a frequency table for the pseudo-attribute *temperature* < 65 (Figure 8.3(a)).

Class	*temperature* < 65	*temperature* ≥ 65	Class total
play	1 *	8	**9**
don't play	0 *	5	**5**
Column sum	1	13	**14**

Figure 8.3(a) Frequency Table for *golf* Example

In this and the other frequency tables in this section the counts of play and don't play in the 'temperature < xxx' column are marked with an asterisk. The entries in the final column are fixed (the same for all attributes) and are shown in bold. All the other entries are calculated from these by simple addition and subtraction. Once the frequency table has been constructed, the values of measures such as Information Gain and Gain Ratio can be calculated from it, as described in Chapter 6.

Figure 8.3(b) shows the frequency table resulting after the next row of the sorted instances table has been examined. The counts are now $play = 1$, $don't$ $play = 1$.

Class	$temperature < 68$	$temperature \geq 68$	Class total
play	1 *	8	9
don't play	1 *	4	5
Column sum	2	12	14

Figure 8.3(b)   Frequency Table for *golf* Example

The value of Information Gain (or the other measures) can again be calculated from this table. The important point here is how easily this second frequency table can be derived from the first. Only the *don't play* row has changed by moving just one instance from the 'greater than or equal to' column to the 'less than' column.

We proceed in this way processing rows 3, 4, 5 and 6 and generating a new frequency table (and hence a new value of measure) for each one. When we come to the seventh row ($temperature = 72$) we note that the value of temperature for the next instance is the same as for the current one (both 72), so we do not create a new frequency table but instead go on to row 8. As the value of temperature for this is different from that for the next instance we construct a frequency table for the latter value, i.e. for pseudo-attribute $temperature < 75$ (Figure 8.3(c)).

Class	$temperature < 75$	$temperature \geq 75$	Class total
play	5 *	4	9
don't play	3 *	2	5
Column sum	8	6	14

Figure 8.3(c)   Frequency Table for *golf* Example

We go on in this way until we have processed row 13 (out of 14). This ensures that frequency tables are constructed for all the distinct values of temperature except the first. There are 11 of these candidate cut values, corresponding to pseudo-attributes $temperature < 65$, $temperature < 68$, ..., $temperature < 85$.

The value of this method is that the 11 frequency tables are generated from each other one by one, by a single pass through the sorted instances table.

At each stage it is only necessary to update the relevant count of instances in the appropriate class to move from one frequency table to the next. Having duplicated attribute values is a complication, but it is easily overcome.

8.3.2 Computational Efficiency

This section looks at three efficiency issues associated with the method described in Section 8.3.1.

(a) *Sorting continuous values into ascending numerical order*

This is the principal overhead on the use of the method and thus the principal limitation on the maximum size of training set that can be handled. This is also true of almost any other conceivable method of discretising continuous attributes. For this algorithm it has to be carried out once for each continuous attribute at each node of the decision tree.

It is important to use an efficient method of sorting, especially if the number of instances is large. The one most commonly used is probably Quicksort, descriptions of which are readily available from books (and websites) about sorting. Its most important feature is that the number of operations required is approximately a constant multiple of $n \times \log_2 n$, where n is the number of instances. We say it *varies as* $n \times \log_2 n$. This may not seem important but there are other sorting algorithms that vary as n^2 (or worse) and the difference is considerable.

Figure 8.4 shows the values of $n \times \log_2 n$ and n^2 for different values of n. It is clear from the table that a good choice of sorting algorithm is essential.

n	$n \times \log_2 n$	n^2
100	664	10,000
500	4,483	250,000
1,000	9,966	1,000,000
10,000	132,877	100,000,000
100,000	1,660,964	10,000,000,000
1,000,000	19,931,569	1,000,000,000,000

Figure 8.4   Comparison of Values of $n \log_2 n$ and n^2

The difference between the values in the second and third columns of this table is considerable. Taking the final row for illustration, if we imagine a sorting task for 1,000,000 items (not a huge number) that takes 19,931,569 steps and assume that each step takes just one microsecond to perform, the time required would be 19.9 seconds. If we used an alternative method to perform the same task that takes 1,000,000,000,000 steps, each lasting a microsecond, the time would increase to over 11.5 days.

(b) *Calculating the measure value for each frequency table*

For any given continuous attribute, generating the frequency tables takes just one pass through the training data. The number of such tables is the same as the number of cut values, i.e. the number of distinct attribute values (ignoring the first). Each table comprises just $2 \times 2 = 4$ entries in its main body plus two column sums. Processing many of these small tables should be reasonably manageable.

(c) *Number of candidate cut points*

As the method was described in Section 8.3.1 the number of candidate cut points is always the same as the number of distinct values of the attribute (ignoring the first). For a large training set the number of distinct values may also be large. One possibility is to reduce the number of candidate cut points by making use of class information.

Figure 8.5 is the sorted instances table for the *golf* training set and attribute *temperature*, previously shown in Section 8.3.1, with the eleven cut values indicated with asterisks (where there are repeated attribute values only the last occurrence is treated as a cut value).

We can reduce this number by applying the rule 'only include attribute values for which the class value is different from that for the previous attribute value'. Thus attribute value 65 is included because the corresponding class value (don't play) is different from the class corresponding to temperature 64, which is play. Attribute value 69 is excluded because the corresponding class (play) is the same as that for attribute value 68. Figure 8.6 shows the result of applying this rule.

The instances with temperature value 65, 68, 71, 81 and 85 are included. Instances with value 69, 70 and 83 are excluded.

However, repeated attribute values lead to complications. Should 72, 75 and 80 be included or excluded? We cannot apply the rule 'only include attribute values for which the class value is different from that for the previous attribute value' to the two instances with attribute value 72 because one of their class values (don't play) is the same as for the previous attribute value and the other (play) is not. Even though both instances with temperature 75 have class play,

Temperature	Class
64	play
65 *	don't play
68 *	play
69 *	play
70 *	play
71 *	don't play
72	play
72 *	don't play
75	play
75 *	play
80 *	don't play
81 *	play
83 *	play
85 *	don't play

Figure 8.5 Sorted Instances with Candidate Cut Values

Temperature	Class
64	play
65 *	don't play
68 *	play
69	play
70	play
71 *	don't play
72	play
72 ?	don't play
75	play
75 ?	play
80 ?	don't play
81 *	play
83	play
85 *	don't play

Figure 8.6 Sorted Instances with Candidate Cut Values (revised)

we still cannot apply the rule. Which of the instances for the previous attribute value, 72, would we use? It seems reasonable to include 80, as the class for both occurrences of 75 is play, but what if they were a combination of play and don't play?

There are other combinations that can occur, but in practice none of this need cause us any problems. It does no harm to examine more candidate cut points than the bare minimum and a simple amended rule is: 'only include attribute values for which the class value is different from that for the previous attribute value, together with any attribute which occurs more than once and the attribute immediately following it'.

This gives the final version of the table shown in Figure 8.7, with eight candidate cut values.

Temperature	Class
64	play
65 *	don't play
68 *	play
69	play
70	play
71 *	don't play
72	play
72 *	don't play
75	play
75 *	play
80 *	don't play
81 *	play
83	play
85 *	don't play

Figure 8.7   Sorted Instances with Candidate Cut Values (final)

8.4 Using the ChiMerge Algorithm for Global Discretisation

ChiMerge is a well-known algorithm for global discretisation introduced by Randy Kerber, an American researcher [1]. It uses a statistical technique for discretising each continuous attribute separately.

The first step in discretising a continuous attribute is to sort its values into ascending numerical order, with the corresponding classifications sorted into the same order.

The next step is to construct a frequency table giving the number of occurrences of each distinct value of the attribute for each possible classification. It then uses the distribution of the values of the attribute within the different classes to generate a set of intervals that are considered statistically distinct at a given level of significance.

As an example, suppose that A is a continuous attribute in a training set with 60 instances and three possible classifications $c1$, $c2$ and $c3$. A possible distribution of the values of A arranged in ascending numerical order is shown in Figure 8.8. The aim is to combine the values of A into a number of ranges. Note that some of the attribute values occur just once, whilst others occur several times.

Value of A	Observed frequency for class			Total
	$c1$	$c2$	$c3$	
1.3	1	0	4	5
1.4	0	1	0	1
1.8	1	1	1	3
2.4	6	0	2	8
6.5	3	2	4	9
8.7	6	0	1	7
12.1	7	2	3	12
29.4	0	0	1	1
56.2	2	4	0	6
87.1	0	1	3	4
89.0	1	1	2	4

Figure 8.8 ChiMerge: Initial Frequency Table

Each row can be interpreted not just as corresponding to a single attribute value but as representing an *interval*, i.e. a range of values starting at the value given and continuing up to but excluding the value given in the row below. Thus the row labelled 1.3 corresponds to the interval $1.3 \leq A < 1.4$. We can regard the values 1.3, 1.4 etc. as *interval labels*, with each label being used to indicate the lowest number in the range of values included in that interval. The final row corresponds to all values of A from 89.0 upwards.

The initial frequency table could be augmented by an additional column showing the interval corresponding to each row (Figure 8.9).

Value of A	Interval	Observed frequency for class			Total
		c1	c2	c3	
1.3	$1.3 \leq A < 1.4$	1	0	4	5
1.4	$1.4 \leq A < 1.8$	0	1	0	1
1.8	$1.8 \leq A < 2.4$	1	1	1	3
2.4	$2.4 \leq A < 6.5$	6	0	2	8
6.5	$6.5 \leq A < 8.7$	3	2	4	9
8.7	$8.7 \leq A < 12.1$	6	0	1	7
12.1	$12.1 \leq A < 29.4$	7	2	3	12
29.4	$29.4 \leq A < 56.2$	0	0	1	1
56.2	$56.2 \leq A < 87.1$	2	4	0	6
87.1	$87.1 \leq A < 89.0$	0	1	3	4
89.0	$89.0 \leq A$	1	1	2	4

Figure 8.9 ChiMerge: Initial Frequency Table with Intervals Added

In practice, the 'Interval' column is generally omitted as it is implied by the entries in the Value column.

Starting with the initial frequency table, ChiMerge systematically applies statistical tests to combine pairs of adjacent intervals until it arrives at a set of intervals that are considered statistically different at a given level of significance.

ChiMerge tests the following hypothesis for each pair of adjacent rows in turn.

Hypothesis
The class is independent of which of the two adjacent intervals an instance belongs to.

If the hypothesis is confirmed, there is no advantage in treating the intervals separately and they are merged. If not, they remain separate.

ChiMerge works through the frequency table from top to bottom, examining each pair of adjacent rows (intervals) in turn in order to determine whether the relative class frequencies of the two intervals are significantly different. If not, the two intervals are considered to be similar enough to justify merging them into a single interval.

The statistical test applied is the χ^2 test, pronounced (and often written) as the 'Chi square' test. χ is a Greek letter, which is written as Chi in the Roman alphabet. It is pronounced like 'sky', without the initial 's'.

For each pair of adjacent rows a *contingency table* is constructed giving the observed frequencies of each combination of the two variables A and 'class'. For the adjacent intervals labelled 8.7 and 12.1 in Figure 8.8 the contingency table is shown below as Figure 8.10(a).

Value of A	Observed frequency for class			Total observed
	$c1$	$c2$	$c3$	
8.7	6	0	1	7
12.1	7	2	3	12
Total	13	2	4	19

Figure 8.10(a) Observed Frequencies for Two Adjacent Rows of Figure 8.8

The 'row sum' figures in the right-hand column and the 'column sum' figures in the bottom row are called 'marginal totals'. They correspond respectively to the number of instances for each value of A (i.e. with their value of attribute A in the corresponding interval) and the number of instances in each class for both intervals combined. The grand total (19 instances in this case) is given in the bottom right-hand corner of the table.

The contingency table is used to calculate the value of a variable called χ^2 (or 'the χ^2 statistic' or 'the Chi-square statistic'), using a method that will be described in Section 8.4.1. This value is then compared with a *threshold value T*, which depends on the number of classes and the level of statistical significance required. The threshold will be described further in Section 8.4.2. For the current example we will use a significance level of 90% (explained below). As there are three classes this gives a threshold value of 4.61.

The significance of the threshold is that if we assume that the classification is independent of which of the two adjacent intervals an instance belongs to, there is a 90% probability that χ^2 will be less than 4.61.

If χ^2 is less than 4.61 it is taken as supporting the hypothesis of independence at the *90% significance level* and the two intervals are merged. On the other hand, if the value of χ^2 is greater than 4.61 we deduce that the class and interval are not independent, again at the 90% significance level, and the two intervals are left unchanged.

8.4.1 Calculating the Expected Values and χ^2

For a given pair of adjacent rows (intervals) the value of χ^2 is calculated using the 'observed' and 'expected' frequency values for each combination of class and row. For this example there are three classes so there are six such combinations. In each case, the observed frequency value, denoted by O, is the frequency that actually occurred. The expected value E is the frequency value that would be expected to occur by chance given the assumption of independence.

If the row is i and the class is j, then let the total number of instances in row i be $rowsum_i$ and let the total number of occurrences of class j be $colsum_j$. Let the grand total number of instances for the two rows combined be sum. Assuming the hypothesis that the class is independent of which of the two rows an instance belongs to is true, we can calculate the expected number of instances in row i for class j as follows. There are a total of $colsum_j$ occurrences of class j in the two intervals combined, so class j occurs a proportion of $colsum_j/sum$ of the time. As there are $rowsum_i$ instances in row i, we would expect $rowsum_i \times colsum_j/sum$ occurrences of class j in row i.

To calculate this value for any combination of row and class, we just have to take the product of the corresponding row sum and column sum divided by the grand total of the observed values for the two rows.

For the adjacent intervals labelled 8.7 and 12.1 in Figure 8.8 the six values of O and E (one pair of values for each class/row combination) are given in Figure 8.10(b).

Value of A	Frequency for class						Total observed
	$c1$		$c2$		$c3$		
	O	E	O	E	O	E	
8.7	6	4.79	0	0.74	1	1.47	7
12.1	7	8.21	2	1.26	3	2.53	12
Total	13		2		4		19

Figure 8.10(b) Observed and Expected Values for Two Adjacent Rows of Figure 8.8

The O values are taken from Figure 8.8 or Figure 8.10(a). The E values are calculated from the row and column sums. Thus for row 8.7 and class $c1$, the expected value E is $13 \times 7/19 = 4.79$.

Having calculated the value of O and E for all six combinations of class and row, the next step is to calculate the value of $(O - E)^2/E$ for each of the six combinations. These are shown in the Val columns in Figure 8.11.

The value of χ^2 is then the sum of the six values of $(O - E)^2/E$. For the pair of rows shown in Figure 8.11 the value of χ^2 is 1.89.

If the independence hypothesis is correct the observed and expected values O and E would ideally be the same and χ^2 would be zero. A small value of χ^2 would also support the hypothesis, but the larger the value of χ^2 the more reason there is to suspect that the hypothesis may be false. When χ^2 exceeds

Value	Frequency for class									Total
of A	$c1$			$c2$			$c3$			observed
	O	E	Val*	O	E	Val*	O	E	Val*	
8.7	6	4.79	0.31	0	0.74	0.74	1	1.47	0.15	7
12.1	7	8.21	0.18	2	1.26	0.43	3	2.53	0.09	12
Total	13			2			4			19

* Val columns give the value of $(O - E)^2/E$

Figure 8.11 O, E and Val values for two adjacent rows of Figure 8.8

the threshold value we consider that it is so unlikely for this to have occurred
by chance that the hypothesis is rejected.

The value of χ^2 is calculated for each adjacent pair of rows (intervals). When
doing this, a small but important technical detail is that an adjustment has to
be made to the calculation for any value of E less than 0.5. In this case the
denominator in the calculation of $(O - E)^2/E$ is changed to 0.5.

The results for the initial frequency table are summarised in Figure 8.12(a).

Value of A	Frequency for class			Total	Value of χ^2
	$c1$	$c2$	$c3$		
1.3	1	0	4	5	3.11
1.4	0	1	0	1	1.08
1.8	1	1	1	3	2.44
2.4	6	0	2	8	3.62
6.5	3	2	4	9	4.62
8.7	6	0	1	7	1.89
12.1	7	2	3	12	1.73
29.4	0	0	1	1	3.20
56.2	2	4	0	6	6.67
87.1	0	1	3	4	1.20
89.0	1	1	2	4	
Total	27	12	21	60	

Figure 8.12(a)   Initial Frequency Table with χ^2 Values Added

In each case, the χ^2 value given in a row is the value for the pair of adjacent
intervals comprising that row and the one below. No χ^2 value is calculated for
the final interval, because there is not one below it. As the table has 11 intervals
there are 10 χ^2 values.

ChiMerge selects the smallest value of χ^2, in this case 1.08, corresponding to the intervals labelled 1.4 and 1.8 and compares it with the threshold value, which in this case is 4.61.

The value 1.08 is less than the threshold value so the independence hypothesis is supported and the two intervals are merged. The combined interval is labelled 1.4, i.e. the smaller of the two previous labels.

This gives us a new frequency table, which is shown in Figure 8.12(b). There is one fewer row than before.

Value of A	Frequency for class			Total
	$c1$	$c2$	$c3$	
1.3	1	0	4	5
1.4	1	2	1	4
2.4	6	0	2	8
6.5	3	2	4	9
8.7	6	0	1	7
12.1	7	2	3	12
29.4	0	0	1	1
56.2	2	4	0	6
87.1	0	1	3	4
89.0	1	1	2	4

Figure 8.12(b)   ChiMerge: Revised Frequency Table

The χ^2 values are now calculated for the revised frequency table. Note that the only values that can have changed from those previously calculated are those for the two pairs of adjacent intervals of which the newly merged interval (1.4) is one. These values are shown in bold in Figure 8.12(c).

Now the smallest value of χ^2 is 1.20, which again is below the threshold value of 4.61. So intervals 87.1 and 89.0 are merged.

ChiMerge proceeds iteratively in this way, merging two intervals at each stage until a minimum χ^2 value is reached which is greater than the threshold, indicating that an irreducible set of intervals has been reached. The final table is shown as Figure 8.12(d).

The χ^2 values for the two remaining pairs of intervals are greater than the threshold value. Hence no further merging of intervals is possible and the discretisation is complete. Continuous attribute A can be replaced by a categorical attribute with just three values, corresponding to the ranges (for the 90% significance level):

Value of A	Frequency for class			Total	Value of χ^2
	$c1$	$c2$	$c3$		
1.3	1	0	4	5	**3.74**
1.4	1	2	1	4	**5.14**
2.4	6	0	2	8	3.62
6.5	3	2	4	9	4.62
8.7	6	0	1	7	1.89
12.1	7	2	3	12	1.73
29.4	0	0	1	1	3.20
56.2	2	4	0	6	6.67
87.1	0	1	3	4	1.20
89.0	1	1	2	4	
Total	27	12	21	60	

Figure 8.12(c)   Revised Frequency Table with χ^2 Values Added

Value of A	Frequency for class			Total	Value of χ^2
	$c1$	$c2$	$c3$		
1.3	24	6	16	46	10.40
56.2	2	4	0	6	5.83
87.1	1	2	5	8	
Total	27	12	21	60	

Figure 8.12(d)   Final Frequency Table

$$1.3 \leq A < 56.2$$
$$56.2 \leq A < 87.1$$
$$A \geq 87.1$$

A possible problem with using these ranges for classification purposes is that for an unseen instance there might be a value of A that is substantially less than 1.3 (the smallest value of A for the training data) or substantially greater than 87.1. (Although the final interval is given as $A \geq 87.1$ the largest value of A for the training data was just 89.0.) In such a case we would need to decide whether to treat such a low or high value of A as belonging to either the first or last of the ranges as appropriate or to treat the unseen instance as unclassifiable.

8.4.2 Finding the Threshold Value

Threshold values for the χ^2 test can be found in statistical tables. The value depends on two factors:

1. The significance level. 90% is a commonly used significance level. Other commonly used levels are 95% and 99%. The higher the significance level, the higher the threshold value and the more likely it is that the hypothesis of independence will be supported and thus that the adjacent intervals will be merged.

2. The number of *degrees of freedom* of the contingency table. A full explanation of this is outside the scope of this book, but the general idea is as follows. If we have a contingency table such as Figure 8.10(a) with 2 rows and 3 columns, how many of the $2 \times 3 = 6$ cells in the main body of the table can we fill independently given the marginal totals (row and column sums)? The answer to this is just 2. If we put two numbers in the $c1$ and $c2$ columns of the first row ($A = 8.7$), the value in the $c3$ column of that row is determined by the row sum value. Once all three values in the first row are fixed, those in the second row ($A = 12.1$) are determined by the three column sum values.

In the general case of a contingency table with N rows and M columns the number of independent values in the main body of the table is $(N-1) \times (M-1)$. For the ChiMerge algorithm the number of rows is always two and the number of columns is the same as the number of classes, so the number of degrees of freedom is $(2-1) \times$ (number of classes -1) = number of classes -1, which in this example is 2. The larger the number of degrees of freedom is, the higher the threshold value.

For 2 degrees of freedom and a 90% significance level, the χ^2 threshold value is 4.61. Some other values are given in Figure 8.13 below.

Choosing a higher significance level will increase the threshold value and thus may make the merging process continue for longer, resulting in categorical attributes with fewer and fewer intervals.

8.4.3 Setting *minIntervals* and *maxIntervals*

A problem with the ChiMerge algorithm is that the result may be a large number of intervals or, at the other extreme, just one interval. For a large training set an attribute may have many thousands of distinct values and the method may produce a categorical attribute with hundreds or even thousands of values. This is likely to be of little or no practical value. On the other hand,

Degrees of freedom	90% Significance level	95% Significance level	99% Significance level
1	2.71	3.84	6.64
2	4.61	5.99	9.21
3	6.25	7.82	11.34
4	7.78	9.49	13.28
5	9.24	11.07	15.09
6	10.65	12.59	16.81
7	12.02	14.07	18.48
8	13.36	15.51	20.09
9	14.68	16.92	21.67
10	15.99	18.31	23.21
11	17.28	19.68	24.72
12	18.55	21.03	26.22
13	19.81	22.36	27.69
14	21.06	23.69	29.14
15	22.31	25.00	30.58
16	23.54	26.30	32.00
17	24.77	27.59	33.41
18	25.99	28.87	34.80
19	27.20	30.14	36.19
20	28.41	31.41	37.57
21	29.62	32.67	38.93
22	30.81	33.92	40.29
23	32.01	35.17	41.64
24	33.20	36.42	42.98
25	34.38	37.65	44.31
26	35.56	38.89	45.64
27	36.74	40.11	46.96
28	37.92	41.34	48.28
29	39.09	42.56	49.59
30	40.26	43.77	50.89

Figure 8.13 χ^2 Threshold Values

if the intervals are eventually merged into just one that would suggest that the attribute value is independent of the classification and the attribute would best be deleted. Both a large and a small number of intervals can simply reflect setting the significance level too low or too high.

Kerber [1] proposed setting two values, *minIntervals* and *maxIntervals*. This form of the algorithm always merges the pair of intervals with the lowest value of χ^2 as long as the number of intervals is more than *maxIntervals*. After that the pair of intervals with the smallest value of χ^2 is merged at each stage until *either* a χ^2 value is reached that is greater than the threshold value *or* the number of intervals is reduced to *minIntervals*. In either of those cases the algorithm stops. Although this is difficult to justify in terms of the statistical theory behind the χ^2 test it can be very useful in practice to give a manageable number of categorical values. Reasonable settings for *minIntervals* and *maxIntervals* might be 2 or 3 and 20, respectively.

8.4.4 The ChiMerge Algorithm: Summary

With the above extension, the ChiMerge algorithm is summarised in Figure 8.14.

8.4.5 The ChiMerge Algorithm: Comments

The ChiMerge algorithm works quite well in practice despite some theoretical problems relating to the statistical technique used, which will not be discussed here (Kerber's paper [1] gives further details). A serious weakness is that the method discretises each attribute independently of the values of the others, even though the classifications are clearly not determined by the values of just a single attribute.

Sorting the values of each continuous attribute into order can be a significant processing overhead for a large dataset. However this is likely to be an overhead for any method of discretisation, not just ChiMerge. In the case of ChiMerge it needs to be performed only once for each continuous attribute.

1. Set values of *minIntervals* and *maxIntervals* ($2 \leq minIntervals \leq max$-*Intervals*).

2. Decide on a significance level (say 90%). Using this and the number of degrees of freedom (i.e. number of classes -1) look up the threshold value to use.

3. For each continuous attribute in turn:

(a) Sort the values of the attribute into ascending numerical order.

(b) Create a frequency table containing one row for each distinct attribute value and one column for each class. Label each row with the corresponding attribute value. Enter the number of occurrences of each attribute value/class combination in the training set in the cells of the table.

(c) If (number of rows = *minIntervals*) then stop, otherwise go on to next step.

(d) For each pair of adjacent rows in the frequency table in turn:
For each combination of row and class:

(i) calculate O, the observed frequency value for that combination

(ii) calculate E, the expected frequency value for that combination, from the product of the row and column sums divided by the total number of occurrences in the two rows combined

(iii) calculate the value of $(O - E)^2/E$ *

Add the values of $(O - E)^2/E$ to give χ^2 for that pair of adjacent rows.

(e) Find the pair of adjacent rows with the lowest value of χ^2.

(f) If the lowest value of χ^2 is less than the threshold value OR (number of rows > *maxIntervals*), merge the two rows, setting the attribute value label for the merged row to that of the first of the two constituent rows, reduce the number of rows by one and go back to step (c). Otherwise stop.

---

* If $E < 0.5$, replace E in the denominator of this formula by 0.5.

Figure 8.14 The ChiMerge Algorithm

8.5 Comparing Global and Local Discretisation for Tree Induction

This section describes an experiment aimed at comparing the effectiveness of using the local discretisation method for TDIDT described in Section 8.3 with that of using ChiMerge for global discretisation of continuous attributes followed by using TDIDT for rule generation, with all attributes now categorical.

For convenience information gain will be used for attribute selection throughout.

Seven datasets are used for the experiment, all taken from the UCI Repository. Basic information about each dataset is given in Figure 8.15.

Dataset	Instances	Attributes		Classes
		Categ.	Contin.	
glass	214	0	9	7
hepatitis	155	13	6	2
hypo	2514	22	7	5
iris	150	0	4	3
labor-ne	40	8	8	2
pima-indians	768	0	8	2
sick-euthyroid	3163	18	7	2

Figure 8.15 Datasets Used in ChiMerge Experiments

The version of ChiMerge used is a re-implementation by the present author of Kerber's original algorithm.

The value of each set of classification rules can be measured by the number of rules generated and the percentage of instances that they correctly classify. The methodology chosen for these experiments is *10-fold cross-validation*. First the training set is divided into 10 groups of instances of equal size. TDIDT is then run 10 times with a different 10% of the instances omitted from the rule generation process for each run and used subsequently as an unseen test set. Each run produces a percentage of correct classifications over the unseen test set and a number of rules. These figures are then combined to give an average number of rules and the percentage of correct classifications. The 'default to largest class' strategy is used throughout.

Figure 8.16 shows the results of applying TDIDT directly to all the datasets, compared with first using ChiMerge to discretise all the continuous attributes globally (90% significance level).

The percentage of correct classifications for the global discretisation approach is comparable with those achieved by local discretisation. However, local discretisation seems to produce an appreciably smaller number of rules, at least for these datasets. This is particularly the case for the *pima-indians* and *sick-euthyroid* datasets.

On the other hand, the global discretisation approach has the considerable advantage that the data only has to be discretised once and can then be used as the input to any data mining algorithm that accepts categorical attributes, not only TDIDT.

Dataset	Local discretisation		Global discretisation	
	Number of rules	Correct %	Number of of rules	Correct %
glass	38.3	69.6	88.2	72.0
hepatitis	18.9	81.3	42.0	81.9
hypo	14.2	99.5	46.7	98.7
iris	8.5	95.3	15.1	94.7
labor-ne	4.8	85.0	7.6	85.0
pima-indians	121.9	69.8	328.0	74.0
sick-euthyroid	72.7	96.6	265.1	96.6

Figure 8.16 TDIDT with Information Gain. Local Discretisation v Global Discretisation by ChiMerge (90% significance level). Results from 10-fold Cross-validation

8.6 Chapter Summary

This chapter looks at the question of how to convert a continuous attribute to a categorical one, a process known as *discretisation*. This is important as many data mining algorithms, including TDIDT, require all attributes to take categorical values.

Two different types of discretisation are distinguished, known as local and global discretisation. The process of extending the TDIDT algorithm by adding local discretisation of continuous attributes is illustrated in detail, followed by a description of the ChiMerge algorithm for global discretisation. The effectiveness of the two methods is compared for the TDIDT algorithm for a number of datasets.

8.7 Self-assessment Exercises for Chapter 8

1. Using the amended form of the rule given in Section 8.3.2, what are the candidate cut points for the continuous attribute *humidity* in the *golf* training set given in Chapter 4?

2. Starting at Figure 8.12(c) and the resulting merger of intervals 87.1 and 89.0, find the next pair of intervals to be merged.

Reference

[1] Kerber, R. (1992). ChiMerge: discretization of numeric attributes. In *Proceedings of the 10th national conference on artificial intelligence* (pp. 123–128). Menlo Park: AAAI Press.

9

Avoiding Overfitting of Decision Trees

The Top-Down Induction of Decision Trees (TDIDT) algorithm described in previous chapters is one of the most commonly used methods of classification. It is well known, widely cited in the research literature and an important component of many successful commercial packages. However, like many other methods, it suffers from the problem of *overfitting* to the training data, resulting in some cases in excessively large rule sets and/or rules with very low predictive power for previously unseen data.

A classification algorithm is said to *overfit* to the training data if it generates a decision tree (or any other representation of the data) that depends too much on irrelevant features of the training instances, with the result that it performs well on the training data but relatively poorly on unseen instances.

Realistically, overfitting will always occur to a greater or lesser extent simply because the training set does not contain all possible instances. It only becomes a problem when the classification accuracy on unseen instances is significantly downgraded. We always need to be aware of the possibility of significant overfitting and to seek ways of reducing it.

In this chapter we look at ways of adjusting a decision tree either while it is being generated, or afterwards, in order to increase its predictive accuracy. The idea is that generating a tree with fewer branches than would otherwise be the case (known as *pre-pruning*) or removing parts of a tree that has already been generated (known as *post-pruning*) will give a smaller and simpler tree. This tree is unlikely to be able to predict correctly the classification of some of the instances in the training set. As we already know what those values should be this is of little or no importance. On the other hand the simpler tree may be

© Springer-Verlag London Ltd., part of Springer Nature 2020
M. Bramer, *Principles of Data Mining*, Undergraduate Topics
in Computer Science, DOI 10.1007/978-1-4471-7493-6_9

able to predict the correct classification more accurately for unseen data — a case of 'less means more'.

We will start by looking at a topic that at first sight is unrelated to the subject of this chapter, but will turn out to be important: how to deal with inconsistencies in a training set.

9.1 Dealing with Clashes in a Training Set

If two (or more) instances in a training set have the same combination of attribute values but different classifications the training set is inconsistent and we say that a *clash* occurs.

There are two main ways this can happen.

1. One of the instances has at least one of its attribute values or its classification incorrectly recorded, i.e. there is noise in the data.

2. The clashing instances are both (or all) correct, but it is not possible to discriminate between them on the basis of the attributes recorded.

In the second case the only way of discriminating between the instances is by examining the values of further attributes, not recorded in the training set, which in most cases is impossible. Unfortunately there is usually no way except 'intuition' of distinguishing between cases (1) and (2).

Clashes in the training set are likely to prove a problem for any method of classification but they cause a particular problem for tree generation using the TDIDT algorithm because of the 'adequacy condition' introduced in Chapter 4. For the algorithm to be able to generate a classification tree from a given training set, it is only necessary for one condition to be satisfied: no two or more instances may have the same set of attribute values but different classifications. This raises the question of what to do when the adequacy condition is not satisfied.

It is generally desirable to be able to generate a decision tree even when there are clashes in the training data, and the basic TDIDT algorithm can be adapted to do this.

9.1.1 Adapting TDIDT to Deal with Clashes

Consider how the TDIDT algorithm will perform when there is a clash in the training set. The method will still produce a decision tree but (at least) one of the branches will grow to its greatest possible length (i.e. one term for each of the possible attributes), with the instances at the lowest node having more than one classification. The algorithm would like to choose another attribute to split on at that node but there are no 'unused' attributes and it is not permitted to choose the same attribute twice in the same branch. When this happens we will call the set of instances represented by the lowest node of the branch the *clash set*.

A typical clash set might have one instance with classification *true* and one with classification *false*. In a more extreme case there may be several possible classifications and several instances with each classification in the clash set, e.g. for an object recognition example there might be three instances classified as *house*, two as *tree* and two as *lorry*.

Figure 9.1 shows an example of a decision tree generated from a training set with three attributes x, y and z, each with possible values 1 and 2, and three classifications $c1$, $c2$ and $c3$. The node in the bottom row labelled 'mixed' represents a clash set, i.e. there are instances with more than one of the three possible classifications, but no more attributes to split on.

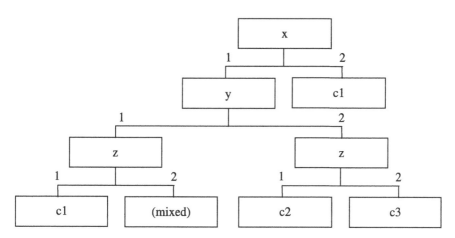

Figure 9.1 Incomplete Decision Tree (With Clash Set)

There are many possible ways of dealing with clashes but the two principal ones are:

(a) The 'delete branch' strategy: discard the branch to the node from the node above. This is similar to removing the instances in the clash set from the training set (but not necessarily equivalent to it, as the order in which the attributes were selected might then have been different).

Applying this strategy to Figure 9.1 gives Figure 9.2. Note that this tree will be unable to classify unseen instances for which $x = 1$, $y = 1$ and $z = 2$, as previously discussed in Section 6.7.

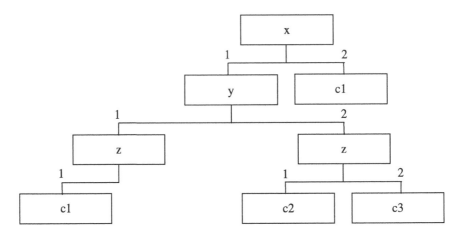

Figure 9.2 Decision Tree Generated from Figure 9.1 by 'Delete Branch' Strategy

(b) The 'majority voting' strategy: label the node with the most common classification of the instances in the clash set. This is similar to changing the classification of some of the instances in the training set (but again not necessarily equivalent, as the order in which the attributes were selected might then have been different).

Applying this strategy to Figure 9.1 gives Figure 9.3, assuming that the most common classification of the instances in the clash set is $c3$.

The decision on which of these strategies to use varies from one situation to another. If there were, say, 99 instances classified as *yes* and one instance classified as *no* in the training set, we would probably assume that the *no* was a misclassification and use method (b). If the distribution in a weather forecasting application were 4 *rain*, 5 *snow* and 3 *fog*, we might prefer to discard the instances in the clash set altogether and accept that we are unable to make a prediction for that combination of attribute values.

A middle approach between the 'delete branch' and the 'majority voting' strategies is to use a *clash threshold*. The clash threshold is a percentage from 0 to 100 inclusive.

The 'clash threshold' strategy is to assign all the instances in a clash set to the most commonly occurring class for those instances provided that the proportion of instances in the clash set with that classification is at least equal to the clash threshold. If it is not, the instances in the clash set (and the corresponding branch) are discarded altogether.

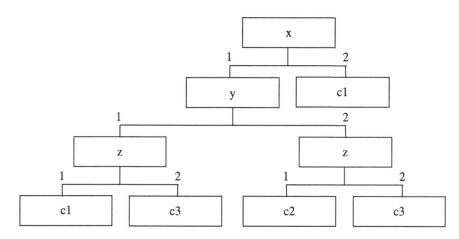

Figure 9.3 Decision Tree Generated from Figure 9.1 by 'Majority Voting' Strategy

Setting the clash threshold to zero gives the effect of *always* assigning to the most common class, i.e. the 'majority voting' strategy. Setting the threshold to 100 gives the effect of *never* assigning to the most common class, i.e. the 'delete branch' strategy.

Clash threshold values between 0 and 100 give a middle position between these extremes. Reasonable percentage values to use might be 60, 70, 80 or 90.

Figure 9.4 shows the result of using different clash thresholds for the same dataset. The dataset used is the *crx* 'credit checking' dataset modified by deleting all the continuous attributes to ensure that clashes will occur. The modified training set does not satisfy the adequacy condition.

The results were all generated using TDIDT with attributes selected using information gain in 'train and test' mode.

Clash threshold	Training set			Test set		
	Correct	Incorr.	Unclas	Correct	Incorr.	Unclas
0% Maj. Voting	651	39	0	184	16	0
60%	638	26	26	182	10	8
70%	613	13	64	177	3	20
80%	607	11	72	176	2	22
90%	552	0	138	162	0	38
100% Del. Branch	552	0	138	162	0	38

Figure 9.4 Results for *crx* (Modified) With Varying Clash Thresholds

From the results given it is clear that when there are clashes in the training data it is no longer possible to obtain a decision tree that gives 100% predictive accuracy on the training set from which it was generated.

The 'delete branch' option (threshold = 100%) avoids making any errors but leaves many of the instances unclassified. The 'majority voting' strategy (threshold = 0%) avoids leaving instances unclassified but gives many classi-fication errors. The results for threshold values 60%, 70%, 80% and 90% lie between these two extremes. However, the predictive accuracy for the train-ing data is of no importance — we already know the classifications! It is the accuracy for the test data that matters.

In this case the results for the test data are very much in line with those for the training data: reducing the threshold value increases the number of correctly classified instances but it also increases the number of incorrectly classified instances and the number of unclassified instances falls accordingly.

If we use the 'default classification strategy' and automatically allocate each unclassified instance to the largest class in the original training set, the picture changes considerably.

Clash threshold	Training set			Test set	
	Correct	Incorr.	Unclas	Correct	Incorr.
0% maj. voting	651	39	0	184	16
60%	638	26	26	188	12
70%	613	13	64	189	11
80%	607	11	72	189	11
90%	552	0	138	180	20
100% del. branch	552	0	138	180	20

Figure 9.5 Results for *crx* (Modified) With Varying Clash Thresholds (Using Default to Largest Class)

Figure 9.5 shows the results given in Figure 9.4 modified so that for the test data any unclassified instances are automatically assigned to the largest class. The highest predictive accuracy is given for clash thresholds 70% and 80% in this case.

Having established the basic method of dealing with clashes in a training set, we now turn back to the main subject of this chapter: the problem of avoiding the overfitting of decision trees to data.

9.2 More About Overfitting Rules to Data

Let us consider a typical rule such as

IF $a = 1$ and $b = $ yes and $z = $ red THEN class $= $ OK

Adding an additional term to this rule will *specialise* it, for example the augmented rule

IF $a = 1$ and $b = $ yes and $z = $ red and $k = $ green THEN class $= $ OK

will normally refer to fewer instances than the original form of the rule (possibly the same number, but certainly no more).

In contrast, removing a term from the original rule will *generalise* it, for example the depleted rule

IF $a = 1$ and $b = $ yes THEN class $= $ OK

will normally refer to more instances than the original form of the rule (possibly the same number, but certainly no fewer).

The principal problem with TDIDT and other algorithms for generating classification rules is that of *overfitting*. Every time the algorithm splits on an attribute an additional term is added to each resulting rule, i.e. tree generation is a repeated process of specialisation.

If a decision tree is generated from data containing noise or irrelevant attributes it is likely to capture erroneous classification information, which will tend to make it perform badly when classifying unseen instances.

Even when that is not the case, beyond a certain point, specialising a rule by adding further terms can become counter-productive. The generated rules give a perfect fit for the instances from which they were generated but in some cases are too specific (i.e. specialised) to have a high level of predictive accuracy for other instances. To put this point another way, if the tree is over-specialised, its ability to generalise, which is vital when classifying unseen instances, will be reduced.

Another consequence of excessive specificity is that there is often an unnecessarily large number of rules. A smaller number of more general rules may have greater predictive accuracy on unseen data.

The standard approach to reducing overfitting is to sacrifice classification accuracy on the training set for accuracy in classifying (unseen) test data. This can be achieved by pruning the decision tree. There are two ways to do this:

- **Pre-pruning** (or *forward pruning*)
  Prevent the generation of non-significant branches

- **Post-pruning** (or *backward pruning*)
  Generate the decision tree and then remove non-significant branches.

Pre- and post-pruning are both methods to increase the generality of decision trees.

9.3 Pre-pruning Decision Trees

Pre-pruning a decision tree involves using a 'termination condition' to decide when it is desirable to terminate some of the branches prematurely as the tree is generated.

Each branch of the evolving tree corresponds to an incomplete rule such as

IF $x = 1$ AND $z =$ yes AND $q > 63.5$ ... THEN ...

and also to a subset of instances currently 'under investigation'.

If all the instances have the same classification, say c1, the end node of the branch is treated by the TDIDT algorithm as a leaf node labelled by c1. Each such completed branch corresponds to a (completed) rule, such as

IF $x = 1$ AND $z =$ yes AND $q > 63.5$ THEN class $=$ c1

If not all the instances have the same classification the node would normally be expanded to a subtree by splitting on an attribute, as described previously. When following a pre-pruning strategy the node (i.e. the subset) is first tested to determine whether or not a termination condition applies. If it does not, the node is expanded as usual. If it does, the subset is treated as a clash set in the way described in Section 9.1, using a 'delete branch', a 'majority voting' or some other similar strategy. The most common strategy is probably the 'majority voting' one, in which case the node is treated as a leaf node labelled with the most frequently occurring classification for the instances in the subset (the 'majority class').

The set of pre-pruned rules will wrongly classify some of the instances in the training set. However, the classification accuracy for the test set may be greater than for the unpruned set of rules.

There are several criteria that can be applied to a node to determine whether or not pre-pruning should take place. Two of these are:

- **Size Cutoff**
  Prune if the subset contains fewer than say 5 or 10 instances

- **Maximum Depth Cutoff**
  Prune if the length of the branch is say 3 or 4.

Figure 9.6 shows the results obtained for a variety of datasets using TDIDT with information gain for attribute selection. In each case 10-fold cross-validation is used, with a size cutoff of 5 instances, 10 instances or no cutoff (i.e. unpruned). Figure 9.7 shows the results with a maximum depth cutoff of 3, 4 or unlimited instead. The 'majority voting' strategy is used throughout.

	No cutoff		5 Instances		10 Instances	
	Rules	% Acc.	Rules	% Acc.	Rules	% Acc.
breast-cancer	93.2	89.8	78.7	90.6	63.4	91.6
contact_lenses	16.0	92.5	10.6	92.5	8.0	90.7
diabetes	121.9	70.3	97.3	69.4	75.4	70.3
glass	38.3	69.6	30.7	71.0	23.8	71.0
hypo	14.2	99.5	11.6	99.4	11.5	99.4
monk1	37.8	83.9	26.0	75.8	16.8	72.6
monk3	26.5	86.9	19.5	89.3	16.2	90.1
sick-euthyroid	72.8	96.7	59.8	96.7	48.4	96.8
vote	29.2	91.7	19.4	91.0	14.9	92.3
wake_vortex	298.4	71.8	244.6	73.3	190.2	74.3
wake_vortex2	227.1	71.3	191.2	71.4	155.7	72.2

Figure 9.6 Pre-pruning With Varying Size Cutoffs

	No cutoff		Length 3		Length 4	
	Rules	% Acc.	Rules	% Acc.	Rules	% Acc.
breast-cancer	93.2	89.8	92.6	89.7	93.2	89.8
contact_lenses	16.0	92.5	8.1	90.7	12.7	94.4
diabetes	121.9	70.3	12.2	74.6	30.3	74.3
glass	38.3	69.6	8.8	66.8	17.7	68.7
hypo	14.2	99.5	6.7	99.2	9.3	99.2
monk1	37.8	83.9	22.1	77.4	31.0	82.2
monk3	26.5	86.9	19.1	87.7	25.6	86.9
sick-euthyroid	72.8	96.7	8.3	97.8	21.7	97.7
vote	29.2	91.7	15.0	91.0	19.1	90.3
wake_vortex	298.4	71.8	74.8	76.8	206.1	74.5
wake_vortex2	227.1	71.3	37.6	76.3	76.2	73.8

Figure 9.7 Pre-pruning With Varying Maximum Depth Cutoffs

The results obtained clearly show that the choice of pre-pruning method is important. However, it is essentially *ad hoc*. No choice of size or depth cutoff consistently produces good results across all the datasets.

This result reinforces the comment by Quinlan [1] that the problem with pre-pruning is that the 'stopping threshold' is "not easy to get right — too high a threshold can terminate division before the benefits of subsequent splits become evident, while too low a value results in little simplification". It would be highly desirable to find a more principled choice of cutoff criterion to use with pre-pruning than the size and maximum depth approaches used previously, and if possible one which can be applied completely automatically without the need for the user to select any cutoff threshold value. A number of possible ways of doing this have been proposed, but in practice the use of post-pruning, to which we now turn, has proved more popular.

9.4 Post-pruning Decision Trees

Post-pruning a decision tree implies that we begin by generating the (complete) tree and then adjust it with the aim of improving the classification accuracy on unseen instances.

There are two principal methods of doing this. One method that is widely used begins by converting the tree to an equivalent set of rules. This will be described in Chapter 11.

Another commonly used approach aims to retain the decision tree but to replace some of its subtrees by leaf nodes, thus converting a complete tree to a smaller pruned one which predicts the classification of unseen instances at least as accurately. This method has several variants, such as *Reduced Error Pruning, Pessimistic Error Pruning, Minimum Error Pruning* and *Error Based Pruning*. A comprehensive study and numerical comparison of the effectiveness of different variants is given in [2].

The details of the methods used vary considerably, but the following example gives the general idea. Suppose we have a complete decision tree generated by the TDIDT algorithm, such as Figure 9.8 below.

Here the customary information about the attribute split on at each node, the attribute value corresponding to each branch and the classification at each leaf node are all omitted. Instead the nodes of the tree are labelled from A to M (A being the root) for ease of reference. The numbers at each node indicate how many of the 100 instances in the training set used to generate the tree correspond to each of the nodes. At each of the leaf nodes in the complete tree all the instances have the same classification. At each of the other nodes the corresponding instances have more than one classification.

The branch from the root node A to a leaf node such as J corresponds to a decision rule. We are interested in the proportion of unseen instances to which that rule applies that are incorrectly classified. We call this the *error rate* at node J (a proportion from 0 to 1 inclusive).

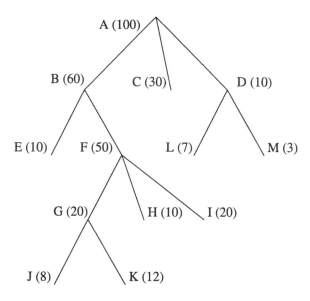

Figure 9.8 Initial Decision Tree

If we imagine the branch from the root node A to an internal node such as G were to terminate there, rather than being split two ways to form the two branches A to J and A to K, this branch would correspond to an incomplete rule of the kind discussed in Section 9.3 on pre-pruning. We will assume that the unseen instances to which a truncated rule of this kind applies are classified using the 'majority voting' strategy of Section 9.1.1, i.e. they are all allocated to the class to which the largest number of the instances in the training set corresponding to that node belong.

When post-pruning a decision tree such as Figure 9.8 we look for non-leaf nodes in the tree that have a descendant subtree of depth one (i.e. all the nodes one level down are leaf nodes). All such subtrees are candidates for post-pruning. If a pruning condition (which will be described below) is met the subtree hanging from the node can be replaced by the node itself. We work from the bottom of the tree upwards and prune one subtree at a time. The method continues until no more subtrees can be pruned.

For Figure 9.8 the only candidates for pruning are the subtrees hanging from nodes G and D.

Working from the bottom of the tree upwards we start by considering the replacement of the subtree 'hanging from' node G by G itself, as a leaf node in a pruned tree. How does the error rate of the branch (truncated rule) ending at G compare with the error rate of the two branches (complete rules) ending at J and K? Is it beneficial or harmful to the predictive accuracy of the tree to split at node G? We might consider truncating the branch earlier, say at node F. Would that be beneficial or harmful?

To answer questions such as these we need some way of estimating the error rate at any node of a tree. One way to do this is to use the tree to classify the instances in some set of previously unseen data called a *pruning set* and count the errors. Note that it is imperative that the pruning set is *additional to* the 'unseen test set' used elsewhere in this book. The test set must not be used for pruning purposes. Using a pruning set is a reasonable approach but may be unrealistic when the amount of data available is small. An alternative that takes a lot less execution time is to use a formula to estimate the error rate. Such a formula is likely to be probability-based and to make use of factors such as the number of instances corresponding to the node that belong to each of the classes and the prior probability of each class.

Figure 9.9 shows the estimated error rates at each of the nodes in Figure 9.8 using a (fictitious) formula.

Node	Estimated error rate
A	0.3
B	0.15
C	0.25
D	0.19
E	0.1
F	0.129
G	0.12
H	0.05
I	0.2
J	0.2
K	0.1
L	0.2
M	0.1

Figure 9.9 Estimated Error Rates at Nodes in Figure 9.8

Using Figure 9.9 we see that the estimated error rates at nodes J and K are 0.2 and 0.1, respectively. These two nodes correspond to 8 and 12 instances, respectively (of the 20 at node G).

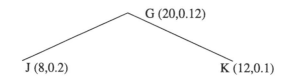

Figure 9.10   Subtree Descending From Node G^1

To estimate the error rate of the subtree hanging from node G (Figure 9.10) we take the weighted average of the estimated error rates at J and K. This value is $(8/20) \times 0.2 + (12/20) \times 0.1 = 0.14$. We will call this the *backed-up estimate* of the error rate at node G because it is computed from the estimated error rates of the nodes below it.

We now need to compare this value with the value obtained from Figure 9.9, i.e. 0.12, which we will call the *static estimate* of the error rate at that node.[2]

In the case of node G the static value is less than the backed-up value. This means that splitting at node G increases the error rate at that node, which is obviously counter-productive. We prune the subtree descending from node G to give Figure 9.11.

The candidates for pruning are now the subtrees descending from nodes F and D. (Node G is now a leaf node of the partly pruned tree.)

We can now consider whether or not it is beneficial to split at node F (Figure 9.12). The static error rates at nodes G, H and I are 0.12, 0.05 and 0.2. Hence the backed-up error rate at node F is $(20/50) \times 0.12 + (10/50) \times 0.05 + (20/50) \times 0.2 = 0.138$.

The static error rate at node F is 0.129, which is smaller than the backed-up value, so we again prune the tree, giving Figure 9.13.

The candidates for pruning are now the subtrees hanging from nodes B and D. We will consider whether to prune at node B (Figure 9.14).

The static error rates at nodes E and F are 0.1 and 0.129, respectively, so the backed-up error rate at node B is $(10/60) \times 0.1 + (50/60) \times 0.129 = 0.124$. This is less than the static error rate at node B, which is 0.15. Splitting at node B reduces the error rate, so we do not prune the subtree.

We next need to consider pruning at node D (Figure 9.15). The static error rates at nodes L and M are 0.2 and 0.1, respectively, so the backed-up error

---

[1] In Figure 9.10 and similar figures, the two figures in parentheses at each node give the number of instances in the training set corresponding to that node (as in Figure 9.8) and the estimated error rate at the node, as given in Figure 9.9.

[2] From now on, for simplicity we will generally refer to the 'backed-up' error rate and the 'static error rate' at a node, without using the word 'estimated' every time. However it is important to bear in mind that they are only estimates not the accurate values, which we have no way of knowing.

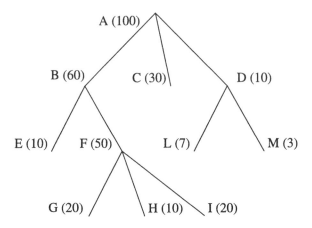

Figure 9.11   Decision Tree With One Subtree Pruned

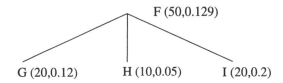

Figure 9.12   Subtree Descending From node F

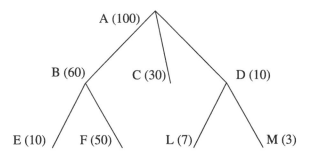

Figure 9.13   Decision Tree With Two Subtrees Pruned

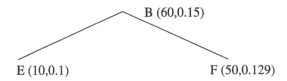

Figure 9.14   Subtree Descending From Node B

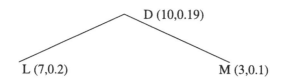

Figure 9.15 Subtree Descending From Node D

rate at node D is $(7/10) \times 0.2 + (3/10) \times 0.1 = 0.17$. This is less than the static error rate at node D, which is 0.19, so we do not prune the subtree. There are no further subtrees to consider. The final post-pruned tree is Figure 9.13.

In an extreme case this method could lead to a decision tree being post-pruned right up to its root node, indicating that using the tree is likely to lead to a higher error rate, i.e. more incorrect classifications, than simply assigning every unseen instance to the largest class in the training data. Luckily such poor decision trees are likely to be very rare.

Post-pruning decision trees would appear to be a more widely used and accepted approach than pre-pruning them. No doubt the ready availability and popularity of the C4.5 classification system [1] has had a large influence on this. However, an important practical objection to post-pruning is that there is a large computational overhead involved in generating a complete tree only then to discard some or possibly most of it. This may not matter with small experimental datasets, but 'real-world' datasets may contain many millions of instances and issues of computational feasibility and scaling up of methods will inevitably become important.

The decision tree representation of classification rules is widely used and it is therefore desirable to find methods of pruning that work well with it. However, the tree representation is itself a source of overfitting, as will be demonstrated in Chapter 11.

9.5 Chapter Summary

This chapter begins by examining techniques for dealing with clashes (i.e. inconsistent instances) in a training set. This leads to a discussion of methods for avoiding or reducing *overfitting* of a decision tree to training data. Overfitting arises when a decision tree is excessively dependent on irrelevant features of the training data with the result that its predictive power for unseen instances is reduced.

Two approaches to avoiding overfitting are distinguished: *pre-pruning* (generating a tree with fewer branches than would otherwise be the case) and *post-*

pruning (generating a tree in full and then removing parts of it). Results are given for pre-pruning using either a size or a maximum depth cutoff. A method of post-pruning a decision tree based on comparing the static and backed-up estimated error rates at each node is also described.

9.6 Self-assessment Exercise for Chapter 9

What post-pruning of the decision tree shown in Figure 9.8 would result from using the table of estimated error rates given below rather than the values given in Figure 9.9?

Node	Estimated error rate
A	0.2
B	0.35
C	0.1
D	0.2
E	0.01
F	0.25
G	0.05
H	0.1
I	0.2
J	0.15
K	0.2
L	0.1
M	0.1

References

[1] Quinlan, J. R. (1993). *C4.5: programs for machine learning.* San Mateo: Morgan Kaufmann.

[2] Esposito, F., Malerba, D., & Semeraro, G. (1997). A comparative analysis of methods for pruning decision trees. *IEEE Transactions on Pattern Analysis and Machine Intelligence, 19*(5), 476–491.

More About Entropy

10.1 Introduction

In this chapter we return to the subject of the *entropy* of a training set, which was introduced in Chapter 5. The idea of entropy is not only used in data mining; it is a very fundamental one, which is widely used in Information Theory as the basis for calculating efficient ways of representing messages for transmission by telecommunication systems.

We will start by explaining what is meant by the entropy of a set of distinct values and then come back to look again at the entropy of a training set.

Suppose we are playing a game of the 'twenty questions' variety where we try to identify one of M possible values by asking a series of yes/no questions. The values in which we are really interested are mutually exclusive classifications of the kind discussed in Chapter 3 and elsewhere, but the same argument can be applied to any set of distinct values.

We will assume at present that all M values are equally likely and for reasons that will soon become apparent we will also assume that M is an exact power of 2, say 2^N, where $N \geq 1$.

As a concrete example we will take the task of identifying an unknown capital city from the eight possibilities: London, Paris, Berlin, Warsaw, Sofia, Rome, Athens and Moscow (here $M = 8 = 2^3$).

There are many possible ways of asking questions, for example random guessing:

© Springer-Verlag London Ltd., part of Springer Nature 2020
M. Bramer, *Principles of Data Mining*, Undergraduate Topics
in Computer Science, DOI 10.1007/978-1-4471-7493-6_10

> Is it Warsaw? *No*
> Is it Berlin? *No*
> Is it Rome? *Yes*

This works well if the questioner makes a lucky guess early on, but (unsurprisingly) it is inefficient in the general case. To show this, imagine that we make our guesses in the fixed order: London, Paris, Berlin etc. until we guess the correct answer. We never need guess further than Athens, as a 'no' answer will tell us the city must be Moscow.

If the city is London, we need 1 question to find it.
If the city is Paris, we need 2 questions to find it.
If the city is Berlin, we need 3 questions to find it.
If the city is Warsaw, we need 4 questions to find it.
If the city is Sofia, we need 5 questions to find it.
If the city is Rome, we need 6 questions to find it.
If the city is Athens, we need 7 questions to find it.
If the city is Moscow, we need 7 questions to find it.

Each of these possibilities is equally likely, i.e. has probability $1/8$, so on average we need $(1 + 2 + 3 + 4 + 5 + 6 + 7 + 7)/8$ questions, i.e. $35/8 = 4.375$ questions.

A little experiment will soon show that the best strategy is to keep dividing the possibilities into equal halves. Thus we might ask

> Is it London, Paris, Athens or Moscow? *No*
> Is it Berlin or Warsaw? *Yes*
> Is it Berlin?

Whether the third question is answered yes or no, the answer will tell us the identity of the 'unknown' city.

The halving strategy always takes three questions to identify the unknown city. It is considered to be the 'best' strategy not because it invariably gives us the answer with the smallest number of questions (random guessing will occasionally do better) but because if we conduct a long series of 'trials' (each a game to guess a city, selected at random each time) the halving strategy will invariably find the answer and will do so with a smaller number of questions on average than any other strategy. With this understanding we can say that the smallest number of yes/no questions needed to determine an unknown value from 8 equally likely possibilities is three.

It is no coincidence that 8 is 2^3 and the smallest number of yes/no questions needed is 3. If we make the number of possible values M a higher or a lower power of two the same occurs. If we start with 8 possibilities and halve the number by the first question, that leaves 4 possibilities. We can determine the unknown value with 2 further questions. If we start with 4 possibilities and halve the number down to 2 by the first question we can determine the unknown value by just one further question ('is it the first one?'). So for $M = 4$ the smallest number of questions is 2 and for $M = 2$ the smallest number of questions is 1.

We can extend the argument to look at higher values of M, say 16. It takes one 'halving' question to reduce the number of possibilities to 8, which we know we can handle with 3 further questions. So the number of questions needed in the case of 16 values ($M = 16$) must be 4.

In general, we have the following result. **The smallest number of yes/no questions needed to determine an unknown value from $M = 2^N$ equally likely possibilities is N.**

Using the mathematical function $\log_2$,[1] we can rewrite the last result as: the smallest number of yes/no questions needed to determine an unknown value from M equally likely possibilities is $\log_2 M$ (provided M is a power of 2; see Figure 10.1).

M	$\log_2 M$
2	1
4	2
8	3
16	4
32	5
64	6
128	7
256	8
512	9
1024	10

Figure 10.1   Some values of $\log_2 M$ (where M is a power of 2)

We will define a quantity called the **entropy** of a set of M distinct values as follows.

> The **entropy** of a set of M distinct values that are equally likely is the smallest number of yes/no questions needed to determine an unknown value drawn from the M possibilities. As before, the words 'in all cases' are implicit and by smallest we mean the smallest number of questions averaged over a series of trials, not just one single trial (game).

---

[1] The $\log_2$ function is defined in Appendix A for readers who are unfamiliar with it.

In the phrase 'the smallest number of yes/no questions needed' in the definition of entropy, it is implicit that each question needs to divide the remaining possibilities into two equally probable halves. If they do not, for example with random guessing, a larger number will be needed.

It is not sufficient that each question looked at in isolation is a 'halving question'. For example, consider the sequence

---

Is it Berlin, London, Paris or Warsaw? *Yes*
Is it Berlin, London, Paris or Sofia? *Yes*

Both questions are 'halving questions' in their own right, but the answers leave us after two questions still having to discriminate amongst three possibilities, which cannot be done with one more question.

It is not sufficient that each question asked is a halving question. It is necessary to find a *sequence* of questions that take full advantage of the answers already given to divide the remaining possibilities into two equally probable halves. We will call this a 'well-chosen' sequence of questions.

So far we have established that the entropy of a set of M distinct values is $\log_2 M$, provided that M is a power of 2 and all values are equally likely. We have also established the need for questions to form a 'well-chosen' sequence. This raises three questions:

– What if M is not a power of 2?

– What if the M possible values are not equally likely?

– Is there a systematic way of finding a sequence of well-chosen questions?

It will be easier to answer these questions if we first introduce the idea of coding information using bits.

10.2 Coding Information Using Bits

There is an obvious everyday sense in which the more questions that are answered the more *information* we have. We can formalise this by saying that the answer to a question that can only be answered yes or no (with equal probability) can be considered as containing one *unit of information*. The basic unit of information is called a *bit* (short for 'binary digit'). This usage of the word 'bit' has a close connection with its use for the basic unit of storage in computer memory. It is a fundamental two-valued unit that corresponds to a switch being open or closed, a light being on or off, an electric current flowing or not flowing, or the dot and dash of Morse code.

The unit of information can also be looked at as the amount of information that can be *coded* using only a zero or a one. If we have two possible values, say male and female, we might use the coding

0 = male
1 = female

We can encode four possible values (say: man, woman, dog, cat) using two bits, e.g.

00 = man
01 = woman
10 = dog
11 = cat

To code eight values, say the eight capital cities, we need to use three bits, for example

000 = London
001 = Paris
010 = Berlin
011 = Warsaw
100 = Sofia
101 = Rome
110 = Athens
111 = Moscow

Coding the 2^N equally likely possibilities with N binary digits shows that it is always possible to discriminate amongst the values with a sequence of N well-chosen questions, for example:

| Is the first bit zero? |
| Is the second bit zero? |
| Is the third bit zero? |
| and so on. |

This leads to the following alternative (and equivalent) definition of entropy:

| The **entropy** of a set of M distinct values is the number of bits needed to encode the values in the most efficient way. |

As for the previous definition, the words 'in all cases' are implicit and by 'the most efficient way' we mean the smallest number of bits averaged over a series of trials, not just one single trial. This second definition also explains why the entropy is often given not as a number but as so many 'bits of information'.

10.3 Discriminating Amongst M Values (M Not a Power of 2)

So far we have established that the entropy of a set of M distinct values that are equally likely is $\log_2 M$ for cases where M is a power of 2. We now need to consider the case when it is not.

Is there any sense in which we can say that the entropy is $\log_2 M$ bits of information? We cannot have a non-integer number of questions or encode with a non-integer number of bits.

To answer this we need to think of identifying not just one value out of M possibilities but a sequence of k such values (each one chosen independently of the others). We will denote the smallest number of yes/no questions needed to determine a sequence of k unknown values drawn independently from M possibilities, i.e. the entropy, by V_{kM}. This is the same as the number of questions needed to discriminate amongst M^k distinct possibilities.

To take a concrete example, say M is 7 and k is 6 and the task is to identify a sequence of six days of the week, for example {Tuesday, Thursday, Tuesday, Monday, Sunday, Tuesday}. A possible question might be

> Is the first day Monday, Tuesday or Wednesday
> and the second day Thursday
> and the third day Monday, Saturday, Tuesday or Thursday
> and the fourth day Tuesday, Wednesday or Friday
> and the fifth day Saturday or Monday
> and the sixth day Monday, Sunday or Thursday?

There are $7^6 = 117649$ possible sequences of six days. The value of $\log_2 117649$ is 16.84413. This is between 16 and 17 so to determine any possible value of a sequence of 6 days of the week would take 17 questions. The average number of questions for each of the six days of the week is $17/6 = 2.8333$. This is reasonably close to $\log_2 7$, which is approximately 2.8074.

A better approximation to the entropy is obtained by taking a larger value of k, say 21. Now $\log_2 M^k$ is $\log_2(7^{21}) = 58.95445$, so 59 questions are needed for the set of 21 values, making an average number of questions per value of $59/21 = 2.809524$.

Finally, for a set of 1000 values ($k = 1000$), $\log_2 M^k$ is $\log_2(7^{1000}) = 2807.3549$, so 2808 questions are needed for the set of 1000 values, making an average per value of 2.808, which is very close to $\log_2 7$.

It is not a coincidence that these values appear to be converging to $\log_2 7$, as is shown by the following argument for the general case of sequences of length k drawn from M distinct equally likely values.

There are M^k possible sequences of k values. Assuming now that M is *not* a power of 2, the number of questions needed, V_{kM} is the next integer above $\log_2 M^k$. We can put lower and upper bounds on the value of V_{kM} by the relation

$$\log_2 M^k \leq V_{kM} \leq \log_2 M^k + 1$$

Using the property of logarithms that $\log_2 M^k = k \log_2 M$ leads to the relation

$$k \log_2 M \leq V_{kM} \leq k \log_2 M + 1$$

so $\log_2 M \leq V_{kM}/k \leq \log_2 M + 1/k$.

V_{kM}/k is the average number of questions needed to determine each of the k values. By choosing a large enough value of k, i.e. a long enough sequence, the value of $1/k$ can be made as small as we wish. Thus the average number of questions needed to determine each value can be made arbitrarily close to $\log_2 M$. Thus the entropy of a set of M distinct values can be said to be $\log_2 M$, even when M is not a power of 2 (see Figure 10.2).

M	$\log_2 M$
2	1
3	1.5850
4	2
5	2.3219
6	2.5850
7	2.8074
8	3
9	3.1699
10	3.3219

Figure 10.2 $\log_2 M$ for M from 2 to 10

10.4 Encoding Values That Are Not Equally Likely

We finally come to the general case of encoding M distinct values that are not equally likely. (We assume that values that never occur are not included.)

When M possible values are equally likely the entropy has previously been shown to be $\log_2 M$. When M values are unequally distributed the entropy will always have a lower value than $\log_2 M$. In the extreme case where only one value ever occurs, there is no need to use even one bit to represent the value and the entropy is zero.

We will write the frequency with which the ith of the M values occurs as p_i where i varies from 1 to M. Then we have $0 \leq p_i \leq 1$ for all p_i and

$$\sum_{i=1}^{i=M} p_i = 1.$$

For convenience we will give an example where all the p_i values are the reciprocal of an exact power of 2, i.e. 1/2, 1/4 or 1/8, but the result obtained can be shown to apply for other values of p_i using an argument similar to that in Section 10.3.

Suppose we have four values A, B, C and D which occur with frequencies 1/2, 1/4, 1/8 and 1/8 respectively. Then $M = 4$, $p_1 = 1/2$, $p_2 = 1/4$, $p_3 = 1/8$, $p_4 = 1/8$.

When representing A, B, C and D we could use the standard 2-bit encoding described previously, i.e.

A 10
B 11
C 00
D 01

However, we can improve on this using a *variable length encoding*, i.e. one where the values are not always represented by the same number of bits. There are many possible ways of doing this. The best way turns out to be the one shown in Figure 10.3.

A	1
B	01
C	001
D	000

Figure 10.3 Most Efficient Representation for Four Values with Frequencies 1/2, 1/4, 1/8 and 1/8

If the value to be identified is A, we need examine only one bit to establish this. If it is B we need to examine two bits. If it is C or D we need to examine 3 bits. In the average case we need to examine $1/2 \times 1 + 1/4 \times 2 + 1/8 \times 3 + 1/8 \times 3 = 1.75$ bits.

This is the most efficient representation. Flipping some or all of the bits consistently will give other equally efficient representations that are obviously equivalent to it, such as

A 0
B 11
C 100
D 101

Any other representation will require more bits to be examined on average. For example we might choose

A 01
B 1
C 001
D 000

With this representation, in the average case we need to examine $1/2 \times 2 + 1/4 \times 1 + 1/8 \times 3 + 1/8 \times 3 = 2$ bits (the same as the number for the fixed length representation).

Some other representations, such as

A 101
B 0011
C 10011
D 100001

are much worse than the 2-bit representation. This one requires $1/2 \times 3 + 1/4 \times 4 + 1/8 \times 5 + 1/8 \times 6 = 3.875$ bits to be examined on average.

The key to finding the most efficient coding is to use a string of N bits to represent a value that occurs with frequency $1/2^N$. Writing this another way, represent a value that occurs with frequency p_i by a string of $\log_2(1/p_i)$ bits (see Figure 10.4).

p_i	$\log_2(1/p_i)$
1/2	1
1/4	2
1/8	3
1/16	4

Figure 10.4 Values of $\log_2(1/p_i)$

This method of coding ensures that we can determine any value by asking a sequence of 'well-chosen' yes/no questions (i.e. questions for which the two possible answers are equally likely) about the value of each of the bits in turn.

Is the first bit 1?
If not, is the second bit 1?

If not, is the third bit 1?

etc.

So in Figure 10.3 value A, which occurs with frequency $1/2$ is represented by 1 bit, value B which occurs with frequency $1/4$ is represented by 2 bits and values C and D are represented by 3 bits each.

If there are M values with frequencies p_1, p_2, ..., p_M the average number of bits that need to be examined to establish a value, i.e. the entropy, is the frequency of occurrence of the ith value multiplied by the number of bits that need to be examined if that value is the one to be determined, summed over all values of i from 1 to M. Thus we can calculate the value of entropy E by

$$E = \sum_{i=1}^{M} p_i \log_2(1/p_i)$$

This formula is often given in the equivalent form

$$E = - \sum_{i=1}^{M} p_i \log_2(p_i)$$

There are two special cases to consider. When all the values of p_i are the same, i.e. $p_i = 1/M$ for all values of i from 1 to M, the above formula reduces to

$$E = - \sum_{i=1}^{M} (1/M) \log_2(1/M)$$
$$= - \log_2(1/M)$$
$$= \log_2 M$$

which is the formula given in Section 10.3.

When there is only one value with a non-zero frequency, $M = 1$ and $p_1 = 1$, so $E = -1 \times \log_2 1 = 0$.

10.5 Entropy of a Training Set

We can now link up the material in this chapter with the definition of the entropy of a training set given in Chapter 5. In that chapter the formula for entropy was simply stated without motivation. We can now see the entropy of a training set in terms of the number of yes/no questions needed to determine an unknown classification.

If we know that the entropy of a training set is E, it does not imply that we can find an unknown classification with E 'well-chosen' yes/no questions. To do so we would have to ask questions about the classification itself, e.g. 'Is the classification A or B, rather than C or D?' Obviously we cannot find a way of predicting the classification of an unseen instance by asking questions of this kind. Instead we ask a series of questions about the value of a set of attributes measured for each of the instances in a training set, which collectively determine the classification. Sometimes only one question is necessary, sometimes many more.

Asking any question about the value of an attribute effectively divides the training set into a number of subsets, one for each possible value of the attribute (any empty subsets are discarded). The TDIDT algorithm described in Chapter 4 generates a decision tree from the top down by repeatedly splitting on the values of attributes. If the training set represented by the root node has M possible classifications, each of the subsets corresponding to the end nodes of each branch of the developing tree has an entropy value that varies from $\log_2 M$ (if the frequencies of each of the classifications in the subset are identical) to zero (if the subset has attributes with only one classification).

When the splitting process has terminated, all the 'uncertainty' has been removed from the tree. Each branch corresponds to a combination of attribute values and for each branch there is a single classification, so the overall entropy is zero.

Although it is possible for a subset created by splitting to have an entropy greater than its 'parent', at every stage of the process splitting on an attribute reduces the average entropy of the tree or at worst leaves it unchanged. This is an important result, which is frequently assumed but seldom proved. We will consider it in the next section.

10.6 Information Gain Must Be Positive or Zero

The Information Gain attribute selection criterion was described in Chapter 5. Because of its name, it is sometimes assumed that Information Gain must always be positive, i.e. information is always gained by splitting on a node during the tree generation process.

However this is not correct. Although it is generally true that information gain is positive it is also possible for it to be zero. The following demonstration that information gain can be zero is based on the principle that for C possible classifications, the entropy of a training set takes the value $\log_2 C$ (its largest possible value) when the classes are balanced, i.e. there are the same number of instances belonging to each of the classes.

The training set shown in Figure 10.5 has two equally balanced classes. The probability of each class is 0.5, so we have

$$E_{start} = -(1/2)\log_2(1/2) - (1/2)\log_2(1/2) = -\log_2(1/2) = \log_2(2) = 1$$

X	Y	Class
1	1	A
1	2	B
2	1	A
2	2	B
3	2	A
3	1	B
4	2	A
4	1	B

Figure 10.5   Training Set for 'Information Gain Can be Zero' Example

This is the value of $\log_2 C$ for $C = 2$ classes.

The training set has been constructed to have the property that whichever attribute is chosen for splitting, each of the branches will also be balanced.

For splitting on attribute X the frequency table is shown in Figure 10.6(a).

	Attribute value			
Class	1	2	3	4
A	1	1	1	1
B	1	1	1	1
Total	2	2	2	2

Figure 10.6(a)   Frequency Table for Attribute X

Each column of the frequency table is balanced and it can easily be verified that $E_{new} = 1$.

For splitting on attribute Y the frequency table is shown in Figure 10.6(b).

	Attribute value	
Class	1	2
A	2	2
B	2	2
Total	4	4

Figure 10.6(b)   Frequency Table for Attribute Y

Again both columns are balanced and $E_{new} = 1$. Whichever value is taken, E_{new} is 1 and so the Information Gain $= E_{start} - E_{new} = 0$.

The absence of information gain does not imply that there is no value in splitting on either of the attributes. Whichever one is chosen, splitting on the other attribute for all the resulting branches will produce a final decision tree with each branch terminated by a leaf node and thus having an entropy of zero.

Although we have shown that Information Gain can sometimes be zero, it can never be negative. Intuitively it would seem wrong for it to be possible to lose information by splitting on an attribute. Surely that can only give more information (or occasionally the same amount)?

The result that Information Gain can never be negative is stated by many authors and implied by others. The name Information *Gain* gives a strong suggestion that information loss would not be possible, but that is far from being a formal proof.

The present author's inability to locate a proof of this crucial result led him to issue a challenge to several British academics to find a proof in the technical literature or generate one themselves. An excellent response to this came from two members of the University of Ulster in Northern Ireland who produced a detailed proof of their own [1]. The proof is too difficult to reproduce here but is well worth obtaining and studying in detail.

10.7 Using Information Gain for Feature Reduction for Classification Tasks

We conclude this chapter by looking at a further use for entropy, in the form of Information Gain, this time as a means of reducing the number of features (i.e. attributes) that a classification algorithm (of any kind) needs to consider.

The method of feature reduction described here is specific to classification tasks. It uses information gain, which was introduced in Chapter 5 as a criterion for selecting attributes at each stage of the TDIDT tree generation algorithm. However for purposes of feature reduction, information gain is applied at the top level only as an initial pre-processing stage. Only the attributes meeting a specified criterion are retained for use by the classification algorithm. There is no assumption that the classification algorithm used is TDIDT. It can potentially be any algorithm.

Broadly the method amounts to asking for each attribute in turn 'how much information is gained about the classification of an instance by knowing the value of this attribute?' Only the attributes with the largest values of information gain are retained for use with the preferred classification algorithm. There are three stages.

1. Calculate the value of information gain for each attribute in the original dataset.
2. Discard all attributes that do not meet a specified criterion.
3. Pass the revised dataset to the preferred classification algorithm.

The method of calculating information gain for categorical attributes using frequency tables was described in Chapter 6. A modification that enables the method to be used for continuous attributes by examining alternative ways of splitting the attribute values into two parts was described in Chapter 8. The latter also returns a 'split value', i.e. the value of the attribute that gives the largest information gain. This value is not needed when information gain is used for feature reduction. It is sufficient to know the largest information gain achievable for the attribute with any split value.

There are many possible criteria that can be used for determining which attributes to retain, for example:

– Only retain the best 20 attributes

– Only retain the best 25% of the attributes

– Only retain attributes with an information gain that is at least 25% of the highest information gain of any attribute

– Only retain attributes that reduce the initial entropy of the dataset by at least 10%.

There is no one choice that is best in all situations, but analysing the information gain values of all the attributes can help make an informed choice.

10.7.1 Example 1: The *genetics* Dataset

As an example we will consider the *genetics* dataset, which is available from the UCI Repository. Some basic information about this is given in Figure 10.7.

Although 60 attributes is hardly a large number, it may still be more than is needed for reliable classification and is large enough to make overfitting a realistic possibility.

There are three classifications, distributed 767, 768 and 1655 amongst the three classes for the 3190 instances. The relative proportions are 0.240, 0.241 and 0.519, so the initial entropy is: $-0.240 \times \log_2(0.240) - 0.241 \times \log_2(0.241) - 0.519 \times \log_2(0.519) = 1.480$.

The values of information gain for some of the attributes A0 to A59 are shown in Figure 10.8.

The *genetics* Dataset: Basic Information

The *genetics* dataset contains 3190 instances. Each instance comprises the values of a sequence of 60 DNA elements and is classified into one of three possible categories: *EI*, *IE* and *N*. Each of the 60 attributes (named A0 to A59) is categorical and has 8 possible values: *A*, *T*, *G*, *C*, *N*, *D*, *S* and *R*.

For further information see [2].

Figure 10.7 *genetics* Dataset: Basic Information

Attribute	Information Gain
A0	0.0062
A1	0.0066
A2	0.0024
A3	0.0092
A4	0.0161
A5	0.0177
A6	0.0077
A7	0.0071
A8	0.0283
A9	0.0279
......	......
A27	0.2108
A28	0.3426
A29	0.3896
A30	0.3296
A31	0.3322
......	......
A57	0.0080
A58	0.0041
A59	0.0123

Figure 10.8 *genetics* Dataset: Information Gain for Some of the Attributes

The largest information gain is for A29. A gain of 0.3896 implies that the initial entropy would be reduced by more than a quarter if the value of A29 were known. The second largest information gain is for attribute A28.

Comparing values written as decimals to four decimal places is awkward (for people). It is probably easier to make sense of this table if it is adjusted by dividing all the information gain values by 0.3896 (the largest value), making a proportion from 0 to 1, and then multiplying them all by 100. The resulting values are given in Figure 10.9. An adjusted information gain of 1.60 for attribute A0 means that the information gain for A0 is 1.60% of the size of the largest value, which was the one obtained for A29.

Attribute	Info. Gain (adjusted)
A0	1.60
A1	1.70
A2	0.61
A3	2.36
A4	4.14
A5	4.55
A6	1.99
A7	1.81
A8	7.27
A9	7.17
. . . . . .	. . . . . .
A27	54.09
A28	87.92
A29	100.00
A30	84.60
A31	85.26
. . . . . .	. . . . . .
A57	2.07
A58	1.05
A59	3.16

Figure 10.9 *genetics* Dataset: Information Gain as Percentage of Largest Value

From this table it is clear that not only is the information gain for A29 the largest, it is considerably larger than most of the other values. Only a small number of other information gain values are even 50% as large.

Another way of looking at the information gain values is to consider *frequencies*. We can divide the range of possible adjusted values (0 to 100% in this case) into a number of ranges, generally known as *bins*. These might be labelled 10, 20, 30, 40, 50, 60, 70, 80, 90 and 100. (It is not essential for the bins to be equally spaced.)

Each of the information gain values is then assigned to one of the bins. The first bin corresponds to values from 0 to 10 inclusive, the second bin corresponds to values greater than 10 but less than or equal to 20, and so on.

The frequency for each of the 10 bins is shown in Figure 10.10. The final two columns show the *cumulative frequency* (i.e. the number of values that are less than or equal to the bin label) and the cumulative frequency expressed as a percentage of the total number of values (i.e. 60).

Bin	Frequency	Cumulative frequency	Cumulative frequency (%)
10	41	41	68.33
20	9	50	83.33
30	2	52	86.67
40	2	54	90.00
50	0	54	90.00
60	2	56	93.33
70	0	56	93.33
80	0	56	93.33
90	3	59	98.33
100	1	60	100.00
Total	60		

Figure 10.10 *genetics* Dataset: Information Gain Frequencies

As many as 41 of the 60 attributes have an information gain that is no more than 10% as large as that of A29. Only six attributes have an information gain that is more than 50% of that of A29.

It is tempting to discard all but the best six attributes. Although this is not necessarily the best policy, it is interesting to look at the change in predictive accuracy that results if we do.

Using TDIDT with the entropy attribute selection criterion for classification, the predictive accuracy obtained using 10-fold cross-validation is 89.5% when all 60 attributes are used. This increases to 91.8% when only the best six attributes are used. Although this improvement is quite small, it certainly is an improvement and is obtained using only 6 out of the original 60 attributes.

10.7.2 Example 2: The *bcst96* Dataset

The next example makes use of a much larger dataset. The dataset *bcst96* has been used for experiments on automatic classification of web pages. Some basic information about it is given in Figure 10.11.

The *bcst96* Dataset: Basic Information

The *bcst96* dataset comprises 1186 instances (training set) and a further 509 instances (test set). Each instance corresponds to a web page, which is classified into one of two possible categories, B or C, using the values of 13,430 attributes, all continuous.

There are 1,749 attributes that each have only a single value for the instances in the training set and so can be deleted, leaving 11,681 continuous attributes.

Figure 10.11   *bcst96* Dataset: Basic Information

In this case the original number of attributes is more than 11 times as large as the number of instances in the training set. It seems highly likely that a large number of the attributes could safely be deleted, but which ones?

The initial value of entropy is 0.996, indicating that the two classes are fairly equally balanced.

As can be seen in Figure 10.11, having deleted the attributes that have a single value for all instances in the training set, there are 11,681 continuous attributes remaining.

Next we calculate the information gain for each of these 11,681 attributes. The largest value is 0.381.

The frequency table is shown in Figure 10.12.

The most surprising result is that as many as 11,135 of the attributes (95.33%) have an information gain in the 5 bin, i.e. no more than 5% of the largest information gain available. Almost 99% of the values are in the 5 and 10 bins.

Using TDIDT with the entropy attribute selection criterion for classification, the algorithm generates 38 rules from the original training set and uses these to predict the classification of the 509 instances in the test set. It does this with 94.9% accuracy (483 correct and 26 incorrect predictions). If we discard all but the best 50 attributes, the same algorithm generates a set of 62 rules, which again give 94.9% predictive accuracy on the test set (483 correct and 26 incorrect predictions).

Bin	Frequency	Cumulative frequency	Cumulative frequency (%)
5	11,135	11,135	95.33
10	403	11,538	98.78
15	76	11,614	99.43
20	34	11,648	99.72
25	10	11,658	99.80
30	7	11,665	99.86
35	4	11,669	99.90
40	1	11,670	99.91
45	2	11,672	99.92
50	1	11,673	99.93
55	1	11,674	99.94
60	2	11,676	99.96
65	2	11,678	99.97
70	0	11,678	99.97
75	1	11,679	99.98
80	0	11,679	99.98
85	1	11,680	99.99
90	0	11,680	99.99
95	0	11,680	99.99
100	1	11,681	100.00
Total	11,681		

Figure 10.12 *bcst96* Dataset: Information Gain Frequencies

In this case just 50 out of 11,681 attributes (less than 0.5%) suffice to give the same predictive accuracy as the whole set of attributes. However, the difference in the amount of processing required to produce the two decision trees is considerable. With all the attributes the TDIDT algorithm will need to examine approximately $1,186 \times 11,681 = 13,853,666$ attribute values at each node of the evolving decision tree. If only the best 50 attributes are used the number drops to just $1,186 \times 50 = 59,300$.

Although feature reduction cannot always be guaranteed to produce results as good as those in these two examples, it should always be considered, especially when the number of attributes is large.

10.8 Chapter Summary

This chapter returns to the subject of the entropy of a training set. It explains the concept of entropy in detail using the idea of coding information using bits. The important result that when using the TDIDT algorithm information gain must be positive or zero is discussed, followed by the use of information gain as a method of feature reduction for classification tasks.

10.9 Self-assessment Exercises for Chapter 10

1. What is the entropy of a training set of 100 instances with four classes that occur with relative frequencies 20/100, 30/100, 25/100 and 25/100? What is the entropy of a training set of 10,000 instances with those frequencies for its four classes?

2. Given the task of identifying an unknown person in a large group using only yes/no questions, which question is it likely to be best to ask first?

References

[1] McSherry, D., & Stretch, C. (2003). *Information gain* (University of Ulster Technical Note).

[2] Noordewier, M. O., Towell, G. G., & Shavlik, J. W. (1991). Training knowledge-based neural networks to recognize genes in DNA sequences. In *Advances in neural information processing systems* (Vol. 3). San Mateo: Morgan Kaufmann.

11

Inducing Modular Rules for Classification

Generating classification rules via the intermediate form of a decision tree is a widely used technique, which formed the main topic of the first part of this book. However, as pointed out in Chapter 9, like many other methods it suffers from the problem of overfitting to the training data. We begin this chapter by describing the 'rule post-pruning' method, which is an alternative to the post-pruning method discussed in Chapter 9. This leads on to the important topic of *conflict resolution*.

We go on to suggest that the decision tree representation is itself a major cause of overfitting and then look at an algorithm which generates rules directly without using the intermediate representation of a decision tree.

11.1 Rule Post-pruning

The Rule Post-pruning method begins by converting a decision tree to an equivalent set of rules and then examines the rules with the aim of simplifying them without any loss of (and preferably with a gain in) predictive accuracy.

Figure 11.1 shows the decision tree for the *degrees* dataset given in Chapter 4. It consists of five branches, each ending with a leaf node labelled with one of the valid classifications, i.e. FIRST or SECOND.

Each branch of the tree corresponds to a classification rule and so the rules equivalent to the decision tree can be extracted from it branch by branch. The order in which the branches are taken is arbitrary as for any unseen instance

© Springer-Verlag London Ltd., part of Springer Nature 2020
M. Bramer, *Principles of Data Mining*, Undergraduate Topics
in Computer Science, DOI 10.1007/978-1-4471-7493-6_11

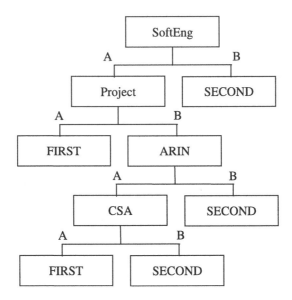

Figure 11.1 Decision Tree for the *degrees* Dataset

only one rule (at most) can ever apply. The five rules corresponding to Figure 11.1 are as follows (in arbitrary order):

IF SoftEng = A AND Project = B AND
    ARIN = A AND CSA = A THEN Class = FIRST
IF SoftEng = A AND Project = A THEN Class = FIRST
IF SoftEng = A AND Project = B AND ARIN = A AND
    CSA = B THEN Class = SECOND
IF SoftEng = A AND Project = B AND ARIN = B THEN
    Class = SECOND
IF SoftEng = B THEN Class = SECOND

We now examine each of the rules in turn to consider whether removing each of its terms increases or reduces its predictive accuracy. Thus for the first rule given above we consider the four terms 'SoftEng = A', 'Project = B', 'ARIN = A' and 'CSA = A'. We need some way of estimating whether removing each of these terms singly would increase or decrease the accuracy of the resulting rule set. Assuming we have such a method, we remove the term that gives the largest increase in predictive accuracy, say 'Project = B'. We then consider the removal of each of the other three terms. The processing of a rule ends when removing any of the terms would reduce (or leave unchanged) the predictive accuracy. We then go on to the next rule.

This description relies on there being some means of estimating the effect on the predictive accuracy of a ruleset of removing a single term from one of the rules. We may be able to use a probability-based formula to do this or we can simply use the original and revised rulesets to classify the instances in an unseen *pruning set* and compare the results. (Note that it would be methodologically unsound to improve the ruleset using a test set and then examine its performance on the same instances. For this method there needs to be three sets: training, pruning and test.)

11.2 Conflict Resolution

A second important issue raised by the use of rule post-pruning is of much wider applicability. Once even one term has been removed from a rule the property that for any unseen instance only one rule (at most) can ever apply is no longer valid.

The method of post-pruning described in Chapter 9, i.e. working bottom-up, repeatedly replacing a subtree by a single node has the very desirable property that the resulting branches will still fit together in a tree structure. For example the method might (probably unwisely) lead to the replacement of the test on the value of ARIN in Figure 11.1 and the subtree that hangs from it by a single node labelled SECOND. The result will still be a tree, as shown in Figure 11.2.

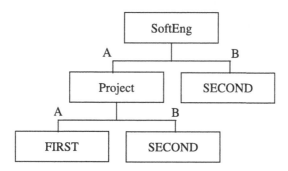

Figure 11.2 Decision Tree for the *degrees* Dataset (revised)

Instead of this, suppose that, as part of a process such as rule post-pruning, we wish to remove the link corresponding to 'SoftEng = A' near the top of the tree, giving Figure 11.3.

If we do so, we will no longer have a tree — just two disconnected trees. It is unclear whether and how these can be used. The five rules listed in Section

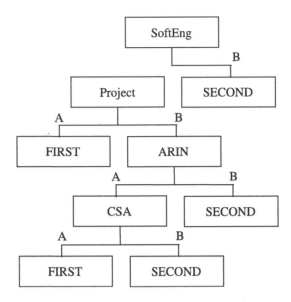

Figure 11.3 Decision Tree for the *degrees* Dataset (revised – version 2)

11.1 have now become the following (the first four rules have changed).

IF Project = B AND ARIN = A AND CSA = A THEN Class = FIRST
IF Project = A THEN Class = FIRST
IF Project = B AND ARIN = A AND CSA = B
    THEN Class = SECOND
IF Project = B AND ARIN = B THEN Class = SECOND
IF SoftEng = B THEN Class = SECOND

We will say that a rule *fires* if its condition part is satisfied for a given instance. If a set of rules fits into a tree structure there is only one rule that can fire for any instance. In the general case of a set of rules that do not fit into a tree structure, it is entirely possible for several rules to fire for a given test instance, and for those rules to give contradictory classifications.

Suppose that for the *degrees* application we have an unseen instance for which the values of SoftEng, Project, ARIN and CSA are 'B', 'B', 'A' and 'A', respectively. Both the first and the last rules will fire. The first rule concludes 'Class = FIRST'; the last rule concludes 'Class = SECOND'. Which one should we take?

The problem can be illustrated outside the context of the *degrees* dataset by considering just two rules from some imaginary ruleset:

IF $x = 4$ THEN Class = a

IF $y = 2$ THEN Class $= b$

What should the classification be for an instance with $x = 4$ and $y = 2$? One rule gives class a, the other class b.

We can easily extend the example with other rules such as

IF $w = 9$ and $k = 5$ THEN Class $= b$
IF $x = 4$ THEN Class $= a$
IF $y = 2$ THEN Class $= b$
IF $z = 6$ and $m = 47$ THEN Class $= b$

What should the classification be for an instance with $w = 9$, $k = 5$, $x = 4$, $y = 2$, $z = 6$ and $m = 47$? One rule gives class a, the other three rules give class b.

We need a method of choosing just one classification to give to the unseen instance. This method is known as a *conflict resolution strategy*. There are various strategies we can use, including:

– 'majority voting' (e.g. there are three rules predicting class b and only one predicting class a, so choose class b)

– giving priority to certain types of rule or classification (e.g. rules with a small number of terms or predicting a rare classification might have a higher weighting than other rules in the voting)

– using a measure of the 'interestingness' of each rule (of the kind that will be discussed in Chapter 16), give priority to the most interesting rule.

It is possible to construct quite elaborate conflict resolution strategies but most of them have the same drawback: they require the condition part of *all* the rules to be tested for each unseen instance, so that all the rules that fire are known before the strategy is applied. By contrast, we need only work through the rules generated from a decision tree until the first one fires (as we know no others can).

A very basic but widely used conflict resolution strategy is to work through the rules in order and to take the first one that fires. This can reduce the amount of processing required considerably, but makes the order in which the rules are generated very important.

Whilst it is possible using a conflict resolution strategy to post-prune a decision tree to give a set of rules that do not fit together in a tree structure, it seems an unnecessarily indirect way of generating a set of rules. In addition if we wish to use the 'take the first rule that fires' conflict resolution strategy, the order in which the rules are extracted from the tree is likely to be of crucial importance, whereas it ought to be arbitrary.

In Section 11.4 we will describe an algorithm that dispenses with tree generation altogether and produces rules that are 'free standing', i.e. do not fit together into a tree structure, directly. We will call these *modular rules*.

11.3 Problems with Decision Trees

Although very widely used, the decision tree representation has a serious potential drawback: the rules derived from the tree may be much more numerous than necessary and may contain many redundant terms.

In a PhD project at the Open University, supervised by the present author, Cendrowska [1], [2] criticised the principle of generating decision trees which can then be converted to decision rules, compared with the alternative of generating decision rules directly from the training set. She comments as follows [the original notation has been changed to be consistent with that used in this book]:

"[The] decision tree representation of rules has a number of disadvantages. . . . [Most] importantly, there are rules that cannot easily be represented by trees.

Consider, for example, the following rule set:

Rule 1: IF $a = 1$ AND $b = 1$ THEN Class = 1
Rule 2: IF $c = 1$ AND $d = 1$ THEN Class = 1

Suppose that Rules 1 and 2 cover all instances of Class 1 and all other instances are of Class 2. These two rules cannot be represented by a single decision tree as the root node of the tree must split on a single attribute, and there is no attribute which is common to both rules. The simplest decision tree representation of the set of instances covered by these rules would necessarily add an extra term to one of the rules, which in turn would require at least one extra rule to cover instances excluded by the addition of that extra term. The complexity of the tree would depend on the number of possible values of the attributes selected for partitioning. For example, let the four attributes a, b, c and d each have three possible values 1, 2 and 3, and let attribute a be selected for partitioning at the root node. The simplest decision tree representation of Rules 1 and 2 is shown [in Figure 11.4].

The paths relating to Class 1 can be listed as follows:

IF $a = 1$ AND $b = 1$ THEN Class = 1
IF $a = 1$ AND $b = 2$ AND $c = 1$ AND $d = 1$ THEN Class = 1
IF $a = 1$ AND $b = 3$ AND $c = 1$ AND $d = 1$ THEN Class = 1
IF $a = 2$ AND $c = 1$ AND $d = 1$ THEN Class = 1

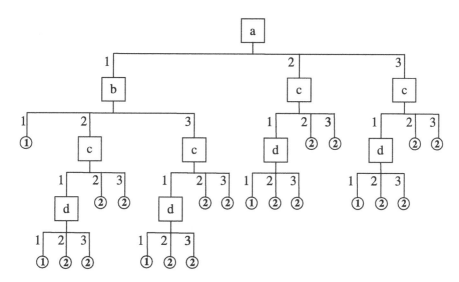

Figure 11.4 Simplest Decision Tree Representation of Rules 1 and 2

IF $a = 3$ AND $c = 1$ AND $d = 1$ THEN Class $= 1$

Clearly, the consequence of forcing a simple rule set into a decision tree representation is that the individual rules, when extracted from the tree, are often too specific (i.e. they reference attributes which are irrelevant). This makes them highly unsuitable for use in many domains."

The phenomenon of unnecessarily large and confusing decision trees described by Cendrowska is far from being merely a rare hypothetical possibility. It will occur whenever there are two (underlying) rules with no attribute in common, a situation that is likely to occur frequently in practice.

All the rules corresponding to the branches of a decision tree must begin in the same way, i.e. with a test on the value of the attribute selected at the top level. Leaving aside issues of overfitting, this effect will inevitably lead to the introduction of terms in rules (branches) which are unnecessary except for the sole purpose of enabling a tree structure to be constructed.

Issues of the size and compactness of a rule set may not seem important when the training sets are small, but may become very important as they scale up to many thousands or millions of instances, especially if the number of attributes is also large.

Although in this book we have generally ignored issues of the practicality of and/or cost associated with finding the values of attributes, considerable practical problems can arise when the values of some attributes are unknown for an instance that needs to be classified or can only be obtained by means of tests that carry an unusually high cost or risk to health. For many real-world applications a method of classifying unseen instances that avoided making unnecessary tests would be highly desirable.

11.4 The Prism Algorithm

The Prism algorithm was introduced by Cendrowska [1], [2]. The aim is to induce modular classification rules directly from the training set. The algorithm assumes that all the attributes are categorical. When there are continuous attributes they can first be converted to categorical ones (as described in Chapter 8). Alternatively the algorithm can be extended to deal with continuous attributes in much the same way as was described for TDIDT in Section 8.3.

Prism uses the 'take the first rule that fires' conflict resolution strategy when the resulting rules are applied to unseen data, so it is important that as far as possible the most important rules are generated first.

The algorithm generates the rules concluding each of the possible classes in turn. Each rule is generated term by term, with each term of the form 'attribute = value'. The attribute/value pair added at each step is chosen to maximise the probability of the target 'outcome class'.

In its basic form, the Prism algorithm is shown in Figure 11.5. Note that the training set is restored to its original state for each new class.

For each classification (class = i) in turn and starting with the complete training set each time:

1. Calculate the probability that class = i for each attribute/value pair.

2. Select the pair with the largest probability and create a subset of the training set comprising all the instances with the selected attribute/value combination (for all classifications).

3. Repeat 1 and 2 for this subset until a subset is reached that contains only instances of class i. The induced rule is then the conjunction of all the attribute/value pairs selected.

4. Remove all instances covered by this rule from the training set.

Repeat 1–4 until all instances of class i have been removed

Figure 11.5 The Basic Prism Algorithm

We will illustrate the algorithm by generating rules for the *lens24* dataset (classification 1 only). The algorithm generates two classification rules for that class.

The initial training set for *lens24* comprises 24 instances, shown in Figure 11.6.

age	specRx	astig	tears	class
1	1	1	1	3
1	1	1	2	2
1	1	2	1	3
1	1	2	2	1
1	2	1	1	3
1	2	1	2	2
1	2	2	1	3
1	2	2	2	1
2	1	1	1	3
2	1	1	2	2
2	1	2	1	3
2	1	2	2	1
2	2	1	1	3
2	2	1	2	2
2	2	2	1	3
2	2	2	2	3
3	1	1	1	3
3	1	1	2	3
3	1	2	1	3
3	1	2	2	1
3	2	1	1	3
3	2	1	2	2
3	2	2	1	3
3	2	2	2	3

Figure 11.6 The *lens24* Training Set

First Rule

Figure 11.7 shows the probability of class = 1 occurring for each attribute/value pair over the whole training set (24 instances).

The maximum probability is when *astig* = 2 or *tears* = 2.

Choose *astig* = 2 arbitrarily.

Incomplete rule induced so far:

IF astig = 2 THEN class = 1

Attribute/value pair	Frequency for class = 1	Total frequency (out of 24 instances)	Probability
age = 1	2	8	0.25
age = 2	1	8	0.125
age = 3	1	8	0.125
specRx = 1	3	12	0.25
specRx = 2	1	12	0.083
astig = 1	0	12	0
astig = 2	4	12	0.33
tears = 1	0	12	0
tears = 2	4	12	0.33

Figure 11.7 First Rule: Probability of Attribute/value Pairs (Version 1)

The subset of the training set covered by this incomplete rule is given in Figure 11.8.

age	specRx	astig	tears	class
1	1	2	1	3
1	1	2	2	1
1	2	2	1	3
1	2	2	2	1
2	1	2	1	3
2	1	2	2	1
2	2	2	1	3
2	2	2	2	3
3	1	2	1	3
3	1	2	2	1
3	2	2	1	3
3	2	2	2	3

Figure 11.8 First Rule: Subset of Training Set Covered by Incomplete Rule (Version 1)

Figure 11.9 shows the probability of each attribute/value pair (not involving attribute *astig*) occurring for this subset.

The maximum probability is when *tears* = 2.

Incomplete rule induced so far:

Attribute/value pair	Frequency for class = 1	Total frequency (out of 12 instances)	Probability
age = 1	2	4	0.5
age = 2	1	4	0.25
age = 3	1	4	0.25
specRx = 1	3	6	0.5
specRx = 2	1	6	0.17
tears = 1	0	6	0
tears = 2	4	6	0.67

Figure 11.9 First Rule: Probability of Attribute/value Pairs (Version 2)

IF astig = 2 and tears = 2 THEN class = 1

The subset of the training set covered by this rule is shown in Figure 11.10.

age	specRx	astig	tears	class
1	1	2	2	1
1	2	2	2	1
2	1	2	2	1
2	2	2	2	3
3	1	2	2	1
3	2	2	2	3

Figure 11.10 First Rule: Subset of Training Set Covered by Incomplete Rule (Version 2)

Figure 11.11 shows the probability of each attribute/value pair (not involving attributes *astig* or *tears*) occurring for this subset.

The maximum probability is when *age* = 1 or *specRx* = 1.
Choose (arbitrarily) *age* = 1.

Incomplete rule induced so far:

IF astig = 2 and tears = 2 and age = 1 THEN class = 1

The subset of the training set covered by this rule is given in Figure 11.12.
This subset contains only instances of class 1.
The final induced rule is therefore

IF astig = 2 and tears = 2 and age = 1 THEN class = 1

Attribute/value pair	Frequency for class = 1	Total frequency (out of 6 instances)	Probability
age = 1	2	2	1.0
age = 2	1	2	0.5
age = 3	1	2	0.5
specRx = 1	3	3	1.0
specRx = 2	1	3	0.33

Figure 11.11   First Rule: Probability of Attribute/value Pairs (Version 3)

age	specRx	astig	tears	class
1	1	2	2	1
1	2	2	2	1

Figure 11.12   First Rule: Subset of Training Set Covered by Incomplete Rule (Version 3)

Second Rule

   Removing the two instances covered by the first rule from the training set gives a new training set with 22 instances. This is shown in Figure 11.13.

   The table of frequencies is now as given in Figure 11.14 for attribute/value pairs corresponding to $class = 1$.

   The maximum probability is achieved by $astig = 2$ and $tears = 2$.
Choose $astig = 2$ arbitrarily.

   Incomplete rule induced so far:

IF astig=2 THEN class = 1

   The subset of the training set covered by this rule is shown in Figure 11.15.
   This gives the frequency table shown in Figure 11.16.
   The maximum probability is achieved by $tears = 2$.
   Incomplete rule induced so far:

IF astig = 2 and tears = 2 then class = 1

   The subset of the training set covered by this rule is shown in Figure 11.17.
   This gives the frequency table shown in Figure 11.18.
   The maximum probability is for $specRx = 1$.
   Incomplete rule induced so far:

IF astig = 2 and tears = 2 and specRx = 1 THEN class = 1

age	specRx	astig	tears	class
1	1	1	1	3
1	1	1	2	2
1	1	2	1	3
1	2	1	1	3
1	2	1	2	2
1	2	2	1	3
2	1	1	1	3
2	1	1	2	2
2	1	2	1	3
2	1	2	2	1
2	2	1	1	3
2	2	1	2	2
2	2	2	1	3
2	2	2	2	3
3	1	1	1	3
3	1	1	2	3
3	1	2	1	3
3	1	2	2	1
3	2	1	1	3
3	2	1	2	2
3	2	2	1	3
3	2	2	2	3

Figure 11.13 The *lens24* Training Set (Reduced)

Attribute/value pair	Frequency for class = 1	Total frequency (out of 22 instances)	Probability
age = 1	0	6	0
age = 2	1	8	0.125
age = 3	1	8	0.125
specRx = 1	2	11	0.18
specRx = 2	0	11	0
astig = 1	0	12	0
astig = 2	2	10	0.2
tears = 1	0	12	0
tears = 2	2	10	0.2

Figure 11.14 Second Rule: Probability of Attribute/value Pairs (Version 1)

age	specRx	astig	tears	class
1	1	2	1	3
1	2	2	1	3
2	1	2	1	3
2	1	2	2	1
2	2	2	1	3
2	2	2	2	3
3	1	2	1	3
3	1	2	2	1
3	2	2	1	3
3	2	2	2	3

Figure 11.15 Second Rule: Subset of Training Set Covered by Incomplete Rule (Version 1)

Attribute/value pair	Frequency for class = 1	Total frequency (out of 10 instances)	Probability
age = 1	0	2	0
age = 2	1	4	0.25
age = 3	1	4	0.25
specRx = 1	0	5	0
specRx = 2	2	5	0.4
tears = 1	0	6	0
tears = 2	2	4	0.5

Figure 11.16 Second Rule: Probability of Attribute/value Pairs (Version 2)

age	specRx	astig	tears	class
2	1	2	2	1
2	2	2	2	3
3	1	2	2	1
3	2	2	2	3

Figure 11.17 Second Rule: Subset of Training Set Covered by Incomplete Rule (Version 2)

Attribute/value pair	Frequency for class = 1	Total Frequency (out of 4 instances)	Probability
age = 1	0	0	–
age = 2	1	2	0.5
age = 3	1	2	0.5
specRx = 1	2	2	1.0
specRx = 2	0	2	0

Figure 11.18 Second Rule: Probability of Attribute/value Pairs (Version 3)

age	specRx	astig	tears	class
2	1	2	2	1
3	1	2	2	1

Figure 11.19 Second Rule: Subset of Training Set Covered by Incomplete Rule (Version 3)

The subset of the training set covered by this rule is shown in Figure 11.19. This subset contains only instances of class 1. So the final induced rule is:

IF astig = 2 and tears = 2 and specRx = 1 THEN class = 1

Removing the two instances covered by this rule from the current version of the training set (which has 22 instances) gives a training set of 20 instances from which all instances of class 1 have now been removed. So the Prism algorithm terminates (for classification 1).

The final pair of rules induced by Prism for class 1 are:

IF astig = 2 and tears = 2 and age = 1 THEN class = 1
IF astig = 2 and tears = 2 and specRx = 1 THEN class = 1

The algorithm will now go on to generate rules for the remaining classifications. It produces 3 rules for class 2 and 4 for class 3. Note that the training set is restored to its original state for each new class.

11.4.1 Changes to the Basic Prism Algorithm

1. *Tie-breaking*

   The basic algorithm can be improved slightly by choosing between attribute/value pairs which have equal probability not arbitrarily as above but by taking the one with the highest total frequency.

2. *Clashes in the Training Data*

The original version of Prism does not include any method of dealing with clashes in the training set encountered during rule generation.

However, the basic algorithm can easily be extended to deal with clashes as follows.

Step 3 of the algorithm states:

Repeat 1 and 2 for this subset until a subset is reached that contains only instances of class i.

To this needs to be added 'or a subset is reached which contains instances of more than one class, although values of all the attributes have already been used in creating the subset'.

The simple approach of assigning all instances in the subset to the majority class does not fit directly into the Prism framework. A number of approaches to doing so have been investigated, and the most effective would appear to be as follows.

If a clash occurs while generating the rules for class i:

1. Determine the majority class for the subset of instances in the clash set.

2. If this majority class is class i, then complete the induced rule by assigning all the instances in the clash set to class i. If not, discard the rule.

11.4.2 Comparing Prism with TDIDT

Both the additional features described in Section 11.4.1 are included in a reimplementation of Prism by the present author [3].

The same paper describes a series of experiments to compare the performance of Prism with that of TDIDT on a number of datasets. The author concludes "The experiments presented here suggest that the Prism algorithm for generating modular rules gives classification rules which are at least as good as those obtained from the widely used TDIDT algorithm. There are generally fewer rules with fewer terms per rule, which is likely to aid their comprehensibility to domain experts and users. This result would seem to apply even more strongly when there is noise in the training set. As far as classification accuracy on unseen test data is concerned, there appears to be little to choose between the two algorithms for noise-free datasets, including ones with a significant proportion of clash instances in the training set. The main difference is that Prism generally has a preference for leaving a test instance as 'unclassified' rather than giving it a wrong classification. In some domains this may be an important feature. When it is not, a simple strategy such as assigning unclassified instances to the majority class would seem to suffice. When noise is present, Prism would seem to give consistently better classification accuracy than TDIDT, even when there is a high level of noise in the training set.... The reasons why Prism should be more tolerant to noise than TDIDT are not entirely clear, but may be related to the presence of fewer terms per rule in most cases. The computational effort involved in generating rules using Prism ... is greater than for TDIDT. However, Prism would seem to have considerable potential for efficiency improvement by parallelisation."

These very positive conclusions are of course based on only a fairly limited number of experiments and need to be verified for a much wider range of datasets. In practice, despite the drawbacks of a decision tree representation and the obvious potential of Prism and other similar algorithms, TDIDT is far more frequently used to generate classification rules. The ready availability of C4.5 [4] and related systems is no doubt a significant factor in this.

In Chapter 16 we go on to look at the use of modular rules for predicting associations between attribute values rather than for classification.

11.5 Chapter Summary

This chapter begins by considering a method of post-pruning decision rules generated via a decision tree, which has the property that the pruned rules will not generally fit together to form a tree. Rules of this kind are known as *modular rules*. When using modular rules to classify unseen test data a *conflict resolution strategy* is needed and several possibilities for this are discussed. The use of a decision tree as an intermediate representation for rules is identified as a source of overfitting.

The Prism algorithm induces modular classification rules directly from a training set. Prism is described in detail, followed by a discussion of its performance as a classification algorithm relative to TDIDT.

11.6 Self-assessment Exercise for Chapter 11

What would be the first rule generated by Prism for the *degrees* dataset given in Chapter 4, Figure 4.3, for class 'FIRST'?

References

[1] Cendrowska, J. (1987). PRISM: an algorithm for inducing modular rules. *International Journal of Man-Machine Studies*, *27*, 349–370.

[2] Cendrowska, J. (1990). *Knowledge acquisition for expert systems: inducing modular rules from examples*. PhD Thesis, The Open University.

[3] Bramer, M. A. (2000). Automatic induction of classification rules from examples using N-prism. In *Research and development in intelligent systems XVI* (pp. 99–121). Berlin: Springer.

[4] Quinlan, J. R. (1993). *C4.5: programs for machine learning*. San Mateo: Morgan Kaufmann.

12

Measuring the Performance of a Classifier

Up to now we have generally assumed that the best (or only) way of measuring the performance of a classifier is by its *predictive accuracy*, i.e. the proportion of unseen instances it correctly classifies. However this is not necessarily the case.

There are many other types of classification algorithm as well as those discussed in this book. Some require considerably more computation or memory than others. Some require a substantial number of training instances to give reliable results. Depending on the situation the user may be willing to accept a lower level of predictive accuracy in order to reduce the run time/memory requirements and/or the number of training instances needed.

A more difficult trade-off occurs when the classes are severely unbalanced. Suppose we are considering investing in one of the leading companies quoted on a certain stock market. Can we predict which companies will become bankrupt in the next two years, so we can avoid investing in them? The proportion of such companies is obviously small. Let us say it is 0.02 (a fictitious value), so on average out of every 100 companies 2 will become bankrupt and 98 will not. Call these 'bad' and 'good' companies respectively.

If we have a very 'trusting' classifier that always predicts 'good' under all circumstances its predictive accuracy will be 0.98, a very high value. Looked at only in terms of predictive accuracy this is a very successful classifier. Unfortunately it will give us no help at all in avoiding investing in bad companies.

On the other hand, if we want to be very safe we could use a very 'cautious' classifier that always predicted 'bad'. In this way we would never lose our money in a bankrupt company but would never invest in a good one either. This is

© Springer-Verlag London Ltd., part of Springer Nature 2020
M. Bramer, *Principles of Data Mining*, Undergraduate Topics
in Computer Science, DOI 10.1007/978-1-4471-7493-6_12

similar to the ultra-safe strategy for air traffic control: ground all aeroplanes, so you can be sure that none of them will crash. In real life, we are usually willing to accept the risk of making some mistakes in order to achieve our objectives.

It is clear from this example that neither the very trusting nor the very cautious classifier is any use in practice. Moreover, where the classes are severely unbalanced (98% to 2% in the company example), predictive accuracy on its own is not a reliable indicator of a classifier's effectiveness.

12.1 True and False Positives and Negatives

The idea of a confusion matrix was introduced in Chapter 7. When there are two classes, which we will call positive and negative (or simply $+$ and $-$), the confusion matrix consists of four cells, which can be labelled TP, FP, FN and TN as in Figure 12.1.

		Predicted class		Total
		$+$	$-$	instances
Actual class	$+$	TP	FN	P
	$-$	FP	TN	N

Figure 12.1   True and False Positives and Negatives

TP: true positives
The number of positive instances that are classified as positive

FP: false positives
The number of negative instances that are classified as positive

FN: false negatives
The number of positive instances that are classified as negative

TN: true negatives
The number of negative instances that are classified as negative

P = TP + FN
The total number of positive instances

N = FP + TN
The total number of negative instances

It is often useful to distinguish between the two types of classification error: false positives and false negatives.

False positives (also known as *Type 1 Errors*) occur when instances that should be classified as negative are classified as positive.

False negatives (also known as *Type 2 Errors*) occur when instances that should be classified as positive are classified as negative.

Depending on the application, errors of these two types are of more or less importance.

In the following examples we will make the assumption that there are only two classifications, which will be called positive and negative, or + and −. The training instances can then be considered as positive and negative examples of a concept such as 'good company', 'patient with brain tumour' or 'relevant web page'.

Bad Company Application. Here we would like the number of false positives (bad companies that are classified as good) to be as small as possible, ideally zero. We would probably be willing to accept a high proportion of false negatives (good companies classified as bad) as there are a large number of possible companies to invest in.

Medical Screening Application. It would not be possible in any realistic system of healthcare to screen the entire population for a condition that occurs only rarely, say a brain tumour. Instead the doctor uses his or her experience to judge (based on symptoms and other factors) which patients are most likely to be suffering from a brain tumour and sends them to a hospital for screening.

For this application we might be willing to accept quite a high proportion of false positives (patients screened unnecessarily) perhaps as high as 0.90, i.e. only 1 in 10 of patients screened has a brain tumour, or even higher. However we would like the proportion of false negatives (patients with a brain tumour who are not screened) to be as small as possible, ideally zero.

Information Retrieval Application. A web search engine can be looked at as a kind of classifier. Given a specification such as 'pages about American poetry' it effectively classifies all pages on the web that are known to it as either 'relevant' or 'not relevant' and displays the URLs of the 'relevant' ones to the user. Here we may be willing to accept a high proportion of false negatives (relevant pages left out), perhaps 30% or even higher, but probably do not want too many false positives (irrelevant pages included), say no more than 10%. In such information retrieval applications the user is seldom aware of the false negatives (relevant pages not found by the search engine) but false positives are visible, waste time and irritate the user.

These examples illustrate that, leaving aside the ideal of perfect classification accuracy, there is no single combination of false positives and false negatives that is ideal for every application and that even a very high level of predictive accuracy may be unhelpful when the classes are very unbalanced. To go further we need to define some improved measures of performance.

12.2 Performance Measures

We can now define a number of performance measures for a classifier applied to a given test set. The most important ones are given in Figure 12.2. Several measures have more than one name, depending on the technical area (signal processing, medicine, information retrieval etc.) in which they are used.

For information retrieval applications the most commonly used measures are Recall and Precision. For the search engine application, Recall measures the proportion of relevant pages that are retrieved and Precision measures the proportion of retrieved pages that are relevant. The F1 Score combines Precision and Recall into a single measure, which is their product divided by their average. This is known as the *harmonic mean* of the two values.

The values of P and N, the number of positive and negative instances, are fixed for a given test set, whichever classifier is used. The values of the measures given in Figure 12.2 will generally vary from one classifier to another. Given the values of True Positive Rate and False Positive Rate (as well as P and N) we can derive all the other measures.

We can therefore characterise a classifier by its True Positive Rate (TP Rate) and False Positive Rate (FP Rate) values, which are both proportions from 0 to 1 inclusive. We start by looking at some special cases.

A: The Perfect Classifier

Here every instance is correctly classified. $TP = P$, $TN = N$ and the confusion matrix is:

		Predicted class		Total
		+	−	instances
Actual class	+	P	0	P
	−	0	N	N

True Positive Rate or Hit Rate or Recall or Sensitivity or TP Rate	TP/P	The proportion of positive instances that are correctly classified as positive
False Positive Rate or False Alarm Rate or FP Rate	FP/N	The proportion of negative instances that are erroneously classified as positive
False Negative Rate or FN Rate	FN/P	The proportion of positive instances that are erroneously classified as negative $= 1 -$ True Positive Rate
True Negative Rate or Specificity or TN Rate	TN/N	The proportion of negative instances that are correctly classified as negative
Precision or Positive Predictive Value	TP/(TP+FP)	Proportion of instances classified as positive that are really positive
F1 Score	$(2 \times$ Precision $\times$ Recall$)$ $/($Precision $+$ Recall$)$	A measure that combines Precision and Recall
Accuracy or Predictive Accuracy	(TP + TN)/(P + N)	The proportion of instances that are correctly classified
Error Rate	(FP + FN)/(P + N)	The proportion of instances that are incorrectly classified

Figure 12.2 Some Performance Measures for a Classifier

TP Rate (Recall) $= P/P = 1$
FP Rate $= 0/N = 0$
Precision $= P/P = 1$
F1 Score $= 2 \times 1/(1+1) = 1$
Accuracy $= (P+N)/(P+N) = 1$

B: The Worst Possible Classifier

Every instance is wrongly classified. $TP = 0$ and $TN = 0$. The confusion matrix is:

		Predicted class		Total
		+	−	instances
Actual class	+	0	P	P
	−	N	0	N

TP Rate (Recall) $= 0/P = 0$
FP Rate $= N/N = 1$
Precision $= 0/N = 0$
F1 Score is not applicable (as Precision + Recall $= 0$)
Accuracy $= 0/(P+N) = 0$

C: The Ultra-liberal Classifier

This classifier always predicts the positive class. The True Positive rate is 1 but the False Positive rate is also 1. The False Negative and True Negative rates are both zero. The confusion matrix is:

		Predicted class		Total
		+	−	instances
Actual class	+	P	0	P
	−	N	0	N

TP Rate (Recall) $= P/P = 1$
FP Rate $= N/N = 1$
Precision $= P/(P+N)$
F1 Score $= 2 \times P/(2 \times P + N)$
Accuracy $= P/(P+N)$, which is the proportion of positive instances in the test set.

D: The Ultra-conservative Classifier

This classifier always predicts the negative class. The False Positive rate is zero, but so is the True Positive rate. The confusion matrix is:

		Predicted class		Total
		+	−	instances
Actual class	+	0	P	P
	−	0	N	N

TP Rate (Recall) $= 0/P = 0$
FP Rate $= 0/N = 0$
Precision is not applicable (as $TP + FP = 0$)
F1 Score is also not applicable
Accuracy $= N/(P + N)$, which is the proportion of negative instances in the test set.

12.3 True and False Positive Rates versus Predictive Accuracy

One of the strengths of characterising a classifier by its TP Rate and FP Rate values is that they do not depend on the relative sizes of P and N. The same applies to using the FN Rate and TN Rate values or any other combination of two 'rate' values calculated from *different* rows of the confusion matrix. In contrast, Predictive Accuracy and all the other measures listed in Figure 12.2 are derived from values in *both* rows of the table and so are affected by the relative sizes of P and N, which can be a serious weakness.

To illustrate this, suppose that the positive class corresponds to those who pass a driving test at the first attempt and that the negative class corresponds to those who fail. Assume that the relative proportions in the real world are 9 to 10 (a fictitious value) and the test set correctly reflects this.

Then the confusion matrix for a particular classifier on a given test set might be

		Predicted class		Total
		$+$	$-$	instances
Actual class	$+$	8, 000	1, 000	9, 000
	$-$	2, 000	8, 000	10, 000

This gives a true positive rate of 0.89 and a false positive rate of 0.2, which we will assume is a satisfactory result.

Now suppose that the number of successes grows considerably over a period of time because of improved training, so that there is a higher proportion of passes. With this assumption a possible confusion matrix for a future series of trials would be as follows.

		Predicted class		Total
		$+$	$-$	instances
Actual class	$+$	80, 000	10, 000	90, 000
	$-$	2, 000	8, 000	10, 000

The classifier will of course still work exactly as well as before to predict the correct classification of either a pass or a fail with which it is presented. For both confusion matrices the values of TP Rate and FP Rate are the same (0.89 and 0.2 respectively). However the values of the Predictive Accuracy measure are different.

For the original confusion matrix, Predictive Accuracy is $16,000/19,000 = 0.842$. For the second one, Predictive Accuracy is $88,000/100,000 = 0.88$.

An alternative possibility is that over a period of time there is a large increase in the relative proportion of failures, perhaps because of an increase in the number of younger people being tested. A possible confusion matrix for a future series of trials would be as follows.

		Predicted class		Total
		+	−	instances
Actual class	+	8,000	1,000	9,000
	−	20,000	80,000	100,000

Here the Predictive Accuracy is $88,000/109,000 = 0.807$.

Whichever of these test sets was used with the classifier the TP Rate and FP Rate values would be the same. However the three Predictive Accuracy values would vary from 81% to 88%, reflecting changes in the relative numbers of positive and negative values in the test set, rather than any change in the quality of the classifier.

12.4 ROC Graphs

The TP Rate and FP Rate values of different classifiers on the same test set are often represented diagrammatically by a *ROC Graph*. The abbreviation ROC Graph stands for 'Receiver Operating Characteristics Graph', which reflects its original uses in signal processing applications.

On a ROC Graph, such as Figure 12.3, the value of FP Rate is plotted on the horizontal axis, with TP Rate plotted on the vertical axis.

Each point on the graph can be written as a pair of values (x, y) indicating that the FP Rate has value x and the TP Rate has value y.

The points $(0, 1)$, $(1, 0)$, $(1, 1)$ and $(0, 0)$ correspond to the four special cases A, B, C and D in Section 12.2, respectively. The first is located at the best possible position on the graph, the top left-hand corner. The second is at the worst possible position, the bottom right-hand corner. If all the classifiers are good ones, all the points on the ROC Graph are likely to be around the top left-hand corner.

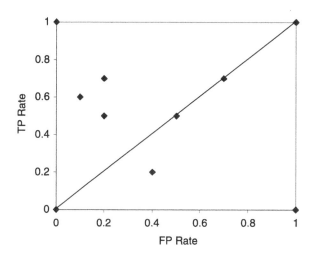

Figure 12.3 Example of ROC Graph

The other six points shown are $(0.1, 0.6)$, $(0.2, 0.5)$, $(0.4, 0.2)$, $(0.5, 0.5)$, $(0.7, 0.7)$ and $(0.2, 0.7)$.

One classifier is better than another if its corresponding point on the ROC Graph is to the 'north-west' of the other's. Thus the classifier represented by $(0.1, 0.6)$ is better than the one represented by $(0.2, 0.5)$. It has a lower FP Rate and a higher TP Rate. If we compare points $(0.1, 0.6)$ and $(0.2, 0.7)$, the latter has a higher TP Rate but also a higher FP Rate. Neither classifier is superior to the other on both measures and the one chosen will depend on the relative importance given by the user to the two measures.

The diagonal line joining the bottom left and top right-hand corners corresponds to random guessing, whatever the probability of the positive class may be. If a classifier guesses positive and negative at random with equal frequency, it will classify positive instances correctly 50% of the time and negative instances as positive, i.e. incorrectly, 50% of the time. Thus both the TP Rate and the FP Rate will be 0.5 and the classifier will lie on the diagonal at point $(0.5, 0.5)$.

Similarly, if a classifier guesses positive and negative at random with positive selected 70% of the time, it will classify positive instances correctly 70% of the time and negative instances as positive, i.e. incorrectly, 70% of the time. Thus both the TP Rate and the FP Rate will be 0.7 and the classifier will lie on the diagonal at point $(0.7, 0.7)$.

We can think of the points on the diagonal as corresponding to a large number of random classifiers, with higher points on the diagonal corresponding to higher proportions of positive classifications generated on a random basis.

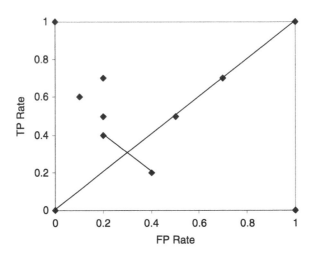

Figure 12.4 Example of ROC Graph (Amended)

The upper left-hand triangle corresponds to classifiers that are better than random guessing. The lower right-hand triangle corresponds to classifiers that are worse than random guessing, such as the one at $(0.4, 0.2)$.

A classifier that is worse than random guessing can be converted to one that is better than random guessing simply by reversing its predictions, so that every positive prediction becomes negative and vice versa. By this method the classifier at $(0.4, 0.2)$ can be converted to the new one at $(0.2, 0.4)$ in Figure 12.4. The latter point is the former reflected about the diagonal line.

12.5 ROC Curves

In general, each classifier corresponds to a single point on a ROC Graph. However there are some classification algorithms that lend themselves to 'tuning', so that it is reasonable to think of a *series* of classifiers, and thus points on a ROC Graph, one for each value of some variable, generally known as a *parameter*. For a decision tree classifier such a parameter might be the 'depth cutoff' (see Chapter 9) which can vary from 1, 2, 3 etc.

In such a case the points can be joined to form a *ROC Curve* such as Figure 12.5.

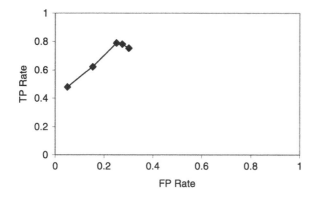

Figure 12.5 Example of ROC Curve

Examining ROC curves can give insights into the best way of tuning a classification algorithm. In Figure 12.5 performance clearly degrades after the third point in the series.

The performance of different types of classifier with different parameters can be compared by inspecting their ROC curves.

12.6 Finding the Best Classifier

There is no infallible way of finding the best classifier for a given application, unless we happen to find one that gives perfect performance, corresponding to the $(0, 1)$ point on the ROC Graph. One approach that is sometimes used is to measure the distance of a classifier on the ROC Graph from the perfect classifier.

Figure 12.6 shows the points $(fprate, tprate)$ and $(0, 1)$. The Euclidean distance between them is $\sqrt{fprate^2 + (1 - tprate)^2}$.

We can write $Euc = \sqrt{fprate^2 + (1 - tprate)^2}$.

The smallest possible value of Euc is zero, when $fprate = 0$ and $tprate = 1$ (the perfect classifier). The largest value is $\sqrt{2}$, when $fprate$ is 1 and $tprate$ is zero (the worst possible classifier). We could hypothesise that the smaller the value of Euc the better the classifier.

Euc is a useful measure but does not take into account the relative importance of true and false positives. There is no best answer to this. It depends on the use to which the classifier will be put.

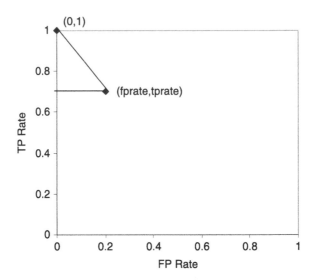

Figure 12.6 Measuring the Distance from the Perfect Classifier

We can specify the relative importance of making *tprate* as close to 1 as possible and making *fprate* as close to zero as possible by a weight w from 0 to 1 and define the *Weighted Euclidean Distance* as

$WEuc = \sqrt{(1-w)fprate^2 + w(1-tprate)^2}$

If $w = 0$ this reduces to $WEuc = fprate$, i.e. we are only interested in minimising the value of *fprate*.

If $w = 1$ it reduces to $WEuc = 1 - tprate$, i.e. we are only interested in minimising the difference between *tprate* and 1 (thus maximising *tprate*).

If $w = 0.5$ the formula reduces to

$WEuc = \sqrt{0.5 * fprate^2 + 0.5 * (1 - tprate)^2}$

which is a constant multiple of

$\sqrt{fprate^2 + (1 - tprate)^2}$, so the effect when comparing one classifier with another is the same as if there were no weighting at all.

12.7 Chapter Summary

This chapter looks at the use of true and false positive and negative classifications as a better way of measuring the performance of a classifier than predictive accuracy alone. Other performance measures can be derived from these four basic ones, including *true positive rate* (or hit rate), *false positive rate* (or false alarm rate), *precision*, *accuracy* and *F1 score*.

The values of true positive rate and false positive rate are often represented diagrammatically by a *ROC graph*. Joining the points on a ROC graph to form a ROC curve can often give insight into the best way of tuning a classifier. A Euclidean distance measure of the difference between a given classifier and the performance of a hypothetical perfect classifier is described.

12.8 Self-assessment Exercise for Chapter 12

Four classifiers are generated for the same training set, which has 100 instances. They have the following confusion matrices.

		Predicted class	
		+	−
Actual class	+	50	10
	−	10	30

		Predicted class	
		+	−
Actual class	+	55	5
	−	5	35

		Predicted class	
		+	−
Actual class	+	40	20
	−	1	39

		Predicted class	
		+	−
Actual class	+	60	0
	−	20	20

Calculate the values of true positive rate and false positive rate for each classifier and plot them on a ROC graph. Calculate the value of the Euclidean distance measure *Euc* for each one. Which classifier would you consider the best if you were equally concerned with avoiding false positive and false negative classifications?

13

Dealing with Large Volumes of Data

13.1 Introduction

In the not too far distant past, datasets with a few hundred or a few thousand records would have been considered normal and those with tens of thousands of records would probably have been considered very large. The 'data explosion' that is so evident all around us has changed all that. In some fields only quite a small amount of data is available and that is unlikely to change very much (perhaps fossil data or data about patients with rare illnesses); in other fields (such as retailing, bioinformatics, branches of science such as chemistry, cosmology and particle physics, and the ever-growing area of mining data held by Internet applications such as blogs and social networking sites) the volume has greatly increased and seems likely to go on increasing rapidly.

Some of the best–known data mining methods were developed in those far-off days and were originally tested on datasets such as the UCI Repository [1]. It is certainly not self-evident that they will all scale up to much larger datasets with acceptable runtimes or memory requirements. The most obvious answer to this problem is to take a sample from a large dataset and use that for data mining. Taking a 1% sample chosen at random from a 100 million record dataset would leave 'only' a million records to analyse but that is itself a substantial number. Also, however random the 1% selection process itself may be, that does not guarantee that what results will be a random sample from the underlying (probably far larger) population of possible records for that task area, as that will depend on how the original data was collected. All that will be certain is that 99 million data records will have been discarded.

© Springer-Verlag London Ltd., part of Springer Nature 2020
M. Bramer, *Principles of Data Mining*, Undergraduate Topics
in Computer Science, DOI 10.1007/978-1-4471-7493-6_13

In this chapter we will concentrate on classification rule induction as a particularly important and widely-used area of data mining, but many of the comments made will be more generally applicable.

Back in 1991, the Australian researcher Jason Catlett wrote a PhD thesis entitled *Megainduction: machine learning on very large databases* [2] in which he criticised the practice of sampling data before a classification rule induction algorithm was applied, showing that the accuracy of an induced classifier increases with an increasing size of training sample. The datasets that Catlett regarded as very large would now be considered small, or at most 'normal', but his warning remains a potent one. To add to this there is the consideration that some application areas (especially in science) are concerned with the discovery of new knowledge, where discarding a large proportion of the data is a very risky business. For other applications, even a small sample of the available data may still be massive.

For the purposes of this chapter we shall assume that you have a very large dataset (which may be a sample from an even larger one) and want to analyse it all. To tackle this problem, the methods of parallel and distributed computing are increasingly likely to be used. This is a large and complex field which goes far beyond data mining but in this chapter we will describe some of the issues and illustrate them by some recent work.

We will start by assuming that the approach adopted is to use a distributed local area network of personal computers (technically called a *loosely-coupled* architecture), as for many organisations this will be a much cheaper and more realistic option than the alternative of buying a high-performance supercomputer. Both 'desktop' and 'notebook' size computers are routinely sold in high-street stores at readily affordable prices. Organisations such as schools and university departments frequently throw away or give away 'out of date' models that are still perfectly usable. It is entirely realistic to think that even an individual working alone with a small budget could build up a network of say 20 machines at very low cost, each one of them with a speed and capacity which in past years would have qualified them to be called supercomputers.

In this chapter we will use the term *processor* to also include a local memory. It will be assumed that each classification (or other data mining) program is executed on a single processor using its local memory. Processors do not necessarily all have to have the same processing speed and memory capacity, but for simplicity we will generally assume that they do. We will sometimes use the term 'machine' to mean a processor plus its local memory.

With a network of processors it is tempting for the naïve newcomer to think that by dividing a task up to be performed by a network of say 100 identical processors it would be achievable in one hundredth of the time it would take for one processor alone. A little experience will soon dispel this illusion. In reality it can easily be the case that 100 processors take considerably longer to do the job than just 10, because of communication and other overheads amongst them. We might invent the term 'the two many cooks principle' to describe this.

There are several ways in which a classification task could be distributed over a number of processors.

(1) If all the data is together in one very large dataset, we can distribute it on to p processors, run an identical classification algorithm on each one and combine the results.

(2) The data may inherently 'live' in different datasets on different processors, for example in different parts of a company or even in different co-operating organisations. As for (1) we could run an identical classification algorithm on each one and combine the results.

(3) An extreme case of a large data volume is *streaming data* arriving in effectively a continuous infinite stream in real time, e.g. from a CCTV. If the data is all coming to a single source, different parts of it could be processed by different processors acting in parallel. If it is coming into several different processors, it could be handled in a similar way to (2).

(4) An entirely different situation arises where we have a dataset that is not particularly large, but we wish to generate several or many different classifiers from it and then combine the results by some kind of 'voting' system in order to classify unseen instances. In this case we might have the whole dataset on a single processor, accessed by different classification programs (possibly identical or possibly different) accessing all or part of the data. Alternatively, we could distribute the data in whole or in part to each processor before running a set of either identical or different classification programs on it. This topic is discussed in Chapter 14 'Ensemble Classification'.

A common feature of all these approaches is that there needs to be some kind of 'control module' to combine the results obtained on the p processors. Depending on the application, the control module may also need to distribute the data to different processors, initiate the processing on each processor and perhaps synchronise the p processors' work. The control module might be running on an additional processor or as a separate process on one of the p processors mentioned previously.

In the next section we will focus on the first category of application, i.e. all the data is together in one very large dataset, a part of which we can distribute on to each of p processors, then run an identical classification algorithm on each one and combine the results.

13.2 Distributing Data onto Multiple Processors

Large data volumes are generally large in one of two ways:

– There are far more instances (records) than attributes. We will call such datasets 'portrait style' and think about dividing them horizontally (called *horizontal partitioning*) on to different processors. This is illustrated in Figure 13.1 for a dataset with 17 instances × 4 attributes, divided into 5 parts.

– There are far more attributes than instances. We will call such datasets 'landscape style' and think about dividing them vertically (called *vertical partitioning*) on to different processors. This is illustrated in Figure 13.2 for a dataset with 3 instances × 25 attributes, divided into 7 parts.

Naturally a dataset can also be divided both horizontally and vertically depending on the circumstances.

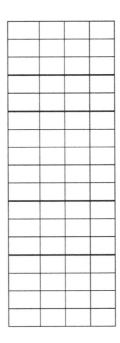

Figure 13.1 A Portrait-style Dataset with Horizontal Partitioning

This leads to a very rough outline for a possible way of distributing a classification task to a network of processors. For simplicity we will assume that the aim is to generate a set of classification rules corresponding to a given dataset, rather than some other form of classification model.

Figure 13.2 A Landscape-style Dataset with Vertical Partitioning

(a) The data is divided up either vertically or horizontally (or perhaps both) amongst the processors.

(b) The same algorithm is executed on each processor to analyse the corresponding portion of the data.

(c) Finally the results obtained by each processor are passed to a 'control module', which combines the results into a set of rules. It will also have been responsible for initiating steps (a) and (b) and for whatever action was necessary to keep the processors in step during step (b).

A general model for distributed data mining of this kind is provided by the Cooperating Data Mining (CDM) model introduced by Provost [3]. Figure 13.3 shows the basic architecture (reproduced from [4] with permission).

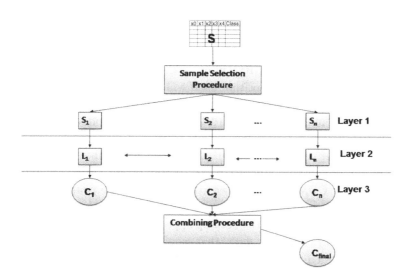

Figure 13.3 Cooperating Data Mining

The model has three *layers*:

– **Layer 1:** the *sample selection procedure*, which partitions the data sample S into subsamples (one for each of the processors available)

– **Layer 2:** For each processor there is a corresponding *learning algorithm* L_i which runs on the corresponding subsample S_i and generates a concept description C_i.

– **Layer 3:** the concept descriptions are then merged by a *combining procedure* to form a final concept description C_{final} (such as a set of classification rules).

The model allows for the learning algorithms L_i to communicate with each other but does not specify how.

13.3 Case Study: PMCRI

Some rule generation algorithms lend themselves considerably better to parallelisation than others. An early attempt to parallelise the TDIDT decision tree induction algorithm is described in [5]. The Prism algorithm for generating modular rules described in Chapter 11 is also one that lends itself well to this approach. The PMCRI (Parallel Modular Classification Rule Induction) framework [4, 6, 7] was developed by the German researcher Dr. Frederic Stahl in association with the present author as a distributed version of Prism. In this and the following section PMCRI will be used as a vehicle for explaining some general principles, but the algorithm itself will not be described in detail here. The account in these two sections draws heavily from [4]. Figures 13.5 to 13.7 are reproduced from [4] and Figures 13.4 and 13.8 are reproduced from [6] with permission.

PMCRI uses a variant of the Prism algorithm described in Chapter 11, called PrismTCS, but the differences are not important here. The important point is how the CDM model is used to control the rule generation process. Assuming that there are p processors, all roughly identical, the sample selection procedure at **Layer 1** divides the data up approximately evenly amongst them. If we focus on landscape-style data, that is achieved by giving each processor all the instances for $1/p$ th of the total number of attributes.

Without repeating the details of the original Prism algorithm here, the main point is that each classification rule is generated term-by-term. For example we may start with an outline rule

IF ...... THEN class = 1

with an empty left-hand side and expand it progressively to

IF X = large ...... THEN class = 1

IF X = large AND $Z < 124.7$ ...... THEN class = 1

IF $X = $ large AND $Z < 124.7$ AND $Q < 12.0$ ...... THEN class $= 1$
IF $X = $ large AND $Z < 124.7$ AND $Q < 12.0$ AND $M = $ green
    THEN class $= 1$

which is its final form.

As each term of each rule is generated at **Layer 2** there are a number of possible attribute/value pairs to consider, e.g. $X = $ large or $Y < 23.4$ and we need to calculate the probability of each one. If we suppose that there are, say, 200 attributes and 10 processors it is straightforward to allocate 20 attributes to each of the ten processors. As each new term comes to be generated each processor looks at all possible attribute/value pairs for its group of 20 attributes, finds the one with highest probability as a 'locally best rule term' and notifies the probability (but not the term itself) to the control module by means of the *Blackboard* described below, as a kind of bid, essentially saying (for example) 'the best term processor 3 can find has a probability of 0.9'. It is easy for the control program to combine the 'bids' from all 10 processors to find the overall highest probability, corresponding to the 'globally best rule term', at each stage.

PMCRI implements communication amongst the learning algorithms in the second CDM layer by means of a distributed *blackboard* architecture, inspired by the DARBS distributed blackboard system [8].

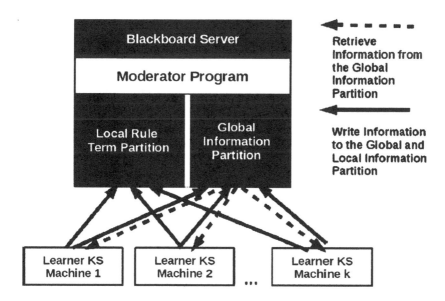

Figure 13.4 The architecture of the PMCRI framework using a distributed blackboard system

A Blackboard can be thought of as similar to a blackboard (on an easel) of the sort that teachers used to write on (and some still possibly do) with a piece of chalk in an old-fashioned classroom. A group of experts all work on a common problem, but the only way they can communicate with each other is by writing to or reading from the blackboard. Naturally, the 'experts' are not human ones and in the case of PMCRI the experts (described as 'Learner KS Machines' in Figure 13.4, for reasons that need not concern us) are just the processors referred to previously, each working out the probabilities for all possible attribute/value pairs for the attributes assigned to it. The Blackboard is just a reserved storage area on one of the processors, or perhaps some separate processor. There is a *Local Rule Term Partition* of the Blackboard to which the experts write the probabilities corresponding to their 'locally best rule terms' (although not the terms themselves). There is also a moderator program (previously called a control module) which can write to the Global Information Partition to tell the experts which one of them posted the highest probability (implying that the corresponding term was the 'globally best') and/or what to do next, e.g. start working on the next rule term or the next rule. The moderator can also read from the local rule term partition so that when all the probabilities (corresponding to the locally best term found by each expert) have been posted it can examine them and find the highest (corresponding to the globally best rule term).

The advantage of the PMCRI approach is that the workloads on the processors stay in the same proportion as the rule generation process goes on.

Once the rule generation process is finished, each expert will hold zero, one or more of the constituent terms for each of the rules in its memory. These are the terms corresponding to the probabilities it placed on the Blackboard that turned out to be the highest 'bids'. As an example, for expert number 3 the terms might be $z < 48.3$ and $q =$ green for rule 2, $x < 99.1$, $w < 62.3$ and $j < 82.67$ for rule 9 and $z < 112.9$ for rule 17.

Next the 'Combining Procedure' in **Layer 3** is started. Each expert submits its rule terms to the Global Information Partition, the moderator reads the submitted terms (rule fragments) and constructs the full ruleset from them.

Full details of the PMCRI algorithm are given in [4]. The aim of this chapter is not to describe PMCRI in detail, but to sketch out a general approach.

13.4 Evaluating the Effectiveness of a Distributed System: PMCRI

A distributed data mining system such as PMCRI can be evaluated in terms of three kinds of performance: its *scale-up*, its *size-up* and its *speed-up*. We will consider each of these in turn.

In what follows we will assume that all the processors in the distributed system are identical. We will use the term *runtime* to refer to the elapsed time taken by the entire system to complete a specified data mining task, excluding the time taken to load the data (Layer 1), which is a fixed overhead on any system of this kind.

We will use the term the *workload* of a processor to mean the number of instances held in its associated memory. Note however that a value of, say, 10,000 may mean 10,000 instances with all their attributes, or 20,000 instances with half of the attributes each, or 100,000 instances with one tenth of the attributes each, etc. We will assume that the workload is the same for each processor that is in use in the network.

Finally we will use the term *total workload of the system* to mean the sum of the workloads for each of the processors in use in the network, again measured as a number of instances.

Scale-Up

Scale-up experiments evaluate the performance of the system with respect to the number of processors for a fixed workload per processor. We keep the workload per processor constant and measure the runtime as additional processors are added. Ideally the runtime measured this way would remain constant, as for example, doubling the number of processors would double the amount of data to be processed by the system as a whole but there would be twice the number of processors to do it. A constant runtime would be indicated by a horizontal line on a graph of runtime against the number of processors.

Figure 13.5 is one of several showing results obtained for PMCRI. The runtime is plotted against the number of processors, increasing from 2 to 10, for three values of the workload per processor: 130K, 300K and 850K instances. We can see that rather than remaining horizontal, each plot increases as the number of processors increases. This is caused by an additional communications overhead in the network as more processors need to communicate information via the blackboard. Unsurprisingly, the runtime even for just two processors is greater when the workload per processor is larger. It is easier to see what

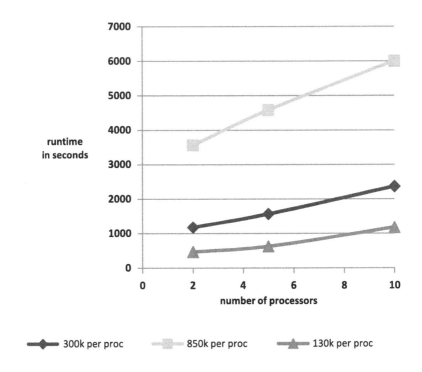

Figure 13.5 Scale-up of PMCRI

is happening if we plot on the vertical axis not runtime but relative runtime, i.e. (for each of the three plots) the runtime divided by the runtime for just 2 processors. This gives us Figure 13.6. Now each plot starts with a relative runtime of one (for two processors) and we have added the 'ideal' situation of a horizontal line of height one to the graph accordingly.

We can now see that the relative runtime is greatest for the smallest workload per processor (130K) and smallest for the largest workload (850K). So with this algorithm, the effect of the communication overhead in increasing the runtime above the ideal is lower as the workload per processor increases. As we wish to be able to deal with very large datasets this is a most desirable result.

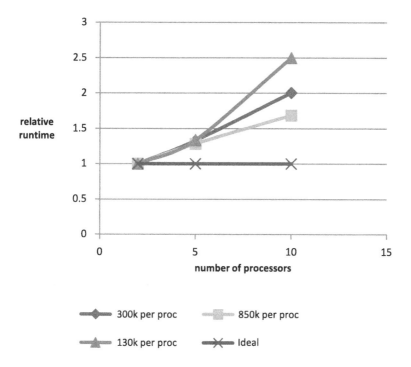

Figure 13.6 Scale-up of PMCRI Using Relative Runtimes

Size-Up

Size-up experiments evaluate the performance of the system with respect to its total workload for a fixed configuration of processors. We keep the number of processors constant and measure the runtime as the total number of training instances is increased.

Figure 13.7 shows a graph of relative runtime against number of instances, increasing from 17K to 8,000K, plotted for 1, 2, 5 and 10 processors. (Relative runtime is the runtime divided by the runtime for 17K instances.) Each plot shows an approximately linear size-up, i.e. the runtime is approximately a linear function of the size of the training data.

We have added a plot of the 'ideal' size-up where increasing the number of instances by a factor of N increases the relative runtime by a factor of N. It can be seen that the serial (i.e. one processor) plot is worse (i.e. has a greater runtime) than the ideal size-up, but the 2, 5 and 10 processor plots are all appreciably better than the 'ideal' size-up. This is possible because of

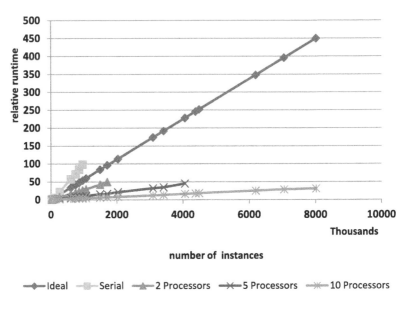

Figure 13.7 Size-up of PMCRI Using Relative Runtimes

the way the system handles the communication overheads. This is a very good result.

Speed-Up

Speed-up experiments evaluate the performance of the system with respect to the number of processors for a fixed total workload.

We keep the total workload of the system constant and measure the runtime as the number of processors is increased. This shows how much a distributed algorithm is faster than the serial (one processor) version, as a large dataset is distributed to more and more processors.

We can define two performance metrics associated with speed-up.

– The *speedup factor* S_p is defined by $S_p = R_1/R_p$, where R_1 and R_p are the runtimes of the algorithm on a single processor and on p processors, respectively. This measures how much the runtime is faster using p processors than just one. The ideal case is that $S_p = p$, but the usual situation is that $S_p < p$ because of communication or other overheads in the system.

– The *efficiency* E_p of using p processors rather than one is defined by $E_p = S_p/p$ (i.e. the speedup factor divided by the number of processors). E_p is usually a number between 0 and 1 but can occasionally be a value greater than one, in the case of what is known as a *superlinear* speedup.

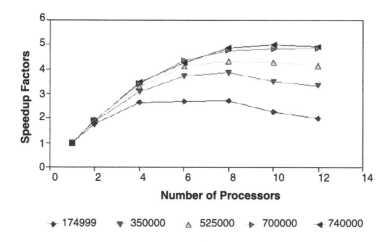

Figure 13.8 Speed-up of PMCRI

Figure 13.8 shows a graph of speedup factor against number of processors, increasing from 1 to 12, plotted for a total workload from 174,999 to 740,000 instances. This form of display is often preferred to the more obvious plot of runtime versus number of processors, as it makes it straightforward to see the largest number of processors that has a positive impact on the runtime, for a fixed workload.

We can see from Figure 13.8 that having more than four processors either does not increase or reduces the speedup factor for the smallest workload (174,999 instances) but using a larger number of processors (up to at least 10) is beneficial for the two largest workloads. Thus the PMCRI approach appears to be of most value with larger numbers of instances, which is clearly desirable.

13.5 Revising a Classifier Incrementally

In this book we have generally assumed that all the data needed to generate a classifier has already been collected and is available in a training set, possibly one that is so large that it needs to be sampled and/or distributed to a number of processors.

A very different situation arises when a classifier has been constructed and then a large volume of additional data comes in, for example data about customer choices in a retailing application. We may have a classifier constructed using a training set of 100,000 instances and then receive an additional 10,000 instances of classified data every evening about that day's transactions. After a few weeks the amount of additional data will be much greater than the amount in the training set from which the classifier was constructed, but even a small number of additional instances (in an extreme case, even just one) can make a considerable difference to a classifier such as a decision tree. In the interests of reliable classification, we should take advantage of the availability of the additional data by generating a new classifier but how often should we do this? Once a day? Once a week? However often we do it, we would certainly not want to have to re-process all the data that has already been used to generate the classifier, starting 'from scratch' each time with an ever-growing volume of data.

To deal with the frequent arrival of new training data we need to use a classification algorithm that is *incremental*, i.e. where a classifier already constructed can be updated using new data without needing to re-process data already used. Once processed the training data can then be discarded, if it is not needed for other purposes.

An extreme version of this situation arises with *streaming* data, i.e. data that arrives in real time as effectively an infinite stream, e.g. images from CCTV or messages from telemetry devices or a news or information feed (such as the latest share prices) or the transactions from a high-volume application such as purchases made in a supermarket or by credit card.

Given an incremental classification algorithm, it is not realistic to update the classifier for each single new instance that arrives, so we will generally batch incoming instances into groups of N and update the classifier as each batch is completed. Two important questions about this approach are:

1. How accurately will a classifier produced in this way approximate the classifier that would have been constructed if all the data had been available for processing at the beginning as a single job?

2. To what extent does the choice of batch size N affect the answer to (1)?

A collection of algorithms and tools for mining streaming data is described in [9] for those with a knowledge of the Java programming language.

In the remainder of this section we will consider a method of classification which lends itself very well to an incremental approach: the Naïve Bayes classifier which was described in Chapter 3. In this case processing the data as batches of whatever size involves no loss of accuracy compared with collecting a potentially vast amount of data together and processing it all as a single job. This is a highly desirable property.

We will only briefly summarise the description of the Naïve Bayes classification algorithm here, using an example from Chapter 3. Given a training set such as Figure 13.9:

day	season	wind	rain	class
weekday	spring	none	none	on time
weekday	winter	none	slight	on time
weekday	winter	none	slight	on time
weekday	winter	high	heavy	late
saturday	summer	normal	none	on time
weekday	autumn	normal	none	very late
holiday	summer	high	slight	on time
sunday	summer	normal	none	on time
weekday	winter	high	heavy	very late
weekday	summer	none	slight	on time
saturday	spring	high	heavy	cancelled
weekday	summer	high	slight	on time
saturday	winter	normal	none	late
weekday	summer	high	none	on time
weekday	winter	normal	heavy	very late
saturday	autumn	high	slight	on time
weekday	autumn	none	heavy	on time
holiday	spring	normal	slight	on time
weekday	spring	normal	none	on time
weekday	spring	normal	slight	on time

Figure 13.9 The *train* Dataset

We construct a probability table giving conditional probabilities (in the body of the table) and prior probabilities (in the bottom row) corresponding to the training data (Figure 13.10).

	class			
	on time	late	very late	cancelled
day = weekday *	$9/14 = 0.64$	$1/2 = 0.5$	$3/3 = 1$	$0/1 = 0$
day = saturday	$2/14 = 0.14$	$1/2 = 0.5$	$0/3 = 0$	$1/1 = 1$
day = sunday	$1/14 = 0.07$	$0/2 = 0$	$0/3 = 0$	$0/1 = 0$
day = holiday	$2/14 = 0.14$	$0/2 = 0$	$0/3 = 0$	$0/1 = 0$
season = spring	$4/14 = 0.29$	$0/2 = 0$	$0/3 = 0$	$1/1 = 1$
season = summer *	$6/14 = 0.43$	$0/2 = 0$	$0/3 = 0$	$0/1 = 0$
season = autumn	$2/14 = 0.14$	$0/2 = 0$	$1/3 = 0.33$	$0/1 = 0$
season = winter	$2/14 = 0.14$	$2/2 = 1$	$2/3 = 0.67$	$0/1 = 0$
wind = none	$5/14 = 0.36$	$0/2 = 0$	$0/3 = 0$	$0/1 = 0$
wind = high *	$4/14 = 0.29$	$1/2 = 0.5$	$1/3 = 0.33$	$1/1 = 1$
wind = normal	$5/14 = 0.36$	$1/2 = 0.5$	$2/3 = 0.67$	$0/1 = 0$
rain = none	$5/14 = 0.36$	$1/2 = 0.5$	$1/3 = 0.33$	$0/1 = 0$
rain = slight	$8/14 = 0.57$	$0/2 = 0$	$0/3 = 0$	$0/1 = 0$
rain = heavy *	$1/14 = 0.07$	$1/2 = 0.5$	$2/3 = 0.67$	$1/1 = 1$
Prior Probability	$14/20 = 0.70$	$2/20 = 0.10$	$3/20 = 0.15$	$1/20 = 0.05$

Figure 13.10 Probability Table for the *train* Dataset

Then the score for each class for an unseen instance such as

weekday	summer	high	heavy	????

can be calculated from the values in the rows shown above that are marked with asterisks.

class = on time $0.70 * 0.64 * 0.43 * 0.29 * 0.07 = 0.0039$
class = late $0.10 * 0.5 * 0 * 0.5 * 0.5 = 0$
class = very late $0.15 * 1 * 0 * 0.33 * 0.67 = 0$
class = cancelled $0.05 * 0 * 0 * 1 * 1 = 0$

The class with the largest score is selected, in this case class = *on time*. (There are complications with zero values which will be ignored here.)

First we note that there is no need to store all the values shown above. All that needs to be stored for each of the attributes is a frequency table showing the number of instances with each possible combination of the attribute value and classification. For attribute *day* the table would be as shown in Figure 13.11.

	class			
	on time	late	very late	cancelled
weekday	9	1	3	0
saturday	2	1	0	1
sunday	1	0	0	0
holiday	2	0	0	0

Figure 13.11 Frequency Table for Attribute *day*

Together with a table for each attribute there needs to be a row showing the frequencies of each of the four classes, as shown for this example in
Figure 13.12.

	class			
	on time	late	very late	cancelled
TOTAL	14	2	3	1

Figure 13.12 Class Frequencies

The values in the TOTAL row are used as the denominators when the values
in the frequency table for each attribute are used in calculations, e.g. for the
frequency table for attribute *day*, the value used for *weekday/on time* is 9/14.
The Prior Probability row in Figure 13.10 does not need to be stored at all as
in each case the value is the frequency of the corresponding class divided by
the total number of instances (20 in this example).

Even when the volume of data is very large the number of classes is often
small and even when there are a very large number of categorical attributes, the
number of possible attribute values for each one is likely to be quite small, so
overall it seems entirely practical to store a frequency table such as Figure 13.11
for each attribute plus a single table of class frequencies.

With this tabular representation for the probability model generated by
the Naïve Bayes algorithm, incrementally updating a classifier becomes trivial.
Suppose that based on 100,000 instances we have a frequency table for attribute
A as shown in Figure 13.13.

The frequency counts for the four classes are 50120, 19953, 14301 and 15626
making a grand total of 100,000.

Suppose that we now want to process a batch of 50,000 more instances with
a frequency table for attribute *A* as shown in Figure 13.14.

	class = c1	class = c2	class = c3	class = c4
a1	8201	8412	5907	8421
a2	34202	7601	6201	5230
a3	7717	3940	2193	1975

Figure 13.13 Frequency table for attribute A (first 100,000 instances)

	class = c1	class = c2	class = c3	class = c4
a1	4017	5412	2907	6421
a2	15002	2601	4201	2230
a3	2289	1959	2208	753

Figure 13.14 Frequency table for attribute A (next 50,000 instances)

For these new instances the frequency counts of the classes are 21308, 9972, 9316 and 9404, making a total of 50,000.

In order to obtain the same classification for any unseen instance with the training data received in two parts as if all 150,000 instances had been used together to generate the classifier as a single job, it is only necessary to add the two frequency tables for each attribute together element-by-element and to add together the frequency totals for each class. This is simple to do with no loss of accuracy involved.

Returning to the topic of distributing data to a number of processors by vertical partitioning, i.e. allocating a portion of the attributes to each processor, that approach fits well with the Naïve Bayes algorithm. All that each processor would have to do is to count the frequency of each attribute value/class combination for each of the attributes allocated to it and pass a small table for each one to the 'control module' whenever requested.

Experiments have shown that the classification accuracy of Naïve Bayes is generally competitive with that of other methods. Its main drawbacks are that it only applies when the attribute values are all categorical and that the probability model generated is not as explicit as a decision tree, say. Depending on the application, the explicitness of the model may or may not be a significant issue.

13.6 Chapter Summary

This chapter is concerned with issues relating to large volumes of data, in particular the ability of classification algorithms to scale up to be usable for such volumes.

Some of the ways in which a classification task could be distributed over a local area network of personal computers are described and a case study using an extended version of the Prism rule induction algorithm known as PMCRI is presented. Techniques for evaluating a distributed system of this kind are then illustrated.

The issue of streaming data is also considered, leading to a discussion of a classification algorithm that lends itself well to an incremental approach: the Naïve Bayes classifier.

13.7 Self-assessment Exercises for Chapter 13

After the data in the *train* dataset given in Figure 13.9 has been collected records for another 10 days are collected, as shown in the table below.

day	season	wind	rain	class
weekday	summer	none	none	cancelled
weekday	winter	none	none	on time
weekday	winter	none	none	on time
weekday	summer	high	heavy	late
saturday	summer	normal	none	on time
weekday	summer	normal	slight	very late
holiday	summer	high	slight	on time
sunday	summer	normal	none	on time
weekday	winter	high	heavy	very late
weekday	summer	none	slight	on time

1. Construct a frequency table for each of the four attributes and a class frequency table, using the data in the two *train* datasets combined.

2. Using these new tables find the most likely classification for the unseen instance given below.

weekday	summer	high	heavy	????

References

[1] Dua, D., & Graff, C. (2019). *UCI Machine Learning Repository*. Irvine: University of California, School of Information and Computer Science. `https://archive.ics.uci.edu/ml/`.

[2] Catlett, J. (1991). *Megainduction: machine learning on very large databases.* Sydney: University of Technology.

[3] Provost, F. (2000). Distributed data mining: scaling up and beyond. In H. Kargupta & P. Chan (Eds.), *Advances in distributed data mining.* San Mateo: Morgan Kaufmann.

[4] Stahl, F., Bramer, M., & Adda, M. (2009). PMCRI: a parallel modular classification rule induction framework. In *LNAI: Vol. 5632. Machine learning and data mining in pattern recognition* (pp. 148–162). Berlin: Springer.

[5] Shafer, J. C., Agrawal, R., & Mehta, M. (1996). SPRINT: a scalable parallel classifier for data mining. In *Twenty-second international conference on very large data bases.*

[6] Stahl, F. T., Bramer, M. A., & Adda, M. (2010). J-PMCRI: a methodology for inducing pre-pruned modular classification rules. In *Artificial intelligence in theory and practice III* (pp. 47–56). Berlin: Springer.

[7] Stahl, F., & Bramer, M. (2013). *Computationally efficient induction of classification rules with the PMCRI and J-PMCRI frameworks. Knowledge based systems.* Amsterdam: Elsevier.

[8] Nolle, L., Wong, K. C. P., & Hopgood, A. (2002). DARBS: a distributed blackboard system. In M. A. Bramer, F. Coenen, & A. Preece (Eds.), *Research and development in intelligent systems XVIII.* Berlin: Springer.

[9] Bifet, A., Holmes, G., Kirkby, R., & Pfahringer, B. (2010). MOA: massive online analysis, a framework for stream classification and clustering. *Journal of Machine Learning Research, 99*, 1601–1604.

14
Ensemble Classification

14.1 Introduction

The idea of *ensemble classification* is to learn not just one classifier but a set of classifiers, called an *ensemble* of classifiers, and then to combine their predictions for the classification of unseen instances using some form of voting. This is illustrated in Figure 14.1 below. It is hoped that the ensemble will collectively have a higher level of predictive accuracy than any one of the individual classifiers, but that is not guaranteed.

The term *ensemble learning* is often used to mean the same as ensemble classification, but the former is a more general technique where a set of models is learnt that collectively can be applied to solving a problem of potentially any kind, not just classification.

The individual classifiers in an ensemble are known as *base classifiers*. If the base classifiers are all of the same kind (e.g. decision trees) the ensemble is known as *homogeneous*. Otherwise it is known as *heterogeneous*.

A simple form of ensemble classification algorithm is:

1. Generate N classifiers for a given dataset

2. For an unseen instance X

    a) Compute the predicted classification of X for each of the N classifiers

    b) Select the classification that is most frequently predicted.

This is a *majority voting* model where each time a classifier predicts a particular classification for an unseen instance it counts as one 'vote' for that

© Springer-Verlag London Ltd., part of Springer Nature 2020
M. Bramer, *Principles of Data Mining*, Undergraduate Topics
in Computer Science, DOI 10.1007/978-1-4471-7493-6_14

classification. With N classifiers in the ensemble there will be a total of N votes and the classification with most votes wins, i.e. is deemed to be the ensemble's prediction of the correct classification.

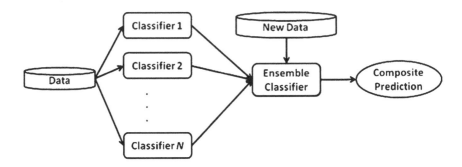

Figure 14.1   Ensemble Classification

The obvious objection to an ensemble classifier approach is that generating N classifiers takes much longer than only one and this additional effort is only justified if the performance of the ensemble is substantially better than that of just a single classifier. There is no guarantee that this will be the case for a given set of test data and far less so for an individual unseen instance, but intuitively it seems reasonable to believe that N classifiers 'working together' have the potential to give better predictive accuracy than one on its own. In practice this is likely to depend on how the classifiers are generated and how their predictions are combined (majority voting or otherwise).

In this chapter we will restrict our attention to the homogeneous case, where all the classifiers are of the same kind, say decision trees. There are several ways in which an ensemble can be formed, for example:

- N trees generated using the same tree generation algorithm, with different parameter settings, all using the same training data.

- N trees generated using the same tree generation algorithm, all with different training data and either with the same or with different parameter settings.

- N trees generated using a variety of different tree generation algorithms, either with the same or with different training data.

- N trees generated using a different subset of the attributes for each one.

If the additional effort needed to generate an ensemble of classifiers is to be worthwhile, the best approach is unlikely to be to generate trees that are all very similar, as they are all likely to give a very similar 'standard' performance. A better strategy is likely to be to generate trees (or other classifiers) that are diverse, in the hope that some will give much better than 'standard' performance, even if others are much worse. Those in the latter category should not be included in the ensemble; those in the former should be retained. This leads naturally to the idea of generating a large number of classifiers in some random way and then retaining only the best.

Two pioneering pieces of work in this field are the Random Decision Forests system developed by Tin Kam Ho [1] and the Random Forests system of Leo Breiman [2]. Both use the approach of generating a large number of decision trees in a way that has a substantial random element, measuring their performance and then selecting the best trees for the ensemble. To quote Stahl and Bramer [3]: "Ho argues that traditional trees often cannot be grown over a certain level of complexity without risking a loss of generalisation caused by overfitting on the training data. Ho proposes inducing multiple trees in randomly selected subsets of the feature space. He claims that the combined classification will improve, as the individual trees will generalise better on the classification for their subset of the feature space".

Ho's work introduced the idea of making a random selection of the attributes to use when generating each classifier. Breiman added to this by introducing a technique known as *bagging* for generating multiple different but related training sets from a single set of training data, with the aim of reducing overfitting and improving classification accuracy [4].

Naturally this is computationally expensive to do. Ho's and Breiman's papers are both important contributions to the field and are well worth studying in detail. However as usual there are many other ways of implementing the same general ideas once they have been set out and the description given in this chapter is our own.

To develop the idea of basing an ensemble on random classifiers further we need:

– A means of generating a large number of classifiers (say 100) in a random fashion and

– A way of measuring the performance of each one.

The final step is to choose all those that meet some criterion to include in an ensemble. There are several ways of doing this. For example we may select, say, the 10 classifiers with the best performance or all the classifiers with performance above some threshold of accuracy.

14.2 Estimating the Performance of a Classifier

Elsewhere in this book we have described the standard methodology for developing and estimating the performance of a classifier: divide the available data into a training set and a test set, use the training set to develop the classifier and then use the test set to estimate how the classifier will perform on (genuinely) unseen data.

For an ensemble classifier the procedure requires an extra dataset called a *validation dataset* associated with each classifier. The method is as follows:

1. Divide the available data into a test set and the remainder.

2. For each candidate classifier

   a) Divide the remaining data from step (1) into training data and validation data in some suitable fashion.

   b) Generate a classifier using the training data.

   c) Run the classifier against the validation data to give an estimate of its performance.

3. Use the performance estimates to find the best classifiers, e.g. all those with predictive accuracy greater than a specified percentage or perhaps the best X. If the number of classifiers remaining from this step is M, together they comprise an ensemble of size M.

4. Use the ensemble to classify each of the instances in the test set selected at step (1) and use the result as an estimate of the performance of the ensemble on (genuinely) unseen data.

The method used to predict the classification of unseen instances at step (4) is generally to use each of the M classifiers independently and then to combine their 'votes' for the correct classification (see Section 14.5 below).

How many classifiers to use in an ensemble is a matter for experiment, but to take advantage of the opportunity given by introducing a random element into the classifier generation process, i.e. that some particularly good classifiers will emerge by chance, a reasonable number might be, say, 100 with perhaps the best 10 chosen to form the ensemble itself.

14.3 Selecting a Different Training Set for Each Classifier

One problem that arises when implementing step (2)(a) of the algorithm in the previous section 'divide the remainder of the data into training data and validation data, in some suitable fashion' is how best to do this a large number of times, each giving a different division into the two datasets.

An approach to this which was implemented by Breiman [4] in a different context and later used in his Random Forests system is called *bagging*. (Bagging is short for 'bootstrap aggregating', but the significance of this term will not be explained here.)

Let us assume that the data described as the 'remaining data' in the last section, i.e. all the available data less instances removed to form a test set, comprises N instances. The bagging method is then as follows, applied to form each candidate classifier in turn.

– Randomly select N instances, one-by-one, at each stage selecting from the full set of instances (we call this *sampling with replacement*). This will lead to a training set of N instances in which inevitably some of the instances will appear more than once, perhaps several times, and others will not appear at all.

– There are likely to be many instances left unselected by this process. Collect them together to form a validation set.

It is extremely unlikely that sampling with replacement N times from a collection of N instances will lead to each instance being selected exactly once. The opposite extreme, where a single instance happens to be selected N times, is also extremely unlikely. To see what is likely to happen in the usual case we start by asking what is the probability that a particular instance in the 'remaining data' is never picked.

The probability of a particular instance being selected at the first 'pick' is $1/N$, so the probability that it is not selected is $1 - 1/N$. Each of the N picks is independent of the others, as all N instances are available for picking each time, so the probability of a particular instance never being picked as the training set of N instances is assembled is $(1 - 1/N)^N$. As N becomes large, this value can be proved to become extremely close to the value $1/e$ (mathematicians call this its *limiting value*). The symbol e represents a well-known 'mathematical constant' with the value 2.71828. Thus the limiting value is $1/e = 0.368$. The value of $(1 - 1/N)^N$ approximates this value to two decimal places for values of N as small as 64.

Since the same calculation applies to all instances and those never selected form the validation dataset for the classifier, it follows that for a reasonably large dataset of 'remaining data' we can expect that the validation dataset will comprise (on average) 36.8% of the instances. It follows that the other 63.2% go into the training set, some of them many times, to make a training set of N instances.

The significance of the training set being 'padded out' to N instances with duplicate values is far from negligible. Depending on the algorithm used, the classifier generated may be substantially different from the one obtained if duplicate values are deleted from the training set, which is a possible alternative approach.

14.4 Selecting a Different Set of Attributes for Each Classifier

One of the ideas introduced in Ho's Random Decision Forests system was that of processing only a subset of the available attributes (he uses the equivalent term 'features'), selected at random for each decision tree. The general idea is that combining classifiers produced by trees generated this way will give greater accuracy than a single classifier as the individual trees will generalise better on their subset of the available features.

One way of selecting attributes at random is just to choose a random subset from the total number available, with a different subset for each classifier. Another more complex approach would be similar to that for selecting instances for a training set in the previous section. If there are a total of N attributes, then N attributes are picked one at a time, in each case from the full collection of N possibilities. The analysis given in the previous section demonstrates that on average approximately 63.2% of the attributes will be selected for each decision tree by this method. In this case, the attributes not selected would simply be discarded. Duplicates of attributes already selected would also be discarded.

A random selection of attributes can be made just once for each decision tree. An alternative would be to make a further random selection at each node of an evolving decision tree from the attributes remaining under consideration at that point.

14.5 Combining Classifications: Alternative Voting Systems

Having constructed an ensemble of N classifiers, how can their predictions of the correct classification of an unseen instance (whether one in the test set or a genuinely unseen instance) best be combined into a single prediction?

The method adopted in both Ho's Random Decision Forests paper and Breiman's Random Forests paper is simply to treat each prediction as a vote for a particular classification, giving a total of N votes, with the prediction collecting the most votes being considered the winner. We will call this approach *majority voting* or *simple majority voting*. As with real-world voting systems for elections it is quite easy to point to possible flaws in this approach.

Classifier	Predicted Class
1	A
2	B
3	A
4	B
5	A
6	C
7	C
8	A
9	C
10	B

Figure 14.2 Predicted Classes for an Ensemble of 10 Classifiers

Figure 14.2 shows a possible situation. Classification A gained 4 votes, against 3 for B and 3 for C and so is 'elected', even though only 4 out of 10 classifiers made that prediction. Winning with a minority of the votes cast may (or may not) be acceptable for elections where the government of a country is at stake. For the purposes of this book, the important question is how reliable a prediction made this way is likely to be – to which the obvious answer is 'not very'.

Figure 14.3 is the same as Figure 14.2 but with an additional column: 'Accuracy'. This shows the predictive accuracy of the classifier on its validation dataset during the ensemble creation process, expressed as a proportion from 0 to 1. All the values are quite high, or the classifier would not have been included in the ensemble, but some are appreciably higher than others.

Classifier	Accuracy	Predicted Class
1	0.65	A
2	0.90	B
3	0.65	A
4	0.85	B
5	0.70	A
6	0.70	C
7	0.90	C
8	0.65	A
9	0.80	C
10	0.95	B
Total	7.75	

Figure 14.3 An Ensemble of Classifiers with Predictive Accuracy Information

We can now adopt a *weighted majority voting* approach, with each vote for a classification weighted by the proportion given in the middle column.

– Now classifier A gains $0.65 + 0.65 + 0.7 + 0.65 = 2.65$ votes.

– Classifier B gains $0.9 + 0.85 + 0.95 = 2.7$ votes.

– Classifier C gains $0.7 + 0.9 + 0.8 = 2.4$ votes.

– The total number of votes available is $0.65 + 0.9 + \ldots + 0.95 = 7.75$.

With this approach classifier B is now the winner. This seems reasonable as it gained the votes of three of the best classifiers, judged by their performance on their validation datasets (which vary from one classifier to another), whereas candidate classifier A gained the votes of four relatively weak classifiers. In this case choosing B as the winning classifier seems justified.

However it is possible to make the situation more complex still. An overall predictive accuracy figure of say 0.85 can conceal considerable variation in performance. We will focus on classifier 4 with overall predictive accuracy of 0.85 and consider a possible confusion matrix for it, assuming there were exactly 1,000 instances in its validation dataset. (Confusion matrices are discussed in Chapter 7.)

From Figure 14.4 we can see that classification B was quite rare in the validation dataset for classifier 4. Of the 100 instances with that classification only 50 were correctly predicted. Even worse, if we look at the 120 times that classification B was predicted by classifier 4, only 50 times was the prediction correct. Now it seems as if giving classifier 4 a weighted value of 0.85 for its

		Predicted Class			Total
		A	B	C	
Actual Class	A	550	30	20	600
	B	20	50	30	100
	C	10	40	250	300
Total		580	120	300	1000

Figure 14.4 Confusion Matrix for Classifier 4

prediction of classification B was far too optimistic. Perhaps it should have been just $50/120 = 0.417$.

Looking at confusion matrices gives us an approach to combining votes from multiple classifiers, which we will call 'track record voting'. For classifier 4, when it predicts class B: 30 times out of 120 the correct classification is A (25%), 50 times out of 120 the correct classification is B (41.7%) and 40 times out of 120 the correct classification is C (33.3%)

We say that a prediction of B by classifier 4 gives votes of 0.25, 0.417 and 0.333 for classifications A, B and C respectively. Note that these figures are all far below the overall predictive accuracy of the classifier (0.85). The explanation is that classifier 4 is very reliable when it predicts class A (correct 550 times out of $580 = 94.8\%$) and class C (correct 250 times out of $300 = 83.3\%$) but very unreliable when it predicts class B (correct only 50 times out of $120 = 41.7\%$).

Classifier	Predicted Class	Vote for Class			Total
		A	B	C	
1	A	0.80	0.05	0.15	1.0
2	B	0.10	0.80	0.10	1.0
3	A	0.75	0.20	0.05	1.0
4	B	0.25	0.42	0.33	1.0
5	A	0.40	0.20	0.40	1.0
6	C	0.05	0.05	0.90	1.0
7	C	0.10	0.10	0.80	1.0
8	A	0.75	0.20	0.05	1.0
9	C	0.10	0.00	0.90	1.0
10	B	0.10	0.80	0.10	1.0
Total		3.40	2.82	3.78	10.0

Figure 14.5 Ensemble of Classifiers with Voting Based on 'Track Record'

Figure 14.5 is a revised version of Figure 14.3. Now each classifier again has one vote, which it casts as three proportions. For example classifier 4 predicts class B for the unseen instance under consideration. This produces not a single vote for class B, but a vote split into three parts cast for all three classes A, B and C, in this case the values 0.25, 0.42 and 0.33 respectively. These proportions are derived from the 'Predicted Class B' column of the confusion matrix for classifier 4 (Figure 14.4).

Adding the votes for each of the three classes in Figure 14.5, the winner now (rather surprisingly) is class C, mainly because of the three high votes of 0.9 twice and 0.8.

Which of the three methods illustrated in this section is the most reliable? The first predicted class A, the second class B and the third class C. There is no clear-cut answer to this. The point is that there are a number of ways the votes can be combined in an ensemble classifier rather than just one.

Looking again at Figure 14.5 there are further complications to take into account. Classifier 5, which predicts class A has 'votes' of 0.4, 0.2 and 0.4. This means that for its validation data when it predicted class A, only 40% of the instances were actually of class A, 20% of the instances were class B and 40% of the instances were class C. What credibility can be given to a prediction of class A by that classifier? We can look at the three proportions for classifier 5 as indications of its 'track record' when predicting class A. On that basis there seems no reason at all to trust it and we might consider eliminating that classifier from consideration any time its prediction is A, as well as eliminating classifier 4 when its prediction is class B. However, if we do so, we will have implicitly moved from a 'democratic' model – one classifier, one vote – to something closer to a 'community of experts' approach.

Suppose the 10 classifiers represent 10 medical consultants in a hospital and A, B and C are three treatments to give a patient with a life-threatening condition. The consultants are trying to predict which treatment is most likely to prove effective. Why should anyone trust consultants 4 and 5, with their poor track records when predicting B and A respectively?

By contrast consultant 6, whose prediction is that treatment C will prove the most effective at saving the patient, has a track record of 90% success when making that prediction. The only consultant to compare with consultant 6 is number 9, who also has a track record of 90% success when predicting C. With two such experts making the same choice, who would wish to contradict them? Even the act of counting the votes seems not only pointless but unnecessarily risky, just in case the other eight less successful consultants might happen to outvote the two leading experts.

We could go on elaborating this example but will stop here. Clearly it is possible to look at the question of how best to combine the classifications produced by the different classifiers in an ensemble in a variety of different ways. Which way is most likely to give a high level of classification accuracy on unseen data? As so often in data mining, only experimentation with different datasets can give us the answer, but whatever the best approach turns out to be for an 'average' dataset, it is most unlikely that a single method will be best for all datasets or for all unseen instances and it is desirable to have a range of options available.

14.6 Parallel Ensemble Classifiers

As mentioned previously, an important practical obstacle to an ensemble classifier approach is the computation time needed to generate N classifiers rather than just one.

One way of dealing with this is to distribute the work around a local area network of personal computers, with each machine responsible for generating one or more classifiers and estimating its performance using a corresponding validation dataset. This general approach is described in Chapter 13 in the context of dealing with a large volume of data, rather than (as here) generating a large number of classifiers.

Depending on the way in which the ensemble is formed (as discussed in Section 14.1) the machines in the network might all make use of the same data in a central location, or all have identical local copies of the data, or they might begin by taking a sample of a common dataset (e.g. when using a bagging approach, as described in Section 14.3).

If we envisage a network of say 10 machines, we might generate 500 classifiers (50 per machine), estimate the performance of each one using its own validation dataset and retain (say) the 50 best. We might then rearrange the locations of the best 50 classifiers so that there are 5 on each of the 10 machines, or possibly we might put them all together on a single machine, if the volume of unseen data that needs to be processed is expected to be small.

The field of Parallel Ensemble Classifiers is a relatively new one, but appears promising. Two papers that give further information are [5] and [6].

14.7 Chapter Summary

This chapter is concerned with ensemble classification, i.e. using a set of classifiers to classify unseen data rather than just a single one. The classifiers in the ensemble all predict the correct classification of each unseen instance and their predictions are then combined using some form of voting system.

The idea of a random forest of classifiers is introduced and issues relating to the selection of a different training set and/or a different set of attributes from a given dataset when constructing each of the classifiers are discussed.

A number of alternative ways of combining the classifications produced by an ensemble of classifiers are considered. The chapter concludes with a brief discussion of a distributed processing approach to dealing with the large amount of computation often required to generate an ensemble.

14.8 Self-assessment Exercises for Chapter 14

Given the values shown in Figure 14.5:

1. What would be the effect of setting a threshold of 0.5, i.e. discounting any classifier for which the entry in the table (the 'vote') for the predicted class is less than 0.5?

2. What would be the effect of setting a threshold of 0.8?

References

[1] Ho, T. K. (1995). Random decision forests. *International Conference on Document Analysis and Recognition, 1*, 278.

[2] Breiman, L. (2001). Random forests. *Machine Learning, 45*(1), 5–32.

[3] Stahl, F., & Bramer, M. (2011). Random prism: an alternative to random forests. In *Research and development in intelligent systems XXVIII* (pp. 5–18). Springer.

[4] Breiman, L. (1996). Bagging predictors. *Machine Learning, 24*(2), 123–140.

[5] Stahl, F., May, D., & Bramer, M. (2012). Parallel random prism: a computationally efficient ensemble learner for classification. In *Research and development in intelligent systems XXIX*. Springer.

[6] Panda, B., Herbach, J. S., Basu, S., & Bayardo, R. J. (2009). Planet: massively parallel learning of tree ensembles with mapreduce. *Proceedings of the VLDB Endowment, 2*, 1426–1437.

15

Comparing Classifiers

15.1 Introduction

In Chapter 12 we considered how to choose between different classifiers applied to the same dataset. For those with real datasets to analyse this is obviously the principal issue.

However there is an entirely different category of data miner: those who develop new algorithms or what they hope are improvements to existing algorithms designed to give superior performance on not just one dataset but a wide range of possible datasets most of which are not known or do not even exist at the time the new methods are developed. Into this category fall both academic researchers and commercial software developers.

Whatever new methods are developed in the future, we can be certain of this: no one is going to develop a new algorithm that out-performs all established methods of classification (such as those described in this book) for all possible datasets. Data mining packages intended for use in a wide variety of possible application areas will continue to need to include a choice of classification algorithms to use. The aim of further development is to establish new techniques that are generally preferable to well-established ones. To do this it is necessary to compare their performance against at least one established algorithm on a range of datasets.

There are many published papers giving descriptions of interesting new classification algorithms accompanied by a performance table such as Figure 15.1. Each column gives the predictive accuracy, expressed as a percentage, of one of

© Springer-Verlag London Ltd., part of Springer Nature 2020
M. Bramer, *Principles of Data Mining*, Undergraduate Topics
in Computer Science, DOI 10.1007/978-1-4471-7493-6_15

Dataset	Established Classifier A	New Classifier B
dataset 1	80	85
dataset 2	73	70
dataset 3	85	85
dataset 4	68	74
dataset 5	82	71
dataset 6	75	65
dataset 7	73	77
dataset 8	64	73
dataset 9	75	75
dataset 10	69	76
Total	744	751
Average	74.4	75.1

Figure 15.1   Performance of classifiers A and B on 10 datasets

the classifiers on a range of datasets. (Note that for the method of comparison we describe below multiplying all the values in both columns by a constant has no effect on the outcome. Thus it makes no difference whether we represent predictive accuracy by percentages as here or by proportions between 0 and 1, such as 0.8 and 0.85.)

The production of tables of comparative values such as Figure 15.1 is a considerable improvement over the position with some of the older Data Mining literature where new algorithms are either not evaluated at all (leaving the brilliance of the author's ideas to speak for itself, one assumes) or are evaluated on datasets that are only available to the author and/or are not named. As time has gone by collections of 'standard' datasets have been assembled that make it possible for developers to compare their results with those obtained by other methods on the same datasets. In many cases the latter results are only available in the published literature, since with a few honourable exceptions authors do not generally make software implementing their algorithms accessible to other developers and researchers, except in the case of commercial packages.

A very widely-used collection of datasets is the 'UCI Repository' [1] which was introduced in Section 2.6. Being able to compare performance on the same datasets as those used by previous authors clearly makes it far easier to evaluate new algorithms. However the widespread use of such repositories is not an unmixed blessing as will be explained later.

Figure 15.1 shows the predictive accuracy of algorithms A and B on 10 datasets. We can see that in three cases A out-performed B, in two cases the performance was equal and in five cases B out-performed A. The average accuracy of A was 74.4% and the average accuracy of B was 75.1%. What can we conclude from all this?

15.2 The Paired t-Test

A commonly used method of comparing classification algorithms is the *paired t-test*. We will start by illustrating the method and then discuss a number of issues relating to it.

First we add to Figure 15.1 a column of the differences between the A and B values, i.e. B-A, which is traditionally denoted by the letter z. We also construct a column showing the square of the differences, i.e. z^2.

Dataset	Established Classifier A	New Classifier B	Difference z	Square of Difference z^2
dataset 1	80	85	5	25
dataset 2	73	70	-3	9
dataset 3	85	85	0	0
dataset 4	68	74	6	36
dataset 5	82	71	-11	121
dataset 6	75	65	-10	100
dataset 7	73	77	4	16
dataset 8	64	73	9	81
dataset 9	75	75	0	0
dataset 10	69	76	7	49
Total	744	751	7	437
Average	74.4	75.1	0.7	43.7

Figure 15.2 Performance of classifiers A and B on 10 datasets (with z and z^2 values)

We can see that the average difference between A and B is 0.7, i.e. 0.7% in favour of classifier B. This does not seem very much. Is it sufficient to reject the *null hypothesis* that the performance of classifiers A and B is effectively the same? We will address this question using a paired t-test. The word 'paired' in the name refers to the fact that the results fall into natural pairs, i.e. it is sensible to compare the results for dataset 1 for classifiers A and B but these are separate from those for dataset 2 etc.

To perform a paired t-test we need only three values: the total of the values of z, the total of the z^2 values and the number of datasets. We well denote these by $\sum z$, $\sum z^2$, and n, respectively, so $\sum z = 7$, $\sum z^2 = 437$ and $n = 10$.[1]

From these three values we can calculate the value of a statistic which is traditionally represented by the variable t. The t-statistic was introduced in the early 20th century by an English statistician named William Gosset, who is best known by his pen name of 'Student', and so this test is also often known as *Student's t-test*.

The calculation of the value of t can be broken down into the following steps.

Step 1. Calculate the average value of z: $\sum z/n = 7/10 = 0.7$.

Step 2. Calculate the value of $(\sum z)^2/n$. Here this gives $7^2/10 = 4.9$.

Step 3. Subtract the result of step 2 from $\sum z^2$. Here this gives $437 - 4.9 = 432.1$.

Step 4. Divide this value by $(n - 1)$ to give the *sample variance*, which is traditionally denoted by s^2. Here s^2 is $432.1/9 = 48.01$.

Step 5. Take the square root of s^2 to give s, known as the *sample standard deviation*. Here the value of s is $\sqrt{48.01} = 6.93$.

Step 6. Divide s by $\sqrt{n}$ to give the *standard error*. Here the value is $6.93/\sqrt{10} = 2.19$.

Step 7. Finally we divide the average value of z by the standard error to give the value of the t statistic. Here $t = 0.7/2.19 = 0.32$.

The word 'sample' in both 'sample variance' and 'sample standard deviation' refers to the fact that the 10 datasets given in the table are not all the possible datasets that exist to which the two classifiers may be applied. They are just a very small sample of all the possible datasets that exist or may exist in the future. We are using them as 'representatives' of this much larger collection of datasets. We will return to the question of how far this is reasonable.

The terms standard deviation and variance are commonly used in statistics. Standard deviation measures the fluctuation of the values of z about the mean

---

[1] For those not familiar with this notation, which uses the Greek letter $\sum$ (pronounced 'sigma') to denote summation, it is explained in Appendix A.1.1. The simplified variant used here leaves out the subscripts, as the values to be added are obvious. $\sum z$ (read as 'sigma z') denotes the sum of all values of z, which here is 7, $\sum z^2$ (read as 'sigma z squared') represents the sum of all the values of z^2, which is 437. The latter is not to be confused with $(\sum z)^2$, which is the square of $\sum z$, i.e. 49.

value, which here is 0.7. In Figure 15.2 the fluctuation is considerable: the differences between the values of z and the average value (0.7) vary from -11.7 to $+8.3$ and this is reflected in a sample standard deviation, s, value of 6.93, almost 10 times larger than the average itself. The calculation of the standard error value adjusts s to allow for the number of datasets in the sample. Because t is the average value of z divided by the standard error, it follows that the smaller the value of s (i.e. the fluctuation of z values about the average), the larger will be the value of t. (Readers interested in a full explanation of and justification for the t-test are referred to the many statistics textbooks that are available.)

Now we have calculated t, the next step is to use it to determine whether or not to accept the null hypothesis that the performance of classifiers A and B is effectively the same. We ask this question in an equivalent form: is the value of t sufficiently far away from zero to justify rejecting the null hypothesis? We say 'sufficiently far away from zero' rather than 'sufficiently large' because t can have either a positive or a negative value. (The average value of z can be positive or negative; standard error is always positive.)

We can now reformulate our question as: 'how likely is a value of t outside the range from -0.32 to $+0.32$ to occur by chance'? The answer to this depends on the number of datasets n, but statisticians refer instead to the number of *degrees of freedom*, which for our purposes is always one less than the number of datasets, i.e. $n - 1$.

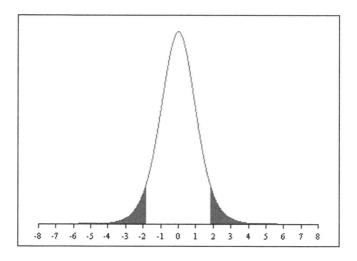

Figure 15.3 *t*-distribution for 9 degrees of freedom

Figure 15.3 shows the distribution of the t-statistic for 9 degrees of freedom (chosen because there are 10 datasets in the tables shown so far).

The left- and right-hand ends of the curve (called its 'tails') go on infinitely in both directions. The area between the entire curve and the horizontal axis, i.e. the t-axis, gives the probability that t will take one of its possible values, which of course is one.

The figure has the values $t = -1.83$ and $t = +1.83$ marked with vertical lines. The area between the parts of the curve that are to the left of $t = -1.83$ or to the right of $t = +1.83$ and the horizontal axis is the probability of the t value being ≤ -1.83 or $\geq +1.83$, i.e. at least as far away from zero as 1.83. We need to look at both tails in this way as a negative value of -1.83 is just as much evidence that the null hypothesis (that the two classifiers are equivalent) is false as the positive value $+1.83$. When we compare two classifiers there is no reason to believe that if A and B are significantly different then B must be better than A; it might also be that B is worse than A.

The area shaded in Figure 15.3, i.e. the probability that t is at least 1.83 either side of zero can be calculated to be 0.1005.

Looking at the probability that $t \leq -1.83$ or $t \geq +1.83$, or in general that $t \leq -a$ or $t \geq +a$, for any positive value a, gives us what is known as a *two-tailed test of significance*.

The value of the area under the two tails $t \leq -a$ and $t \geq +a$ have been calculated for different degrees of freedom and values of a corresponding to probabilities of particular interest. Some of these are summarised in Figure 15.4. Figure 15.4 shows some key values for the t statistic for degrees of freedom from 1 to 19, i.e. for comparisons based on anything from 2 to 20 datasets. (Note that because we are using a two-tailed test, probabilities 0.10, 0.05 and 0.01 in the table correspond to $a = 0.05$, 0.025 and 0.005 respectively in the previous discussion.)

Looking at the values for 9 degrees of freedom (i.e. for $n = 10$) the value of 1.833 in the 'Probability 0.10' column indicates that a value of $t \geq 1.833$ (or ≤ -1.833) would only be expected to happen by chance with probability 0.10 or less, i.e. no more than 1 time out of 10. If we had a t value of 2.1, say, we could reject the null hypothesis 'at the 10% level', implying that such an extreme value of t would only be expected to occur by chance fewer than one time in 10. This is a commonly used criterion for rejecting a null hypothesis and on this basis we could confidently say that classifier B is significantly better than classifier A.

A value of $t \geq 2.262$ (or ≤ -2.262) would enable us to reject the null hypothesis at the 5% level, and a value of $t \geq 3.250$ (or ≤ -3.250) would enable us to reject the null hypothesis at the 1% level, as such values would only be expected to occur by chance one time in 20 and 1 time in 100 respectively.

Degrees of Freedom	Probability 0.10	Probability 0.05	Probability 0.01
1	6.314	12.71	63.66
2	2.920	4.303	9.925
3	2.353	3.182	5.841
4	2.132	2.776	4.604
5	2.015	2.571	4.032
6	1.943	2.447	3.707
7	1.895	2.365	3.499
8	1.860	2.306	3.355
9	1.833	2.262	3.250
10	1.812	2.228	3.169
11	1.796	2.201	3.106
12	1.782	2.179	3.055
13	1.771	2.160	3.012
14	1.761	2.145	2.977
15	1.753	2.131	2.947
16	1.746	2.120	2.921
17	1.740	2.110	2.898
18	1.734	2.101	2.878
19	1.729	2.093	2.861

Figure 15.4 t values for 1 to 19 degrees of freedom (two-tailed test)

Naturally we could use other threshold values and work out a value of t that would only be exceeded by chance one time in six on average, say, but conventionally we use one of the thresholds shown in Figure 15.4. The least restrictive condition generally imposed is that to reject a null hypothesis we require a value of t that would occur no more than 1 time in 10 by chance.

Returning to our example, the value of t calculated was only 0.32, which with 9 degrees of freedom is nowhere near the 10% value of 1.833. We can safely accept the null hypothesis. On the basis of the evidence presented it would be unsafe to say that the performance of classifier B was significantly different from that of classifier A.

It is important to appreciate that the reason for this disappointing result (certainly disappointing to the creator of classifier B) is not the relatively low average value of z (0.7). It is the relatively high value of the standard error (2.19) relative to the average value of z.

To illustrate this we will introduce a new classifier C, which will turn out to be much more successful as a challenger to classifier A.

Dataset	Established Classifier A	New Classifier C	Difference z	Square of Difference z^2
dataset 1	80	81	1	1
dataset 2	73	74	1	1
dataset 3	85	86	1	1
dataset 4	68	69	1	1
dataset 5	82	83	1	1
dataset 6	75	75	0	0
dataset 7	73	75	2	4
dataset 8	64	63	−1	1
dataset 9	75	75	0	0
dataset 10	69	70	1	1
Total	744	751	7	11
Average	74.4	75.1	0.7	1.1

Figure 15.5 Performance of classifiers A and C on 10 datasets

Figure 15.5 shows the percentage accuracy of each classifier on the 10 datasets. Once again the average value of z is 0.7 but this time there is far less spread of z values around the average. The differences between the values of z and the average value (0.7) vary from −1.7 to +1.3.

This time the significant values are $\sum z = 7$, $\sum z^2 = 11$ and $n = 10$. Only the second of these has changed but the effect is considerable. The seven step calculation of t now goes as follows.

Step 1. Calculate the average value of z: $\sum z/n = 7/10 = 0.7$ [as before].

Step 2. Calculate the value of $(\sum z)^2/n$. Here this gives $7^2/10 = 4.9$ [as before].

Step 3. Subtract the result of step 2 from $\sum z^2$. Here this gives $11 - 4.9 = 6.1$.

Step 4. Divide this value by $(n - 1)$ to give the sample variance s^2. Here s^2 is $6.1/9 = 0.68$.

Step 5. Take the square root of s^2 to give the sample standard deviation. Here the value of s is $\sqrt{0.68} = 0.82$.

Step 6. Divide s by $\sqrt{n}$ to give the *standard error*. Here the value is $0.82/\sqrt{10} = 0.26$, which is considerably less than the standard error calculated from Figure 15.2 (i.e. 2.19).

Step 7. Finally we divide the average value of z by the standard error to give the value of the t statistic. Here $t = 0.7/0.26 = 2.69$.

This value of t is greater than the 5% value for 9 degrees of freedom in Figure 15.4. We can say that classifier C is significantly better than classifier A at the 5% level.

The decisive difference between this example and the earlier one using Figure 15.2 was not the average value of z (they were the same) but the much smaller standard error.

15.3 Choosing Datasets for Comparative Evaluation

We will now return to the original problem of whether classifier B is better than (or perhaps worse than) classifier A.

Suppose now that for whatever reason datasets 5 and 6, both of which give results very favourable to classifier A, had been omitted from the sample investigated. We would then have a revised version of Figure 15.2, with only 8 datasets, as shown in Figure 15.6.

Dataset	Established Classifier A	New Classifier B	Difference z	Square of Difference z^2
dataset 1	80	85	5	25
dataset 2	73	70	−3	9
dataset 3	85	85	0	0
dataset 4	68	74	6	36
dataset 7	73	77	4	16
dataset 8	64	73	9	81
dataset 9	75	75	0	0
dataset 10	69	76	7	49
Total	587	615	28	216
Average	73.375	76.875	3.5	27

Figure 15.6 Performance of classifiers A and B with datasets 5 and 6 removed.

Now $\sum z = 28$, $\sum z^2 = 216$ and $n = 8$.

The average value of z is 3.5. The standard error is 1.45 and the value of t is 2.41. This is large enough for classifier B to be declared significantly better than classifier A at the 5% level. (With 7 degrees of freedom the threshold value

for probability 0.05 is 2.365.) The developer of classifier B is clearly fortunate
that datasets 5 and 6 were left out of the analysis.

Suppose now that datasets 5 and 6 were omitted, but two further datasets,
11 and 12, both of which are favourable to classifier B, were included in the
analysis, giving the results shown in Figure 15.7.

Dataset	Established Classifier A	New Classifier B	Difference z	Square of Difference z^2
dataset 1	80	85	5	25
dataset 2	73	70	-3	9
dataset 3	85	85	0	0
dataset 4	68	74	6	36
dataset 7	73	77	4	16
dataset 8	64	73	9	81
dataset 9	75	75	0	0
dataset 10	69	76	7	49
dataset 11	75	80	5	25
dataset 12	82	88	6	36
Total	704	783	39	277
Average	70.4	78.3	3.9	27.7

Figure 15.7 Performance of classifiers A and B with datasets 11 and 12
replacing 5 and 6.

Now $\sum z = 39$, $\sum z^2 = 277$ and $n = 10$.

The average value of z is 3.9. The standard error is 1.18 and the value of t
is 3.31. This is large enough to be significant at the 1% level.

Paradoxically if the results for classifier B with datasets 11 and 12 had
been much better, say 95% and 99% respectively, the value of t would have
been lower at 2.81. Intuitively, we may say that by increasing the fluctuation
around the average value of z we make it more likely that the difference between
the classifiers has occurred by chance. To obtain a significant value of t, it is
generally far more important that the values of z have low variability than that
the average value of z is large.

It is clear that the choice of datasets to include in a performance table such
as Figure 15.1 is of critical importance. A comparison of the t values calculated
from Figures 15.2, 15.6 and 15.7 shows that leaving out (or including) datasets
on which the new algorithm B performs badly (or well) can make the difference
between a 'no significant difference' result and a significant improvement (or

vice versa). Paradoxically, omitting particularly favourable results, by lowering the standard error, can also increase the t value.

Is it too indelicate to raise here the issue of cheating? It would be very easy to leave out a few unfavourable results to make the t-value come out as significant. Naturally no reader of this book would ever be tempted to leave out poor results just to gain public recognition, a higher degree, a pay bonus or promotion, but it is possible that others are not always so scrupulous. Although this is always a possibility, a much bigger problem may be that of 'cheating oneself'. Having obtained good results for a new method, how much incentive is there to hunt for other datasets for which the results may be far worse?

15.3.1 Confidence Intervals

Having established that for the results given in Figure 15.6 classifier B is statistically significantly better than classifier A at the 5% level, and the average improvement for the eight datasets listed is 3.5%, it would be helpful to establish a *confidence interval* for the average improvement to indicate within what limits the true improvement for datasets not included in the table is likely to lie.

For this example the average value of z is 3.5 and the standard error is 1.45. As the t value in the 'Probability 0.05' column of Figure 15.4 for 7 degrees of freedom is 2.365, we can say that the 95% confidence interval for the true average difference is $3.5 \pm (2.365 * 1.45) = 3.5 \pm 3.429$. We can be 95% certain that the true average improvement lies between 0.071% and 6.929%.

For the performance figures given in Figure 15.7 classifier B is significantly better than classifier A at the 1% level. Here the average value of z is 3.9 and the standard error is 1.18. There are 9 degrees of freedom and the value of t in the 'Probability 0.01' column for that number of degrees of freedom is 3.250. We can say that the 99% confidence interval for the true average difference is $3.9 \pm (3.250 * 1.18) = 3.9 \pm 3.835$. We can be 99% certain that the true average improvement lies between 0.065% and 7.735%.

15.4 Sampling

So far we have shown how to test for the significance of a difference in performance between two classifiers on some specified datasets. However in most cases we do this not because we are particularly interested in those datasets but because we would like our new method to be considered better on all possible datasets. This brings us to the issue of *sampling*.

Any collection of datasets can be considered to be a *sample* from the complete collection of all the world's datasets (which is not accessible to us of course), but is it a *representative sample*, i.e. one that accurately reflects the members of the entire population? If not, why should anyone imagine that a classifier's improved performance on datasets 1–10, say, should generalise to imply improved performance on all other (or indeed any other) datasets?

The situation is similar to the world of advertising, where it is common to see claims such as '8 out of 10 women prefer product B to product A'. (The laws of libel prevent us using more realistic examples in this section.)

Does this claim mean that the advertiser has asked exactly 10 women, perhaps all close friends, family members or employees? That would not be very convincing. Why should those 10 speak for all the women of the world? Even if we restrict ourselves to the aim of speaking for, say, all the women in Great Britain, it is obvious that just asking 10 people is hopelessly inadequate.

Some advertisements go further and say (e.g.) 'total number of women asked = 94'. This is better, but how were the 94 selected? If they were all questioned on the same Tuesday morning at the same shopping centre, or sports event say, the bias towards selecting people living in a small geographical area with particular interests and availability for answering surveys on Tuesday mornings is surely obvious.

To make any meaningful statement about the views of the female population of Great Britain we need to sub-divide the population into a number of mutually exclusive and homogeneous sub-groups, based on features such as geographical location, age group and socio-economic status and then ensure we interview a reasonably large group of women that is broken down in the same proportions for each sub-group as the overall population. This is known as *stratified sampling* and is the approach typically adopted by companies conducting opinion surveys.

Returning to data mining, a natural question to ask when faced with a table showing the comparative performance of different classifiers on a number of datasets is how were those datasets selected? It would be good to believe that they were a carefully selected representative sample of all the world's datasets, but that is hardly realistic. Let us suppose that all the datasets were chosen from a standard repository, such as the UCI one, which was established to facilitate comparison with the work of previous software developers. Is there any reason to suppose that they are a representative sample (rather than just a sample) of all the datasets in the UCI Repository?

It would be possible to attempt to achieve this, although unavoidably imprecisely, e.g. by choosing a number of datasets that are believed to include a substantial proportion of noise, a number believed to be noise free, some with all attributes categorical, some with all attributes continuous, and so on.

In practice, most authors make no attempt to claim that their datasets are a representative sample of the UCI Repository. In many cases those chosen were almost certainly just those that were readily available to the developers. This is known as using an *opportunity sample* and is a reasonable way of proceeding in some circumstances, but such a sample is most unlikely to be representative.

When the aim is to make a comparison with results published, perhaps years earlier, by the celebrated Data Mining expert Professor X, there is really little choice but to use the same datasets as were used by X in his or her celebrated work. Developers of new methods can hardly be blamed for doing this, but again it begs the question: how did X select those datasets?

Even assuming that we could find a way of selecting a representative sample of the datasets in the UCI Repository would that guarantee that we had a representative sample of all the world's datasets? Unfortunately not. There is no reason to believe that datasets are entered into the Repository in a random fashion. We might hypothesise that in many cases they are datasets on which well-established methods give good predictive accuracy, placed in a Repository as a challenge for future workers to get even better results. Those who work on 'difficult' datasets and fail to make progress may be assumed to be much less likely to place the datasets in a Repository as a reminder of their failure.

Unfortunately the problems relating to the widespread use of the UCI Repository go far beyond this. They were discussed in a paper by Salzberg [2] as far back as 1997, which refers to a 'community experiments' effect. He says: 'many people are sharing a small repository of datasets and repeatedly using those same datasets for experiments. Thus there is a substantial danger that published results, even when using strict significance criteria and the appropriate significance tests, will be mere accidents of chance. . . . Suppose that 100 different people are studying the effects of algorithms A and B, trying to determine which one is better. Suppose that in fact both have the same mean accuracy (on some very large population of datasets), although the algorithms vary randomly in their performance on specific datasets. Now, if 100 people are studying the effect of algorithms A and B, we would *expect* that five of them will get results that are statistically significant at the [0.05] level, and one will get significance at the 0.01 level! . . . Clearly in this case these results are due to chance, but if the 100 people are working separately, the ones who get significant results will publish, while the others will simply move on to other experiments'.

The problem of the community experiments effect can only have become more severe since. In the short term, it can be countered by creating new repositories, used by fewer people. However, in the long run the large number of people experimenting with classification algorithms and the desirability of producing results that can be compared with those obtained by others in the future mean that the community experiments effect will inevitably affect these new repositories too.

It is perhaps becoming clear why evaluation is the Achilles Heel of much of the published literature about new classification algorithms. At the very least those publishing comparison tables such as Figure 15.1 should explain how the datasets listed were selected – but remarkably few seem to do so.

Faced with these problems, all that can be asked is that developers do the best they can. Publishing results for more datasets is obviously desirable, not only for those trying to judge their work but as benchmarks for future work. Most importantly, developers should always explain how and why they chose the datasets they analysed – and of course that choice should always be made *before* running any new algorithm on them.

15.5 How Bad Is a 'No Significant Difference' Result?

Whilst it is certainly desirable to have a range of classification algorithms available, as no one algorithm can ever be guaranteed to give the best possible performance on all datasets, the comments about 'community experiments' quoted above reflect a situation where many experiments with new classifiers have been and continue to be carried out, most of them giving a very similar performance across a range of familiar datasets.

The world does not need an endless supply of classification algorithms that are not significantly different from well-established ones or give only slightly better performance on a small number of datasets. Nevertheless there are reasons why developing a new classification algorithm may be desirable even though its performance measured by predictive accuracy is not significantly different from that of well-known 'standard' classifiers.

Predictive accuracy is not the only way to judge the quality of a classifier. A new classifier B may be better than an existing classifier A for other reasons, for example:

– B may be better founded in theory than A

– B may be computationally more efficient than A

– B may produce a model that is more human-understandable than A does

– B may give better performance for certain types of dataset than A, for example where there are many missing values or where there is likely to be a high proportion of noise present.

Given a performance table such as Figure 15.1 the question that needs to be addressed is what distinguishes those datasets for which the B value is greater than the A value from those the other way round. Often there may be no discernible reason for the differences but, where there is, a valuable new algorithm for particular types of dataset may have been found.

15.6 Chapter Summary

This chapter considers how to compare the performance of alternative classifiers across a range of datasets. The commonly used paired t-test is described and illustrated with worked examples, leading to the use of confidence intervals when the predictive accuracies of two classifiers are found to be significantly different.

Pitfalls involved in comparing classifiers are discussed, leading to alternative ways of comparing their performance that do not rely on comparisons of predictive accuracy.

15.7 Self-assessment Exercises for Chapter 15

Given the following table showing the percentage accuracy of two classifiers A and B on 20 datasets

1. Calculate the average value of the difference $B - A$.

2. Calculate the value of the standard error and the t-statistic.

3. Determine whether classifier B is significantly better or worse than classifier A at the 5% level.

4. If the answer to question 3 is yes, calculate the 95% confidence interval for the true difference in percentage accuracy between classifiers A and B.

Dataset	Classifier A	Classifier B
1	74	86
2	69	75
3	80	86
4	67	69
5	84	83
6	87	95
7	69	65
8	74	81
9	78	74
10	72	80
11	75	73
12	72	82
13	70	68
14	75	78
15	80	78
16	84	85
17	79	79
18	79	78
19	63	76
20	75	71

References

[1] Dua, D., & Graff, C. (2019). *UCI Machine Learning Repository.* Irvine: University of California, School of Information and Computer Science. https://archive.ics.uci.edu/ml/.

[2] Salzberg, S. L. (1997). On comparing classifiers: pitfalls to avoid and a recommended approach. *Data Mining and Knowledge Discovery, 1,* 317–327. Kluwer.

16

Association Rule Mining I

16.1 Introduction

Classification rules are concerned with predicting the value of a categorical attribute that has been identified as being of particular importance. In this chapter we go on to look at the more general problem of finding *any* rules of interest that can be derived from a given dataset.

We will restrict our attention to IF ... THEN ... rules that have a conjunction of 'attribute = value' terms on both their left- and right-hand sides. We will also assume that all attributes are categorical (continuous attributes can be dealt with by discretising them 'globally' before any of the methods discussed here are used).

Unlike classification, the left- and right-hand sides of rules can potentially include tests on the value of any attribute or combination of attributes, subject only to the obvious constraints that at least one attribute must appear on both sides of every rule and no attribute may appear more than once in any rule. In practice data mining systems often place restrictions on the rules that can be generated, such as the maximum number of terms on each side.

If we have a financial dataset one of the rules extracted might be as follows:

IF Has-Mortgage = yes AND Bank_Account_Status = In_credit
THEN Job_Status = Employed AND Age_Group = Adult_under_65

Rules of this more general kind represent an *association* between the values of certain attributes and those of others and are called *association rules*. The

© Springer-Verlag London Ltd., part of Springer Nature 2020
M. Bramer, *Principles of Data Mining*, Undergraduate Topics
in Computer Science, DOI 10.1007/978-1-4471-7493-6_16

process of extracting such rules from a given dataset is called *association rule mining* (ARM). The term *generalised rule induction* (or GRI) is also used, by contrast with classification rule induction. (Note that if we were to apply the constraint that the right-hand side of a rule has to have only one term which must be an attribute/value pair for a designated categorical attribute, association rule mining would reduce to induction of classification rules.)

For a given dataset there are likely to be few if any association rules that are exact, so we normally associate with each rule a *confidence* value, i.e. the proportion of instances matched by its left- and right-hand sides combined as a proportion of the number of instances matched by the left-hand side on its own. This is the same measure as the predictive accuracy of a classification rule, but the term 'confidence' is more commonly used for association rules.

Association Rule Mining algorithms need to be able to generate rules with confidence values less than one. However the number of possible Association Rules for a given dataset is generally very large and a high proportion of the rules are usually of little (if any) value. For example, for the (fictitious) financial dataset mentioned previously, the rules would include the following (no doubt with very low confidence):

IF Has-Mortgage = yes AND Bank_Account_Status = In_credit
THEN Job_Status = Unemployed

This rule will almost certainly have a very low confidence and is obviously unlikely to be of any practical value.

The main difficulty with association rule mining is computational efficiency. If there are say 10 attributes, each rule can have a conjunction of up to nine 'attribute = value' terms on the left-hand side. Each of the attributes can appear with any of its possible values. Any attribute not used on the left-hand side can appear on the right-hand side, also with any of its possible values. There are a very large number of possible rules of this kind. Generating all of these is very likely to involve a prohibitive amount of computation, especially if there are a large number of instances in the dataset.

For a given unseen instance there are likely to be several or possibly many rules, probably of widely varying quality, predicting different values for any attributes of interest. A conflict resolution strategy of the kind discussed in Chapter 11 is needed that takes account of the predictions from all the rules, plus information about the rules and their quality. However we will concentrate here on rule generation, not on conflict resolution.

16.2 Measures of Rule Interestingness

In the case of classification rules we are generally interested in the quality of a rule set as a whole. It is all the rules working in combination that determine the effectiveness of a classifier, not any individual rule or rules.

In the case of association rule mining the emphasis is on the quality of each individual rule. A single high quality rule linking the values of attributes in a financial dataset or the purchases made by a supermarket customer, say, may be of significant commercial value.

To distinguish between one rule and another we need some measures of rule quality. These are generally known as *rule interestingness measures*. The measures can of course be applied to classification rules as well as association rules if desired.

Several interestingness measures have been proposed in the technical literature. Unfortunately the notation used is not yet very well standardised, so in this book we will adopt a notation of our own for all the measures described.

In this section we will write a rule in the form

if LEFT then RIGHT

We start by defining four numerical values which can be determined for any rule simply by counting:

N_{LEFT} Number of instances matching LEFT
N_{RIGHT} Number of instances matching RIGHT
N_{BOTH} Number of instances matching both LEFT and RIGHT
N_{TOTAL} Total number of instances

We can depict this visually by a figure known as a *Venn diagram*. In Figure 16.1 the outer box can be envisaged as containing all N_{TOTAL} instances under consideration. The left- and right-hand circles contain the N_{LEFT} instances that match LEFT and the N_{RIGHT} instances that match RIGHT, respectively. The hashed area where the circles intersect contains the N_{BOTH} instances that match both LEFT and RIGHT.

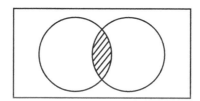

Figure 16.1 Instances matching LEFT, RIGHT and both LEFT and RIGHT

The values N_{LEFT}, N_{RIGHT}, N_{BOTH} and N_{TOTAL} are too basic to be considered as rule interestingness measures themselves but the values of most (perhaps all) interestingness measures can be computed from them.

Three commonly used measures are given in Figure 16.2 below. The first has more than one name in the technical literature.

Confidence (Predictive Accuracy, Reliability)

N_{BOTH} / N_{LEFT}

The proportion of right-hand sides predicted by the rule that are correctly predicted

Support

N_{BOTH}/N_{TOTAL}

The proportion of the training set correctly predicted by the rule

Completeness

N_{BOTH}/N_{RIGHT}

The proportion of the matching right-hand sides that are correctly predicted by the rule

---

Figure 16.2 Basic Measures of Rule Interestingness

We can illustrate this using the financial rule given in Section 16.1.

IF Has-Mortgage = yes AND Bank_Account_Status = In_credit
THEN Job_Status = Employed AND Age_Group = Adult_under_65

Assume that by counting we arrive at the following values:

$N_{LEFT} = 65$
$N_{RIGHT} = 54$
$N_{BOTH} = 50$
$N_{TOTAL} = 100$

From these we can calculate the values of the three interestingness measures given in Figure 16.2.

Confidence = $N_{BOTH}/N_{LEFT} = 50/65 = 0.77$
Support = $N_{BOTH}/N_{TOTAL} = 50/100 = 0.5$
Completeness = $N_{BOTH}/N_{RIGHT} = 50/54 = 0.93$

The confidence of the rule is 77%, which may not seem very high. However it correctly predicts for 93% of the instances in the dataset that match the right-hand side of the rule and the correct predictions apply to as much as 50% of the dataset. This seems like a valuable rule.

Amongst the other measures of interestingness that are sometimes used is *discriminability*. This measures how well a rule discriminates between one class and another. It is defined by:

$$1 - (N_{LEFT} - N_{BOTH})/(N_{TOTAL} - N_{RIGHT})$$

which is

$1 - $ (number of misclassifications produced by the rule)/(number of instances with other classifications)

If the rule predicts perfectly, i.e. $N_{LEFT} = N_{BOTH}$, the value of discriminability is 1.

For the example given above, the value of discriminability is

$$1 - (65 - 50)/(100 - 54) = 0.67.$$

16.2.1 The Piatetsky-Shapiro Criteria and the RI Measure

In an influential paper [1] the American researcher Gregory Piatetsky-Shapiro proposed three principal criteria that should be met by any rule interestingness measure. The criteria are listed in Figure 16.3 and explained in the text that follows.

Criterion 1
The measure should be zero if $N_{BOTH} = (N_{LEFT} \times N_{RIGHT})/N_{TOTAL}$
Interestingness should be zero if the antecedent and the consequent are statistically independent (as explained below).

Criterion 2
The measure should increase monotonically with N_{BOTH}

Criterion 3
The measure should decrease monotonically with each of N_{LEFT} and N_{RIGHT}

For criteria 2 and 3, it is assumed that all other parameters are fixed.

Figure 16.3 Piatetsky-Shapiro Criteria for Rule Interestingness Measures

The second and third of these are more easily explained than the first.

Criterion 2 states that if everything else is fixed the more right-hand sides that are correctly predicted by a rule the more interesting it is. This is clearly reasonable.

Criterion 3 states that if everything else is fixed

(a) the more instances that match the left-hand side of a rule the less interesting it is.

(b) the more instances that match the right-hand side of a rule the less interesting it is.

The purpose of (a) is to give preference to rules that correctly predict a given number of right-hand sides from as few matching left-hand sides as possible (for a fixed value of N_{BOTH}, the smaller the value of N_{LEFT} the better).

The purpose of (b) is to give preference to rules that predict right-hand sides that are relatively infrequent (because predicting common right-hand sides is easier to do).

Criterion 1 is concerned with the situation where the antecedent and the consequent of a rule (i.e. its left- and right-hand sides) are independent. How many right-hand sides would we expect to predict correctly just by chance?

We know that the number of instances in the dataset is N_{TOTAL} and that the number of those instances that match the right-hand side of the rule is N_{RIGHT}. So if we just predicted a right-hand side without any justification whatever we would expect our prediction to be correct for N_{RIGHT} instances out of N_{TOTAL}, i.e. a proportion of N_{RIGHT}/N_{TOTAL} times.

If we predicted the same right-hand side N_{LEFT} times (one for each instance that matches the left-hand side of the rule), we would expect that purely by chance our prediction would be correct $N_{LEFT} \times N_{RIGHT}/N_{TOTAL}$ times.

By definition the number of times that the prediction actually turns out to be correct is N_{BOTH}. So Criterion 1 states that if the number of correct predictions made by the rule is the same as the number that would be expected by chance the rule interestingness is zero.

Piatetsky-Shapiro proposed a further rule interestingness measure called RI, as the simplest measure that meets his three criteria. This is defined by:

$RI = N_{BOTH} - (N_{LEFT} \times N_{RIGHT}/N_{TOTAL})$

RI measures the difference between the actual number of matches and the expected number if the left- and right-hand sides of the rule were independent. Generally the value of RI is positive. A value of zero would indicate that the rule is no better than chance. A negative value would imply that the rule is less successful than chance.

The RI measure satisfies all three of Piatetsky-Shapiro's criteria.

Criterion 1 RI is zero if $N_{BOTH} = (N_{LEFT} \times N_{RIGHT})/N_{TOTAL}$

<u>Criterion 2</u> RI increases monotonically with N_{BOTH} (assuming that all other parameters are fixed).
<u>Criterion 3</u> RI decreases monotonically with each of N_{LEFT} and N_{RIGHT} (assuming that all other parameters are fixed).

Although doubts have been expressed about the validity of the three criteria and much research in this field remains to be done, the RI measure remains a valuable contribution in its own right.

There are several other rule interestingness measures available. Some important ones are described later in this chapter and in Chapter 17.

16.2.2 Rule Interestingness Measures Applied to the *chess* Dataset

Although Rule Interestingness Measures are particularly valuable for association rules, we can also apply them to classification rules if we wish.

The unpruned decision tree derived from the *chess* dataset (with attribute selection using entropy) comprises 20 rules. One of these (numbered rule 19 in Figure 16.4) is

IF inline = 1 AND wr_bears_bk = 2 THEN Class = safe

For this rule

$N_{LEFT} = 162$
$N_{RIGHT} = 613$
$N_{BOTH} = 162$
$N_{TOTAL} = 647$

So we can calculate the values of the various rule interestingness measures as follows:

Confidence = $162/162 = 1$
Completeness = $162/613 = 0.26$
Support = $162/647 = 0.25$
Discriminability = $1 - (162 - 162)/(647 - 613) = 1$
RI = $162 - (162 \times 613/647) = 8.513$

The 'perfect' values of confidence and discriminability are of little value here. They always occur when rules are extracted from an unpruned classification tree (created without encountering any clashes in the training data). The *RI* value indicates that the rule can be expected to correctly predict 8.513 more correct classifications (on average) than would be expected by chance.

Rule	N_{LEFT}	N_{RIGHT}	N_{BOTH}	Conf	Compl	Supp	Discr	RI
1	2	613	2	1.0	0.003	0.003	1.0	0.105
2	3	34	3	1.0	0.088	0.005	1.0	2.842
3	3	34	3	1.0	0.088	0.005	1.0	2.842
4	9	613	9	1.0	0.015	0.014	1.0	0.473
5	9	613	9	1.0	0.015	0.014	1.0	0.473
6	1	34	1	1.0	0.029	0.002	1.0	0.947
7	1	613	1	1.0	0.002	0.002	1.0	0.053
8	1	613	1	1.0	0.002	0.002	1.0	0.053
9	3	34	3	1.0	0.088	0.005	1.0	2.842
10	3	34	3	1.0	0.088	0.005	1.0	2.842
11	9	613	9	1.0	0.015	0.014	1.0	0.473
12	9	613	9	1.0	0.015	0.014	1.0	0.473
13	3	34	3	1.0	0.088	0.005	1.0	2.842
14	3	613	3	1.0	0.005	0.005	1.0	0.158
15	3	613	3	1.0	0.005	0.005	1.0	0.158
16	9	34	9	1.0	0.265	0.014	1.0	8.527
17	9	34	9	1.0	0.265	0.014	1.0	8.527
18	81	613	81	1.0	0.132	0.125	1.0	4.257
19	162	613	162	1.0	0.264	0.25	1.0	8.513
20	324	613	324	1.0	0.529	0.501	1.0	17.026

$N_{TOTAL} = 647$

Figure 16.4 Rule Interestingness Values for Rules Derived from *chess* Dataset

The table of interestingness values of all 20 classification rules derived from the *chess* dataset, given as Figure 16.4, is very revealing.

Judging by the RI values, it looks as if only the last five rules are really of any interest. They are the only rules (out of 20) that correctly predict the classification for at least four instances more than would be expected by chance. Rule 20 predicts the correct classification 324 out of 324 times. Its support value is 0.501, i.e. it applies to over half the dataset, and its completeness value is 0.529. By contrast, Rules 7 and 8 have RI values as low as 0.053, i.e. they predict only slightly better than chance.

Ideally we would probably prefer only to use rules 16 to 20. However in the case of classification rules we cannot just discard the other 15 much lower quality rules. If we do we will have a tree with only five branches that is unable to classify 62 out of the 647 instances in the dataset. This illustrates the general point that an effective classifier (set of rules) can include a number of rules that are themselves of low quality.

16.2.3 Using Rule Interestingness Measures for Conflict Resolution

We can now return briefly to the subject of conflict resolution, when several rules predict different values for one or more attributes of interest for an unseen test instance. Rule interestingness measures give one approach to handling this. For example we might decide to use only the rule with the highest interestingness value, or the most interesting three rules, or more ambitiously we might decide on a 'weighted voting' system that adjusts for the interestingness value or values of each rule that fires.

16.3 Association Rule Mining Tasks

The number of generalised rules that can be derived from a given dataset is potentially very large and in practice the aim is usually either to find all the rules satisfying a specified criterion or to find the best N rules. The latter will be discussed in the next section.

As a criterion for accepting a rule we could use a test on the confidence of the rule, say 'confidence > 0.8', but this is not completely satisfactory. It is quite possible that we can find rules that have a high level of confidence but are applicable very rarely. For example with the financial example used before we might find the rule

IF Age_Group = Over_seventy AND Has-Mortgage = no
THEN Job_Status = Retired

This may well have a high confidence value but is likely to correspond to very few instances in the dataset and thus be of little practical value. One way of avoiding such problems is to use a second measure. One frequently used is support. The value of support is the proportion of the instances in the dataset to which the rule (successfully) applies, i.e. the proportion of instances matched by the left- and right-hand sides together. A rule that successfully applied to only 2 instances in a dataset of 10,000 would have a low value of support (just 0.0002), even if its confidence value were high.

A common requirement is to find all rules with confidence and support above specified threshold values. A particularly important type of association rule application for which this approach is used is known as *market basket analysis*. This involves analysing very large datasets of the kind collected by supermarkets, telephone companies, banks etc. about their customers' transactions (purchases, calls made, etc.) to find rules that, in the supermarket case, find associations between the products purchased by customers. Such datasets are generally handled by restricting attributes to having only the values true or false (indicating the purchase or non-purchase of some product, say) and restricting the rules generated to ones where every attribute included in the rule has the value true.

Market basket analysis will be discussed in detail in Chapter 17.

16.4 Finding the Best N Rules

In this section we will look at a method of finding the best N rules that can be generated from a given dataset. We will assume that the value of N is a small number such as 20 or 50.

We first need to decide on some numerical value that we can measure for any rule which captures what we mean by 'best'. We will call this a *quality measure*. In this section we will use a quality measure (or measure of rule interestingness) known as the *J-measure*.

Next we need to decide on some set of rules in which we are interested. This could be all possible rules with a conjunction of 'attribute = value' terms on both the left- and right-hand sides, the only restriction being that no attribute may appear on both sides of a rule. However a little calculation shows that for even as few as 10 attributes the number of possible rules is huge and in practice we may wish to restrict the rules of interest to some smaller (but possibly still very large) number. For example we might limit the rule 'order', i.e. the number of terms on the left-hand side, to no more than four (say) and possibly also place restrictions on the right-hand side, for example a maximum of two terms or only a single term or even only terms involving a single specified attribute. We will call the set of possible rules of interest the *search space*.

Finally we need to decide on a way of generating the possible rules in the search space in an efficient order, so that we can calculate the quality measure for each one. This is called a *search strategy*. Ideally we would like to find a search strategy that avoids having to generate low-quality rules if possible.

As rules are generated we maintain a table of the best N rules so far found and their corresponding quality measures in descending numerical order. If a new rule is generated that has a quality measure greater than the smallest value in the table the Nth best rule is deleted and the new rule is placed in the table in the appropriate position.

16.4.1 The *J*-Measure: Measuring the Information Content of a Rule

The *J*-measure was introduced into the data mining literature by Smyth and Goodman [2], as a means of quantifying the information content of a rule that is soundly based on theory. Justifying the formula is outside the scope of this book, but calculating its value is straightforward.

Given a rule of the form **If** $Y = y$, **then** $X = x$ using Smyth and Goodman's notation, the information content of the rule, measured in bits of information, is denoted by $J(X; Y = y)$, which is called the *J-measure* for the rule.

The value of the *J*-measure is the product of two terms:

– $p(y)$ The probability that the left-hand side (antecedent) of the rule will occur

– $j(X; Y = y)$ The *j-measure* (note the small letter '*j*') or *cross-entropy*.

The cross-entropy term is defined by the equation:

$$j(X; Y = y) = p(x|y).\log_2\left(\frac{p(x|y)}{p(x)}\right) + (1 - p(x|y)).\log_2\left(\frac{1 - p(x|y)}{1 - p(x)}\right)$$

The value of cross-entropy depends on two values:

– $p(x)$ The probability that the right-hand side (consequent) of the rule will be satisfied if we have no other information (called the *a priori* probability of the rule consequent)

– $p(x|y)$ The probability that the right-hand side of the rule will be satisfied if we know that the left-hand side is satisfied (read as 'probability of x given y').

A plot of the *j*-measure for various values of $p(x)$ is given in Figure 16.5.

In terms of the basic measures introduced in Section 16.2:

$p(y) = N_{LEFT}/N_{TOTAL}$
$p(x) = N_{RIGHT}/N_{TOTAL}$
$p(x|y) = N_{BOTH}/N_{LEFT}$

The *J*-measure has two helpful properties concerning upper bounds. First, it can be shown that the value of $J(X; Y = y)$ is less than or equal to

$p(y).\log_2\left(\frac{1}{p(y)}\right)$.

The maximum value of this expression, given when $p(y) = 1/e$, is $\log_2 e/e$, which is approximately 0.5307 bits.

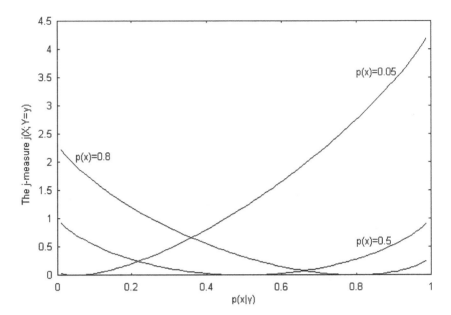

Figure 16.5 Plot of j-Measure for Various Values of $p(x)$

Second (and more important), it can be proved that the J value of any rule obtained by *specialising* a given rule by adding further terms is bounded by the value

$$Jmax = p(y). \max\{p(x|y). \log_2(\tfrac{1}{p(x)}), (1 - p(x|y)). \log_2(\tfrac{1}{1-p(x)})\}$$

Thus if a given rule is known to have a J value of, say, 0.352 bits and the value of $Jmax$ is also 0.352, there is no benefit to be gained (and possibly harm to be done) by adding further terms to the left-hand side, as far as information content is concerned.

We will come back to this topic in the next section.

16.4.2 Search Strategy

There are many ways in which we can search a given search space, i.e. generate all the rules of interest and calculate their quality measures. In this section we will describe a method that takes advantage of the properties of the J-measure.

To simplify the description we will assume that there are ten attributes $a1$, $a2$, ..., $a10$ each with three possible values 1, 2 and 3. The search space comprises rules with just one term on the right-hand side and up to nine terms on the left-hand side.

We start by generating all possible right-hand sides. There are 30 of them, i.e. each of the 10 attributes combined with each of its three values, e.g. $a1 = 1$ or $a7 = 2$.

From these we can generate all possible rules of order one, i.e. with one term on the left-hand side. For each right-hand side, say '$a2 = 2$', there are 27 possible left-hand sides, i.e. the other nine attributes combined with each of their three possible values, and thus 27 possible rules of order one, i.e.

IF $a1 = 1$ THEN $a2 = 2$
IF $a1 = 2$ THEN $a2 = 2$
IF $a1 = 3$ THEN $a2 = 2$
IF $a3 = 1$ THEN $a2 = 2$
IF $a3 = 2$ THEN $a2 = 2$
IF $a3 = 3$ THEN $a2 = 2$

and so on.

We calculate the J-value for each of the 27×30 possible rules. We put the rules with the N highest J-values in the best rule table in descending order of J.

The next step is to specialise the rules of order one to form rules of order two, e.g. to expand

IF $a3 = 3$ THEN $a2 = 2$

to the set of rules

IF $a3 = 3$ AND $a1 = 1$ THEN $a2 = 2$
IF $a3 = 3$ AND $a1 = 2$ THEN $a2 = 2$
IF $a3 = 3$ AND $a1 = 3$ THEN $a2 = 2$
IF $a3 = 3$ AND $a4 = 1$ THEN $a2 = 2$
IF $a3 = 3$ AND $a4 = 2$ THEN $a2 = 2$
IF $a3 = 3$ AND $a4 = 3$ THEN $a2 = 2$

and so on.

We can then go on to generate all rules of order 3 and then all rules of order 4, 5 etc. up to 9. This clearly involves generating a very large number of rules. There are 262,143 possible left-hand sides for each of the 30 possible right-hand sides, making a total of 7,864,290 rules to consider. However, there are two ways in which the process can be made more computationally feasible.

The first is to expand only the best (say) 20 rules of order one with an additional term. The J-values of the resulting rules of order 2 are then calculated and the 'best N rules' table is adjusted as necessary. The best 20 rules of order 2 (whether or not they are in the best N rules table overall) are then expanded by a further term to give rules of order 3 and so on. This technique is known as a *beam search*, by analogy with the restricted width of the beam of a torch.

In this case the *beam width* is 20. It is not necessary for the beam width to be a fixed value. For example it might start at 50 when expanding rules of order one then reduce progressively for rules of higher orders.

It is important to appreciate that using a beam search technique to reduce the number of rules generated is a *heuristic*, i.e. a 'rule of thumb' that is not guaranteed to work correctly in every case. It is not necessarily the case that the best rules of order K are all specialisations of the best rules of order $K - 1$.

The second method of reducing the number of rules to be generated is guaranteed always to work correctly and relies on one of the properties of the J-measure.

Let us suppose that the last entry in the 'best N rules table' (i.e. the entry with lowest J-value in the table) has a J-value of 0.35 and we have a rule with two terms, say

IF $a3 = 3$ AND $a6 = 2$ THEN $a2 = 2$

which has a J-value of 0.28.

In general specialising a rule by adding a further term can either increase or decrease its J-value. So even if the order 3 rule

IF $a3 = 3$ AND $a6 = 2$ AND $a8 = 1$ THEN $a2 = 2$

has a lower J-value, perhaps 0.24, it is perfectly possible that adding a fourth term could give a higher J-value that will put the rule in the top N.

A great deal of unnecessary calculation can be avoided by using the *Jmax* value described in Section 16.4.1. As well as calculating the J-value of the rule

IF $a3 = 3$ AND $a6 = 2$ THEN $a2 = 2$

which was given previously as 0.28, let us assume that we also calculate its *Jmax* value as 0.32. This means that no further specialisation of the rule by adding terms to the left-hand side can produce a rule (for the same right-hand side) with a J-value larger than 0.32. This is less than the minimum of 0.35 needed for the expanded form of the rule to qualify for the best N rules table. Hence the order 2 form of the rule can safely be discarded.

Combining a beam search with rule 'pruning' using the *Jmax* value can make generating rules from even quite a large dataset computationally feasible.

In the next chapter we look at the problem of generating association rules for market basket analysis applications, where the datasets are often huge, but the rules take a restricted form.

16.5 Chapter Summary

This chapter looks at the problem of finding any rules of interest that can be derived from a given dataset, not just classification rules as before. This is known as *Association Rule Mining* or *Generalised Rule Induction*. A number of measures of rule interestingness are defined and criteria for choosing between measures are discussed. An algorithm for finding the best N rules that can be generated from a dataset using the J-measure of the information content of a rule and a 'beam search' strategy is described.

16.6 Self-assessment Exercises for Chapter 16

1. Calculate the values of Confidence, Completeness, Support, Discriminability and RI for rules with the following values.

Rule	N_{LEFT}	N_{RIGHT}	N_{BOTH}	N_{TOTAL}
1	720	800	700	1000
2	150	650	140	890
3	1000	2000	1000	2412
4	400	250	200	692
5	300	700	295	817

2. Given a dataset with four attributes w, x, y and z, each with three values, how many rules can be generated with one term on the right-hand side?

References

[1] Piatetsky-Shapiro, G. (1991). Discovery, analysis and presentation of strong rules. In G. Piatetsky-Shapiro & W. J. Frawley (Eds.), *Knowledge discovery in databases* (pp. 229–248). Menlo Park: AAAI Press.

[2] Smyth, P., & Goodman, R. M. (1992). Rule induction using information theory. In G. Piatetsky-Shapiro & W. J. Frawley (Eds.), *Knowledge discovery in databases* (pp. 159–176). Menlo Park: AAAI Press.

17

Association Rule Mining II

This chapter requires a basic knowledge of mathematical set theory. If you do not already have this, the notes in Appendix A will tell you all you need to know.

17.1 Introduction

This chapter is concerned with a special form of Association Rule Mining, which is known as *Market Basket Analysis*. The rules generated for Market Basket Analysis are all of a certain restricted kind.

Here we are interested in any rules that relate the purchases made by customers in a shop, frequently a large store with many thousands of products, as opposed to those that predict the purchase of one particular item. Although in this chapter ARM will be described in terms of this application, the methods described are not restricted to the retail industry. Other applications of the same kind include analysis of items purchased by credit card, patients' medical records, crime data and data from satellites.

© Springer-Verlag London Ltd., part of Springer Nature 2020
M. Bramer, *Principles of Data Mining*, Undergraduate Topics
in Computer Science, DOI 10.1007/978-1-4471-7493-6_17

17.2 Transactions and Itemsets

We will assume that we have a database comprising n *transactions* (i.e. records), each of which is a set of *items*.

In the case of market basket analysis we can think of each transaction as corresponding to a group of purchases made by a customer, for example {milk, cheese, bread} or {fish, cheese, bread, milk, sugar}. Here milk, cheese, bread etc. are items and we call {milk, cheese, bread} an *itemset*. We are interested in finding rules known as *association rules* that apply to the purchases made by customers, for example 'buying fish and sugar is often associated with buying milk and cheese', but only want rules that meet certain criteria for 'interestingness', which will be specified later.

Including an item in a transaction just means that some quantity of it was bought. For the purposes of this chapter, we are not interested in the quantity of cheese or the number of cans of dog food etc. bought. We do not record the items that a customer did *not* buy and are not interested in rules that include a test of what was *not* bought, such as 'customers who buy milk but do not buy cheese generally buy bread'. We only look for rules that link all the items that were actually bought.

We will assume that there are m possible items that can be bought and will use the letter I to denote the set of all possible items.

In a realistic case the value of m can easily be many hundreds or even many thousands. It partly depends on whether a company decides to consider, say, all the meat it sells as a single item 'meat' or as a separate item for each type of meat ('beef', 'lamb', 'chicken' etc.) or as a separate item for each type and weight combination. It is clear that even in quite a small store the number of different items that could be considered in a basket analysis is potentially very large.

The items in a transaction (or any other itemset) are listed in a standard order, which may be alphabetical or something similar, e.g. we will always write a transaction as {cheese, fish, meat}, not {meat, fish, cheese} etc. This does no harm, as the meaning is obviously the same, but has the effect of greatly reducing and simplifying the calculations we need to do to discover all the 'interesting' rules that can be extracted from the database.

As an example, if a database comprises 8 transactions (so $n = 8$) and there are only 5 different items (an unrealistically low number), denoted by a, b, c, d and e, so we have $m = 5$ and $I = \{a, b, c, d, e\}$, the database might comprise the transactions shown in Figure 17.1.

Note that the details of how the information is actually stored in the database is a separate issue, which is not considered here.

Transaction number	Transactions (itemsets)
1	{a, b, c}
2	{a, b, c, d, e}
3	{b}
4	{c, d, e}
5	{c}
6	{b, c, d}
7	{c, d, e}
8	{c, e}

Figure 17.1 A Database With Eight Transactions

For convenience we write the items in an itemset in the order in which they appear in set I, the set of all possible items, i.e. $\{a, b, c\}$ not $\{b, c, a\}$.

All itemsets are subsets of I. We do not count the empty set as an itemset and so an itemset can have anything from 1 up to m members.

17.3 Support for an Itemset

We will use the term *support count* of an itemset S, or just the *count* of an itemset S, to mean the number of transactions in the database matched by S.

We say that an itemset S *matches* a transaction T (which is itself an itemset) if S is a subset of T, i.e. all the items in S are also in T. For example itemset {bread, milk} matches the transaction {cheese, bread, fish, milk, wine}.

If an itemset $S = \{\text{bread}, \text{milk}\}$ has a support count of 12, written as count$(S) = 12$ or count$(\{\text{bread}, \text{milk}\}) = 12$, it means that 12 of the transactions in the database contain both the items bread and milk.

We define the *support* of an itemset S, written as support(S), to be the proportion of itemsets in the database that are matched by S, i.e. the proportion of transactions that contain all the items in S. Alternatively we can look at it in terms of the frequency with which the items in S occur together in the database. So we have support$(S) = \text{count}(S)/n$, where n is the number of transactions in the database.

17.4 Association Rules

The aim of Association Rule Mining (ARM) is to examine the contents of the database and find rules, known as *association rules*, in the data. For example we might notice that when items c and d are bought item e is often bought too. We can write this as the rule

$$cd \rightarrow e$$

The arrow is read as 'implies', but we must be careful not to interpret this as meaning that buying c and d somehow causes e to be bought. It is better to think of rules in terms of *prediction*: if we know that c and d were bought we can predict that e was also bought.

The rule $cd \rightarrow e$ is typical of most if not all of the rules used in Association Rule Mining in that it is not invariably correct. The rule is satisfied for transactions 2, 4 and 7 in Figure 17.1, but not for transaction 6, i.e. it is satisfied in 75% of cases. For basket analysis it might be interpreted as 'if bread and milk are bought, then cheese is bought too in 75% of cases'.

Note that the presence of items c, d and e in transactions 2, 4, and 7 can also be used to justify other rules such as

$$c \rightarrow ed$$
and
$$e \rightarrow cd$$

which again do not have to be invariably correct.

The number of rules that can be generated from quite a small database is potentially very large. In practice most of them are of little if any practical value. We need some way of deciding which rules to discard and which to retain.

First we will introduce some more terminology and notation. We can write the set of items appearing on the left- and right-hand sides of a given rule as L and R, respectively, and the rule itself as $L \rightarrow R$. L and R must each have at least one member and the two sets must be *disjoint*, i.e. have no common members. The left-hand and right-hand sides of a rule are often called its *antecedent* and *consequent* or its *body* and *head*, respectively.

Note that with the $L \rightarrow R$ notation the left- and right-hand sides of rules are both sets. However we will continue to write rules that do not involve variables in a simplified notation, e.g. $cd \rightarrow e$ instead of the more accurate but also more cumbersome form $\{c, d\} \rightarrow \{e\}$.

The *union* of the sets L and R is the set of items that occur in either L or R. It is written $L \cup R$ (read as 'L union R'). As L and R are disjoint and each has at least one member, the number of items in the itemset $L \cup R$, called the *cardinality* of $L \cup R$, must be at least two.

For the rule $cd \rightarrow e$ we have $L = \{c, d\}$, $R = \{e\}$ and $L \cup R = \{c, d, e\}$. We can count the number of transactions in the database that are matched by the first two itemsets. Itemset L matches four transactions, numbers 2, 4, 6 and 7, and itemset $L \cup R$ matches 3 transactions, numbers 2, 4 and 7, so $\text{count}(L) = 4$ and $\text{count}(L \cup R) = 3$.

As there are 8 transactions in the database we can calculate

$$\text{support}(L) = \text{count}(L)/8 = 4/8$$

and

$$\text{support}(L \cup R) = \text{count}(L \cup R)/8 = 3/8$$

A large number of rules can be generated from even quite a small database and we are generally only interested in those that satisfy given criteria for *interestingness*. There are many ways in which the interestingness of a rule can be measured, but the two most commonly used are *support* and *confidence*. The justification for this is that there is little point in using rules that only apply to a small proportion of the database or that predict only poorly.

The *support* for a rule $L \rightarrow R$ is the proportion of the database to which the rule successfully applies, i.e. the proportion of transactions in which the items in L and the items in R occur together. This value is just the support for itemset $L \cup R$, so we have

$$\text{support}(L \rightarrow R) = \text{support}(L \cup R).$$

The predictive accuracy of the rule $L \rightarrow R$ is measured by its *confidence*, defined as the proportion of transactions for which the rule is satisfied. This can be calculated as the number of transactions matched by the left-hand and right-hand sides combined, as a proportion of the number of transactions matched by the left-hand side on its own, i.e. $\text{count}(L \cup R)/\text{count}(L)$.

Ideally, every transaction matched by L would also be matched by $L \cup R$, in which case the value of confidence would be 1 and the rule would be called *exact*, i.e. always correct. In practice, rules are generally not exact, in which case $\text{count}(L \cup R) < \text{count}(L)$ and the confidence is less than 1.

Since the support count of an itemset is its support multiplied by the total number of transactions in the database, which is a constant value, the confidence of a rule can be calculated either by

$$\text{confidence}(L \rightarrow R) = \text{count}(L \cup R)/\text{count}(L)$$

or by

$$\text{confidence}(L \rightarrow R) = \text{support}(L \cup R)/\text{support}(L)$$

It is customary to reject any rule for which the support is below a minimum threshold value called *minsup*, typically 0.01 (i.e. 1%) and also to reject all rules with confidence below a minimum threshold value called *minconf*, typically 0.8 (i.e. 80%).

For the rule $cd \rightarrow e$, the confidence is $\text{count}(\{c,d,e\})/\text{count}(\{c,d\})$, which is $3/4 = 0.75$.

17.5 Generating Association Rules

There are many ways in which all the possible rules can be generated from a given database. A basic but very inefficient method has two stages.

We will use the term *supported itemset* to mean any itemset for which the value of support is greater than or equal to *minsup*. The terms *frequent itemset* and *large itemset* are often used instead of supported itemset.

---

1. Generate all supported itemsets $L \cup R$ with cardinality at least two.

2. For each such itemset generate all the possible rules with at least one item on each side and retain those for which confidence $\geq$ *minconf*.

Step 2 in this algorithm is fairly straightforward to implement and will be discussed in Section 17.8.

The main problem is with step 1 'generate all supported itemsets $L \cup R$ with cardinality at least 2', assuming we take this to mean that we first generate all possible itemsets of cardinality two or greater and then check which of them are supported. The number of such itemsets depends on the total number of items m. For a practical application this can be very large.

The number of possible itemsets $L \cup R$ is the same as the number of possible subsets of I, the set of all items, which has cardinality m. There are 2^m such subsets. Of these, m have a single element and one has no elements (the empty set). Thus the number of itemsets $L \cup R$ with cardinality at least 2 is $2^m - m - 1$.

If m takes the unrealistically small value of 20 the number of itemsets $L \cup R$ is $2^{20} - 20 - 1 = 1,048,555$. If m takes the more realistic but still relatively small value of 100 the number of itemsets $L \cup R$ is $2^{100} - 100 - 1$, which is approximately 10^{30}.

Generating all the possible itemsets $L \cup R$ and then checking against the transactions in the database to establish which ones are supported is clearly unrealistic or impossible in practice.

Fortunately, a much more efficient method of finding supported itemsets is available which makes the amount of work manageable, although it can still be large in some cases.

17.6 Apriori

This account is based on the very influential *Apriori* algorithm by Agrawal and Srikant [1], which showed how association rules could be generated in a realistic timescale, at least for relatively small databases. Since then a great deal of effort has gone into looking for improvements on the basic algorithm to enable larger and larger databases to be processed.

The method relies on the following very important result.

Theorem 1

If an itemset is supported, all of its (non-empty) subsets are also supported.

Proof

Removing one or more of the items from an itemset cannot reduce and will often increase the number of transactions that it matches. Hence the support for a subset of an itemset must be at least as great as that for the original itemset. It follows that any (non-empty) subset of a supported itemset must also be supported.

This result is sometimes called the *downward closure property* of itemsets.

If we write the set containing all the supported itemsets with cardinality k as L_k then a second important result follows from the above. (The use of the letter L stands for 'large itemsets'.)

Theorem 2

If $L_k = \emptyset$ (the empty set) then L_{k+1}, L_{k+2} etc. must also be empty.

Proof

If any supported itemsets of cardinality $k + 1$ or larger exist, they will have subsets of cardinality k and it follows from Theorem 1 that all of these must be supported. However we know that there are no supported itemsets of cardinality k as L_k is empty. Hence there are no supported subsets of cardinality $k + 1$ or larger and L_{k+1}, L_{k+2} etc. must all be empty.

Taking advantage of this result, we generate the supported itemsets in ascending order of cardinality, i.e. all those with one element first, then all those with two elements, then all those with three elements etc. At each stage, the set L_k of supported items of cardinality k is generated from the previous set L_{k-1}.

The benefit of this approach is that if at any stage L_k is $\emptyset$, the empty set, we know that L_{k+1}, L_{k+2} etc. must also be empty. Itemsets of cardinality $k+1$ or greater do not need to be generated and then tested against the transactions in the database as they are certain to turn out not to be supported.

We need a method of going from each set L_{k-1} to the next L_k in turn. We can do this in two stages.

First we use L_{k-1} to form a *candidate set* C_k containing itemsets of cardinality k. C_k must be constructed in such a way that it is certain to include all the supported itemsets of cardinality k but may contain some other itemsets that are not supported.

Next we need to generate L_k as a subset of C_k. We can generally discard some of the members of C_k as possible members of L_k by inspecting the members of L_{k-1}. The remainder need to be checked against the transactions in the database to establish their support values. Only those itemsets with support greater than or equal to *minsup* are copied from C_k into L_k.

This gives us the *Apriori* algorithm for generating all the supported itemsets of cardinality at least 2 (Figure 17.2).

Create L_1 = set of supported itemsets of cardinality one
Set k to 2
while $(L_{k-1} \neq \emptyset)$ {
    Create C_k from L_{k-1}
    Prune all the itemsets in C_k that are not
        supported, to create L_k
    Increase k by 1
}
The set of all supported itemsets with at least two members is $L_2 \cup \cdots \cup L_{k-2}$

Figure 17.2 The Apriori Algorithm (adapted from [1])

To start the process we construct C_1, the set of all itemsets comprising just a single item, then make a pass through the database counting the number of transactions that match each of these itemsets. Dividing each of these counts by the number of transactions in the database gives the value of support for each single-element itemset. We discard all those with support $<$ *minsup* to give L_1.

The process involved can be represented diagrammatically as Figure 17.3, continuing until L_k is empty.

Agrawal and Srikant's paper also gives an algorithm *Apriori-gen* which takes L_{k-1} and generates C_k without using any of the earlier sets L_{k-2} etc. There are two stages to this. These are given in Figure 17.4.

To illustrate the method, let us assume that L_4 is the list
$\{\{p,q,r,s\}, \{p,q,r,t\}, \{p,q,r,z\}, \{p,q,s,z\}, \{p,r,s,z\}, \{q,r,s,z\},$
$\{r,s,w,x\}, \{r,s,w,z\}, \{r,t,v,x\}, \{r,t,v,z\}, \{r,t,x,z\}, \{r,v,x,y\},$
$\{r,v,x,z\}, \{r,v,y,z\}, \{r,x,y,z\}, \{t,v,x,z\}, \{v,x,y,z\}\}$
which contains 17 itemsets of cardinality four.

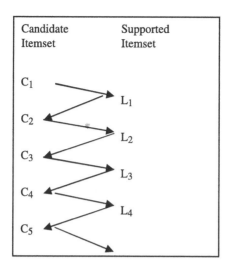

Figure 17.3 Diagram Illustrating the Apriori Algorithm

(Generates C_k from L_{k-1})

Join Step

Compare each member of L_{k-1}, say A, with every other member, say B, in turn. If the first $k-2$ items in A and B (i.e. all but the rightmost elements of the two itemsets) are identical, place set $A \cup B$ into C_k.

Prune Step

For each member c of C_k in turn {

Examine all subsets of c with $k-1$ elements

Delete c from C_k if any of the subsets is not a member of L_{k-1}

}

Figure 17.4 The Apriori-gen Algorithm (adapted from [1])

We begin with the join step.

There are only six pairs of elements that have the first three elements in common. These are listed below together with the set that each combination causes to be placed into C_5.

First itemset	Second itemset	Contribution to C_5
$\{p,q,r,s\}$	$\{p,q,r,t\}$	$\{p,q,r,s,t\}$
$\{p,q,r,s\}$	$\{p,q,r,z\}$	$\{p,q,r,s,z\}$
$\{p,q,r,t\}$	$\{p,q,r,z\}$	$\{p,q,r,t,z\}$
$\{r,s,w,x\}$	$\{r,s,w,z\}$	$\{r,s,w,x,z\}$
$\{r,t,v,x\}$	$\{r,t,v,z\}$	$\{r,t,v,x,z\}$
$\{r,v,x,y\}$	$\{r,v,x,z\}$	$\{r,v,x,y,z\}$

The initial version of candidate set C_5 is

$$\{\{p,q,r,s,t\},\{p,q,r,s,z\},\{p,q,r,t,z\},\{r,s,w,x,z\},\{r,t,v,x,z\},\{r,v,x,y,z\}\}$$

We now go on to the prune step where each of the subsets of cardinality four of the itemsets in C_5 are examined in turn, with the following results.

Itemset in C_5	Subsets all in L_4?
$\{p,q,r,s,t\}$	No, e.g. $\{p,q,s,t\}$ is not a member of L_4
$\{p,q,r,s,z\}$	Yes
$\{p,q,r,t,z\}$	No, e.g. $\{p,q,t,z\}$ is not a member of L_4
$\{r,s,w,x,z\}$	No, e.g. $\{r,s,x,z\}$ is not a member of L_4
$\{r,t,v,x,z\}$	Yes
$\{r,v,x,y,z\}$	Yes

We can eliminate the first, third and fourth itemsets from C_5, making the final version of candidate set C_5

$$\{\{p,q,r,s,z\},\{r,t,v,x,z\},\{r,v,x,y,z\}\}$$

The three itemsets in C_5 now need to be checked against the database to establish which are supported.

17.7 Generating Supported Itemsets: An Example

We can illustrate the entire process of generating supported itemsets from a database of transactions with the following example.

Assume that we have a database with 100 items and a large number of transactions. We begin by constructing C_1, the set of itemsets with a single member. We make a pass though the database to establish the support count for each of the 100 itemsets in C_1 and from these calculate L_1, the set of supported itemsets that comprise just a single member.

Let us assume that L_1 has just 8 of these members, namely $\{a\}$, $\{b\}$, $\{c\}$, $\{d\}$, $\{e\}$, $\{f\}$, $\{g\}$ and $\{h\}$. We cannot generate any rules from these, as they only have one element, but we can now form candidate itemsets of cardinality two.

In generating C_2 from L_1 all pairs of (single-item) itemsets in L_1 are considered to match at the 'join' step, since there is nothing to the left of the rightmost element of each one that might fail to match.

In this case the candidate generation algorithm gives us as members of C_2 all the itemsets with two members drawn from the eight items a, b, c, $\ldots$, h. Note that it would be pointless for a candidate itemset of two elements to include any of the other 92 items from the original set of 100, e.g. $\{a, z\}$, as one of its subsets would be $\{z\}$, which is not supported.

There are 28 possible itemsets of cardinality 2 that can be formed from the items a, b, c, $\ldots$, h. They are

$\{a,b\}, \{a,c\}, \{a,d\}, \{a,e\}, \{a,f\}, \{a,g\}, \{a,h\},$
$\{b,c\}, \{b,d\}, \{b,e\}, \{b,f\}, \{b,g\}, \{b,h\},$
$\{c,d\}, \{c,e\}, \{c,f\}, \{c,g\}, \{c,h\},$
$\{d,e\}, \{d,f\}, \{d,g\}, \{d,h\},$
$\{e,f\}, \{e,g\}, \{e,h\},$
$\{f,g\}, \{f,h\},$
$\{g,h\}.$

As mentioned previously, it is convenient always to list the elements of an itemset in a standard order. Thus we do not include, say, $\{e, d\}$ because it is the same set as $\{d, e\}$.

We now need to make a second pass through the database to find the support counts of each of these itemsets, then divide each of the counts by the number of transactions in the database and reject any itemsets that have support less than *minsup*. Assume in this case that only 6 of the 28 itemsets with two elements turn out to be supported, so $L_2 = \{\{a, c\}, \{a, d\}, \{a, h\}, \{c, g\}, \{c, h\}, \{g, h\}\}$.

The algorithm for generating C_3 now gives just four members, i.e. $\{a, c, d\}$, $\{a, c, h\}$, $\{a, d, h\}$ and $\{c, g, h\}$.

Before going to the database, we first check whether each of the candidates meets the condition that all its subsets are supported. Itemsets $\{a, c, d\}$ and $\{a, d, h\}$ fail this test, because their subsets $\{c, d\}$ and $\{d, h\}$ are not members of L_2. That leaves just $\{a, c, h\}$ and $\{c, g, h\}$ as possible members of L_3.

We now need a third pass through the database to find the support counts for itemsets $\{a, c, h\}$ and $\{c, g, h\}$. We will assume they both turn out to be supported, so $L_3 = \{\{a, c, h\}, \{c, g, h\}\}$.

We now need to calculate C_4. It has no members, as the two members of L_3 do not have their first two elements in common. As C_4 is empty, L_4 must also

be empty, which implies that L_5, L_6 etc. must also be empty and the process
ends.

We have found all the itemsets of cardinality at least two with just three
passes through the database. In doing so we needed to find the support counts
for just $100 + 28 + 2 = 130$ itemsets, which is a huge improvement on checking
through the total number of possible itemsets for 100 items, which is approximately 10^{30}.

The set of all supported itemsets with at least two members is the union
of L_2 and L_3, i.e. $\{\{a,c\}, \{a,d\}, \{a,h\}, \{c,g\}, \{c,h\}, \{g,h\}, \{a,c,h\}, \{c,g,h\}\}$.
It has eight itemsets as members. We next need to generate the candidate rules
from each of these and determine which of them have a confidence value greater
than or equal to *minconf*.

Although using the Apriori algorithm is clearly a significant step forward,
it can run into substantial efficiency problems when there are a large number
of transactions, items or both. One of the main problems is the large number
of candidate itemsets generated during the early stages of the process. If the
number of supported itemsets of cardinality one (the members of L_1) is large,
say N, the number of candidate itemsets in C_2, which is $N(N-1)/2$, can be
a very large number.

A fairly large (but not huge) database may comprise over 1,000 items and
100,000 transactions. If there are, say, 800 supported itemsets in L_1, the number
of itemsets in C_2 is $800 \times 799/2$, which is approximately 320,000.

Since Agrawal and Srikant's paper was published a great deal of research
effort has been devoted to finding more efficient ways of generating supported
itemsets. These generally involve reducing the number of passes through all
the transactions in the database, reducing the number of unsupported itemsets
in C_k, more efficient counting of the number of transactions matched by each
of the itemsets in C_k (perhaps using information collected in previous passes
through the database), or some combination of these.

17.8 Generating Rules for a Supported Itemset

If supported itemset $L \cup R$ has k elements, we can generate all the possible
rules $L \rightarrow R$ systematically from it and then check the value of confidence for
each one.

To do so it is only necessary to generate all possible right-hand sides in turn.
Each one must have at least one and at most $k-1$ elements. Having generated
the right-hand side of a rule all the unused items in $L \cup R$ must then be on the
left-hand side.

For itemset $\{c, d, e\}$ there are 6 possible rules that can be generated, as listed below.

Rule $L \rightarrow R$	count($L \cup R$)	count(L)	confidence($L \rightarrow R$)
$de \rightarrow c$	3	3	1.0
$ce \rightarrow d$	3	4	0.75
$cd \rightarrow e$	3	4	0.75
$e \rightarrow cd$	3	4	0.75
$d \rightarrow ce$	3	4	0.75
$c \rightarrow de$	3	7	0.43

Only one of the rules has a confidence value greater than or equal to *minconf* (i.e. 0.8).

The number of ways of selecting i items from the k in a supported itemset of cardinality k for the right-hand side of a rule is denoted by the mathematical expression $_kC_i$ which has the value $\frac{k!}{(k-i)!i!}$.

The total number of possible right-hand sides L and thus the total number of possible rules that can be constructed from an itemset $L \cup R$ of cardinality k is $_kC_1 + {_kC_2} + \cdots + {_kC_{k-1}}$. It can be shown that the value of this sum is $2^k - 2$.

Assuming that k is reasonably small, say 10, this number is manageable. For $k = 10$ there are $2^{10} - 2 = 1022$ possible rules. However as k becomes larger the number of possible rules rapidly increases. For $k = 20$ it is 1,048,574.

Fortunately we can reduce the number of candidate rules considerably using the following result.

Theorem 3

Transferring members of a supported itemset from the left-hand side of a rule to the right-hand side cannot increase the value of rule confidence.

Proof

For this purpose we will write the original rule as $A \cup B \rightarrow C$, where sets A, B and C all contain at least one element, have no elements in common and the union of the three sets is the supported itemset S.

Transferring the item or items in B from the left to the right-hand side then amounts to creating a new rule $A \rightarrow B \cup C$.

The union of the left- and right-hand sides is the same for both rules, namely the supported itemset S, so we have

confidence($A \rightarrow B \cup C$) = $\frac{\text{support}(S)}{\text{support}(A)}$

confidence($A \cup B \rightarrow C$) = $\frac{\text{support}(S)}{\text{support}(A \cup B)}$

It is clear that the proportion of transactions in the database matched by an itemset A must be at least as large as the proportion matched by a larger itemset $A \cup B$, i.e. support(A) $\geq$ support($A \cup B$).

Hence it follows that confidence($A \rightarrow B \cup C$) $\leq$ confidence($A \cup B \rightarrow C$).

If the confidence of a rule $\geq$ *minconf* we will call the itemset on its right-hand side *confident*. If not, we will call the right-hand itemset *unconfident*. From the above theorem we then have two important results that apply whenever the union of the itemsets on the two sides of a rule is fixed:

> Any superset of an unconfident right-hand itemset is unconfident.
> Any (non-empty) subset of a confident right-hand itemset is confident.

This is very similar to the situation with supported itemsets described in Section 17.6. We can generate confident right-hand side itemsets of increasing cardinality in a way similar to Apriori, with a considerable reduction in the number of candidate rules for which the confidence needs to be calculated. If at any stage there are no more confident itemsets of a certain cardinality there cannot be any of larger cardinality and the rule generation process can stop.

17.9 Rule Interestingness Measures: Lift and Leverage

Although they are generally only a very small proportion of all the possible rules that can be derived from a database, the number of rules with support and confidence greater than specified threshold values can still be large. We would like additional interestingness measures we can use to reduce the number to a manageable size, or rank rules in order of importance. Two measures that are often used for this are *lift* and *leverage*.

The *lift* of rule $L \rightarrow R$ measures how many more times the items in L and R occur together in transactions than would be expected if the itemsets L and R were statistically independent.

The number of times the items in L and R occur together in transactions is just count$(L \cup R)$. The number of times the items in L occur is count(L). The proportion of transactions matched by R is support(R). So if L and R were independent we would expect the number of times the items in L and R occurred together in transactions to be count$(L) \times$ support(R). This gives the formula for lift:

$$\text{lift}(L \rightarrow R) = \frac{\text{count}(L \cup R)}{\text{count}(L) \times \text{support}(R)}$$

This formula can be written in several other forms, including

$$\text{lift}(L \rightarrow R) = \frac{\text{support}(L \cup R)}{\text{support}(L) \times \text{support}(R)}$$

$$\text{lift}(L \rightarrow R) = \frac{\text{confidence}(L \rightarrow R)}{\text{support}(R)}$$

$$\text{lift}(L \to R) = \frac{n \times \text{confidence}(L \to R)}{\text{count}(R)}$$

where n is the number of transactions in the database, and

$$\text{lift}(L \to R) = \frac{\text{confidence}(R \to L)}{\text{support}(L)}$$

Incidentally, from the second of these five formulae, which is symmetric in L and R, we can also see that

$$\text{lift}(L \to R) = \text{lift}(R \to L)$$

Suppose we have a database with 2000 transactions and a rule $L \to R$ with the following support counts

count(L)	count(R)	count($L \cup R$)
220	250	190

We can calculate the values of support and confidence from these:

$$\text{support}(L \to R) = \text{count}(L \cup R)/2000 = 0.095$$

$$\text{confidence}(L \to R) = \text{count}(L \cup R)/\text{count}(L) = 0.864$$

$$\text{lift}(L \to R) = \text{confidence}(L \cup R) \times 2000/\text{count}(R) = 6.91$$

The value of support(R) measures the support for R if we examine the whole of the database. In this example the itemset matches 250 transactions out of 2000, a proportion of 0.125.

The value of confidence($L \to R$) measures the support for R if we only examine the transactions that match L. In this case it is $190/220 = 0.864$. So purchasing the items in L makes it $0.864/0.125 = 6.91$ times more likely that the items in R are purchased.

Lift values greater than 1 are 'interesting'. They indicate that transactions containing L tend to contain R more often than transactions that do not contain L.

Although lift is a useful measure of interestingness it is not always the best one to use. In some cases a rule with higher support and lower lift can be more interesting than one with lower support and higher lift because it applies to more cases.

Another measure of interestingness that is sometimes used is *leverage*. This measures the difference between the support for $L \cup R$ (i.e. the items in L and R occurring together in the database) and the support that would be expected if L and R were independent.

The former is just support$(L \cup R)$. The frequencies (i.e. supports) of L and R are support(L) and support(R), respectively. If L and R were independent the expected frequency of both occurring in the same transaction would be the product of support(L) and support(R).

This gives a formula for leverage:

$$\text{leverage}(L \to R) = \text{support}(L \cup R) - \text{support}(L) \times \text{support}(R).$$

The value of the leverage of a rule is clearly always less than its support.

The number of rules satisfying the support $\geq$ *minsup* and confidence $\geq$ *minconf* constraints can be reduced by setting a leverage constraint, e.g. leverage $\geq$ 0.0001, corresponding to an improvement in support of one occurrence per 10,000 transactions in the database.

If a database has 100,000 transactions and we have a rule $L \to R$ with these support counts

count(L)	count(R)	count$(L \cup R)$
8000	9000	7000

the values of support, confidence, lift and leverage can be calculated to be 0.070, 0.875, 9.722 and 0.063 respectively (all to three decimal places).

So the rule applies to 7% of the transactions in the database and is satisfied for 87.5% of the transactions that include the items in L. The latter value is 9.722 times more frequent than would be expected by chance. The improvement in support compared with chance is 0.063, corresponding to 6.3 transactions per 100 in the database, i.e. approximately 6300 in the database of 100,000 transactions.

17.10 Chapter Summary

This chapter is concerned with a special form of Association Rule Mining known as *Market Basket Analysis*, the most common application of which is to relate the purchases made by the customers in a shop. An approach to finding rules of this kind, with support and confidence measures above specified thresholds, is described. This is based on the idea of *supported itemsets*. The *Apriori* algorithm for finding supported itemsets is described in detail. Further rule interestingness measures, *lift* and *leverage*, which can be used to reduce the number of rules generated are introduced.

17.11 Self-assessment Exercises for Chapter 17

1. Suppose that L_3 is the list

   $\{\{a, b, c\}, \{a, b, d\}, \{a, c, d\}, \{b, c, d\}, \{b, c, w\}, \{b, c, x\},$
   $\{p, q, r\}, \{p, q, s\}, \{p, q, t\}, \{p, r, s\}, \{q, r, s\}\}$

   Which itemsets are placed in C_4 by the join step of the *Apriori-gen* algorithm? Which are then removed by the prune step?

2. Suppose that we have a database with 5000 transactions and a rule $L \rightarrow R$ with the following support counts

   $\text{count}(L)$ $=$ 3400
   $\text{count}(R)$ $=$ 4000
   $\text{count}(L \cup R)$ $=$ 3000

   What are the values of support, confidence, lift and leverage for this rule?

Reference

[1] Agrawal, R., & Srikant, R. (1994). Fast algorithms for mining association rules in large databases. In J. B. Bocca, M. Jarke & C. Zaniolo (Eds.), *Proceedings of the 20th international conference on very large databases (VLDB94)* (pp. 487–499). San Mateo: Morgan Kaufmann. http://citeseer.nj.nec.com/agrawal94fast.html.

18

Association Rule Mining III: Frequent Pattern Trees

18.1 Introduction: FP-Growth

The *Apriori* algorithm described in Chapter 17 is a successful method of deriving association rules from a transaction database. However it has important shortcomings. In this chapter an alternative method, known as the *FP-growth algorithm* is presented, which aims to overcome these. Before expanding on this, we will start by recapping on some of the basic points from Chapter 17.

It is assumed that we have a database of *transactions*, each comprising a number of *items*, such as

milk, fish, cheese
eggs, milk, pork, butter
cheese, cream, bread, milk, fish

Each record corresponds to a transaction such as one person's purchases in a supermarket. A collection of items, such as {*fish, pork, cream*} is known as an *itemset*.

The *support count* (or just *count*) of an itemset is the number of times that the items occur together in a transaction, possibly with other items. Thus for the above database of three transactions $count(\{milk\}) = 3$, $count(\{pork\}) = 1$, $count(\{cheese, milk\}) = 2$, $count(\{fish, milk\}) = 2$ etc.

The *support* of an itemset is defined as the value of the support count divided by the number of transactions in the database.

© Springer-Verlag London Ltd., part of Springer Nature 2020
M. Bramer, *Principles of Data Mining*, Undergraduate Topics
in Computer Science, DOI 10.1007/978-1-4471-7493-6_18

The aim is to find *association rules* linking the items in purchases together, e.g.

eggs, milk → bread, cheese, pork

meaning that transactions that contain eggs and milk generally also include bread, cheese and pork.

We do this in two stages:

1. Find *itemsets* such as {*eggs, milk, bread*} with a sufficiently high value of *support* (defined by the user).

2. For each such itemset, extract one or more association rules, with all the items in the itemset appearing on either the left- or the right-hand side.

This chapter is only concerned with step (1) of this process, i.e. finding the itemsets. A method for extracting the association rules from the itemsets is described in Section 17.8 of Chapter 17.

The term used in Chapter 17 for itemsets with a sufficiently high value of *support* was *supported itemsets*. In view of the title of this chapter we will switch here to using the equivalent term *frequent itemsets*, which is more commonly used in the technical literature, although perhaps less meaningful. (We will use the term frequent itemsets rather than frequent patterns.)

There is another detailed change from Chapter 17. In that chapter the definition of a frequent (or supported) itemset was that the value of the support count divided by the number of transactions in the database, i.e. the *support*, was greater than or equal to a threshold value defined by the user, such as 0.01, called *minsup*. This is equivalent to saying that the support count must be greater than or equal to the number of transactions multiplied by the value of *minsup*. For a database with a million transactions the value of *minsup* multiplied by the number of transactions would be a large number such as 10,000.

> In this chapter we will define a *frequent itemset* as one for which the support count is greater than or equal to a user-defined integer which we will call *minsupportcount*.

These two definitions are clearly equivalent. The value of *minsupportcount* will typically be a large integer, but for the example used in the remainder of this chapter we will set it to the highly unrealistic value of three.

An important result which was established in Chapter 17 is the *downward closure* property of itemsets: if an itemset is frequent, any (non-empty) subset of it is also frequent. This is generally used in a different form: if an itemset is infrequent then any superset of it must also be infrequent. For example if {a, b, c, d} is infrequent then {a, b, c, d, e, f} must also be infrequent. If the latter were frequent, then $\{a, b, c, d\}$ as a subset of it must also be frequent, but we know that it is not. The practical significance of this result is that the only itemsets with, say, 6 elements that are worth considering are those that are created from a frequent itemset with 5 elements by adding an additional item.

We now return to the *Apriori* algorithm. Although very effective, it suffers from two disadvantages.

– The number of candidate itemsets to be considered can be very large, especially those with two elements. If there are n single-item itemsets, e.g. $\{fish\}$ that are frequent, the number of two-item itemsets generated for examination will be approximately $n^2/2$. As n might easily be tens of thousands this is a lot of itemsets to process, the large majority of which are likely to prove infrequent.

– Even though *Apriori* reduces the number of database scans considerably compared with more primitive methods, the number of scans can still be substantial and this can place a large processing overhead on the system, especially for large transaction databases.

One of the most popular alternative approaches to generating association rules is the *FP-Growth* (standing for *Frequent Pattern Growth*) algorithm, which was introduced by Han et al. [1]. The aim is to find all the frequent itemsets that can be extracted from the transaction database as efficiently as possible. One way of improving on the efficiency of the *Apriori* algorithm is to reduce the number of database scans. Another is to examine as few of the infrequent itemsets as possible. The number of possible (non-empty) itemsets for a database with n different items is $2^n - 1$, of which only a relatively small number are likely to be frequent, so reducing the number of infrequent ones examined is very important. Even for the very small transaction database with just three items shown above there are 8 different items, giving $2^8 - 1 = 255$ possible itemsets. For even quite a small supermarket the number of items could easily be several thousand.

The *FP-growth* algorithm has two stages.

– First the transaction database is processed to produce a data structure called a *FP-tree* (Frequent Pattern Tree) which captures the essence of the database as far as extracting frequent itemsets is concerned.

– Next the FP-tree is processed recursively, by constructing a sequence of reduced trees known as *conditional FP-trees*.

The transaction database is only processed at the first of these stages and is only scanned twice. As for virtually any conceivable alternative method the database would have to be scanned at least once, reducing the number of scans to just two is a very valuable feature of this algorithm.

In [1] it is claimed that *FP-growth* is an order of magnitude faster than *Apriori*. Naturally this depends on a number of factors, for example whether the FP-tree can be represented in a way that is compact enough to fit into main memory. Like virtually all the algorithms in this book, there are a number of variants of both *Apriori* and *FP-growth* that aim to make them less memory or computationally expensive and there will no doubt be more in the future.

In the following sections the *FP-growth* algorithm is described and illustrated by a series of figures showing the FP-tree corresponding to an example transaction database, followed by a sequence of conditional FP-trees from which it is straightforward to extract the frequent itemsets.

18.2 Constructing the FP-tree

18.2.1 Pre-processing the Transaction Database

To illustrate the process we will use the transaction data from [1]. There are just five transactions held in a transaction database, with each item represented by a single letter:

| f, a, c, d, g, i, m, p |
| a, b, c, f, l, m, o |
| b, f, h, j, o |
| b, c, k, s, p |
| a, f, c, e, l, p, m, n |

The first step is to make a scan through the transaction database to count the number of occurrences of each item, which is the same as the support count of the corresponding single-item itemset. The result is as follows.

f, c: 4

a, m, p, b: 3

l, o: 2

d, g, i, h, j, k, s, e and n: 1

> The user now needs to decide on a value for *minsupportcount*. As the amount of data is so small, in this example we will use the highly unrealistic value: **minsupportcount = 3**.

There are only six items for which the corresponding single-item itemset has a support count of *minsupportcount* or more. In descending order of support count they are: f, c, a, b, m and p. We store them in an array named *orderedItems* (Figure 18.1).

index	orderedItems
0	f
1	c
2	a
3	b
4	m
5	p

Figure 18.1 *orderedItems* array

As far as extracting frequent itemsets is concerned the items that are not in the *orderedItems* array may as well not exist, as they cannot occur in any frequent itemset. For example, if item g were a member of a frequent itemset then by the downward closure property of itemsets any non-empty subset of that itemset would also be frequent, so $\{g\}$ would have to be frequent, but we know by counting that it is not.

> It is conventional and very important from a computational point of view that the items in an itemset are written in a fixed order. In the case of *FP-growth* they are written in descending order of their position in the *orderedItems* array, i.e. in descending order of the number of transactions in which each of them occurs. Thus $\{c, a, m\}$ is a valid itemset, which may be frequent or infrequent, but $\{m, c, a\}$ and $\{c, m, a\}$ are invalid. We are only interested in whether itemsets that are valid in this sense are frequent or infrequent.

We next make the second and final scan through the transaction database. As each transaction is read all items that are not in *orderedItems* are removed and the remaining items are sorted into descending order (i.e. the order of the items in *orderedItems*) before being passed to the FP-tree construction process.

This gives the same effect as if the transaction data were originally the five transactions

> f, c, a, m, p
> f, c, a, b, m
> f, b
> c, b, p
> f, c, a, m, p

but the transaction database itself is left unchanged.

We now go on to describe the process of creating the FP-tree and extracting frequent itemsets from it. Although the transaction data is taken from [1] this description and especially the method of representing the evolving trees by arrays is the current author's own and the responsibility for any accidental errors or distortions is his alone.

18.2.2 Initialisation

Diagrammatically we can represent the initial state of the FP-tree by a single node, representing the root.

We will also represent the evolving tree by the contents of four arrays:

– Two two-dimensional arrays *nodes* and *child*, with a numerical index that will correspond to the numbering of the nodes in the tree (zero indicates the root node). The names given to the columns of these arrays are shown in Figure 18.2. Note that *child* can have an indefinite number of columns, but only the first two are needed for this example.

– Single-dimensional arrays *startlink* and *endlink* indexed by the names of the itemsets in the *orderedItems* array, i.e. f, c, a, b, m and p.

index	*item name*	*count*	*linkto*	*parent*
0	*root*			

nodes array

child1	*child2*

child array

index	*startlink*	*endlink*
f		
c		
a		
b		
m		
p		

link arrays

Figure 18.2 Arrays Corresponding to Initial Form of FP-tree: Root Node Only

18.2.3 Processing Transaction 1: f, c, a, m, p

Item f As this is the first item for the transaction we take the 'current node' to be the root node. In this case the current node does not have a descendant node with item name f, so a new node for item f is added numbered 1, with its parent node numbered 0 (indicating the root node) in Figure 18.4. Note that an item with name f and support count 1 is indicated by $f/1$ in Figure 18.3.

Adding a new node numbered N, for an item with name *Item* with its parent node numbered P

- A new node numbered N is added to the tree with item name *Item* and support count 1 as a descendant of the node numbered P.

- A new row, numbered N, is added to the *nodes* array with *itemname*, *count* and *parent* values *Item*, 1 and P respectively. The first unused *child* value for node P is set to N.

- The value of the row with index *Item* in both array *startlink* and array *endlink* is set to N.

Item c

The current node is now node 1, which does not have a descendant node with item name c, so a new node is added numbered 2, for item c with its parent node numbered 1.

Item a

The current node is now node 2, which does not have a descendant node with item name a, so a new node is added numbered 3, for item a with its parent node numbered 2.

Item m

The current node is now node 3, which does not have a descendant node with item name m, so a new node is added numbered 4, for item m with its parent node numbered 3.

Item p

The current node is now node 4, which does not have a descendant node with item name p, so a new node is added numbered 5, for item p with its parent node numbered 4.

This gives the partial tree and corresponding tables shown below.

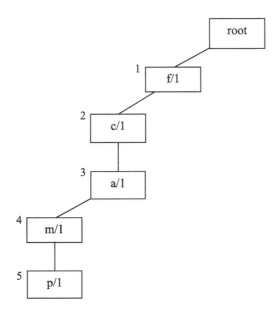

Figure 18.3 FP-tree After Processing Transaction 1

index	item name	count	linkto	parent
0	root			
1	f	1		0
2	c	1		1
3	a	1		2
4	m	1		3
5	p	1		4

nodes array

child1	child2
1	
2	
3	
4	
5	

child array

index	startlink	endlink
f	1	1
c	2	2
a	3	3
b		
m	4	4
p	5	5

link arrays

Figure 18.4 Arrays Corresponding to FP-tree After Processing Transaction 1

18.2.4 Processing Transaction 2: *f, c, a, b, m*

Items f, c and a

There is already a chain of nodes from the root to f, c, and a nodes in turn, so no changes are needed except to increase the counts of nodes 1, 2 and 3 and the corresponding rows of array *nodes* by one, giving Figures 18.5 and 18.6.

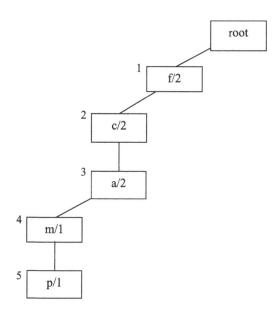

Figure 18.5 FP-tree After Processing First Three Items of Transaction 2

index	item name	count	linkto	parent
0	root			
1	f	2		0
2	c	2		1
3	a	2		2
4	m	1		3
5	p	1		4

nodes array

child1	child2
1	
2	
3	
4	
5	

child array

index	startlink	endlink
f	1	1
c	2	2
a	3	3
b		
m	4	4
p	5	5

link arrays

Figure 18.6 Arrays Corresponding to FP-tree After Processing First Three Items of Transaction 2

Item *b*

There is no descendant of the current node (the last node accessed), i.e. node 3, that has item name *b*, so a new node numbered 6 is added for item *b* with its parent node numbered 3 (Figures 18.7 and 18.8).

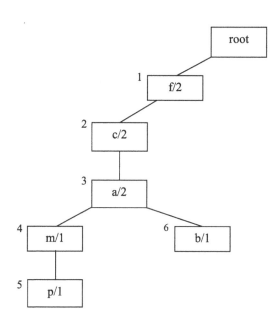

Figure 18.7 FP-tree After Processing First Four Items of Transaction 2

index	item name	count	linkto	parent
0	root			
1	f	2		0
2	c	2		1
3	a	2		2
4	m	1		3
5	p	1		4
6	b	1		3

nodes array

child1	child2
1	
2	
3	
4	6
5	

child array

index	startlink	endlink
f	1	1
c	2	2
a	3	3
b	6	6
m	4	4
p	5	5

link arrays

Figure 18.8 Arrays Corresponding to FP-tree After Processing First Four Items of Transaction 2

Item *m*

A new node numbered 7 is added for item *m* with its parent node numbered 6.

For the first time in this example the *endlink* array has a non-null value for a newly added node, as *endlink[m]* is 4. Because of this, a dashed line link is made from node 4 to node 7 for item *m* (Figures 18.9 and 18.10).

Making a 'dashed line' link for item *Item* across the tree from node *A* to node *B*

The *linkto* value in row *A* of the *nodes* array and the value of *endlink[Item]* are both set to *B*.

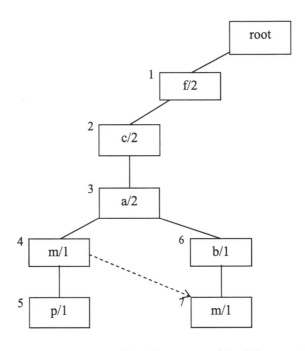

Figure 18.9 FP-tree After Processing All of Transaction 2

index	item name	count	linkto	parent
0	root			
1	f	2		0
2	c	2		1
3	a	2		2
4	m	1	7	3
5	p	1		4
6	b	1		3
7	m	1		6

nodes array

child1	child2
1	
2	
3	
4	6
5	
7	

child array

index	startlink	endlink
f	1	1
c	2	2
a	3	3
b	6	6
m	4	7
p	5	5

link arrays

Figure 18.10 Arrays Corresponding to FP-tree After Processing All of Transaction 2

18.2.5 Processing Transaction 3: *f, b*

Item *f*

The count value for node 1 in the tree and row 1 in the *nodes* array are both increased by 1.

Item *b*

There is no descendant of the current node, node 1, with item name *b* so a new node numbered 8 is added for item *b* with its parent node numbered 1.

The *endlink* array has a non-null value for the new node, as *endlink[b]* is 6. A dashed line link is made from node 6 to node 8 for item *b* (Figures 18.11 and 18.12).

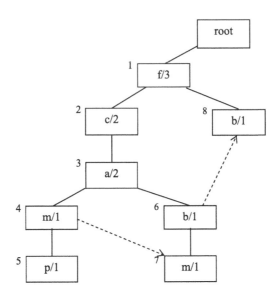

Figure 18.11 FP-tree After Processing All of Transaction 3

index	item name	count	linkto	parent
0	root			
1	f	3		0
2	c	2		1
3	a	2		2
4	m	1	7	3
5	p	1		4
6	b	1	8	3
7	m	1		6
8	b	1		1

nodes array

child1	child2
1	
2	8
3	
4	6
5	
7	

child array

index	startlink	endlink
f	1	1
c	2	2
a	3	3
b	6	8
m	4	7
p	5	5

link arrays

Figure 18.12 Arrays Corresponding to FP-tree After Processing All of Transaction 3

18.2.6 Processing Transaction 4: *c*, *b*, *p*

Item *c*
The current node (the root node) does not have a descendant node with item
name *c*, so a new node is added numbered 9, for item *c* with its parent node
numbered 0 (indicating the root node). A dashed line link is made from node
2 to node 9.

Item *b*
The current node is now node 9, which does not have a descendant node with
item name *b*, so a new node is added numbered 10, for item *b* with its parent
node numbered 9. A dashed line link is made from node 8 to node 10.

Item *p*
The current node is now node 10, which does not have a descendant node
with item name *p*, so a new node is added numbered 11, for item *p* with its
parent node numbered 10. A dashed line link is made from node 5 to node 11
(Figures 18.13 and 18.14).

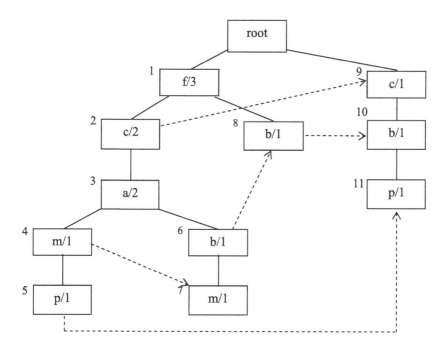

Figure 18.13 FP-tree After Processing Transaction 4

index	item name	count	linkto	parent
0	root			
1	f	3		0
2	c	2	9	1
3	a	2		2
4	m	1	7	3
5	p	1	11	4
6	b	1	8	3
7	m	1		6
8	b	1	10	1
9	c	1		0
10	b	1		9
11	p	1		10

nodes array

child1	child2
1	9
2	8
3	
4	6
5	
7	
10	
11	

child array

index	startlink	endlink
f	1	1
c	2	9
a	3	3
b	6	10
m	4	7
p	5	11

link arrays

Figure 18.14 Arrays Corresponding to FP-tree After Processing Transaction 4

18.2.7 Processing Transaction 5: *f, c, a, m, p*

There is already a chain of nodes from the root to *f*, *c*, *a*, *m* and *p* in turn, so
no changes are needed except to increase the counts of nodes 1, 2, 3, 4 and 5
and the corresponding rows of array *nodes* by one. This gives the final FP-tree
and corresponding set of arrays as follows (Figures 18.15 and 18.16).

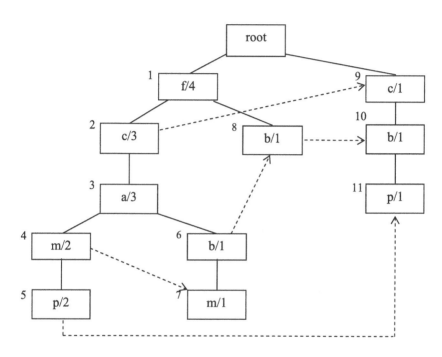

Figure 18.15 Final FP-tree After Processing Transaction 5

index	item name	count	linkto	parent		child1	child2
0	root					1	9
1	f	4		0		2	8
2	c	3	9	1		3	
3	a	3		2		4	6
4	m	2	7	3		5	
5	p	2	11	4			
6	b	1	8	3		7	
7	m	1		6			
8	b	1	10	1			
9	c	1		0		10	
10	b	1		9		11	
11	p	1		10			

nodes array   child array

index	startlink	endlink
f	1	1
c	2	9
a	3	3
b	6	10
m	4	7
p	5	11

link arrays

Figure 18.16 Arrays Corresponding to Final FP-tree After Processing Transaction 5

Once the FP-tree has been created arrays *child* and *endlink* can be discarded. The contents of the tree are fully represented by arrays *nodes* and *startlink*.

18.3 Finding the Frequent Itemsets from the FP-tree

Having constructed the FP-tree, which is shown diagrammatically in Figure 18.15 and is represented by the arrays *nodes* and *startlink* shown in Figure 18.16, we can now analyse it to extract all the frequent itemsets for the transaction database.

We will illustrate the process by a series of diagrams and describe how the frequent itemset extraction process can be implemented in a recursive fashion by constructing a number of tables that are equivalent to reduced versions of the FP-tree.

We start by observing some general points.

- The dashed lines (links) in Figure 18.15 are not part of the tree itself (if there were links across the tree it would no longer be a tree structure). Rather, they are a way of keeping track of all the nodes with a particular name, e.g. b, wherever they occur in the tree. This will be very useful in what follows.

- The items used to label the nodes in each branch of the tree from the root downwards are always in the same order as the items in the *orderedItems* array, i.e. f, c, a, b, m, p. This is descending order of the support counts of the corresponding itemsets (e.g. $\{f\}$) in the transaction database, or equivalently the order of the items in the *orderedItems* array, which is repeated as Figure 18.17. (Not every branch of the tree includes all six of the items.)

- Although the nodes in Figure 18.15 are labelled with the names c, m, p etc. these are just the rightmost items in the itemsets to which the nodes correspond. Thus nodes 1, 2, 3, 4 and 5 correspond to the itemsets $\{f\}$, $\{f, c\}$, $\{f, c, a\}$, $\{f, c, a, m\}$ and $\{f, c, a, m, p\}$ respectively.

The *orderedItems* array is repeated here for convenience as Figure 18.17.

index	orderedItems
0	f
1	c
2	a
3	b
4	m
5	p

Figure 18.17 *orderedItems* array

The process of extracting all the frequent itemsets from the FP-tree is essentially a recursive one which can be represented by a call to a recursively-defined function *findFrequent* that takes four arguments:

- Two arrays representing the tree. Initially these are arrays *nodes* and *startlink*, corresponding to the original FP-tree. For future calls to the function these will be replaced by arrays *nodes2* and *startlink2* corresponding to a conditional FP-tree, as will be explained subsequently.

- Integer variable *lastitem*, which initially is set to the number of elements in the *orderedItems* array (6 in this example).

- A set named *originalItemset*, which is initially empty, i.e. {}.

We will start with an 'original itemset' with no members, i.e. {} and generate all possible one-item itemsets derived from it by adding a new item to its leftmost position in ascending order of the elements of *orderedItems*, i.e. {p}, {m}, {b}, {a}, {c} and {f} in that order[1]. For each of the itemsets that is frequent[2], say {m}, we next examine itemsets with an additional item in the leftmost position, e.g. {b, m}, {a, m} or {c, m} to find any that are frequent. Note that the additional item must be above m in the *orderedItems* array to preserve the conventional ordering of the items in an itemset. If we find a frequent itemset, e.g. {a, m}, we next construct itemsets with a further item in the leftmost position, e.g. {c, a, m}, check whether each one is frequent and so on. The effect is that having found a single-item itemset that is frequent we will go on to find all the frequent itemsets that end in the corresponding item before examining the next single-item itemset.

Constructing new itemsets by adding one new item at a time to the left, maintaining the same order as in the *orderedItems* array, is a very efficient way of proceeding. Having established that say {c, a} is frequent, the only other itemset that needs checking is {f, c, a} as f is the only item above c in *orderedItems*. It may be true (and it is true in this case) that some other itemset such as {c, a, m} is also frequent but that will already have been dealt with at another stage.

Examining itemsets in this order also takes advantage of the downward closure property of itemsets. If we find that an itemset, say {b, m} is infrequent

---

[1] This rather convoluted way of describing the generation of the itemsets {p}, {m}, {b}, {a}, {c} and {f} is for consistency with the description of the generation of two-item, three-item etc. itemsets that follows.

[2] All the single item itemsets must inevitably be frequent, as the items in the initial tree were selected from those in the transaction database on that basis. However this will often not be the case as we go on to use *findFrequent* recursively to analyse reduced versions of the FP-tree.

there is no point in examining any other itemsets with further items added. If any of them, say $\{f, c, b, m\}$ were frequent then by the downward closure property $\{b, m\}$ must be too, but we already know that it is not.

This strategy for generating frequent itemsets can be implemented in function *findFrequent* by a loop for variable *thisrow* through values from *lastitem*-1 down to zero.

- We set variable *nextitem* to *orderedItems[thisrow]* and then set *firstlink* to *startlink[nextitem]*.

- If *firstlink* is null we go on to the next value of *thisrow*.

- Otherwise we set variable *thisItemset* to be an expanded version of *originalItemset* with item *nextitem* as its leftmost item and then call function *condfptree* which takes four arguments: *nodes*, *firstlink*, *thisrow* and *thisItemset*.

- Function *condfptree* first sets variable *lastitem* to the value of *thisrow*. It then checks whether *thisItemset* is frequent. If it is, it goes on to generate a *conditional FP-tree* for that itemset in the form of arrays *nodes2* and *startlink2* and then calls *findFrequent* recursively with the two replacement arrays, together with *lastitem* and *thisItemset*, as arguments.

18.3.1 Itemsets Ending with Item p

Itemset $\{p\}$ – expanded from original itemset $\{\}$
We start by establishing whether itemset $\{p\}$ is frequent. We can determine this from the FP-tree by examining the two linked p nodes (nodes 5 and 11) with support counts 2 and 1 respectively. The total count is 3, which is greater than or equal to the value of *minsupportcount* (i.e. 3 for this example). So **itemset $\{p\}$ is frequent**.

It is straightforward to find the chain of p nodes from arrays *nodes* and *startlink* in the FP-tree (Figure 18.16). The value of *startlink[p]* is 5, the value in the *linkto* column of row 5 of the *nodes* array is 11 and the value in the *linkto* column of row 11 of the *nodes* array is null, indicating 'no further nodes'. Thus there is a chain of p nodes from node 5 to node 11.

Generating a conditional FP-tree for itemset $\{p\}$

Rather than going on, at this stage, to examine the frequency of other single-item itemsets $\{m\}$, $\{b\}$, $\{a\}$, $\{c\}$ and $\{f\}$, the algorithm first generates a sequence of two-item itemsets by extending the itemset $\{p\}$ by adding an item in the leftmost position. It does this for all the items that are above p in the *orderedItems* array in turn. Thus the two-item itemsets $\{m, p\}$, $\{b, p\}$, $\{a, p\}$, $\{c, p\}$ and $\{f, p\}$ are examined in turn. If any of them is frequent its conditional FP-tree is constructed and a sequence of three-item itemsets is generated by extending the two-item itemset by adding an item in the leftmost position. The process continues in this fashion until the whole tree structure has been examined. At each stage when the current itemset is expanded by adding an extra item in the leftmost position, only those items in the *orderedItems* array (Figure 18.17) above the one previously in the leftmost position are considered.

We now need to check whether any two-item itemsets formed by adding an additional item to itemset $\{p\}$ are also frequent. To do this we first construct a *conditional FP-tree* for itemset $\{p\}$. This is a reduced version of the original FP-tree that contains only the branches that begin at the root and end at the two nodes labelled p, but with the nodes renumbered and often with different support counts. (It may be helpful to look ahead to Figures 18.20 and 18.21 at this point.)

Initialisation

Diagrammatically we can represent the initial state of the FP-tree by a single unnumbered node, representing the root.

We will represent the evolving tree by the contents of four arrays, all initially empty:

- A two-dimensional array *nodes2*, with a numerical index that will correspond to the numbering of the nodes in the tree. The names given to the columns of this array are the same as those for array *nodes* in Section 18.2.

- A single-dimensional array *oldindex*, which for each node holds the number of the corresponding node in the tree from which the evolving conditional FP-tree is derived (initially the FP-tree shown in Figure 18.15).

- Single-dimensional arrays *startlink2* and *lastlink* indexed by the names of some or all of the itemsets in the *orderedItems* array.

We again work through the chain of linked p nodes, this time adding branches to an evolving conditional FP-tree for itemset $\{p\}$ and values to the four equivalent arrays as we do so.

First Branch

Add the five nodes in the leftmost branch of the FP-tree (Figure 18.15), numbering from the bottom upwards, as a branch leading up to the root, all with the support count of the lowest node (i.e. the one with *itemname p*).

Values corresponding to each node in turn are added to the four arrays, as described in the box below (note that this is not yet a complete description).

Adding a branch that ends in a node with support count *Count*
Version 1

For each node

1. Set variables *thisitem* and *thisparent* to the values of *itemname* and *parent* for the original node, respectively. Add a new row to the *nodes2* array, with the value of *itemname* set to *thisitem*. Set the value of *count* (for all the nodes) to *Count*.

2. Set the value in the *oldindex* array to the number of the node in the tree from which the evolving conditional FP-tree is being derived.

3. Set the values of *startlink2[thisitem]* and *lastlink[thisitem]* to the new row number.

4. If the value of *thisparent* is not zero or null, set the value of *parent* in the *nodes2* array to the number of the following row.

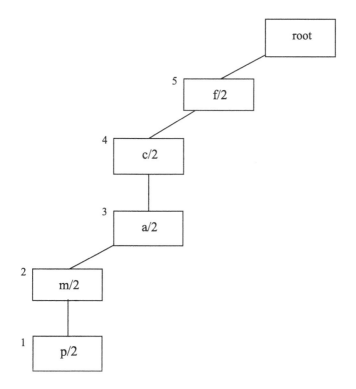

Figure 18.18 Conditional FP-tree for {p} – first branch only

Note that in Figure 18.18 the numbering of the nodes is different from that in Figure 18.15. It reflects the order in which this new tree has been generated, working from bottom (the p node) to top (the root) for each branch. The root node has not been numbered and the other nodes are numbered from 1 onwards.

index	item name	count	linkto	parent	oldindex
1	p	2		2	5
2	m	2		3	4
3	a	2		4	3
4	c	2		5	2
5	f	2			1

nodes2 array   oldindex

index	startlink2	lastlink
p	1	1
m	2	2
a	3	3
c	4	4
f	5	5

link arrays

Figure 18.19 Arrays Corresponding to Conditional FP-tree for $\{p\}$ – first branch only

The values in the *nodes2*, *oldindex*, *startlink2* and *lastlink* arrays corresponding to the first branch are shown in Figure 18.19.

The null value in the *parent* column of node 5 indicates a link to the root node. The use of the *linkto* column in array *nodes2* will be explained when we go on to add the second branch. The use of the array *oldindex* will be explained in Section 18.3.2.

Note that the support counts of the branch in Figure 18.18 are different from those of the corresponding branch in the FP-tree (Figure 18.15). When we constructed the original FP-tree we thought of a node such as node 3 as representing an itemset $\{f, c, a\}$ with support count 3. All the nodes in the branch from node 1 down to node 5 represented itemsets beginning with f, e.g. node 4 represented $\{f, c, a, m\}$. We need to think of a conditional FP-tree in a different way, working from the bottom of each branch to the top. The lowest node (now numbered 1) in Figure 18.18 now represents (part of) itemset $\{p\}$, node 2 represents itemset $\{m, p\}$, nodes 3, 4 and 5 represent itemsets $\{a, m, p\}$, $\{c, a, m, p\}$ and $\{f, c, a, m, p\}$ respectively. In all cases the itemset ends with item p rather than starting with item f. Looking at Figure 18.18 this way, the support counts for the a, c and f nodes cannot be 3, 3 and 4 respectively as they were in the FP-tree. If there are two transactions that include item p there cannot be more than 2 transactions that include items a and p together, or any other such combination.

For this reason the best approach to constructing the conditional FP-tree for $\{p\}$ is to construct the tree bottom-up, branch by branch, using the counts of the p nodes. Each new node entered in the tree 'inherits' the support count of the p node at the bottom of the branch.

<u>Second Branch</u>

We now add the second and final branch that ends in a node with *itemname* p in the FP-tree.

This gives the final version of the conditional FP-tree for itemset $\{p\}$ shown in Figure 18.20.

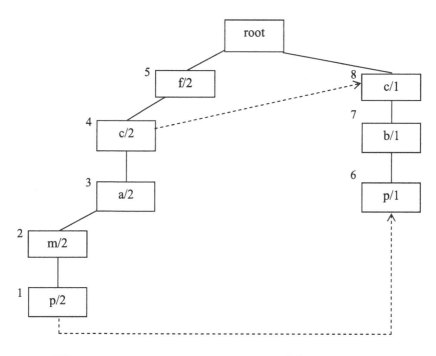

Figure 18.20 Conditional FP-tree for $\{p\}$ – final version

The important difference from adding the first branch is that now the dashed line links have been added for nodes p and c. These are essential for determining whether itemsets are frequent at each stage of the extraction process.

The algorithm for adding additional nodes needs to be augmented to deal with this. For example after node 6 (a second p node) is added, we can tell that there is already a p node in the tree by the non-null value in $lastlink[p]$. The current value of $lastlink[p]$ is 1 so we set both the $linkto$ value for row 1 and the new value of $lastlink[p]$ to the current row number (i.e. 6). This effectively creates a chain of two p nodes from node 1 to node 6. A similar procedure occurs when node 8 (a c node) is added.

A revised version of the algorithm for adding a new branch is given in the box below (but this is still not a complete description).

Adding a branch that ends in a node with support count *Count*
Version 2

For each node

1. Set variables *thisitem* and *thisparent* to the values of *itemname* and *parent* for the original node, respectively. Add a new row to the *nodes2* array, with the value of *itemname* set to *thisitem*. Set the value of *count* (for all the nodes) to *Count*.

2. Set the value in the *oldindex* array to the number of the node in the tree from which the evolving conditional FP-tree is being derived.

3. Set *lastval* to *lastlink[thisitem]*.

   IF *lastval* is not null, set both the *linkto* value in row *lastval* and *lastlink[thisitem]* to the current row number.

   ELSE set the values of *startlink2[thisitem]* and *lastlink[thisitem]* to the current row number.

4. If the value of *thisparent* is not zero or null, set the value of *parent* in the *nodes2* array to the number of the following row.

The values in the *nodes2*, *oldindex*, *startlink2* and *lastlink* arrays corresponding to the final version of the conditional FP-tree for itemset $\{p\}$ are shown in Figure 18.21.

index	item name	count	linkto	parent		oldindex
1	p	2	6	2		5
2	m	2		3		4
3	a	2		4		3
4	c	2	8	5		2
5	f	2				1
6	p	1		7		11
7	b	1		8		10
8	c	1				9

nodes2 array   oldindex

index	startlink2	lastlink
p	1	6
m	2	2
a	3	3
c	4	8
f	5	5
b	7	7

link arrays

Figure 18.21 Arrays Corresponding to Conditional FP-tree for $\{p\}$ – final version

The null values in the *parent* column of nodes 5 and 8 indicate links to the root node. The non-null values in the *linkto* column of array *nodes2* correspond to 'dashed line' links between nodes across the tree.

Two-item Itemsets

Having constructed the conditional FP-tree for itemset $\{p\}$, there are five two-item itemsets to examine, starting with $\{m, p\}$. In each case we do it by extracting the part of the tree that contains only the branches that begin at the root and end at each of the nodes labelled m (or similarly for each of the other items b, a, c, and f in turn). Note that the nodes in the conditional FP-tree are numbered sequentially from 1 (in the order they are generated) each time.

To implement the creation and examination of the two-item itemsets expanded from $\{p\}$ we make a recursive call from function *condfptree* to function *findFrequent* with four arguments: *nodes2*, *startlink2*, *lastitem* and *thisItemset*. The last of these has the value $\{p\}$.

A sequence of itemsets with two items is now generated from the conditional FP-tree for itemset $\{p\}$ by making a loop through the *orderedItems* array from row *lastitem*-1 to row zero. As *lastitem* is now 5, this means that the items used as a new leftmost item for the expanded itemsets are m, b, a, c and f in that order (but not p).

Itemsets $\{m, p\}$, $\{b, p\}$, $\{a, p\}$ and $\{c, p\}$ – expanded from original itemset $\{p\}$

{m, p}: There is only one m node, which has a count of 2. So $\{m, p\}$ is infrequent (Figure 18.22).

{b, p}: There is only one b node, which has a count of 1. So $\{b, p\}$ is infrequent (Figure 18.23).

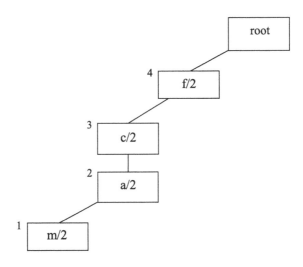

Figure 18.22   Conditional FP-tree for $\{m, p\}$

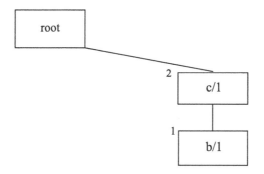

Figure 18.23 Conditional FP-tree for $\{b, p\}$

{a, p}: There is only one a node, which has a count of 2. So $\{a, p\}$ is infrequent (Figure 18.24).

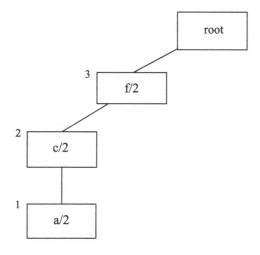

Figure 18.24 Conditional FP-tree for $\{a, p\}$

{c, p}: There are two c nodes, with a total count of 3. So $\{c, p\}$ **is frequent** (Figure 18.25).

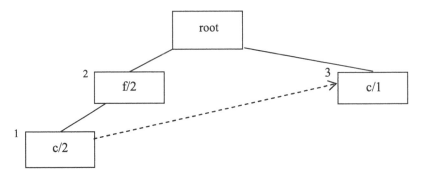

Figure 18.25 Conditional FP-tree for $\{c, p\}$

Before going on to examine $\{f, p\}$ we now generate all **three-item itemsets** formed by adding an additional item to the leftmost position of $\{c, p\}$. We only consider those items above c in the *orderedItems* array. There is only one, i.e. f. So we start by generating the conditional FP-tree for $\{f, c, p\}$.

> We implement this by making a recursive call from function *condfptree* to function *findFrequent* with four arguments: the arrays *nodes2* and *startlink2* that correspond to Figure 18.25, *lastitem* (which is now 1) and *thisItemset*, which is now $\{c, p\}$.

Itemset $\{f, c, p\}$ – expanded from original itemset $\{c, p\}$
There is only one f node, which has a count of 2 (Figure 18.26). So $\{f, c, p\}$ is infrequent. We go back to examining the two-item itemsets, the next of which is $\{f, p\}$.

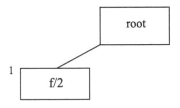

Figure 18.26 *Conditional FP-tree for $\{f, c, p\}$*

Itemset $\{f, p\}$ – expanded from original itemset $\{p\}$
There is only one f node, which has a count of 2. So $\{f, p\}$ is infrequent (Figure 18.27).

We have found two frequent itemsets ending with item p: $\{p\}$ and $\{c, p\}$. There cannot be any other frequent itemsets ending with p. For example if $\{f, c, b, p\}$ were frequent then by the downward closure property all its non-empty subsets would be frequent too. That would include itemset $\{b, p\}$, which we

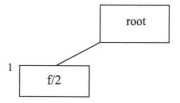

Figure 18.27 *Conditional FP-tree* for $\{f, p\}$

already know is infrequent. There are 32 possible itemsets with p as the right-most item and in descending order of the items in the *orderedItems* array. We have only needed to examine seven of them (two frequent and five infrequent).

For space reasons we will not examine all the other single-item itemsets and those constructed by expanding them by adding additional items in the leftmost position. However we will examine itemset $\{m\}$ and its derivatives as this will illustrate some important additional points.

18.3.2 Itemsets Ending with Item m

Itemset $\{m\}$ – expanded from original itemset $\{\}$
The conditional FP-tree for $\{m\}$ is shown as Figure 18.28.

Note that nodes 2, 3 and 4 inherit a support count of 2 from node 1 and a support count of 1 from node 5. For that reason their (total) support counts are shown as 3.

There are two m nodes, with a total count of 3. So $\{m\}$ **is frequent**.

In constructing the tree bottom-up it is important to distinguish between the case that applies here, where the *parent* of node 6 is an a node (node 2) that has already been entered in the tree and the case where the parent is a different a node, not yet in the tree, which needs to be created.

Figure 18.29 shows the state of the four arrays as node 6 in Figure 18.28 is about to be added to the tree.

The first part of the processing is the same as for all other nodes. The new node is part of a branch that ends in a m node with support count 1. As it happens, the node was also numbered 6 in the original FP-tree, so variables *thisitem* and *thisparent* are taken from row 6 of the *nodes* array and set to b and 3 respectively. A new row, row 6, is added to *nodes2* with the values of *itemname* and *parent* set to b and 3 respectively. The value of element 6 in *oldindex* is set to 6. Next *lastval* is set to *lastlink[b]* which is null, so both *startlink2[b]* and *lastlink[b]* are set to 6.

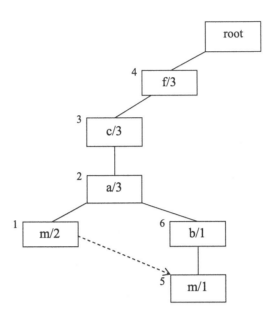

Figure 18.28 Conditional FP-tree for itemset $\{m\}$

index	item name	count	linkto	parent		oldindex
1	m	2	5	2		4
2	a	2		3		3
3	c	2		4		2
4	f	2				1
5	m	1				7

nodes2 array   oldindex

index	startlink2	lastlink
m	1	5
a	2	2
c	3	3
f	4	4

link arrays

Figure 18.29 Arrays corresponding to Conditional FP-tree for itemset $\{m\}$ – first five nodes only

It is at the final stage that the processing of this node differs from the algorithm used up to now. We check whether the value of *thisparent* (i.e. 3) is already in the *oldindex* array. Unlike for all the examples shown previously, it is there in position 2, implying that the *b* node has a parent, node 2, which is already present in the evolving tree structure. This in turn implies that the new node 6 needs to be linked to the part of the tree structure that has already been created. There are three stages to this.

– The value of *parent* in row 6 of *nodes2* is set to 2.

– The adding of additional nodes for the current branch is aborted.

– The chain of parent nodes in the *nodes2* array is followed from row 2, up to immediately before the root, i.e. from 2 to 3 to 4, with the support count being increased by the support count of the node at the bottom of the branch (i.e. by 1) at each stage.

This concludes the construction of the arrays corresponding to the conditional FP-tree for itemset {*m*}, giving Figure 18.30.

index	item name	count	linkto	parent	oldindex
1	m	2	5	2	4
2	a	3		3	3
3	c	3		4	2
4	f	3			1
5	m	1		6	7
6	b	1		2	6

nodes2 array   oldindex

index	startlink2	lastlink
m	1	5
a	2	2
c	3	3
f	4	4
b	6	6

link arrays

Figure 18.30 Arrays corresponding to Conditional FP-tree for itemset {*m*} – all nodes

This leads to a revised and final version of the algorithm for adding a branch.

Adding a branch that ends in a node with support count *Count*

Final version

For each node

1. Set variables *thisitem* and *thisparent* to the values of *itemname* and *parent* for the original node, respectively. Add a new row to the *nodes2* array, with the value of *itemname* set to *thisitem*. Set the value of *count* (for all the nodes) to *Count*.

2. Set the value in the *oldindex* array to the number of the node in the tree from which the evolving conditional FP-tree is being derived.

3. Set *lastval* to *lastlink[thisitem]*.

   IF *lastval* is not null, set both the *linkto* value in row *lastval* and *lastlink[thisitem]* to the current row number.

   ELSE set the values of *startlink2[thisitem]* and *lastlink[thisitem]* to the current row number.

4. If the value of *thisparent* is not zero or null, test whether the value of *thisparent* is already in array *oldindex* at position *pos*.

   If it is {

   (a) Set the value of *parent* for the current row of *nodes2* to *pos*.

   (b) Abort the adding of additional nodes for the current branch.

   (c) Follow the chain of parent nodes in the *nodes2* array from row *pos* up to immediately before the root, increasing the support count by *Count* for each one.

   }

   Otherwise set the value of *parent* for the current row of *nodes2* to the number of the following row.

Having done this the algorithm now goes on to consider the four possible two-item itemsets $\{b, m\}$, $\{a, m\}$, $\{c, m\}$ and $\{f, m\}$ in turn (only items above m in the *orderedItems* array need to be considered for the leftmost position). The relevant conditional FP-trees in the order in which they are constructed are as follows.

Itemsets $\{b, m\}$ and $\{a, m\}$ – expanded from original itemset $\{m\}$

$\{b, m\}$: There is only one b node, which has a count of 1. So $\{b, m\}$ is infrequent. Note that the count of 1 has been inherited from node 1 by nodes 2, 3 and 4 (Figure 18.31).

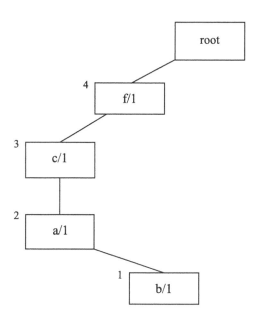

Figure 18.31 Conditional FP-tree for itemset $\{b, m\}$

{a, m}: There is only one a node, which has a count of 3. So **{a, m}** is **frequent** (Figure 18.32).

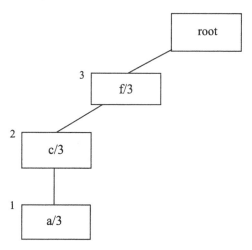

Figure 18.32 Conditional FP-tree for itemset $\{a, m\}$

We now examine all the three-item itemsets constructed by expanding $\{a, m\}$ by adding an item in the leftmost position. Only items above a in the *orderedItems* array need to be considered, i.e. c then f.

Itemset $\{c, a, m\}$ – expanded from original itemset $\{a, m\}$

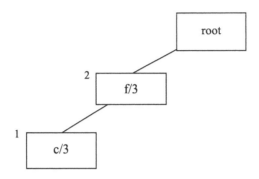

Figure 18.33   Conditional FP-tree for itemset $\{c, a, m\}$

There is only one c node, which has a count of 3 (Figure 18.33). So $\{c, a, m\}$ **is frequent**.

We now examine all the four-item itemsets constructed by expanding $\{c, a, m\}$ by adding an item in the leftmost position. Only items above c in the *orderedItems* array need to be considered, i.e. f.

Itemset $\{f, c, a, m\}$ – expanded from original itemset $\{c, a, m\}$

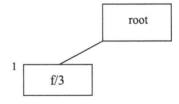

Figure 18.34   Conditional FP-tree for itemset $\{f, c, a, m\}$

There is only one f node, which has a count of 3 (Figure 18.34). So $\{f, c, a, m\}$ **is frequent**.

As there is no item above f in *orderedItems* and there are no other four-item itemsets expanded from $\{c, a, m\}$ to be considered, the examination of itemsets expanded from $\{c, a, m\}$ is concluded.

This can be implemented by adding a test to function *condfptree* so that having established that an itemset is frequent the function only goes on to generate the conditional FP-tree etc. if the value of *lastitem* is greater than zero.

Itemset $\{f, a, m\}$ – expanded from original itemset $\{a, m\}$

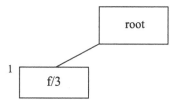

Figure 18.35 Conditional FP-tree for itemset $\{f, a, m\}$

There is only one c node, which has a count of 3 (Figure 18.35). So $\{f,\ a,\ m\}$ **is frequent**.

As there is no item above f in *orderedItems* the examination of itemsets with three items that are expanded versions of $\{a, m\}$ is concluded.

Itemset $\{c, m\}$ – expanded from original itemset $\{m\}$

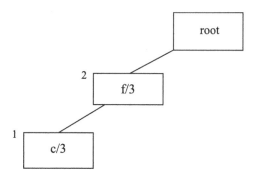

Figure 18.36 Conditional FP-tree for itemset $\{c, m\}$

There is only one c node, which has a count of 3 (Figure 18.36). So $\{c, m\}$ **is frequent**.

We now examine all the three-item itemsets constructed by expanding $\{c, m\}$ by adding an item in the leftmost position. Only items above c in the *orderedItems* array need to be considered, i.e. f.

Itemset $\{f, c, m\}$ – expanded from original itemset $\{c, m\}$

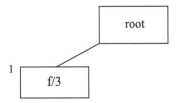

Figure 18.37 Conditional FP-tree for itemset $\{f, c, m\}$

There is only one f node, which has a count of 3 (Figure 18.37). So $\{f, c, m\}$ is frequent.

As there is no item above f in *orderedItems* the examination of itemsets with three items that are expanded versions of $\{c, m\}$ is concluded.

Itemset $\{f, m\}$ – expanded from original itemset $\{m\}$

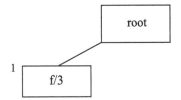

Figure 18.38 *Conditional FP-tree for itemset $\{f, m\}$*

There is only one f node, which has a count of 3 (Figure 18.38). So $\{f, m\}$ is frequent.

As there is no item above f in *orderedItems* and there are no more two-item itemsets to be considered, the examination of itemsets with final item m is concluded.

This time we have found 8 frequent itemsets ending with item m (there cannot be any others) and have examined only one infrequent itemset. There are 16 possible itemsets with m as the rightmost item that are in descending order of the items in the *orderedItems* array. We have only needed to examine a total of nine of them.

18.4 Chapter Summary

This chapter introduces the *FP-growth* algorithm for extracting frequent itemsets from a database of transactions. First the database is processed to produce a data structure called a *FP-tree*, then the tree is processed recursively by constructing a sequence of reduced trees known as *conditional FP-trees*, from which the frequent itemsets are extracted. The algorithm has the very desirable feature of requiring only two scans through the database.

18.5 Self-assessment Exercises for Chapter 18

1. Draw the conditional FP-tree for itemset $\{c\}$.

2. How can the support count for $\{c\}$ be determined from the conditional FP-tree? What is it?

3. Is itemset $\{c\}$ frequent?

4. What are the contents of the four arrays corresponding to the conditional FP-tree for itemset $\{c\}$?

Reference

[1] Han, J., Pei, J., & Yin, Y. (2000). Mining frequent patterns without candidate generation. *SIGMOD Record*, 29(2), 1–12. Proceedings of the 2000 ACM SIGMOD international conference on management of data, ACM Press.

19
Clustering

19.1 Introduction

In this chapter we continue with the theme of extracting information from unlabelled data and turn to the important topic of *clustering*. Clustering is concerned with grouping together objects that are similar to each other and dissimilar to the objects belonging to other clusters.

In many fields there are obvious benefits to be had from grouping together similar objects. For example

– In an economics application we might be interested in finding countries whose economies are similar.

– In a financial application we might wish to find clusters of companies that have similar financial performance.

– In a marketing application we might wish to find clusters of customers with similar buying behaviour.

– In a medical application we might wish to find clusters of patients with similar symptoms.

– In a document retrieval application we might wish to find clusters of documents with related content.

– In a crime analysis application we might look for clusters of high volume crimes such as burglaries or try to cluster together much rarer (but possibly related) crimes such as murders.

© Springer-Verlag London Ltd., part of Springer Nature 2020
M. Bramer, *Principles of Data Mining*, Undergraduate Topics
in Computer Science, DOI 10.1007/978-1-4471-7493-6_19

There are many algorithms for clustering. We will describe two methods for which the similarity between objects is based on a measure of the distance between them.

In the restricted case where each object is described by the values of just two attributes, we can represent them as points in a two-dimensional space (a plane) such as Figure 19.1.

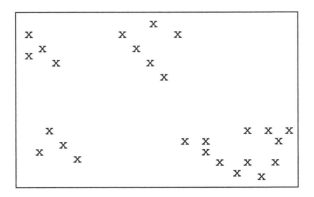

Figure 19.1   Objects for Clustering

It is usually easy to visualise clusters in two dimensions. The points in Figure 19.1 seem to fall naturally into four groups as shown by the curves drawn surrounding sets of points in Figure 19.2.

However there is frequently more than one possibility. For example are the points in the lower-right corner of Figure 19.1 one cluster (as shown in Figure 19.2) or two (as shown in Figure 19.3)?

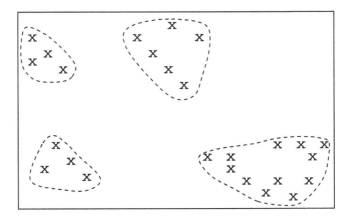

Figure 19.2   Clustering of Objects in Figure 19.1(first version)

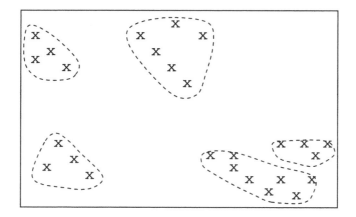

Figure 19.3 Clustering of Objects in Figure 19.1(second version)

In the case of three attributes we can think of the objects as being points in a three-dimensional space (such as a room) and visualising clusters is generally straightforward too. For larger dimensions (i.e. larger numbers of attributes) it soon becomes impossible to visualise the points, far less the clusters.

The diagrams in this chapter will use only two dimensions, although in practice the number of attributes will usually be more than two and can often be large.

Before using a *distance-based clustering algorithm* to cluster objects, it is first necessary to decide on a way of measuring the distance between two points. As for nearest neighbour classification, discussed in Chapter 3, a measure commonly used when clustering is the Euclidean distance. To avoid complications we will assume that all attribute values are continuous. (Attributes that are categorical can be dealt with as described in Chapter 3.)

We next need to introduce the notion of the 'centre' of a cluster, generally called its *centroid*.

Assuming that we are using Euclidean distance or something similar as a measure we can define the centroid of a cluster to be the point for which each attribute value is the average of the values of the corresponding attribute for all the points in the cluster.

So the centroid of the four points (with 6 attributes)

8.0	7.2	0.3	23.1	11.1	−6.1
2.0	−3.4	0.8	24.2	18.3	−5.2
−3.5	8.1	0.9	20.6	10.2	−7.3
−6.0	6.7	0.5	12.5	9.2	−8.4

would be

| 0.125 | 4.65 | 0.625 | 20.1 | 12.2 | −6.75 |

The centroid of a cluster will sometimes be one of the points in the cluster, but frequently, as in the above example, it will be an 'imaginary' point, not part of the cluster itself, which we can take as marking its centre. The value of the idea of the centroid of a cluster will be illustrated in what follows.

There are many methods of clustering. In this book we will look at two of the most commonly used: *k-means clustering* and *hierarchical clustering*.

19.2 *k*-Means Clustering

k-means clustering is an *exclusive clustering algorithm*. Each object is assigned to precisely one of a set of clusters. (There are other methods that allow objects to be in more than one cluster.)

For this method of clustering we start by deciding how many clusters we would like to form from our data. We call this value k. The value of k is generally a small integer, such as 2, 3, 4 or 5, but may be larger. We will come back later to the question of how we decide what the value of k should be.

There are many ways in which k clusters might potentially be formed. We can measure the quality of a set of clusters using the value of an *objective function* which we will take to be the sum of the squares of the distances of each point from the centroid of the cluster to which it is assigned. We would like the value of this function to be as small as possible.

We next select k points (generally corresponding to the location of k of the objects). These are treated as the centroids of k clusters, or to be more precise as the centroids of k potential clusters, which at present have no members. We can select these points in any way we wish, but the method may work better if we pick k initial points that are fairly far apart.

We now assign each of the points one by one to the cluster which has the nearest centroid.

When all the objects have been assigned we will have k clusters based on the original k centroids but the 'centroids' will no longer be the true centroids of the clusters. Next we recalculate the centroids of the clusters, and then repeat the previous steps, assigning each object to the cluster with the nearest centroid etc. The entire algorithm is summarised in Figure 19.4.

1. Choose a value of k.

2. Select k objects in an arbitrary fashion. Use these as the initial set of k centroids.

3. Assign each of the objects to the cluster for which it is nearest to the centroid.

4. Recalculate the centroids of the k clusters.

5. Repeat steps 3 and 4 until the centroids no longer move.

Figure 19.4 The k-Means Clustering Algorithm

19.2.1 Example

We will illustrate the k-means algorithm by using it to cluster the 16 objects with two attributes x and y that are listed in Figure 19.5.

x	y
6.8	12.6
0.8	9.8
1.2	11.6
2.8	9.6
3.8	9.9
4.4	6.5
4.8	1.1
6.0	19.9
6.2	18.5
7.6	17.4
7.8	12.2
6.6	7.7
8.2	4.5
8.4	6.9
9.0	3.4
9.6	11.1

Figure 19.5 Objects for Clustering (Attribute Values)

The 16 points corresponding to these objects are shown diagrammatically in Figure 19.6. The horizontal and vertical axes correspond to attributes x and y, respectively.

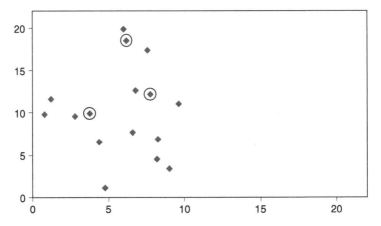

Figure 19.6   Objects for Clustering

Three of the points shown in Figure 19.6 have been surrounded by small circles. We will assume that we have chosen $k = 3$ and that these three points have been selected to be the locations of the initial three centroids. This initial (fairly arbitrary) choice is shown in Figure 19.7.

	Initial	
	x	y
Centroid 1	3.8	9.9
Centroid 2	7.8	12.2
Centroid 3	6.2	18.5

Figure 19.7   Initial Choice of Centroids

The columns headed $d1$, $d2$ and $d3$ in Figure 19.8 show the Euclidean distance of each of the 16 points from the three centroids. For the purposes of this example, we will not normalise or weight either of the attributes, so the distance of the first point $(6.8, 12.6)$ from the first centroid $(3.8, 9.9)$ is simply

$$\sqrt{(6.8 - 3.8)^2 + (12.6 - 9.9)^2} = 4.0 \text{ (to one decimal place)}$$

The column headed 'cluster' indicates the centroid closest to each point and thus the cluster to which it should be assigned.

The resulting clusters are shown in Figure 19.9 below.

The centroids are indicated by small circles. For this first iteration they are also actual points within the clusters. The centroids are those that were used to construct the three clusters but are not the true centroids of the clusters once they have been created.

x	y	$d1$	$d2$	$d3$	cluster
6.8	12.6	4.0	1.1	5.9	2
0.8	9.8	3.0	7.4	10.2	1
1.2	11.6	3.1	6.6	8.5	1
2.8	9.6	1.0	5.6	9.5	1
3.8	9.9	0.0	4.6	8.9	1
4.4	6.5	3.5	6.6	12.1	1
4.8	1.1	8.9	11.5	17.5	1
6.0	19.9	10.2	7.9	1.4	3
6.2	18.5	8.9	6.5	0.0	3
7.6	17.4	8.4	5.2	1.8	3
7.8	12.2	4.6	0.0	6.5	2
6.6	7.7	3.6	4.7	10.8	1
8.2	4.5	7.0	7.7	14.1	1
8.4	6.9	5.5	5.3	11.8	2
9.0	3.4	8.3	8.9	15.4	1
9.6	11.1	5.9	2.1	8.1	2

Figure 19.8 Objects for Clustering (Augmented)

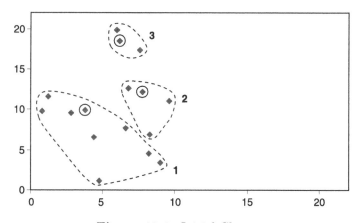

Figure 19.9 Initial Clusters

We next calculate the centroids of the three clusters using the x and y values of the objects currently assigned to each one. The results are shown in Figure 19.10.

The three centroids have all been moved by the assignment process, but the movement of the third one is appreciably less than for the other two.

	Initial		After first iteration	
	x	y	x	y
Centroid 1	3.8	9.9	4.6	7.1
Centroid 2	7.8	12.2	8.2	10.7
Centroid 3	6.2	18.5	6.6	18.6

Figure 19.10 Centroids After First Iteration

We next reassign the 16 objects to the three clusters by determining which centroid is closest to each one. This gives the revised set of clusters shown in Figure 19.11.

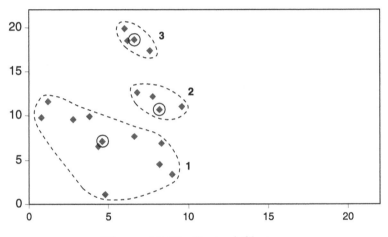

Figure 19.11 Revised Clusters

The centroids are again indicated by small circles. However from now on the centroids are 'imaginary points' corresponding to the 'centre' of each cluster, not actual points within the clusters.

These clusters are very similar to the previous three, shown in Figure 19.9. In fact only one point has moved. The object at $(8.3, 6.9)$ has moved from cluster 2 to cluster 1.

We next recalculate the positions of the three centroids, giving Figure 19.12.

The first two centroids have moved a little, but the third has not moved at all.

We assign the 16 objects to clusters once again, giving Figure 19.13.

These are the same clusters as before. Their centroids will be the same as those from which the clusters were generated. Hence the termination condition of the k-means algorithm 'repeat ... until the centroids no longer move' has

	Initial		After first iteration		After second iteration	
	x	y	x	y	x	y
Centroid 1	3.8	9.9	4.6	7.1	5.0	7.1
Centroid 2	7.8	12.2	8.2	10.7	8.1	12.0
Centroid 3	6.2	18.5	6.6	18.6	6.6	18.6

Figure 19.12 Centroids After First Two Iterations

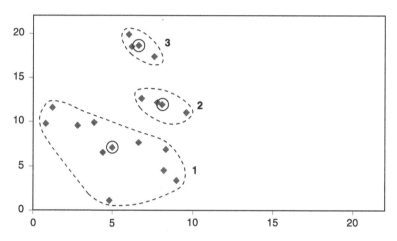

Figure 19.13 Third Set of Clusters

been met and these are the final clusters produced by the algorithm for the initial choice of centroids made.

19.2.2 Finding the Best Set of Clusters

It can be proved that the k-means algorithm will always terminate, but it does not necessarily find the best set of clusters, corresponding to minimising the value of the objective function. The initial selection of centroids can significantly affect the result. To overcome this, the algorithm can be run several times for a given value of k, each time with a different choice of the initial k centroids, the set of clusters with the smallest value of the objective function then being taken.

The most obvious drawback of this method of clustering is that there is no principled way to know what the value of k ought to be. Looking at the final set of clusters in the above example (Figure 19.13), it is not clear that $k = 3$ is the most appropriate choice. Cluster 1 might well be broken into several separate clusters. We can choose a value of k pragmatically as follows.

If we imagine choosing $k = 1$, i.e. all the objects are in a single cluster, with the initial centroid selected in a random way (a very poor idea), the value of the objective function is likely to be large. We can then try $k = 2$, $k = 3$ and $k = 4$, each time experimenting with a different choice of the initial centroids and choosing the set of clusters with the smallest value. Figure 19.14 shows the (imaginary) results of such a series of experiments.

Value of k	Value of objective function
1	62.8
2	12.3
3	9.4
4	9.3
5	9.2
6	9.1
7	9.05

Figure 19.14   Value of Objective Function for Different Values of k

These results suggest that the best value of k is probably 3. The value of the function for $k = 3$ is much less than for $k = 2$, but only a little better than for $k = 4$. It is possible that the value of the objective function drops sharply after $k = 7$, but even if it does $k = 3$ is probably still the best choice. We normally prefer to find a fairly small number of clusters as far as possible.

Note that we are *not* trying to find the value of k with the smallest value of the objective function. That will occur when the value of k is the same as the number of objects, i.e. each object forms its own cluster of one. The objective function will then be zero, but the clusters will be worthless. This is another example of the *overfitting* of data discussed in Chapter 9. We usually want a fairly small number of clusters and accept that the objects in a cluster will be spread around the centroid (but ideally not too far away).

19.3 Agglomerative Hierarchical Clustering

Another very popular clustering technique is called *Agglomerative Hierarchical Clustering*.

As for k-means clustering we need to choose a way of measuring the distance between two objects. Also as for that method a commonly used distance measure is Euclidean distance (defined in Chapter 3). In two dimensions Euclidean distance is just the 'straight line' distance between two points.

The idea behind Agglomerative Hierarchical Clustering is a simple one. We start with each object in a cluster of its own and then repeatedly merge the closest pair of clusters until we end up with just one cluster containing everything. The basic algorithm is given in Figure 19.15.

---

1. Assign each object to its own single-object cluster. Calculate the distance between each pair of clusters.

2. Choose the closest pair of clusters and merge them into a single cluster (so reducing the total number of clusters by one).

3. Calculate the distance between the new cluster and each of the old clusters.

4. Repeat steps 2 and 3 until all the objects are in a single cluster.

Figure 19.15   Agglomerative Hierarchical Clustering: Basic Algorithm

If there are N objects there will be $N - 1$ mergers of two objects needed at Step 2 to produce a single cluster. However the method does not only produce a single large cluster, it gives a *hierarchy* of clusters as we shall see.

Suppose we start with eleven objects A, B, C, ..., K located as shown in Figure 19.16 and we merge clusters on the basis of Euclidean distance.

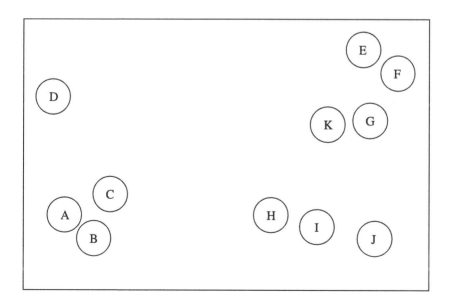

Figure 19.16   Original Data (11 Objects)

It will take 10 'passes' through the algorithm, i.e. repetitions of Steps 2 and 3, to merge the initial 11 single object clusters into a single cluster. Let us assume the process starts by choosing objects A and B as the pair that are closest and merging them into a new cluster which we will call AB. The next step may be to choose clusters AB and C as the closest pair and to merge them. After two passes the clusters then look as shown in Figure 19.17.

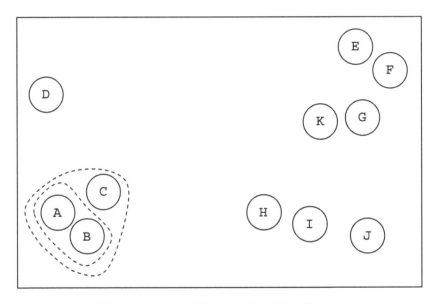

Figure 19.17 Clusters After Two Passes

We will use notation such as A and B → AB to mean 'clusters A and B are merged to form a new cluster, which we will call AB'.

Without knowing the precise distances between each pair of objects, a plausible sequence of events is as follows.

1. A and B → AB
2. AB and C → ABC
3. G and K → GK
4. E and F → EF
5. H and I → HI
6. EF and GK → EFGK
7. HI and J → HIJ
8. ABC and D → ABCD
9. EFGK and HIJ → EFGKHIJ
10. ABCD and EFGKHIJ → ABCDEFGKHIJ

The final result of this hierarchical clustering process is shown in Figure 19.18, which is called a *dendrogram*. A dendrogram is a binary tree (two branches at each node). However, the positioning of the clusters does not correspond to their physical location in the original diagram. All the original objects are placed at the same level (the bottom of the diagram), as leaf nodes. The root of the tree is shown at the top of the diagram. It is a cluster containing all the objects. The other nodes show smaller clusters that were generated as the process proceeded.

If we call the bottom row of the diagram level 1 (with clusters A, B, C, ..., K), we can say that the level 2 clusters are AB, HI, EF and GK, the level 3 clusters are ABC, HIJ and EFGK, and so on. The root node is at level 5.

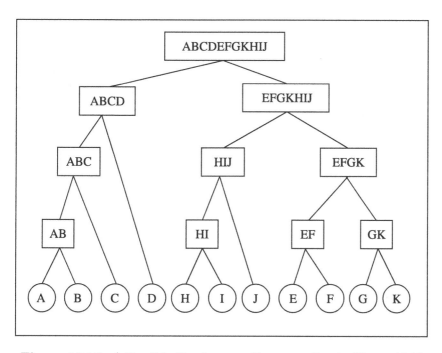

Figure 19.18   A Possible Dendrogram Corresponding to Figure 19.16

19.3.1 Recording the Distance Between Clusters

It would be very inefficient to calculate the distance between each pair of clusters for each pass through the algorithm, especially as the distance between those clusters not involved in the most recent merger cannot have changed.

The usual approach is to generate and maintain a *distance matrix* giving the distance between each pair of clusters.

If we have six objects a, b, c, d, e and f, the initial distance matrix might look like Figure 19.19.

	a	b	c	d	e	f
a	0	12	6	3	25	4
b	12	0	19	8	14	15
c	6	19	0	12	5	18
d	3	8	12	0	11	9
e	25	14	5	11	0	7
f	4	15	18	9	7	0

Figure 19.19 Example of a Distance Matrix

Note that the table is symmetric, so not all values have to be calculated (the distance from c to f is the same as the distance from f to c etc.). The values on the diagonal from the top-left corner to the bottom-right corner must always be zero (the distance from a to a is zero etc.).

From the distance matrix of Figure 19.19 we can see that the closest pair of clusters (single objects) are a and d, with a distance value of 3. We combine these into a single cluster of two objects which we will call ad. We can now rewrite the distance matrix with rows a and d replaced by a single row ad and similarly for the columns (Figure 19.20).

The entries in the matrix for the various distances between b, c, e and f obviously remain the same, but how should we calculate the entries in row and column ad?

	ad	b	c	e	f
ad	0	?	?	?	?
b	?	0	19	14	15
c	?	19	0	5	18
e	?	14	5	0	7
f	?	15	18	7	0

Figure 19.20 Distance Matrix After First Merger (Incomplete)

We could calculate the position of the centroid of cluster ad and use that to measure the distance of cluster ad from clusters b, c, e and f. However for hierarchical clustering a different approach, which involves less calculation, is generally used.

In *single-link clustering* the distance between two clusters is taken to be the shortest distance from any member of one cluster to any member of the other cluster. On this basis the distance from ad to b is 8, the shorter of the distance from a to b (12) and the distance from d to b (8) in the original distance matrix.

Two alternatives to *single-link clustering* are *complete-link clustering* and *average-link clustering*, where the distance between two clusters is taken to be the longest distance from any member of one cluster to any member of the other cluster, or the average such distance respectively.

Returning to the example and assuming that we are using single-link clustering, the position after the first merger is given in Figure 19.21.

	ad	b	c	e	f
ad	0	8	6	11	4
b	8	0	19	14	15
c	6	19	0	5	18
e	11	14	5	0	7
f	4	15	18	7	0

Figure 19.21 Distance Matrix After First Merger

The smallest (non-zero) value in the table is now 4, which is the distance between cluster ad and cluster f, so we next merge these clusters to form a three-object cluster adf. The distance matrix, using the single-link method of calculation, now becomes Figure 19.22.

	adf	b	c	e
adf	0	8	6	7
b	8	0	19	14
c	6	19	0	5
e	7	14	5	0

Figure 19.22 Distance Matrix After Two Mergers

The smallest non-zero is now 5, the distance from cluster c to cluster e. These clusters are now merged into a single new cluster ce and the distance matrix is changed to Figure 19.23.

Clusters adf and ce are now the closest, with distance 6 so we merge them into a single cluster adfce. The distance matrix becomes Figure 19.24.

At the final stage clusters $adfce$ and b are merged into a single cluster $adfceb$ which contains all the original six objects. The dendrogram corresponding to this clustering process is shown in Figure 19.25.

	adf	*b*	*ce*
adf	0	8	6
b	8	0	14
ce	6	14	0

Figure 19.23 Distance Matrix After Three Mergers

	adfce	*b*
adfce	0	8
b	8	0

Figure 19.24 Distance Matrix After Four Mergers

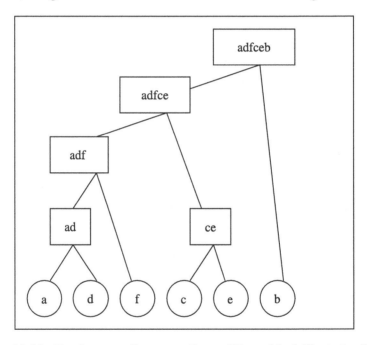

Figure 19.25 Dendrogram Corresponding to Hierarchical Clustering Process

19.3.2 Terminating the Clustering Process

Often we are content to allow the clustering algorithm to produce a complete cluster hierarchy. However we may prefer to end the merger process when we have converted the original N objects to a 'small enough' set of clusters.

We can do this in several ways. For example we can merge clusters until only some pre-defined number remain. Alternatively we can stop merging when a newly created cluster fails to meet some criterion for its compactness, e.g. the average distance between the objects in the cluster is too high.

19.4 Chapter Summary

This chapter continues with the theme of extracting information from unlabelled data. Clustering is concerned with grouping together objects that are similar to each other and dissimilar to objects belonging to other clusters.

There are many methods of clustering. Two of the most widely used, *k-means clustering* and *hierarchical clustering* are described in detail.

19.5 Self-assessment Exercises for Chapter 19

1. Using the method shown in Section 19.2, cluster the following data into three clusters, using the k-means method.

x	y
10.9	12.6
2.3	8.4
8.4	12.6
12.1	16.2
7.3	8.9
23.4	11.3
19.7	18.5
17.1	17.2
3.2	3.4
1.3	22.8
2.4	6.9
2.4	7.1
3.1	8.3
2.9	6.9
11.2	4.4
8.3	8.7

2. For the example given in Section 19.3.1, what would be the distance matrix after each of the first three mergers if complete-link clustering were used instead of single-link clustering?

20
Text Mining

In this chapter we look at a particular type of classification task, where the objects are text documents such as articles in newspapers, scientific papers in journals or perhaps abstracts of papers, or even just their titles. The aim is to use a set of pre-classified documents to classify those that have not yet been seen. This is becoming an increasingly important practical problem as the volume of printed material in many fields keeps increasing and even in specialist fields it can be very difficult to locate relevant documents. Much of the terminology used reflects the origins of this work in librarianship and information science, long before data mining techniques became available.

In principle we can use any of the standard methods of classification (Naïve Bayes, Nearest Neighbour, decision trees etc.) for this task, but datasets of text documents have a number of specific features compared with the datasets we have seen so far, which require separate explanation. The special case where the documents are web pages will be covered in Section 20.9.

20.1 Multiple Classifications

An important issue that distinguishes text classification from the other classification tasks discussed in this book is the possibility of multiple classifications. Up to now we have assumed that there is a set of mutually exclusive categories and that each object must inevitably fit into one and only one of these.

© Springer-Verlag London Ltd., part of Springer Nature 2020
M. Bramer, *Principles of Data Mining*, Undergraduate Topics
in Computer Science, DOI 10.1007/978-1-4471-7493-6_20

Text classification is rather different. In general we may have N categories such as Medicine, Business, Finance, Historical, Biographical, Management and Education and it is perfectly possible for a document to fit into several of these categories, possibly even all of them or possibly none.

Rather than broaden the definition of classification used up to now we prefer to think of the text classification task as N separate binary classification tasks, e.g.

– Is the document about medicine? Yes/No

– Is the document about business? Yes/No

– Is the document about finance? Yes/No

and so on. The need to perform N separate classification tasks adds considerably to the time involved for this form of classification, which even for a single classification is usually computationally expensive.

20.2 Representing Text Documents for Data Mining

For 'standard' data mining tasks the data is presented to the data mining system in the standard form described in Chapter 2, or something similar. There are a fixed number of attributes (or features) which were chosen before the data was collected. For text mining the dataset usually comprises the documents themselves and the features are extracted from the documents automatically based on their content before the classification algorithm is applied. There are generally a very large number of features, most of them only occurring rarely, with a high proportion of noisy and irrelevant features.

There are several ways in which the conversion of documents from plain text to instances with a fixed number of attributes in a training set can be carried out. For example we might count the number of times specified phrases occur, or perhaps any combination of two consecutive words, or we might count the occurrence of two or three character combinations (known as *bigrams* and *trigrams* respectively). For the purposes of this chapter we will assume that a simple word-based representation is used, known as a *bag-of-words representation*. With this representation a document is considered to be simply a collection of the words which occur in it at least once. The order of the words, the combinations in which they occur, paragraph structuring, punctuation and of course the meanings of the words are all ignored. A document is just a collection of words placed in some arbitrary order, say alphabetical, together with a count of how many times each one occurs, or some other measure of the importance of each word.

Assuming that we wish to store an 'importance value' for each word in a document as one instance in a training set, how should we do it? If a given document has say 106 different words, we cannot just use a representation with 106 attributes (ignoring classifications). Other documents in the dataset may use other words, probably overlapping with the 106 in the current instance, but not necessarily so. The unseen documents that we wish to classify may have words that are not used in any of the training documents. An obvious — but extremely bad — approach would be to allocate as many attributes as are needed to allow for all possible words that might be used in any possible unseen document. Unfortunately if the language of the documents is English, the number of possible words is approximately one million, which is a hopelessly impractical number of attributes to use.

A much better approach is to restrict the representation to the words that actually occur in the training documents. This can still be many thousands (or more) and we will look at ways of reducing this number in Sections 20.3 and 20.4 below. We place all the words used at least once in a 'dictionary' and allocate one attribute position in each row of our training set for each one. The order in which we do this is arbitrary, so we can think of it as alphabetical.

The bag-of-words representation is inherently a highly redundant one. It is likely that for any particular document most of the attributes/features (i.e. words) will not appear. For example the dictionary used may have 10,000 words, but a specific document may have just 200 different words. If so, its representation as an instance in the training set will have 9,800 out of 10,000 attributes with value zero, indicating no occurrences, i.e. unused.

If there are multiple classifications there are two possibilities for constructing the dictionary of words for a collection of training documents. Whichever one is used the dictionary is likely to be large.

The first is the *local dictionary* approach. We form a different dictionary for each category, using only those words that appear in documents classified as being in that category. This enables each dictionary to be relatively small at the cost of needing to construct N of them, where there are N categories.

The second approach is to construct a *global dictionary*, which includes all the words that occur at least once in any of the documents. This is then used for classification into each of the N categories. Constructing a global dictionary will clearly be a lot faster than constructing N local dictionaries, but at the cost of making an even more redundant representation to use for classifying into each of the categories. There is some evidence to suggest that using a local dictionary approach tends to give better performance than using a global dictionary.

20.3 Stop Words and Stemming

With the bag-of-words approach, it is possible to have tens of thousands of
different words occurring in a fairly small set of documents. Many of them are
not important for the learning task and their usage can substantially degrade
performance. It is imperative to reduce the size of the *feature space* (i.e. the
set of words included in the dictionary) as far as possible. This can be looked
at as a variant of the methods of data preparation and data cleaning described
in Chapter 2.

One widely used approach is to use a list of common words that are likely to
be useless for classification, known as *stop words*, and remove all occurrences
of these words before creating the bag-of-words representation. There is no
definitive list of stop words that is universally used. The list would obviously
vary from language to language, but in English some obvious choices would be
'a', 'an', 'the', 'is', 'I', 'you' and 'of'. Studying the frequency and distribution
of such words might be very useful for stylistic analysis, i.e. deciding which of
a number of possible authors wrote a novel or a play etc., but for classifying a
document into categories such as Medicine, Finance etc. they are clearly useless.
The University of Glasgow has a list of 319 English stop words beginning with
a, about, above, across, after, afterwards and ending with yet, you, your, yours,
yourself, yourselves. Up to a point the longer the list of stop words the better,
the only risk being the possible loss of useful classifying information if the list
becomes excessive.

Another very important way to reduce the number of words in the representation is to use *stemming*.

This is based on the observation that words in documents often have many
morphological variants. For example we may use the words computing, computer, computation, computes, computational, computable and computability
all in the same document. These words clearly have the same linguistic root.
Putting them together as if they were occurrences of a single word would probably give a strong indication of the content of the document whereas each word
individually might not.

The aim of stemming is to recognise sets of words such as 'computing' and
'computation' or 'applied', 'applying', 'applies' and 'apply' that can be treated
as equivalent. There are many *stemming algorithms* that have been developed
to reduce a word to its *stem* or root form, by which it is then replaced. For
example, 'computing' and 'computation' might both be stemmed to 'comput',
and 'applies' etc. to 'appli'.

The use of stemming can be a very effective way of reducing the number
of words in a bag-of-words representation to a relatively manageable number.
However, as for stop words, there is no standard stemming algorithm that is

universally used and an over-zealous stemming algorithm can remove valuable words from consideration. For example the word 'appliqué' in a document may be an important guide to its classification, but might be reduced by stemming to 'appli', the same stem as if it were a much less significant word such as 'applies' (with which it is very unlikely to have any genuine linguistic connection).

20.4 Using Information Gain for Feature Reduction

Even after removing stop words from a document and replacing each remaining word by its stem, the number of words in a bag-of-words representation of a set of documents can be very large.

One way to reduce the number of words for a given category of documents C_k is to construct a training set where each instance comprises the frequency of each word (or some similar measure) together with the value of the classification C_k which must be a binary yes/no value.

The entropy of this training set can be calculated in the same way as in previous chapters. For example, if 10% of the training documents are in category C_k, the entropy is $-0.1 \times \log_2 0.1 - 0.9 \times \log_2 0.9 = 0.47$.

Using a method such as the frequency table technique described in Chapter 6, we can now calculate the information gain as far as classifying a document as belonging to category C_k or otherwise is concerned that would result from knowing the value of each of the attributes in turn. Having done this we might choose to use only the features with the highest (say) 20, 50 or 100 values of information gain when classifying documents by whether or not they belong to category C_k.

20.5 Representing Text Documents: Constructing a Vector Space Model

We shall now assume that we have decided whether to use a local or a global dictionary and have chosen a representation which replaces each document by a number of features. For a bag-of-words representation each feature is a single word, but for a different representation it may be something else, e.g. a phrase. In the following we will assume that each feature is a *term* of some kind.

Once we have determined that the total number of features is N, we can represent the terms in the dictionary in some arbitrary order as $t_1, t_2, \ldots, t_N$.

We can then represent the ith document as an ordered set of N values, which we will call *an N-dimensional vector* and write as $(X_{i1}, X_{i2}, \ldots, X_{iN})$. These values are just the attribute values in the standard training set format used elsewhere in this book, but with the classification(s) omitted. Writing the values as N-dimensional vectors (i.e. as N values separated by commas and enclosed in parentheses) is simply a more conventional way of looking at the data in this branch of data mining. The complete set of vectors for all documents under consideration is called a *vector space model* or *VSM*.

Up to now we have assumed that the values stored for each feature (attribute) are the number of times each term occurs in the corresponding document. However that does not have to be the case. In general we can say that value X_{ij} is a *weight* measuring the importance of the jth term t_j in the ith document.

One common way of calculating the weights is to count the number of occurrences of each term in the given document (known as *term frequency*). Another possibility is to use a binary representation, where 1 indicates the presence and 0 indicates the absence of the term in the document.

A more complex way of calculating the weights is called TFIDF, which stands for Term Frequency Inverse Document Frequency. This combines term frequency with a measure of the rarity of a term in the complete set of documents. It has been reported as leading to improved performance over the other methods.

The TFIDF value of a weight X_{ij} is calculated as the product of two values, which correspond to the term frequency and the inverse document frequency, respectively.

The first value is simply the frequency of the jth term, i.e. t_j, in document i. Using this value tends to make terms that are frequent in the given (single) document more important than others.

We measure the value of inverse document frequency by $\log_2(n/n_j)$ where n_j is the number of documents containing term t_j and n is the total number of documents. Using this value tends to make terms that are rare across the collection of documents more important than others. If a term occurs in every document its inverse document frequency value is 1. If it occurs in only one document out of every 16, its inverse document frequency value is $\log_2 16 = 4$.

20.6 Normalising the Weights

Before using the set of N-dimensional vectors we first need to normalise the values of the weights, for reasons similar to the need to normalise the value of continuous attributes in Chapter 3.

We would like each value to be between 0 and 1 inclusive and for the values used not to be excessively influenced by the overall number of words in the original document.

We will take a much simplified example to illustrate the point. Suppose we have a dictionary with just 6 members and let us assume that the weights used are just the term frequency values. Then a typical vector would be $(0, 3, 0, 4, 0, 0)$. In the corresponding document the second term appeared 3 times, the fourth term occurred 4 times and the other four terms did not occur at all. Overall only 7 terms occurred in the document, after removal of stop words, stemming etc.

Suppose we now create another document by placing an exact duplicate of its content at the end of the first one. What if by some printing aberration there were other documents where the content of the original one was printed 10 times, or even a hundred times?

In these three cases the vectors would be $(0, 6, 0, 8, 0, 0)$, $(0, 30, 0, 40, 0, 0)$ and $(0, 300, 0, 400, 0, 0)$. These seem to have nothing in common with the original vector, which was $(0, 3, 0, 4, 0, 0)$. This is unsatisfactory. The four documents should obviously be classified in exactly the same way and the vector space representation should reflect this.

The method that is generally used to normalise vectors neatly solves this problem. We calculate the *length* of each vector, defined as the square root of the sum of the squares of its component values. To normalise the values of the weights we divide each value by the length. The resulting vector has the property that its length is always 1.

For the above example the length of $(0, 3, 0, 4, 0, 0)$ is $\sqrt{(3^2 + 4^2)} = 5$, so the normalised vector is $(0, 3/5, 0, 4/5, 0, 0)$, which has length 1. Note that the zero values play no part in the calculations.

The calculations for the other three vectors given are as follows.

$(0, 6, 0, 8, 0, 0)$

The length is $\sqrt{(6^2 + 8^2)} = 10$, so the normalised vector is $(0, 6/10, 0, 8/10, 0, 0) = (0, 3/5, 0, 4/5, 0, 0)$.

$(0, 30, 0, 40, 0, 0)$

The length is $\sqrt{(30^2 + 40^2)} = 50$, so the normalised vector is $(0, 30/50, 0, 40/50, 0, 0) = (0, 3/5, 0, 4/5, 0, 0)$.

$(0, 300, 0, 400, 0, 0)$

The length is $\sqrt{(300^2 + 400^2)} = 500$, so the normalised vector is
$(0, 300/500, 0, 400/500, 0, 0) = (0, 3/5, 0, 4/5, 0, 0)$.

In normalised form all four vectors are the same, as they should be.

20.7 Measuring the Distance Between Two Vectors

One important check on the appropriateness of the normalised vector space model representation of documents described in the last two sections is whether we can make a sensible definition of the distance between two vectors. We would like the distance between two identical vectors to be zero, the distance between two vectors that are as dissimilar as possible to be 1 and the distance between any other two vectors to be somewhere in between.

The standard definition of the distance between two vectors of length one, known as *unit vectors*, meets these criteria.

We define the *dot product* of two unit vectors of the same dimension to be the sum of the products of the corresponding pairs of values.

For example, if we take the two unnormalised vectors $(6, 4, 0, 2, 1)$ and $(5, 7, 6, 0, 2)$, normalising them to unit length converts the values to $(0.79, 0.53, 0, 0.26, 0.13)$ and $(0.47, 0.66, 0.56, 0, 0.19)$.

The dot product is now $0.79 \times 0.47 + 0.53 \times 0.66 + 0 \times 0.56 + 0.26 \times 0 + 0.13 \times 0.19 = 0.74$ approximately.

If we subtract this value from 1 we obtain a measure of the distance between the two values, which is $1 - 0.74 = 0.26$.

What happens if we calculate the distance between two identical unit vectors? The dot product gives the sum of the squares of the values, which must be 1 as the length of a unit vector is 1 by definition. Subtracting this value from 1 gives a distance of zero.

If we take two unit vectors with no values in common (corresponding to no terms in common in the original documents), say $(0.94, 0, 0, 0.31, 0.16)$ and $(0, 0.6, 0.8, 0, 0)$ the dot product is $0.94 \times 0 + 0 \times 0.6 + 0 \times 0.8 + 0.31 \times 0 + 0.16 \times 0 = 0$. Subtracting this value from 1 gives a distance measure of 1, which is the largest distance value achievable.

20.8 Measuring the Performance of a Text Classifier

Once we have converted the training documents into normalised vector form, we can construct a training set of the kind used in previous chapters for each category C_k in turn. We can convert a set of test documents to a test set of instances for each category in the same way as the training documents and apply whatever classification algorithm we choose to the training data to classify the instances in the test set.

For each category C_k we can construct a confusion matrix of the kind discussed in Chapter 7.

		Predicted class	
		C_k	not C_k
Actual	C_k	a	c
class	not C_k	b	d

Figure 20.1 Confusion Matrix for Category C_k

In Figure 20.1 the values a, b, c and d are the number of true positive, false positive, false negative and true negative classifications, respectively. For a perfect classifier b and c would both be zero.

The value $(a+d)/(a+b+c+d)$ gives the predictive accuracy. However, as mentioned in Chapter 12, for information retrieval applications, which include text classification, it is more usual to use some other measures of classifier performance.

Recall is defined as $a/(a+c)$, i.e. the proportion of documents in category C_k that are correctly predicted.

Precision is defined as $a/(a+b)$, i.e. the proportion of documents that are predicted as being in category C_k that are actually in that category.

It is common practice to combine Recall and Precision into a single measure of performance called the *F1 Score*, which is defined by the formula $F1 = 2 \times \text{Precision} \times \text{Recall}/(\text{Precision} + \text{Recall})$. This is just the product of Precision and Recall divided by their average.

Having generated confusion matrices for each of the N binary classification tasks we can combine them in several ways. One method is called *micro-averaging*. The N confusion matrices are added together element by element to form a single matrix from which Recall, Precision, F1 and any other preferred measures can be computed.

20.9 Hypertext Categorisation

An important special case of text classification arises when the documents are web pages, i.e. HTML files. The automatic classification of web pages is usually known as *Hypertext Categorisation* (or *Hypertext Classification*).

Hypertext Categorisation is similar to classifying 'ordinary' text, e.g. articles in newspapers or journals, on the basis of their content, but as we shall see the former can often be considerably harder.

20.9.1 Classifying Web Pages

The most obvious question to ask is why should we bother to do hypertext categorisation, when there are powerful search engines such as Google available for locating web pages of interest.

It has been estimated that the World Wide Web comprises over 13 billion pages and is growing at a rate of several million pages a day. The size of the web will eventually overwhelm the conventional web search engine approach.

The present author lives in a small village in England. When he entered the village name (a unique one for England) into Google a year ago he was astonished to find it returned 87,200 entries — more than 50 times as many as the number of people who live there. This seemed a little excessive. Making the same query today we find that the number of entries has grown to 642,000. We can only speculate on what events have occurred in the village in the intervening year to warrant this much greater attention. For comparison the number of Google entries for Science a few years ago was 459,000,000. A year later it had reached 4,570,000,000.

In practice it is clear that many (probably most) Google users only ever look at the first screenful or two of the entries returned or try a more elaborate search. What else can they do? No one can possibly examine 4,570 million entries on anything. Unfortunately even highly specific queries can easily return many thousands of entries and this number can only grow as time goes by. Looking at only the first screenful or two of entries is placing a huge amount of reliance on the algorithm used by Google to rank the relevance of its entries — far more than can realistically be justified. This is in no way to criticise or denigrate a very successful company — just to point out that the standard approach used by web search engines will not keep working successfully for ever. We can be sure that the search engine companies are well aware of this. It is perhaps not surprising that there are studies that suggest that many users prefer to navigate through directories of pre-classified content and that this frequently enables them to find more relevant information in a shorter time.

When attempting to classify web pages we immediately run into the problem of finding any classified pages to use as training data. Web pages are uploaded by a very large number of individuals, operating in an environment where no widely agreed standard classification scheme exists. Fortunately there are ways of overcoming this problem, at least partially.

The search engine company, Yahoo, uses hundreds of professional classifiers to categorise new web pages into a (nearly) hierarchical structure, comprising 14 main categories, each with many sub-categories, sub-sub-categories etc. The complete structure can be found on the web at `http://dir.yahoo.com`. Users can search through the documents in the directory structure either using a search engine approach or by following links through the structure. For example we might follow the path from 'Science' to 'Computer Science' to 'Artificial Intelligence' to 'Machine Learning' to find a set of links to documents that human classifiers have placed in that category. The first of these (at the time of writing) is to the UCI Machine Learning Repository, which was discussed in Chapter 2.

The Yahoo system demonstrates the potential value of classifying web pages. However, only a very small proportion of the entire web could possibly be classified this way 'manually'. With 1.5 million new pages being added each day the volume of new material will defeat any conceivable team of human classifiers. An interesting area of investigation (which the present author and his research group are currently pursuing) is whether web pages can be classified automatically using the Yahoo classification scheme (or some other similar scheme) by supervised learning methods of the kind described in this book.

Unlike many other task areas for data mining there are few 'standard' datasets available on which experimenters can compare their results. One exception is the *BankSearch* dataset created by the University of Reading, which includes 11,000 web pages pre-classified (by people) into four main categories (Banking and Finance, Programming, Science, Sport) and 11 sub-categories, some quite distinct and some quite similar.

20.9.2 Hypertext Classification versus Text Classification

Classifying hypertext has some important differences from classifying 'standard' text. Only a small number of web pages (manually classified) are available for supervised learning and it is often the case that much of the content of each web page is irrelevant to the topic of the page (links to photographs of the creator's family, train timetables, advertisements etc.).

However one difference is fundamental and unavoidable. In text classification the words that the human reader sees are very similar to the data provided to the classification program. Figure 20.2 is a typical example.

Marley was dead: to begin with. There is no doubt whatever about that. The register of his burial was signed by the clergyman, the clerk, the undertaker, and the chief mourner. Scrooge signed it: and Scrooge's name was good upon 'Change, for anything he chose to put his hand to. Old Marley was as dead as a door-nail.

Mind! I don't mean to say that I know, of my own knowledge, what there is particularly dead about a door-nail. I might have been inclined, myself, to regard a coffin-nail as the deadest piece of ironmongery in the trade. But the wisdom of our ancestors is in the simile; and my unhallowed hands shall not disturb it, or the Country's done for. You will therefore permit me to repeat, emphatically, that Marley was as dead as a door-nail.

Source: Charles Dickens. A Christmas Carol.

Figure 20.2 Text Classification: An Example

Automating the classification of a document based on its content is a hard task (for the example above we might perhaps decide on the categories 'death' and 'ironmongery'). However the problems pale into insignificance compared with classifying even a fairly short piece of hypertext.

Figure 20.3 shows the first few lines of the text form of a well-known web page. It is a small extract from the text that an automatic hypertext categorisation program would need to process. It contains precisely one word of useful information, which occurs twice. The rest is HTML markup and JavaScript that gives no clue to the correct classification of the page.

It is usually considerably easier (for humans) to classify web pages from the 'pictorial' form of the pages displayed by a web browser. In this case, the equivalent web page is a very familiar one (see Figure 20.4).

It is worth noting that most of the words on this page are of little or no use to human classifiers, for example 'images', 'groups', 'news', 'preferences' and 'We're Hiring'. There are only two clues to the correct classification of this page: the phrase 'Searching 8,058,044,651 web pages' and the name of the company. From these we can correctly deduce that it is the home page of a widely used search engine.

A program that attempts to classify this page automatically has to contend with not only the scarcity of useful information in the page, even for human classifiers, but the abundance of irrelevant information in the textual form that it is given.

```
<html><head><meta http-equiv="content-type"
content="text/html; charset=UTF-8">
<title>Google</title><style>
<!--
body,td,a,p,.h{font-family:arial,sans-serif;}
.h{font-size: 20px;}
.q{color:#0000cc;}
//-->
</style>
<script>
<!--
function sf(){document.f.q.focus();}
function clk(el,ct,cd) {if(document.images){(new Image()).src=
"/url?sa=T&ct="+es
cape(ct)+"&cd="+escape(cd)+"&url="
+escape(el.href)+"&ei=gpZNQpzEHaSgQYCUwKoM";}return true;}
// -->
</script>
</head><body bgcolor=#ffffff text=#000000 link=#0000cc vlink=
#551a8b alink=#ff00
00 onLoad=sf()><center><img src="/intl/en_uk/images/logo.gif"
width=276 height=1
10 alt="Google"><br><br>
```

Figure 20.3   Hypertext Classification: An Example

We can deal with the second problem to some extent by removing HTML markup and JavaScript when we create a representation of a document such as a 'bag-of-words', but the scarcity of relevant information on most web pages remains a problem. We must be careful not to assume that HTML markup is always irrelevant noise — the only two useful words in Figure 20.3 (both 'Google') appear in the HTML markup.

Even compared with articles in newspapers, papers in scientific journals etc. web pages suffer from an extremely diverse authorship, with little consistency in style or vocabulary, and extremely diverse content. Ignoring HTML markup, JavaScript, irrelevant advertisements and the like, the content of a web page is often quite small. It is not surprising that classification systems that work well on standard text documents often struggle with hypertext. It is reported that in one experiment, classifiers that were 90% accurate on the widely used Reuters dataset (of standard text documents) scored only 32% on a sample of Yahoo classified pages.

Figure 20.4 Web Page Corresponding to Figure 20.3

To counter the scarcity of textual information in the typical web page we need to try to take advantage of the information given in the tags, links etc. in the HTML markup (whilst of course removing the markup itself before converting the document to a bag-of-words representation or similar).

The information embedded in HTML markup can include:

- a title for the page

- 'metadata' (keywords and a description of the page)

- information about headers etc.

- words considered important enough to place in bold or italic

- the text associated with links to other pages.

How much of this information to include and how to do so is an open research question. We have to beware of 'game playing', where a page deliberately includes misleading information about its content with the aim of fooling internet search engines. Despite this, experience suggests that extracting important words from the markup (especially the 'metadata') and including them in the representation can significantly improve classification accuracy, especially if the words are given greater weighting (say, 3 times greater) than those extracted from the basic text content of the page.

To improve classification accuracy further we could look at the possibility of including some of the information in the 'linked neighbourhood' of each web page, i.e. the pages to which it points and the pages that point to it. However this is considerably beyond the scope of an introductory text.

20.10 Chapter Summary

This chapter looks at a particular type of classification task, where the objects are text documents. A method of processing the documents for use by the classification algorithms given earlier in this book using a *bag-of-words representation* is described.

An important special case of text classification arises when the documents are web pages. The automatic classification of web pages is known as hypertext categorisation. The differences between standard text classification and *hypertext categorisation* are illustrated and issues relating to the latter are discussed.

20.11 Self-assessment Exercises for Chapter 20

1. Given a document, drawn from a collection of 1,000 documents, in which the four terms given in the table below occur, calculate the TFIDF values for each one.

Term	Frequency in current document	Number of documents containing term
dog	2	800
cat	10	700
man	50	2
woman	6	30

2. Normalise the vectors $(20, 10, 8, 12, 56)$ and $(0, 15, 12, 8, 0)$.

   Calculate the distance between the two normalised vectors using the dot product formula.

21
Classifying Streaming Data

21.1 Introduction

One of the most significant developments in Data Mining in recent years has been the huge increase in availability of *streaming data*, i.e. data which arrives (generally in large quantities) from some automatic process over a period of days, months, years or potentially forever.

Some examples of this are:

- Sales transactions in supermarkets
- Data from GPS systems
- Records of changes in share prices
- Logs of telephone calls
- Logs of accesses to webpages
- Records of credit card purchases
- Records of postings to social media
- Data from networks of sensors

For some applications the volume of data received can be as high as tens of millions of records per day, which we can regard as effectively infinite.

As elsewhere in this book we will restrict ourselves to data that is symbolic in nature, as opposed to say images sent from CCTV. We will concentrate on data records that are labelled with a classification and assume that the task is to learn an underlying model in the form of a decision tree. We will further impose the restriction that all attributes are categorical. Continuous

M. Bramer, *Principles of Data Mining*, Undergraduate Topics in Computer Science, DOI 10.1007/978-1-4471-7493-6_21

(numerical) attributes can be handled by some method similar to that discussed in the context of the TDIDT tree generation algorithm in Chapter 8.

As a concrete example, we can think of some supermarket checkout system that has information about a customer (from a loyalty card, say) and records of his/her recent purchases, where the aim is to predict which customers will buy a particular brand of product when they visit the supermarket and which will not. This information will be used in a future sales campaign perhaps to reinforce the behaviour of those who would normally buy the product or to change the behaviour of as many as possible of those who normally would not. In general there is no need to restrict ourselves to just two classifications and in the examples used in this chapter there will be three possibilities available.

We can think of a process which reads a potentially endless stream of labelled data records (instances) as they arrive and uses them to generate a classification tree piece-by-piece possibly over a long period of time. There are some crucial differences between this and generating classification trees as described earlier in this book:

- Because of the large (potentially infinite) volume of data involved it is fundamental that each record is examined, used to update the information recorded in the evolving tree and then discarded – hence it may only be examined once. The original data records are not stored.
- The processing must take place in real-time and must be rapid enough to avoid creating a large backlog of incoming data waiting to be processed, so time-efficient methods are even more important than usual.
- We cannot wait until training is completed before we start using the classification tree for prediction of the classification of previously unseen data. It is important that at any point it is possible to use the incomplete tree to predict the classification of an unseen instance. It must also be possible to evaluate the quality of the evolving tree's classification performance as the tree-building is going on.

The technique to be described in this chapter is adapted from the VFDT method developed by Domingos and Hulten [1]. VFDT stands for 'Very Fast Decision Trees'. As always with popular methods a large number of variants have been developed. The version described here is the present author's own. It is based closely on [1] but uses a substantially different notation and has some simplifications for ease of explanation. It is certainly not claimed to be the fastest (or best) version of the method but should suffice as a basis for further study or development.

The trees constructed by this and similar methods are often known as *Hoeffding Trees* for a reason that will be explained later. To acknowledge this and to avoid any confusion with VFDT, we will call our variant the *H-Tree* algorithm.

21.1.1 Stationary v Time-dependent Data

A crucial assumption made in this chapter is that the underlying process we aim to model is fixed, so that having constructed our decision tree model we can use it repeatedly day-after-day, month-after-month etc. without change. We call data arising from such a fixed process *stationary data*.

Although this is a perfectly correct assumption for some types of data, for other types the underlying model varies from time to time, perhaps seasonally. We call such data *time-dependent data*. Dealing with time-dependent data is the subject of Chapter 22.

One consequence of assuming that the data is stationary is that it seems reasonable to expect it to be possible to generate a classification tree from only a (relatively) small number of records that predicts exactly (or almost) as well as one built using many millions of records. The H-Tree algorithm makes this implicit assumption in the way it generates its trees.

21.2 Building an H-Tree: Updating Arrays

As more and more data records are read a classification tree is developed branch by branch, starting with just one node, numbered zero, which will act as the root of the eventual classification tree. Initially it is treated as a leaf node.[1] When certain conditions are met a leaf node can be *split* on an attribute, meaning that a subtree is created below it with one branch for each possible value of the selected attribute.

It will make it easier to explain the H-Tree algorithm and to illustrate the information that needs to be associated with each node in the classification tree if we start by jumping ahead to a future point where there is a partly developed tree, which is shown below as Figure 21.1.

The nodes in the tree are numbered in the order in which they were created. The system variable *nextnode* holds the number of the next node in sequence for possible future use. In this case *nextnode* is 8.

---

[1] We distinguish between nodes which have or have not previously been split on an attribute. The former are called *internal nodes*; the latter are called *leaf nodes*. We will consider the root node not as a third type of node but as an internal node after it has been split on an attribute and a leaf node before that.

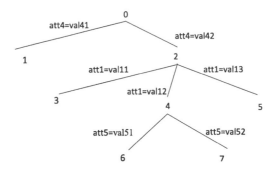

Figure 21.1 A Partly Developed H-Tree

The tree has been created by splitting on attribute *att4* at node 0 (creating nodes 1 and 2), *att1* at node 2 (creating nodes 3, 4 and 5) and *att5* at node 4 (creating nodes 6 and 7). Each attribute can potentially have any number of values but to simplify the figures we will generally assume they have either two or three. We will adopt the convention that if, say, attribute *att5* has two values we will call them *val51* and *val52*.

Although we are not concerned with the fine detail of implementation in this book, it will make the description of the H-Tree algorithm much easier to follow if we think in terms of maintaining six arrays at each node. These will be discussed in the following sections.

21.2.1 Array *currentAtts*

This is a two-dimensional array. The element *currentAtts[N]* is an array containing the names of all the attributes available for splitting on at node *N*, listed in a standard order. This is called the *current attributes array* for that node. In the interest of clarity we will generally use phrases such as 'the current attributes array of node *N*' in preference to 'the array which is the value of *currentAtts[N]*'.

If our data records have the values of seven attributes (an unrealistically small number in most cases) which in standard order are named *att1*, *att2*, *att3*, *att4*, *att5*, *att6* and *att7* then at the root node *currentAtts[0]* is initialised to the array {*att1*, *att2*, *att3*, *att4*, *att5*, *att6*, *att7*}.[2]

When a leaf node is 'expanded' by being split on at an attribute, its im-

---

[2] A note on notation. In this chapter array elements are generally shown enclosed in square brackets, e.g. *currentAtts[2]*. However an array containing a number of constant values will generally be denoted by those values separated by commas and enclosed in braces. So *currentAtts[2]* is {*att1*, *att2*, *att3*, *att5*, *att6*, *att7*}.

mediate descendant nodes inherit the current attributes array of the parent
with the splitting attribute removed. Thus

- *currentAtts*[1] and *currentAtts*[2] are both the array {*att1, att2, att3, att5,
  att6, att7*}
- *currentAtts*[3], *currentAtts*[4] and *currentAtts*[5] are all the array {*att2,
  att3, att5, att6, att7*}
- *currentAtts*[6] and *currentAtts*[7] are both the array {*att2, att3, att6, att7*}.

21.2.2 Array *splitAtt*

For an internal node N, i.e. one that has previously been split on an attribute,
the array element *splitAtt*[N] is the name of the splitting attribute, so

- *splitAtt*[0] is *att4*
- *splitAtt*[2] is *att1*
- *splitAtt*[4] is *att5*.

All the other nodes are leaf nodes at which there are (by definition) no
splitting attributes. The value of *splitAtt*[N] for a leaf node is 'none'.

21.2.3 Sorting a record to the appropriate leaf node

As the data records are received they are processed and discarded, but doing this does not immediately alter the structure (nodes and branches) of the
evolving incomplete tree. As each new record comes in and is processed it is
sorted through the tree to the appropriate leaf node. It is only when a number
of conditions are met at a leaf node that a change to the tree by splitting at
that node is considered.

To illustrate the sorting process let us assume we have the following record
(Figure 21.2):

att1	att2	att3	att4	att5	att6	att7	class
val12	xxx	xxx	val42	val51	xxx	xxx	c2

Figure 21.2 Sample Record (Seven Attribute Values Plus a Classification)

Values that are not relevant to the example are denoted by xxx.)

The record passes (notionally) through the tree starting at the root (node 0). From there because the value of *att4* is val42 it passes on to node 2. Then because *att1* has the value val12 it goes to node 4. Finally, because *att5* has value val51 it arrives at node 6, a leaf. The route taken from root to leaf is 0 to 2 to 4 to 6.

21.2.4 Array *hitcount*

For each leaf node N, *hitcount*[N] is the number of 'hits' on the node since it was created, i.e. the number of records sorted to that leaf node by the process illustrated above. As each new record is sorted to a leaf node L, the value of *hitcount*[L] is increased by 1. The internal nodes 'passed through' in the above example (0, 2 and 4) have their own *hitcount* values, obtained before they were split and became internal nodes. These values are not increased for internal nodes as they play no further part in the tree generation process.

When a new node is created its *hitcount* value is set to zero.

21.2.5 Array *classtotals*

This is another two-dimensional array. If there are three possible classifications named (in a standard order) *c1*, *c2* and *c3* and node N is a leaf node, then *classtotals*[N][*c1*], *classtotals*[N][*c2*] and *classtotals*[N][*c3*] record the number of 'hits' on node N for which the classification is *c1*, *c2* and *c3*, respectively. The sum of these three values is of course *hitcount*[N].

As with array *hitcount*, internal nodes have their own *classtotals* values obtained before they were split and became internal nodes. These values are not increased for internal nodes as they play no part in the tree generation process.

When a new node is created its *classtotals* value is set to zero for all classes.

21.2.6 Array *acvCounts*

This is the most complex of the six arrays. The name stands for 'attribute-class-value counts'. It has four dimensions.

If N is a leaf node then for each attribute A in its current attributes array, *acvCounts*[N][A] is a two-dimensional array which records the number of occurrences of each possible combination of class value and the value of attribute A.

In Figure 21.1, the attributes in the current attributes array for node 6 are *att2*, *att3*, *att6* and *att7*. Assume that *hitcount*[6] is 200 and the values of *classtotals*[6][*c1*], *classtotals*[6][*c2*] and *classtotals*[6][*c3*] are 100, 80 and 20, respectively.

If attribute *att2* has three values, here are some possible values for the array elements at node 6 for attribute *att2*:

- *acvCounts*[6][*att2*][*c1*][*val21*]: 44
- *acvCounts*[6][*att2*][*c1*][*val22*]: 18
- *acvCounts*[6][*att2*][*c1*][*val23*]: 38
- *acvCounts*[6][*att2*][*c2*][*val21*]: 49
- *acvCounts*[6][*att2*][*c2*][*val22*]: 24
- *acvCounts*[6][*att2*][*c2*][*val23*]: 7
- *acvCounts*[6][*att2*][*c3*][*val21*]: 5
- *acvCounts*[6][*att2*][*c3*][*val22*]: 11
- *acvCounts*[6][*att2*][*c3*][*val23*]: 4

It is cumbersome to write the values in this way and it is much easier (and more natural) to depict *acvCounts*[6][*att2*] by a two-dimensional array known as a *frequency table*[3] such as Figure 21.3:

Class	*val21*	*val22*	*val23*
c1	44	18	38
c2	49	24	7
c3	5	11	4

Figure 21.3 Frequency Table for Attribute *att2*

The sum of the values in the *c1* row is the same as *classtotals*[6][*c1*] and similarly for the other classes. The overall total of the numbers in the whole table is the same as *hitcount*[6].

These two-dimensional arrays are precisely what are needed to calculate measures such as Information Gain (discussed in Chapter 5) which are often used to determine which attribute to split on at a node and, as we shall see in Section 21.4, this is how they will be used in developing the H-Tree. As each new record is sorted to a leaf node N, one of the entries in the frequency table corresponding to every attribute in the node's current attributes array is increased by 1.

---

[3]The row and column headings are provided to assist the reader only. The table itself has 3 rows and 3 columns.

As for arrays *hitcount* and *classtotals* internal nodes have their own *acvCounts* values, obtained before they were split and became internal nodes. These values are not increased for internal nodes as they play no part in the H-Tree algorithm.

When a new leaf node is created its *acvCounts* value for each combination of class and attribute value for every attribute in its current attributes array is set to zero.

21.2.7 Array *branch*

This final array, together with the *splitAtt* array provides the 'glue' that keeps the tree structure together.

When leaf node N is split on attribute A, for each value of that attribute a branch leading to a new node is created.

For each value V of attribute A:

- *branch*$[N][A][V]$ is set to *nextnode*
- *nextnode* is increased by 1.

21.3 Building an H-Tree: a Detailed Example

We now return to the starting state with a tree comprising just the root node and will use a detailed example to illustrate the processing involved. As before we will assume that there are three classes, *c1*, *c2* and *c3*, plus seven attributes *att1*, *att2*, ..., *att7*. The number of possible values of an attribute can vary from one to another.

The steps involved in constructing the tree are now as follows.

21.3.1 Step (a): Initialise Root Node 0

We start with a tree with just a single node, numbered zero, and associate five arrays (all except *branch*) with it as described in Section 21.2.

The pseudocode for this is given below.[4]

---

[4]Pseudocode fragments are provided for the benefit of readers who may be interested in developing their own implementations of the H-Tree algorithm. Other readers can safely ignore them.

Pseudocode 1: Initialise Root Node

1. Set *currentAtts*[0] to be an array comprising the names of all the attributes
2. Set *splitAtt*[0] to 'none'
3. Set *hitcount*[0] to zero
4. For each class *C*, set *classtotals*[0][*C*] to zero
5. For each attribute *A* in the node's current attributes array
   - For each combination of class *C* and value *V* of attribute *A*
     - set *acvCounts*[0][*A*][*C*][*V*] to zero
6. Set *nextnode* to 1

21.3.2 Step (b): Begin Reading Records

We now begin reading the incoming records one-by-one, in each case processing the record and then discarding it. (Each record is 'sorted' to node zero as there is only one at present.) We increase one of the numbers in the *classtotals*[0] array by one and the *hitcount* value by one for each record read. We also adjust the contents of the frequency table for each attribute by adding one to one of the values in the table, depending on the combination of the value of the attribute and the specified classification for that record.

Let us assume that by the time the 100th record has been read the *classtotals*[0] array contains $\{63, 17, 20\}$. The sum of the three values in the array will of course be 100. At this stage the frequency table for attribute *att6* might contain the following (Figure 21.4). There will be frequency tables similar to this for each of the other attributes. In each case the right-most column (row sums) will be the same.

Class	*val61*	*val62*	*val63*	*val64*
c1	32	18	4	9
c2	0	5	5	7
c3	0	10	7	3

Figure 21.4 Frequency Table for Attribute *att6*

It will help to interpret this if we add an extra row containing the sum of the numbers in each of the existing columns and a further column containing the sum of the numbers in each row. Note that these additional values do not need to be stored. They are calculated from the values in the stored $3 * 4$ table as and when needed.

The augmented frequency table for attribute *att6* at node 0 looks like this (Figure 21.5):

Class	*val61*	*val62*	*val63*	*val64*	Row sums
c1	32	18	4	9	63
c2	0	5	5	7	17
c3	0	10	7	3	20
Column sums	32	33	16	19	100

Figure 21.5 Augmented Frequency Table for Attribute *att6*

The number in the bottom right-hand corner is the sum of the numbers in the bottom (column sums) row, which is the same as the sum of the numbers in the right-most (row sums) column. This overall total is the same as the number of records sorted to node 0 – in this case 100.

The other values in the right-most column show how many instances have been classified with each of the three possible classes. They are the same as the values in the *classtotals* array, i.e. $\{63, 17, 20\}$.

The first four numbers in the bottom row are the column sums. They show that attribute *att6* had the value *val61* 32 times, *val62* 33 times, *val63* 16 times and *val64* 19 times.

21.3.3 Step (c): Consider Splitting at Node 0

To develop the tree we need to split on an attribute at the root node, but we clearly cannot do this after just one record has been read as the resulting tree would be essentially arbitrary and likely to have extremely low predictive power. Instead we wait until a specified number of records have been sorted to node zero[5] and then make a decision on whether or not to split on an attribute and if so which one.

The specified number is denoted by G and is sometimes referred to as the *grace period*. In this chapter the same value will be used at each leaf node as the tree evolves, but it would be possible to use a larger value at some points in the processing (e.g. at or near the root of the tree) than at others. To make the numbers reasonably small in our examples we will use a value of 100 for G.

---

[5] As initially there are no other nodes, all incoming records will be sorted there.

Once G, i.e. 100 records have been sorted to node 0, we next consider splitting at that node provided that the records sorted to it have more than one classification. If all the classifications were the same we would continue receiving and processing records until the next 100 were received at which time splitting would be considered again. In this example the classifications are not all identical so we go on to determine which attribute to split on, but with 'no split' as one of the options. At present we will assume that we will definitely split and will choose the attribute to split on using a method such as the maximising Information Gain method described in Chapter 5, or one of the other similar methods that use a frequency table for each attribute.

21.3.4 Step (d): Split on Root Node and Initialise New Leaf Nodes

We will say that it is decided to split at node 0 using attribute *att6*. This gives us four branches (one per value of *att6*) leading to four new nodes, numbered from 1 to 4, as shown in Figure 21.6.[6] To achieve this we start by setting array element *branch*[0][*att6*][*val61*] to *nextnode*, i.e. 1, and increasing *nextnode* by 1. We then create the other three branches in a similar way. The value of *nextnode* is now 5.

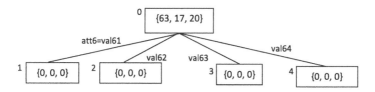

Figure 21.6 H-Tree After Splitting on Node 0 (with current attributes array for each node)

Pseudocode for the process of splitting on an attribute and initialising the resulting new nodes is given below.

---

[6]In Figures 21.6, 21.8 and 21.9 we depart from our usual notation for trees and show the values that are in the *classtotals* array for each node.

Pseudocode 2: Split at Node L Using Attribute A

1. Set $splitAtt[L]$ to A.
2. For each value V of attribute A
   - Set $branch[L][A][V]$ to $nextnode$ (to create a new leaf node)
   - Set $currentAtts[nextnode]$ to be the same array as $currentAtts[L]$ with attribute A removed
   - Initialise arrays $splitAtt$, $hitcount$, $classtotals$ and $acvCounts$ for node $nextnode$ as for Pseudocode 1, steps 2 to 5
   - Increase $nextnode$ by 1

For each of the new nodes 1 to 4 the *classtotals* array is initialised to $\{0, 0, 0\}$, the value of *hitcount* is set to zero and the value of *splitAtt* is set to 'none'.

We create a current attributes array for each of the new nodes, by taking the current attributes array from the parent node (node 0) and removing attribute *att6* from each. This gives all of them the array $\{att1, att2, att3, att4, att5, att7\}$. These are the attributes available for any future splitting at those nodes.

We also create a frequency table for each attribute at each of the three nodes.

For attribute *att2* which has two values, *val21* and *val22*, the values of frequency tables $acvCounts[1][att2]$, $acvCounts[2][att2]$, $acvCounts[3][att2]$ and $acvCounts[4][att2]$ are all initially the same, i.e. (Figure 21.7):

Class	val21	val22
c1	0	0
c2	0	0
c3	0	0

Figure 21.7 Frequency Table for Attribute *att2*

Creating the new frequency tables this way may seem innocuous but it is in fact a major departure from the Information Gain method and the other methods described in Chapter 5 for situations where all the data is available. Ideally we would like the new frequency tables to begin with counts of all the class / attribute value combinations for all the relevant records so far received. However there is no way of doing this. We would need to re-examine the original data, but it has all already been discarded. The best we can do is to start with a table with all zero values for each attribute at each of the nodes, but this will inevitably mean that the tree eventually generated will be different

– perhaps very significantly so – from that which would be generated by the methods given in Chapter 5 if we were somehow able to capture and store all the data.

Before going on it is important to understand that the role of leaf nodes in this method is entirely different from their role in algorithms such as TDIDT described earlier in this book. Here a leaf node has no descendants but not necessarily a single classification such as {84, 0, 0}. The mixture of classifications at a leaf node changes as more records are received and a leaf node can subsequently acquire descendants as the tree building continues.

All the leaf nodes that we will see in this chapter are *expandable* leaf nodes, i.e. ones for which there is a non-empty current attributes array signifying that there are still attributes available for splitting if required. It is possible for a leaf node to be at the end of a long path comprising the same number of branches as there are attributes, with one attribute/value combination pair per branch, although this is not very likely if the number of attributes is large. We call such nodes *non-expandable* leaf nodes. The current attributes array for a non-expandable leaf node will be empty. Naturally we do not consider splitting at a leaf node that is non-expandable.

21.3.5 Step (e): Process the Next Set of Records

We now go on to read and process the next set of records. As each one is read, it is *sorted* to the correct leaf node. We can think of the instance starting at node 0, and then falling down to node 1, 2, 3 or 4 depending on the value of attribute *att6*. In a larger tree it might fall further down to a lower level, but in all cases the instance will be sorted to one of the leaf nodes.

As each record is sorted to a leaf node the values in the *hitcount* and *classtotals* arrays and the frequency table for each attribute in the current attributes array are updated at that node.

Pseudocode for processing a record is given below.

Pseudocode 3: Process Record R with Classification C

1. Set N to the number of the root node
2. While $splitAtt[N] \mathrel{!}= \text{'none'}$
   - Set A to $splitAtt[N]$
   - Set V to value of attribute A in record R
   - Set N to $branch[N][A][V]$
3. Set $L = N$
4. Update arrays at leaf node L:
   - Increase $hitcount[L]$ by 1
   - Increase $classtotals[L][C]$ by 1
   - For each attribute A in the current attributes array for node L
     - set V to the value that the attribute has in record R
     - increase $acvCounts[L][A][C][V]$ by 1
5. If suitable conditions are met consider splitting at node L

Step 5 will be developed further as this section progresses.

Going back to our example, our 'grace period' G is 100 and by the time the 100th record is sorted to node 2 we will assume that the *classtotals* arrays for each of the five nodes are the following:

Node 0: $\{63, 17, 20\}$

Node 1: $\{12, 8, 0\}*$

Node 2: $\{87, 10, 3\}*$

Node 3: $\{0, 0, 0\}*$

Node 4: $\{40, 10, 20\}*$

Leaf nodes are indicated by an asterisk. The *classtotals* array for node 0 has not changed as it is no longer a leaf node. When the records were sorted to leaf nodes 1, 3 and 4 there were fewer than 100 records sorted to each of those nodes so no consideration was given to splitting on an attribute there. Now G (i.e. 100) records have been sorted to node 2 a decision needs to be made whether to split there or not.

21.3.6 Step (f): Consider Splitting at Node 2

We now consider splitting at node 2. The records that have been sorted to that node have more than one classification, so we go on to calculate the Information Gain (or other measure) for each attribute in the node's current attributes array.

This time we will say that attribute *att2*, which has two values, is chosen for splitting, giving the new but still incomplete tree structure shown in Figure 21.8. The new nodes (5 and 6) all have *classtotals* arrays with the value $\{0, 0, 0\}$, *hitcount* values of zero and frequency tables containing all zero values. The *classtotals* and *hitcount* arrays and frequency tables at the other nodes are left unchanged.

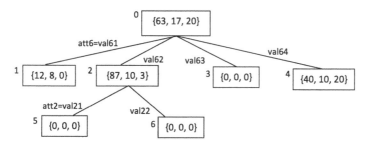

Figure 21.8 H-Tree After Splitting on Node 2

The new nodes 5 and 6 will all have a *currentAtts* array containing $\{att1, att3, att4, att5, att7\}$. The value of *splitAtt* at each node will be 'none'.

21.3.7 Step (g): Process the Next Set of Records

We now continue to read records, sorting each one to the appropriate leaf node, adjusting the values of *classtotals* and the contents of the frequency tables for each attribute each time.

We will assume that at some stage the total number of records sorted to node 4 in Figure 21.8 increases to 100, the value of G, and that at that stage the *classtotals* arrays for the records sorted to the seven nodes are the following:

Node 0: $\{63, 17, 20\}$
Node 1: $\{22, 9, 1\}$*
Node 2: $\{87, 10, 3\}$
Node 3: $\{8, 7, 15\}$*
Node 4: $\{45, 20, 35\}$*
Node 5: $\{25, 12, 31\}$*
Node 6: $\{0, 0, 0\}$*

Leaf nodes are again indicated by an asterisk. The *classtotals* arrays for nodes 0 and 2 have not changed as they are no longer leaf nodes.

We next consider splitting at node 4. If the decision is no, we simply go on to read further records. However we will assume that this time attribute *att2* is chosen for splitting (as it was at node 2), giving the new tree structure shown in Figure 21.9.

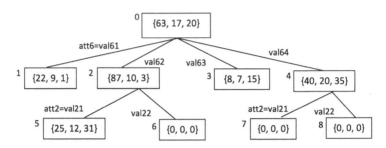

Figure 21.9 H-Tree After Splitting on Node 4

We carry on in this way, expanding at most one leaf node at each stage. Depending on the number of current attributes we have and the number of values each of them has, we may eventually reach a tree where every leaf node is non-expandable. If that happens the tree is now fixed and cannot later be altered. If there are quite a large number of attributes this is highly unlikely to happen. It is far more likely that the tree will initially develop fairly rapidly (or as rapidly as the size of the grace period allows) and then stabilise, i.e. stop evolving or change only slightly as further records are processed.

21.3.8 Outline of the H-Tree Algorithm

The algorithm described above can be summarised by a very simple 'main' algorithm and a revised version of pseudocode fragment 3. Here and subsequently the parts altered are shown in **bold**.

Outline of H-Tree Algorithm

1. Initialise root node (see pseudocode 1)
2. For each record R with classification C that arrives to be processed
   - Process record R with classification C (see pseudocode 3)

Pseudocode 3: Process Record R with Classification C (version 2)

1. Set N to the number of the root node
2. While $splitAtt[N] \mathrel{!}= $ 'none'
   - Set A to $splitAtt[N]$
   - Set V to value of attribute A in record R
   - Set N to $branch[N][A][V]$
3. Set $L = N$
4. Update arrays at leaf node L:
   - Increase $hitcount[L]$ by 1
   - Increase $classtotals[L][C]$ by 1
   - For each attribute A in the current attributes array for node L
     - set V to the value that the attribute has in record R
     - increase $acvCounts[L][A][C][V]$ by 1
5. **If conditions are met at node L**
   - **Determine whether to split on an attribute at node L**
   - **If answer is 'yes', with splitting attribute A, split at node L, using attribute A (see pseudocode 2)**

This leaves two important issues:

(a) What conditions need to be met at node L before checking for a possible split at that node?

(b) How to determine which attribute (if any) to split on at node L?

In answer to (a) there are three conditions that must be met.

(i) The value of $hitcount[L]$ is a multiple of G.

It would be possible to consider splitting at a node every time a new record was sorted to it but that would be computationally expensive and might lead to very poor splits being made. Once a split is made at a node the node cannot be 'unsplit' or 'resplit' on some different attribute. This implies that we need to be cautious and only consider splitting at a leaf node after a significant number of records have been sorted to it.

Note that the test is 'a multiple of G', rather than 'equal to G'. If we consider splitting when the $hitcount$ is G and decide not to do so, we do not consider it again at that node until a further G hits have been received there.

(ii) The classifications of the records that have been sorted to the node are not all the same.

If all the classifications are identical, say $c1$, the entropy at the leaf node is zero and the entropy resulting from splitting on any attribute will also inevitably be zero. For example if the *classtotals* array is $\{100, 0, 0\}$ the frequency table for attribute *att6*, which has four values, might look like this (Figure 21.10):

Class	*val61*	*val62*	*val63*	*val64*	Row sums
c1	28	0	30	42	100
c2	0	0	0	0	0
c3	0	0	0	0	0
Column sums	28	0	30	42	100

Figure 21.10   Frequency Table for Attribute *att6*

This table has an entropy value of zero. The contribution from each of the non-zero values in the main body of the table will be cancelled out by the contribution from the corresponding column sum. This is a general feature of any frequency table with either zero or one positive entries in each column of the table. The result is that the entropy will be identical (i.e. zero) for each attribute so there will be no basis for making a split on one attribute rather than another and no benefit at all from splitting.

(iii) The node must be expandable, i.e. its current attributes array must not be empty.

This leads to another revised version of pseudocode fragment 3.

Pseudocode 3: Process Record R with Classification C (version 3)

1. Set N to the number of the root node
2. While $splitAtt[N]$!= 'none'
   - Set A to $splitAtt[N]$
   - Set V to value of attribute A in record R
   - Set N to $branch[N][A][V]$
3. Set $L = N$
4. Update arrays at leaf node L:
   - Increase $hitcount[L]$ by 1
   - Increase $classtotals[L][C]$ by 1
   - For each attribute A in the current attributes array for node L
     - set V to the value that the attribute has in record R
     - increase $acvCounts[L][A][C][V]$ by 1
5. **If $hitcount[L]$ is a multiple of G and the classifications of the records sorted to node L are not all the same and $currentAtts[L]$ is not empty**
   - Determine whether to split on an attribute at node L (**see pseudocode 4**)
   - If answer is 'yes', with splitting attribute A, split at node L, using attribute A (see pseudocode 2)

Issue (b), i.e. how to determine which attribute to split on (if any) at node L forms the topic of the next two sections. (At step 5 there is a forward reference to pseudocode fragment 4, which will be given in Section 21.5.)

21.4 Splitting on an Attribute: Using Information Gain

We will start by assuming that we definitely want to split on an attribute at leaf node L and illustrate the method of doing so using the Information Gain criterion, as described in Chapters 5 and 6. Other splitting criteria such as those also mentioned in Chapter 6 (Gini Index, Gain Ratio etc.) may also be used but for definiteness we will assume in this chapter that the criterion used is always Information Gain.

We will not repeat the detailed explanation in previous chapters but will summarise the method for splitting at leaf node L briefly here:

- Calculate the 'initial entropy' E_{start} at node L.
- For each attribute A
- Calculate the (weighted average) entropy E_{new} at the new nodes that would result from splitting on attribute A
- Calculate the value of $E_{start} - E_{new}$. This value is the Information Gain.
- Split on the attribute with the highest value of Information Gain.

As an example, suppose the *classtotals* array at node L, i.e. *classtotals*[L], contains the values $\{100, 150, 250\}$. We will illustrate the method without justification. Full details are given in Chapters 5 and 6.

The total class count is 500, so we calculate E_{start} at node L as

$$-(100/500) * \log_2(100/500) - (150/500) * \log_2(150/500)$$
$$-(250/500) * \log_2(250/500)$$

which is $0.464 + 0.521 + 0.5 = 1.4855$ to 4 decimal places.

It can be proved that Information Gain must always be positive or zero.

To calculate the entropy resulting from splitting on an attribute, say attribute *att3* which has three values, we use a frequency table, which in our notation would be the two-dimensional array *acvCounts*[L][*att3*]. Augmented with column sums and headings it might look like this (Figure 21.11):

	att3 = val31	att3 = val32	att3 = val33
Class *c1*	64	4	32
Class *c2*	50	50	50
Class *c3*	200	25	25
Column sum	314	79	107

Figure 21.11 Augmented Frequency Table for Attribute *att3*

Note that the row sums for classes *c1*, *c2* and *c3* are 100, 150, 250, respectively, and the overall total of all the values in the main body of the table (i.e. not including those in the column sum row) is 500.

We now form a sum as follows:

(a) For every non-zero value V in the main body of the table subtract $V * \log_2 V$.
(b) For each non-zero value S in the column sum row add $S * \log_2 S$.
(c) Finally divide the total sum by the overall total of all the values in the main body of the table.

This gives us the value of E_{new}:

$$-64 * \log_2 64 - 4 * \log_2 4 - 32 * \log_2 32$$
$$-50 * \log_2 50 - 50 * \log_2 50 - 50 * \log_2 50$$
$$-200 * \log_2 200 - 25 * \log_2 25 - 25 * \log_2 25$$
$$+314 * \log_2 314 + 79 * \log_2 79 + 107 * \log_2 107$$

all divided by 500.

This gives $Enew = 1.3286$ to 4 decimal places. The value of Information Gain for splitting on attribute *att3* at node L is $E_{start} - E_{new} = 0.1569$ to 4 decimal places.

We calculate the Information Gain for all the attributes in the current attributes array for node L, i.e. *currentAtts[L]*, and select the attribute which gives the highest value.

21.5 Splitting on An Attribute: Using a Hoeffding Bound

We now come to the issue of whether or not to split at a leaf node.

A built-in problem with the evolving classification tree approach described in this chapter is that once a leaf node is split on an attribute it cannot be 'unsplit' back to a leaf node or 'resplit' using some other attribute. This makes the outcome particularly sensitive to the choices of splitting attribute near the top of the tree, especially the very first split on the original root/leaf node, node 0.

One way of avoiding poor splits at an early stage is to start with a value of G much larger than its ultimately intended value and only reduce it to its 'correct' value once the first few splits have been made. Another is to start the tree generation process not with just one node but with part or all of a classification tree generated using a method such as TDIDT (described in Chapter 4) using say 10,000 initial records. All leaf nodes in such a 'startup tree' would be subject to splitting in the usual way as more records arrive.

As the evolving classification tree is sensitive to the order of the initial records processed it is important to ensure as far as possible that there is nothing special or unusual about the initial records, e.g. the data stream does not happen to start with 5,000 records with identical classifications. If the data is taken from an artificial source, rather than a live stream of input it may be worthwhile to randomise the order of the records before use.

However these startup issues are handled, the general problem remains and can apply at any point in an evolving tree: there is a risk of making an inappropriate split at a leaf node when it would give more accurate predictions to leave it as a leaf and possibly split at that node on a different attribute at a later stage when more records have been sorted to it. We need a method of deciding when we should and should not split at a node that is more cautious than the method adopted so far.

In Section 21.3.8 we gave three conditions that must be met before we consider splitting on an attribute at node L. Here we will add a further condition: splitting only takes place if the best value of the measure that can be obtained, assumed to be by splitting on attribute X, is significantly better than the second best value, assumed to be obtained by splitting on attribute Y. We will assume for the remainder of this chapter that the measure used is Information Gain and will write these two values as $IG(X)$ and $IG(Y)$ respectively.

By 'significantly better' we mean that the difference between $IG(X)$ and $IG(Y)$ is greater than some value that we will call a *bound*. If the difference is smaller than the bound we will consider the difference between splitting on X and splitting on Y not to be significant and will leave the leaf node unexpanded. (It may be expanded at a later stage.)

The bound used for the difference between $IG(X)$ and $IG(Y)$ is not a fixed number, but depends on a number of factors. The one we will use is called the *Hoeffding Bound*, which finally explains the term Hoeffding Tree used at the start of the chapter. The Hoeffding Bound was developed by the Finnish statistician Wassily Hoeffding [2] in a different context and was adapted for use with classification trees by Domingos and Hulten [1]. In its revised form (and in our notation) *Hoeffding's inequality* states that with probability *Prob* attribute X is the correct choice of attribute to split on at a leaf node, based on *nrec* records sorted to that node, provided that $IG(X) - IG(Y)$ is greater than a value that depends on *Prob* and *nrec*. That value is called the *Hoeffding Bound*.

Before going on to define the Hoeffding Bound we will first set out three criteria that any such bound needs to meet:

(a) The larger the range of values that the measure we use can take, the larger the bound needs to be.

(b) The higher the value we choose for probability *Prob*, the larger the bound needs to be.

(c) The larger the number of records on which the split is based, the more reliable the choice of splitting attribute is and so the smaller the bound needs to be.

The formula for the Hoeffding Bound meets all these criteria. The bound is denoted by ϵ (the Greek letter 'epsilon') and is defined by the formula

$$\epsilon = R * \sqrt{\frac{ln(1/\delta)}{2 * nrec}}$$

In this formula $nrec$ is the number of records sorted to the given node, i.e. $hitcount[L]$ in our array notation. This is usually the same as G, the 'grace period' but may be a multiple of G. The Greek letter δ (pronounced 'delta') is used to represent the value of 1-$Prob$.

Figure 21.12 shows the value of $ln(1/\delta)$ for various common values of the probability $Prob$. The ln function is called the *natural logarithm function* and is often written as log_e.

Probability $Prob$	$\delta = 1\text{-}Prob$	$ln(1/\delta)$
0.9	0.1	2.3026
0.95	0.05	2.9957
0.99	0.01	4.6052
0.999	0.001	6.9078

Figure 21.12 Values of $ln(1/\delta)$ for Various Probability Values

The value R corresponds to the range of values of the measure we are using to decide which attribute to split on, which we will assume is Information Gain. The smallest value of Information Gain that can be obtained by splitting at a node is zero and the largest value is the 'initial entropy' E_{start} at the node. We will use the value of E_{start} for R.

Number of classes c	Maximum value of R $= log_2 c$
2	1
3	1.5850
4	2
5	2.3219
6	2.5850
7	2.8074
8	3

Figure 21.13 Maximum Values of R for Various Numbers of Classes

The largest value that R can ever take occurs when all the classes are equally frequent at a node, in which case, assuming there are c classes, the value of the entropy and hence the value of R is $\log_2 c$. Even with a very large number of streaming records the number of classifications is likely to be a small number. The maximum values of R corresponding to some small values of c are given in Figure 21.13.

Putting all this together, if we have three classes distributed evenly (so $R = 1.5850$) and want to be 95% certain that attribute X is the best choice, Figure 21.14 shows the value of the bound ϵ for each of several possible values of *nrec*.

Number of records *nrec*	100	200	1,000	2,000	10,000	20,000
Bound ϵ	0.1940	0.1372	0.0613	0.0434	0.0194	0.0137

Figure 21.14 Values of Hoeffding Bound for $R = 1.5850$ and $Prob = 0.95$

For each value of *nrec*, only if the difference between the information gains of the best attribute X and the second best attribute Y is greater than ϵ will a split on X be made. As the number of records, *nrec*, becomes larger the Hoeffding Bound requirement becomes progressively easier to meet.

If we want to adopt a more cautious approach, i.e. require a higher probability of certainty before splitting, the value of the bound will be correspondingly larger (making it more difficult to achieve). Figure 21.15 shows the values of the Hoeffding Bound for $R = 1.5850$ and $Prob = 0.999$ for different values of *nrec*.

Number of records *nrec*	100	200	1,000	2,000	10,000	20,000
Bound ϵ	0.2946	0.2083	0.0931	0.0659	0.0295	0.0208

Figure 21.15 Values of Hoeffding Bound for $R = 1.5850$ and $Prob = 0.999$

We can consider the value of ϵ as a multiple of the value of the range R. If we denote ϵ/R by *mult* then

$$mult = \sqrt{\frac{ln(1/\delta)}{2 * nrec}}$$

Rearranging this we have

$$. nrec = \frac{ln(1/\delta)}{2 * mult^2}$$

A value of $mult = 0.1$ (indicating that ϵ is 10% of R) is given when $nrec = 115$ for $Prob = 0.9$, $nrec = 150$ for $Prob = 0.95$, $nrec = 230$ for $Prob = 0.99$ and $nrec = 345$ for $Prob = 0.999$.

The choice of values for probability $Prob$ and grace period G determines the shape and size of the evolving tree. The most appropriate settings are likely to vary from one application to another.

There are two further adjustments that we can choose to make to the splitting process:

- We might decide only to split if $IG(X)$, the measure associated with the best attribute X, is greater than some specified multiple of the value of R.
- If we decide to make a split we might eliminate any attributes with low values of the measure from the *currentAtts* arrays of the descendant nodes. If there are many attributes, this may speed up subsequent processing of that part of the tree considerably.

This concludes the description of the process of deciding whether or not to spilt on an attribute at node L and if so which attribute to choose. It can be summarised by the following pseudocode.

Pseudocode 4: Choose Attribute to Split on at Node L

1. Calculate the initial entropy at node L
2. For every attribute att in node L's current attributes array calculate the Information Gain $IG(att)$
3. Denote the attributes with the largest and second largest IG values by X and Y respectively
4. Calculate the Hoeffding Bound ϵ for node L:
   - Set R to the initial entropy at node L
   - Set δ to the value of 1-$Prob$
   - Set $nrec$ to $hitcount[L]$
   - Calculate
     $$\epsilon = R * \sqrt{\frac{ln(1/\delta)}{2 * nrec}}$$
5. If $IG(X) - IG(Y) > \epsilon$ return X, otherwise return 'none'

If there is only one attribute in node L's current attributes list, attribute Y will be taken to be the 'null attribute', equivalent to not splitting at all, with an Information Gain value of zero.

21.6 H-Tree Algorithm: Final Version

The final form of the outline 'main' algorithm given in Section 21.3.8 is now as follows. It has an additional initial step to set the values of G and *Prob*.

H-Tree Algorithm: Final Version

1. **Set values of G and *Prob***
2. Initialise root node (see pseudocode 1)
3. For each record R with classification C that arrives to be processed
   - Process record R with classification C (see pseudocode 3)

The main algorithm uses pseudocode fragments 1 and 3, the latter of which uses numbers 2 and 4.

The final versions of all four pseudocode fragments are repeated here for ease of reference.

Pseudocode 1: Initialise Root Node

1. Set *currentAtts*[0] to be an array comprising the names of all the attributes
2. Set *splitAtt*[0] to 'none'
3. Set *hitcount*[0] to zero
4. For each class C, set *classtotals*[0][C] to zero
5. For each attribute A in the node's current attributes array
   - For each combination of class C and value V of attribute A
     - set *acvCounts*[0][A][C][V] to zero
6. Set *nextnode* to 1

Pseudocode 2: Split at Node L Using Attribute A

1. Set *splitAtt*[L] to A.
2. For each value V of attribute A
   - Set *branch*[L][A][V] to *nextnode* (to create a new leaf node)
   - Set *currentAtts*[*nextnode*] to be the same array as *currentAtts*[L] with attribute A removed
   - Initialise arrays *splitAtt*, *hitcount*, *classtotals* and *acvCounts* for node *nextnode* as for Pseudocode 1, steps 2 to 5
   - Increase *nextnode* by 1

Pseudocode 3: Process Record R with Classification C

1. Set N to the number of the root node
2. While $splitAtt[N]$!= 'none'
   - Set A to $splitAtt[N]$
   - Set V to value of attribute A in record R
   - Set N to $branch[N][A][V]$
3. Set $L = N$
4. Update arrays at leaf node L:
   - Increase $hitcount[L]$ by 1
   - Increase $classtotals[L][C]$ by 1
   - For each attribute A in the current attributes array for node L
     − set V to the value that the attribute has in record R
     − increase $acvCounts[L][A][C][V]$ by 1
5. If $hitcount[L]$ is a multiple of G and the classifications of the records sorted to node L are not all the same and $currentAtts[L]$ is not empty
   - Determine whether to split on an attribute at node L (see pseudocode 4)
   - If answer is 'yes', with splitting attribute A, split at node L, using attribute A (see pseudocode 2)

Pseudocode 4: Choose Attribute to Split on at Node L

1. Calculate the initial entropy at node L
2. For every attribute att in node L's current attributes array calculate the Information Gain $IG(att)$
3. Denote the attributes with the largest and second largest IG values by X and Y respectively
4. Calculate the Hoeffding Bound ϵ for node L:
   - Set R to the initial entropy at node L
   - Set δ to the value of 1-$Prob$
   - Set $nrec$ to $hitcount[L]$
   - Calculate
   $$\epsilon = R * \sqrt{\frac{ln(1/\delta)}{2 * nrec}}$$
5. If $IG(X) - IG(Y) > \epsilon$ return X, otherwise return 'none'

21.7 Using an Evolving H-Tree to Make Predictions

In this section we will look at the issue of predicting the classification of an unseen instance from an evolving classification tree.

One of the unavoidable requirements forced on us by streaming data is to be able to use the classification tree while it is still incomplete. This runs the risk that any prediction we obtain from it might have been different if we had made it at a later stage, but realistically we have to accept this.

Suppose that we have the incomplete tree shown in Figure 21.9 in Section 21.3 and we want to classify an unseen instance that is sorted to node 5, i.e. has attribute values $att6 = val62$ and $att2 = val21$. How should we classify it? We could use the *classtotals* array for node 5 and take the largest class, but that approach would not be appropriate in other cases such as for an unseen instance sorted to node 7, which has *a classtotals* array comprising all zeroes.

A simple but effective approach is to look at all the nodes on the path from the root node (node 0) down to node 5 and combine their *classtotals* arrays. The three arrays are $\{63, 17, 20\}$ at node 0, $\{87, 10, 3\}$ at node 2 and $\{25, 12, 31\}$ at node 5, giving combined counts of $\{175, 39, 54\}$. We can accumulate these values in an array *totalClassCounts* with three elements, one for each class.

For our example, the largest count in the *totalClassCounts* array is for the first class, i.e. $c1$, so that is the value predicted for the unseen instance. As more (labelled) records arrive at node 5, the values in array *classtotals* will change and some other class may become the majority one.

Pseudocode for this process is given below.

H-Tree Prediction Algorithm for Record R

1. Set array *totalClassCounts* to zero for each class
2. Set N to the number of the root node
3. While *splitAtt*$[N]$!= 'none'
   - Add values in array *classtotals*$[N]$ to those in *totalClassCounts* for each class in turn
   - Set A to *splitAtt*$[N]$
   - Set V to value of attribute A in record R
   - Set N to *branch*$[N][A][V]$
4. Set $L = N$
5. Add values in array *classtotals*$[L]$ to those in *totalClassCounts* for each class in turn
6. Predict the class which has the largest value in *totalClassCounts*

21.7.1 Evaluating the Performance of an H-Tree

The above method can be adapted to give us a way of evaluating the performance of an evolving H-Tree. One possibility is to keep back a file of records that are not used for building the tree and then use them as a test set, i.e. treat them as if we did not know the classifications and record the predicted and actual classes in a confusion matrix.[7] (In this case we do not change the values of the arrays at the nodes to which they are sorted.)

After the last test record has been examined we might have a confusion matrix such as the one shown in Figure 21.16 (assuming that the test file has 1,000 records).

Actual Class	Predicted Class		
	c1	*c2*	*c3*
c1	263	2	21
c2	2	187	8
c3	4	9	504

Figure 21.16 Confusion Matrix

From this we can calculate predictive accuracy or other measures of

---

[7]Confusion matrices were described in Chapter 7.

accuracy and track how the values vary if we repeat the test every hour, every day etc.

A second possibility is to evaluate the performance of the tree each time a node is expanded, using the same records that were used to develop the tree, rather than a separate test set, but recording in the confusion matrix only the actual versus predicted classifications of those records that have arrived since the previous split. (With this approach, the values in arrays *hitcount*, *classtotals* and *acvCounts* are updated for each new record.)

We create a confusion matrix with all zero values immediately after each split on a node. Using the example in Figure 21.9 (Section 21.3), if the next record that arrives is sorted to node 5 with actual classification *c2* but predicted classification *c1*, we increase the count in row *c2*, column *c1* of the confusion matrix by one.

This method gives a straightforward way of tracking the performance of the classifier from one split to another in terms of the records that have arrived in that period, rather than on a fixed set of test data. This is probably preferable in view of the phenomenon of *concept drift*, which will be described in Chapter 22.

21.8 Experiments: H-Tree versus TDIDT

According to Domingos and Hulten [1]: 'A key property of the Hoeffding tree algorithm is that it is possible to guarantee ... that the trees it produces are asymptotically arbitrarily close to the ones produced by a batch learner (i.e. a learner that uses all the examples to choose a test at each node)'. Such a learning algorithm is TDIDT, which was described in Chapters 4–6.

It is difficult to test empirically whether this aim is achieved with very large datasets as there is no possibility of being able to process such datasets using TDIDT or any similar 'batch learner'. However we can make at least a partial comparison of the results achieved by TDIDT and H-Tree by a simple trick: using a small dataset repeatedly to give the effect of using a large one.

21.8.1 The lens24 Dataset

We will start with an extremely small dataset: *lens24*, an ophthalmological dataset which was described in Chapter 5. It has a mere 24 records, with four attributes: *age*, *specRx*, *astig* and *tears* and three classes: 1, 2 and 3.

If all 24 records are input to H-Tree many times, in batches of 24 and in the same order each time, so the total number of records input is say 2,400, 24,000 or 24,000,000, we can examine the trees produced and compare them with those produced by TDIDT. For any exact number of replications of the original data records TDIDT will give the same result as if they had only been processed once.

We will compare the algorithms by extracting rules from the trees generated, each rule corresponding to the path from the root node to a leaf node, working from left to right.

There are nine rules generated by the TDIDT algorithm:

1. IF $tears = 1$ THEN Class $= 3$
2. IF $tears = 2$ AND $astig = 1$ AND $age = 1$ THEN Class $= 2$
3. IF $tears = 2$ AND $astig = 1$ AND $age = 2$ THEN Class $= 2$
4. IF $tears = 2$ AND $astig = 1$ AND $age = 3$ AND $specRx = 1$ THEN Class $= 3$
5. IF $tears = 2$ AND $astig = 1$ AND $age = 3$ AND $specRx = 2$ THEN Class $= 2$
6. IF $tears = 2$ AND $astig = 2$ AND $specRx = 1$ THEN Class $= 1$
7. IF $tears = 2$ AND $astig = 2$ AND $specRx = 2$ AND $age = 1$ THEN Class $= 1$
8. IF $tears = 2$ AND $astig = 2$ AND $specRx = 2$ AND $age = 2$ THEN Class $= 3$
9. IF $tears = 2$ AND $astig = 2$ AND $specRx = 2$ AND $age = 3$ THEN Class $= 3$

The results below show the rules generated by H-Tree with G and *Prob* set to 500 and 0.999 respectively for varying numbers of records (all multiples of 24).

2400 records

At this stage there are just three rules, listed below.

1. IF $tears = 1$ THEN Class $= 3$
2. IF $tears = 2$ AND $astig = 1$ THEN Class $= \{0, 187, 38\}$
3. IF $tears = 2$ AND $astig = 2$ THEN Class $= \{149, 0, 76\}$

The arrays shown for rules 2 and 3 give the class totals for the three classes (1, 2 and 3) in order.

Rules 2 and 3 look as if they may be 'compressed' versions of TDIDT rules 2–5 and 6–9 respectively. How will they develop as more records are processed?

4800 records

At this stage H-Tree has generated six rules as follow.

1. IF $tears = 1$ THEN Class $= 3$
2. IF $tears = 2$ AND $astig = 1$ AND $age = 1$ THEN Class $= 2$
3. IF $tears = 2$ AND $astig = 1$ AND $age = 2$ THEN Class $= 2$
4. IF $tears = 2$ AND $astig = 1$ AND $age = 3$ THEN Class $= \{0, 55, 54\}$
5. IF $tears = 2$ AND $astig = 2$ AND $specRx = 1$ THEN Class $= 1$
6. IF $tears = 2$ AND $astig = 2$ AND $specRx = 2$ THEN Class $= \{54, 0, 109\}$

Now rules 4 and 6 look as if they may be compressed versions of TDIDT rules 4–5 and 7–9 respectively.

7200 records

At this stage there are the same six rules as for 4800 records, except that the arrays for rules 4 and 6 are now {0, 155, 154} and {154, 0, 309}, respectively.

9600 records

Now H-Tree has generated nine rules, reproduced below. They are exactly the same as the rules produced by TDIDT.

1. IF *tears* = 1 THEN Class = 3
2. IF *tears* = 2 AND *astig* = 1 AND *age* = 1 THEN Class = 2
3. IF *tears* = 2 AND *astig* = 1 AND *age* = 2 THEN Class = 2
4. IF *tears* = 2 AND *astig* = 1 AND *age* = 3 AND *specRx* = 1 THEN Class = 3
5. IF *tears* = 2 AND *astig* = 1 AND *age* = 3 AND *specRx* = 2 THEN Class = 2
6. IF *tears* = 2 AND *astig* = 2 AND *specRx* = 1 THEN Class = 1
7. IF *tears* = 2 AND *astig* = 2 AND *specRx* = 2 AND *age* = 1 THEN Class = 1
8. IF *tears* = 2 AND *astig* = 2 AND *specRx* = 2 AND *age* = 2 THEN Class = 3
9. IF *tears* = 2 AND *astig* = 2 AND *specRx* = 2 AND *age* = 3 THEN Class = 3

Running H-Tree with large numbers of additional repetitions of the original data appears to produce no further changes to the tree.

21.8.2 The vote Dataset

The *vote* 'US congressional voting' dataset has 300 records, with 16 attributes and 2 classes. TDIDT generates 34 rules from this dataset.

Records	Rules
12,000	9
24,000	14
36,000	17
72,000	24
120,000	27
360,000	28
480,000	28
720,000	28

Figure 21.17 Number of Records Generated for *vote* Dataset

Figure 21.17 shows the number of rules generated by the H-Tree algorithm for different numbers of records, all multiple repetitions of the original 300 records.

In this case inspection shows that the H-Tree seems to be converging towards the 34 rules generated by TDIDT. Out of the H-Tree's 28 rules, 24 are the same as those generated by TDIDT, but even after 720,000 records have been processed (2,400 repetitions of the original 300), there are still four of H-Tree's rules with mixed classifications that have not (yet?) been expanded into rules generated by TDIDT. In each case there would seem to be an obvious way in which the rule could be expanded and it is entirely possible that the four H-Tree rules with mixed classifications might evolve into ten rules with single classifications as they are for TDIDT given yet more repetitions of the original 300 records.

It would seem that the tree produced by H-Tree is converging towards the one generated by TDIDT, albeit very slowly.[8]

21.9 Chapter Summary

This chapter is concerned with the classification of *streaming data*, i.e. data which arrives (generally in large quantities) from some automatic process over a period of days, months, years or potentially forever. Generating a classification tree for streaming data requires a different approach from the TDIDT algorithm described earlier in this book. The algorithm given here, *H-Tree*, is a variant of the popular VFDT algorithm which generates a type of decision tree called a *Hoeffding Tree*. The algorithm is described and explained in detail with accompanying pseudocode for the benefit of readers who may be interested in developing their own implementations. An example is given to illustrate a way of comparing the rules generated by H-Tree with those from TDIDT.

21.10 Self-assessment Exercises for Chapter 21

1. Why can the TDIDT algorithm not be used directly with streaming data?
2. What benefit is gained by using a Hoeffding Bound when generating an H-Tree?
3. How does the availability of a potentially infinite amount of streaming data compensate for being unable to store all the data?

---

[8]For some practical applications, to have a tree with a smaller number of leaf nodes which predicts the same or almost the same classifications as the complete TDIDT decision tree might be considered preferable, but we will not pursue that issue here.

4. Assume that we are considering splitting on an attribute at node Z. The values of *classtotals*[Z] and *currentAtts*[Z] are the arrays $\{20, 30, 50\}$ and $\{att1, att3, att4, att7\}$ respectively. Also assume that the values of G and *Prob* are 100 and 0.999 respectively and that the Information Gain associated with splitting on each of the four attributes is as follows:

   IG(*att1*): 0.1614

   IG(*att3*): 1.3286

   IG(*att4*): 1.0213

   IG(*att7*): 0.8783

   Calculate the value of the Hoeffding Bound and determine whether or not we should split on an attribute at node Z and, if so, which one.

References

[1] Domingos, P., & Hulten, G. (2000). Mining high-speed data streams. In *Proceedings of the sixth ACM SIGKDD international conference on knowledge discovery and data mining* (pp. 71–80). New York: ACM.

[2] Hoeffding, W. (1963). Probability inequalities for sums of bounded random variables. *Journal of the American Statistical Association, 58* (301), 13–30.

Classifying Streaming Data II: Time-Dependent Data

22.1 Stationary versus Time-dependent Data

In all the discussion of classification techniques in this book up to now, there has been an implicit assumption, which it will now be helpful to make explicit.

We are assuming throughout that there is some underlying process which leads to an instance (or record) with a given set of attributes having a particular classification rather than another one. The classification is not just random – there is a reason (unknown to us) why a share price goes up or down, why a customer does or does not buy breakfast cereal, why a US congressman votes one way or another, why an earthquake does or does not occur on a given day and so on. We can refer to the process that determines the classification in a given domain as the *underlying causal model*.

The world is very complex and in many domains it may well be that we will never fully know the underlying model. To express it fully may involve a very complex mathematical formalism – possibly one that has not yet been invented. If we knew it in full detail we would probably realise that we had not recorded all the attributes needed to make an accurate calculation of the correct classification in each case and also that we had recorded some attributes that were entirely irrelevant to the result.

This all sounds very complicated and it is. The task of the data miner is

© Springer-Verlag London Ltd., part of Springer Nature 2020   379
M. Bramer, *Principles of Data Mining*, Undergraduate Topics
in Computer Science, DOI 10.1007/978-1-4471-7493-6_22

to produce a model which approximates to the true underlying one using a formalism of our choice: a decision tree, a set of rules or perhaps some other formalism not discussed in this book such as a Neural Net or a Support Vector Machine. The accuracy of our approximation will probably depend crucially on which of the various available formalisms we use but in most cases we have no way of knowing which one to choose, although experience may act as a guide.

We now come to the reason for making all this explicit. Up to now we have assumed that however complex the underlying model may be it is *fixed*. Whatever the process is that produced the original classification it will be the same tomorrow, next week and next year as it is today. If data is collected and then analysed and re-analysed, perhaps over a period of years, then the underlying model we try to approximate is inevitably fixed. We generally assume that if we collect more data over time it will simply be more samples generated by the same underlying model. We will call such data *stationary data*.

The situation with classifying streaming data where we are classifying records over a long (potentially infinite) period of time is significantly different. Although it is perfectly possible that the underlying model is fixed (and this is the assumption made in Chapter 21) it is also possible that the model may change from time to time. For example if we are predicting which customers in a supermarket will buy a particular food product the underlying model may vary considerably from mid-summer to mid-winter, possibly changing gradually as time goes by but also possibly changing rapidly if there is an effective advertising campaign that boosts sales or a contaminated food alarm that causes them serious damage. We will call data resulting from a model that changes across time *time-dependent data*. The underlying model is often referred to as the concept we need to model and the phenomenon of a changing model is known as *concept drift*.

Although the H-Tree algorithm described in Chapter 21 works well with streaming data, if the model is fixed, it has a major weakness when faced with streaming data that is time-dependent: once a tree has been created it can only be changed by further splitting on nodes. There is no way of 'unsplitting', i.e. converting an internal node back to a leaf node or changing a split on attribute X at a given node to a split on attribute Y.

The H-Tree algorithm produces trees that are generally stable: once a reasonable number of records have been processed a large number of additional records can be processed with little or no further change to the tree. With time-dependent data such stability is highly undesirable – a tree that predicts with a high level of accuracy today may predict steadily less accurately as the underlying concept drifts. We need some way of revisiting decisions previously made when building our tree. This may involve replacing the subtree hanging from a node by another subtree that is more appropriate for the changed concept.

Four crucial features that distinguish algorithms for classifying streaming data from the TDIDT algorithm described in Chapters 4–6, which we will call a *batch model*, are:

- We cannot collect all the data before generating a classification tree as the volume is potentially infinite.
- We cannot store all the data and revisit it repeatedly as we can do with TDIDT, once again as the volume is potentially infinite.
- We cannot wait until we have a fixed classification tree before we use the tree to predict the classification for previously unseen data. We must be able to use it for prediction with a high level of accuracy at any time, except for possibly a fairly short start-up phase.
- The algorithm must be able to operate in real-time and thus the amount of processing needed as each record comes in must be quite small. This is particularly important if we want to allow for data that arrives in high volume day-by-day such as data recording supermarket transactions or withdrawals from bank ATMs.

The H-Tree algorithm (based on Domingos and Hulten's VFDT algorithm [1]) meets these four criteria. In this chapter we will develop a revised version of the algorithm that meets the same criteria and also deals with data that is time-dependent. It is based closely on an algorithm introduced by Hulten, Spencer and Domingos [2] called CVFDT, standing for Concept-adapting Very Fast Decision Tree learner. As always with influential algorithms there are many published variants that purport to be improvements. Our own version, which will be described in this chapter, is based closely on CVFDT but incorporates some detailed changes and simplifications. To avoid confusion we will call it the CDH-Tree algorithm, standing for 'Concept Drift Hoeffding Tree'.

We will start by reviewing the H-Tree algorithm and then change it piece by piece to become the final version of CDH-Tree. The next section summarises the key points of the H-Tree algorithm without explanation. It is assumed that there is a constant stream of records arriving and that each one is processed as it arrives and is then thrown away. **If you have not yet read Chapter 21 you are strongly encouraged to do so before going on.**

22.2 Summary of the H-Tree Algorithm

This section gives a brief summary of the H-Tree algorithm developed in Chapter 21 as a reminder of the main points.

As data records are read a classification tree is developed branch by branch, starting with just one node, numbered zero, which will act as the root of the eventual classification tree.

As the records are received they are processed and discarded, but doing this does not immediately alter the structure (nodes and branches) of the evolving incomplete tree. As each new record comes in and is processed it is sorted through the tree to the appropriate leaf node. It is only when G records have been sorted to a leaf node and some other conditions are met that a change to the tree by splitting at that node is considered (G stands for 'Grace Period').

When a leaf node is *split* on an attribute, a subtree is created below it with one branch for each possible value of the selected attribute. Once a node has been split on an attribute it cannot later be 'unsplit' or 'resplit' on a different attribute.

Figure 22.1 shows a partly developed H-Tree.

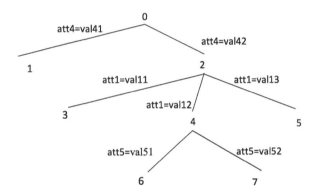

Figure 22.1 A Partly Developed H-Tree

The nodes in the tree are numbered in the order in which they were created. The system variable *nextnode* holds the number of the next node in sequence for possible future use. In this case *nextnode* is 8.

The tree has been created by splitting on attribute *att4* at node 0 (creating nodes 1 and 2), *att1* at node 2 (creating nodes 3, 4 and 5) and *att5* at node 4 (creating nodes 6 and 7).

There are six arrays maintained at every node. They are listed below.

22.2.1 Array *currentAtts*

This is a two-dimensional array. The element *currentAtts[N]* is an array containing the names of all the attributes available for splitting on at node N, listed in a standard order. This is called the *current attributes array* for that node.

If our data records have the values of seven attributes *att1*, *att2*, *att3*, *att4*, *att5*, *att6* and *att7* then at the root node *currentAtts*[0] is initialised to the array {*att1*, *att2*, *att3*, *att4*, *att5*, *att6*, *att7*}.

When a leaf node is 'expanded' by being split on at an attribute, its immediate descendant nodes inherit the current attributes array of the parent with the splitting attribute removed. Thus

- *currentAtts*[1] and *currentAtts*[2] are both the array {*att1*, *att2*, *att3*, *att5*, *att6*, *att7*}
- *currentAtts*[3], *currentAtts*[4] and *currentAtts*[5] are all the array {*att2*, *att3*, *att5*, *att6*, *att7*}
- *currentAtts*[6] and *currentAtts*[7] are both the array {*att2*, *att3*, *att6*, *att7*}.

22.2.2 Array *splitAtt*

For an internal node N, i.e. one that has previously been split on an attribute, the array element *splitAtt*[N] is the name of the splitting attribute, so *splitAtt*[0] is *att4*, *splitAtt*[2] is *att1* and *splitAtt*[4] is *att5*. All the other nodes are leaf nodes at which there are (by definition) no splitting attributes. The value of *splitAtt*[N] for a leaf node is 'none'.

22.2.3 Array *hitcount*

For each leaf node N, *hitcount*[N] is the number of 'hits' on the node since it was created, i.e. the number of records sorted to that leaf node. As each new record is sorted to a leaf node L, the value of *hitcount*[L] is increased by 1. These values are not increased for internal nodes as they play no further part in the tree generation process. When a new node is created its *hitcount* value is set to zero.

22.2.4 Array *classtotals*

This is another two-dimensional array. If there are three possible classifications named *c1*, *c2* and *c3* and node N is a leaf node, then *classtotals*[N][*c1*], *classtotals*[N][*c2*] and *classtotals*[N][*c3*] record the number of 'hits' on node N for which the classification is *c1*, *c2* and *c3*, respectively. When a new node is created its *classtotals* value is set to zero for all classes.

22.2.5 Array *acvCounts*

The name stands for 'attribute-class-value counts'. It has four dimensions. If N is a leaf node then for each attribute A in its current attributes array, $acvCounts[N][A]$ is a two-dimensional array known as a frequency table, which records the number of occurrences of each possible combination of class value and the value of attribute A. When a new leaf node is created its *acvCounts* value for each combination of class and attribute value for every attribute in its current attributes array is set to zero.

22.2.6 Array *branch*

When leaf node N is split on attribute A a branch leading to a new node is created for each value of that attribute. For each value V of attribute A $branch[N][A][V]$ is set to *nextnode* and *nextnode* is increased by 1.

22.2.7 Pseudocode for the H-Tree Algorithm

The algorithm for processing records developed in Chapter 21 can be summarised by the following pseudocode fragments. These are not intended as a replacement for the explanation in Chapter 21 but are provided for the benefit of readers who may be interested in developing their own implementations of the algorithm. Other readers can safely ignore them.

H-Tree Algorithm: Final Version

1. Set values of G and *Prob*
2. Initialise root node (see pseudocode 1)
3. For each record R with classification C that arrives to be processed
   - Process record R with classification C (see pseudocode 3)

Pseudocode 1: Initialise Root Node

1. Set *currentAtts*[0] to be an array comprising the names of all the attributes
2. Set *splitAtt*[0] to 'none'
3. Set *hitcount*[0] to zero
4. For each class *C*, set *classtotals*[0][*C*] to zero
5. For each attribute *A* in the node's current attributes array
   - For each combination of class *C* and value *V* of attribute *A*
     - set *acvCounts*[0][*A*][*C*][*V*] to zero
6. Set *nextnode* to 1

Pseudocode 2: Split at Node *L* Using Attribute *A*

1. Set *splitAtt*[*L*] to *A*.
2. For each value *V* of attribute *A*
   - Set *branch*[*L*][*A*][*V*] to *nextnode* (to create a new leaf node)
   - Set *currentAtts*[*nextnode*] to be the same array as *currentAtts*[*L*] with attribute *A* removed
   - Initialise arrays *splitAtt*, *hitcount*, *classtotals* and *acvCounts* for node *nextnode* as for Pseudocode 1, steps 2 to 5
   - Increase *nextnode* by 1

Pseudocode 3: Process Record R with Classification C

1. Set N to the number of the root node
2. While $splitAtt[N]$!= 'none'
   - Set A to $splitAtt[N]$
   - Set V to value of attribute A in record R
   - Set N to $branch[N][A][V]$
3. Set $L = N$
4. Update arrays at leaf node L:
   - Increase $hitcount[L]$ by 1
   - Increase $classtotals[L][C]$ by 1
   - For each attribute A in the current attributes array for node L
     - set V to the value that the attribute has in record R
     - increase $acvCounts[L][A][C][V]$ by 1
5. If $hitcount[L]$ is a multiple of G and the classifications of the records sorted to node L are not all the same and $currentAtts[L]$ is not empty
   - Determine whether to split on an attribute at node L (see pseudocode 4)
   - If answer is 'yes', with splitting attribute A, split at node L, using attribute A (see pseudocode 2)

Pseudocode 4: Choose Attribute to Split on at Node L

1. Calculate the initial entropy at node L
2. For every attribute att in node L's current attributes array calculate the Information Gain $IG(att)$
3. Denote the attributes with the largest and second largest IG values by X and Y respectively
4. Calculate the Hoeffding Bound ϵ for node L:
   - Set R to the initial entropy at node L
   - Set δ to the value of 1-$Prob$
   - Set $nrec$ to $hitcount[L]$
   - Calculate
   $$\epsilon = R * \sqrt{\frac{ln(1/\delta)}{2 * nrec}}$$
5. If $IG(X) - IG(Y) > \epsilon$ return X, otherwise return 'none'

We will consider all the pseudocode and other information in this section to be the 'initial draft' (version 1) of a specification for CDH-Tree and will progressively refine it in what follows.

22.3 From H-Tree to CDH-Tree: Overview

The two key ideas incorporated in the CDH-Tree algorithm that make it suitable for use with time-dependent data are:

- The values of arrays *hitcount* and *acvCounts* at each node are based on the most recent records to be processed, not all records ever received.
- There is a facility for changing the evolving classification tree by 'resplitting' at a node using a different attribute.

Before turning to these we begin by changing the counts recorded in arrays *hitcount* and *acvCounts* at internal nodes.

22.4 From H-Tree to CDH-Tree: Incrementing Counts

The first step in the transition from H-Tree to CDH-Tree is to increment the *acvCounts* and *hitcount* arrays not only for a leaf node L but also for each of the internal nodes (including the root) through which each record passes on its path from the root to node L.

Assuming there are no other changes, incrementing those values at the internal nodes will not alter the structure of the evolving tree. Only the values at leaf nodes will do that. Although the change will make no difference at this stage, it will turn out to be very useful as we go on adjusting the algorithm until it eventually becomes the final version of CDH-Tree. The key point is that at each internal node the *hitcount* and *acvCounts* arrays will now hold the values that they would have had if they had remained unsplit, thus opening up the possibility of being split on a different attribute at a later stage.

The first revision to the H-Tree algorithm in its transition to CDH-Tree is to replace pseudocode fragment 3 by:

Pseudocode 3: Process Record R with Classification C (version 2)

1. Set N to the number of the root node
2. **Set Continue to 'yes'**
3. **While (Continue = 'yes')**
   a) **Update arrays at node N**
      - **Increase** $hitcount[N]$ **by 1**
      - **For each attribute Att in the current attributes array for node N**
        - **set Val to the value that the attribute has in record R**
        - **increase $acvCounts[N][Att][C][Val]$ by 1**
   b) **If** $splitAtt[N]$ **= 'none' set Continue to 'no'**
      else
      - Set A to $splitAtt[N]$
      - Set V to value of attribute A in record R
      - Set N to $branch[N][A][V]$
4. Set $L = N$
5. **Increase** $classtotals[L][C]$ **by 1**
6. If $hitcount[L]$ is a multiple of G and the classifications of the records sorted to node L are not all the same and $currentAtts[L]$ is not empty
   - Determine whether to split on an attribute at node L (see pseudocode 4)
   - If answer is 'yes', with splitting attribute A, split at node L, using attribute A (see pseudocode 2)

Here and subsequently the parts altered are shown in **bold**. Note that array *classtotals* is only updated at leaf nodes. It is not used when making decisions about splitting or unsplitting but has an important role when using the classification tree for prediction, so its value needs to be increased only at the leaf node to which each record is sorted.

Pseudocode fragments 1, 2 and 4 remain unaltered.

22.5 The Sliding Window Method

Up to now we have built the tree using all the records that have so far arrived. From now on we will use only the most recent W records, say the most recent 10,000. We can think of this as looking at the records going past through a 'window' of fixed size W. We call this the *sliding window* method and call W the *window size*.

This change means that we now need to store the most recent W records[1]. When initially the first W records are processed they are stored in a table of W rows (or some equivalent form), working from row 1 down to row W. When the next record is read its values go into row 1 and the record that previously occupied that row (i.e. the oldest record) is discarded. When the next record is read, it goes into row 2 (which is now the oldest record), the previous occupant of that row is discarded and so on. After $2 * W$ records have been processed none of the original W records will remain in the window.

When a new record is added to the window the *acvCounts* and *hitcount* arrays are incremented for all the nodes it passes through on its path from the root node to the appropriate leaf (including the root node and leaf node) and the *classtotals* array is incremented for the leaf node itself. When an old record is removed from the window it is not merely discarded, it is *forgotten*. Forgetting a record means decreasing by one the values in the *acvCounts* and *hitcount* arrays for all the nodes it passed through on its path from the root node to the appropriate leaf node when it was first added to the window and decreasing by one the values in the *classtotals* array for the leaf node itself.

Since at present we are keeping to the principle that once we have split on an attribute at a given node that decision is never changed, it is still only the values of the *acvCounts* and *hitcount* arrays at the leaf nodes that affect the evolving tree. In [2] it is argued that if the data is stationary, adding records to or removing records from the sliding window should have little effect on the evolving tree.

Our aim in this chapter is to create an algorithm that will deal with data that is time-dependent and the value of introducing a sliding window will become apparent soon.

The revised version of the pseudocode for the main CDH-Tree algorithm now looks like this.

---

[1]We will assume that each record comprises a set of attribute values together with a classification.

CDH-Tree Algorithm
(version 2)

1. Set values of G, *Prob* and **W**
2. Initialise root node (see pseudocode 1)
3. For each record R with classification C that arrives to be processed
   a) **If the number of records in the window $< W$ add R to the window**
      else
      i. **take a copy of the oldest record in the window R_{old} with classification C_{old}**
      ii. **replace R_{old} by R**
      iii. **'forget' record R_{old} with classification C_{old} (see pseudocode 5)**
   b) Process record R with classification C (see pseudocode 3)

Steps (a) and (b) of the algorithm are often described as the grow/forget stage.

Pseudocode fragment 5 is based on fragment 3 but of course it does not need to include any possibility of splitting on the leaf node. *Warning – this version contains an error.*

Pseudocode 5: Forget Record R_{old} with Classification C_{old}

1. Set N to the number of the root node
2. Set Continue to 'yes'
3. While (Continue = 'yes')
   a) Update arrays at node N
      i. decrease $hitcount[N]$ by 1
      ii. for each attribute Att in the current attributes array for node N
         - set Val to the value that the attribute has in record R
         - decrease $acvCounts[N][Att][C_{old}][Val]$ by 1
   b) If $splitAtt[N] = $ 'none' set Continue to 'no'
      else
      i. Set A to $splitAtt[N]$
      ii. Set V to value of attribute A in record R_{old}
      iii. Set N to $branch[N][A][V]$
4. Decrease $classtotals[N][C_{old}]$ by 1

This form of the algorithm is not quite correct. It ignores an important complication that can occur when we forget a record.

Suppose when we added a record to the window the tree looked like Figure 22.2 and the record was sorted to leaf node 4 following the path $0 \rightarrow 2 \rightarrow 4$.

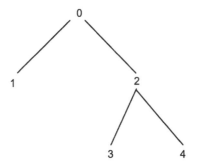

Figure 22.2 A Small Decision Tree

When we come to forget the record the tree may have evolved to look like this (Figure 22.3).

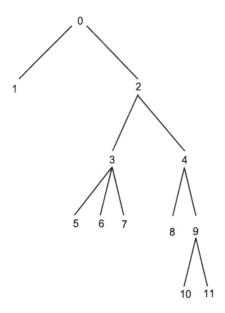

Figure 22.3 Decision Tree at a Later Stage

During the forgetting process (as so far described) the record might now be sorted to leaf node 10 following the path $0 \rightarrow 2 \rightarrow 4 \rightarrow 9 \rightarrow 10$.

It would clearly be wrong to decrement the various counts at nodes 9 and 10 as the record never reached there at the 'grow' stage and so the counts at those nodes were never increased.

To deal with this problem we note that node numbers are allocated sequentially as new nodes are created. The record that we are currently 'forgetting' was originally sorted to leaf node 4. Any further nodes added to any part of the tree after that happened must inevitably have a number that is greater than 4.

So we adopt the strategy that whenever a record is added to the window we store the number of the leaf node to which it is sorted in the window with it. In this case the number is 4. In the general case we will call the value *idMax*.

This revised version of pseudocode fragment 3 shows the change needed.

Pseudocode 3: Process Record R with Classification C (version 3)

As version 2 but with a new Step 6

6. Store the value of L in the window as the *idMax* value of the newest record R

and the previous Step 6 renumbered as Step 7

Now when we forget a record we first retrieve its corresponding *idMax* value and follow the record's path to its (possibly new) corresponding leaf node (decrementing the counts at each node as we do so) only as long as the number of each node is less than or equal to *idMax*.

It will prove convenient to place the retrieve part of this in the 'main' algorithm which becomes

---

Outline of CDH-Tree Algorithm (version 3)

As version 2 but with the following added as the second stage of the 'else' part of Step 3(a)

- set $idMax_{old}$ to the *idMax* value of record R_{old}

Pseudocode fragment 5 now looks as follows.

Pseudocode 5: Forget Record R_{old} with Classification C_{old} (version 2)

1. Set N to the number of the root node
2. **If $N \leq idMax_{old}$**
   a) Set Continue to 'yes'
   b) While (Continue = 'yes')
      i. Update arrays at node N
         - decrease $hitcount[N]$ by 1
         - for each attribute Att in the current attributes array for node N
            – set Val to the value that the attribute has in record R
            – decrease $acvCounts[N][Att][C_{old}][Val]$ by 1
      ii. **Set N_{last} to N**
      iii. If $splitAtt[N]$ = 'none' set Continue to 'no'
         else
         - Set A to $splitAtt[N]$
         - Set V to value of attribute A in record R_{old}
         - Set N to $branch[N][A][V]$
         - **If $N > idMax_{old}$ set Continue to 'no'**
   c) **Decrease $classtotals[N_{last}][C_{old}]$ by 1**

22.6 Resplitting at Nodes

We now come to the most important change in the transition from the H-Tree algorithm to CDH-Tree, which the previous sections have been building up to.

The fundamental problem with the method described when the data is time-dependent is that once a split is made at a node it can never be reversed or changed. We now need to address this issue.

The general idea is that periodically all the internal nodes of the tree are checked to determine for each one whether the attribute on which it was split previously would still be chosen if the decision were being made now, using the counts currently recorded, which relate only to the records currently in the window. If it would not still be chosen and a condition involving the Hoeffding Bound is met by a different attribute, this is taken as a possible indication of concept drift and the node (which will necessarily have a subtree hanging from it) is treated as 'suspect'. We will defer until later sections the issue of what to do with suspect nodes.

22.7 Identifying Suspect Nodes

We will set another parameter D, representing the number of records between checks for concept drift. After each D records have been processed we conduct a review of each of the internal nodes in the tree in turn, to check whether the attribute that was selected to split on there would still be selected if the decision were being made now, based on the records in the current sliding window. Any node which fails this test and at which a different attribute passes a test involving the Hoeffding Bound is treated as 'suspect'.

This requires some minor changes to the main algorithm. We will use variable *recordnum* to store the number of each record to be processed, counting from zero.

Outline of CDH-Tree Algorithm
(version 4)

1. Set values of G, *Prob* and W **and D**
   Set *recordnum* to zero
2. Initialise root node (see pseudocode 1)
3. For each record R with classification C that arrives to be processed
   a) if the number of records in the window $< W$ add R to the window
      else
      i. take a copy of the oldest record in the window: R_{old} with classification C_{old}
      ii. set $idMax_{old}$ to the $idMax$ value of record R_{old}
      iii. replace R_{old} by R
      iv. 'forget' record R_{old} with classification C_{old} (see pseudocode 5)
   b) process record R with classification C (see pseudocode 3)
   c) **increase *recordnum* by 1**
   d) **if *recordnum* is a multiple of D review node 'root' and all**
      its descendants that are internal nodes (see pseudocode 6)

Pseudocode fragment 6 will be developed later in this section.

It is straightforward to identify all the internal nodes in the tree systematically by starting at the root node and using the contents of the *splitAtt* and *branch* arrays. Figure 22.4 illustrates the method[2].

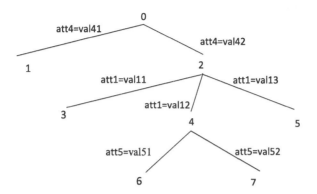

Figure 22.4 A Partly Developed CDH-Tree

The splitting attribute at node zero (the root) is *att4*, which has two values: *val41* and *val42*. These lead to nodes 1 and 2 using the *branch* array: $branch[0][att4][val41]$ is 1 and $branch[0][att4][val42]$ is 2. We look at each of these nodes in turn. Node 1 is a leaf node (we know this from examining $splitAtt[1]$), so we take no action at that node. Node 2 is an internal node. It is split on attribute *att1*, which has three values: *val11*, *val12* and *val13*. The first and third of these lead to leaf nodes 3 and 5 respectively, but the second branch leads to node 4 which is an internal node, and so the process continues, until every path eventually leads to a leaf node and ends.

At each internal node we calculate the Information Gain corresponding to each attribute available for splitting. If the one that was chosen for splitting, attribute A, does not have the largest value, we find the two attributes with the largest Information Gain values and calculate the Hoeffding Bound. If the difference between the values of Information Gain for the best attribute X and the second best attribute Y is greater than the value of the Hoeffding Bound, the node is considered suspect and attribute X is considered to be the alternative splitting attribute for that node.

Whether the node is deemed 'suspect' or not it remains split on attribute A at present. We go on to examine its direct descendants using the contents of array *branch*.

All this gives two new fragments of pseudocode: 6 and 7.

---

[2]Figure 22.4 is identical to Figure 22.1. It is repeated for ease of reference.

Pseudocode 6: Review Node N and all its Descendants that are Internal Nodes

1. If N is a leaf node stop
   else
   a) Examine internal node N (see pseudocode 7)
   b) If node N is suspect with alternative attribute X *To be discussed in Section 22.8*
   c) Set A to *splitAtt*$[N]$
   d) For each value V of attribute A
      i. set *N1* to *branch*$[N][A][V]$
      ii. review node *N1* and all its descendants that are internal nodes

---

Pseudocode 7: Examine Internal Node N

1. Let A be the attribute currently split on at node N, i.e. *splitAtt*$[N]$
2. Find the value of Information Gain for each attribute in node N's current attribute array
3. If A has the largest value of Information Gain, return 'not suspect'
   else
   a) Find the two attributes with the largest values of Information Gain. Call them X and Y respectively
   b) Calculate the value of the Hoeffding Bound ϵ for node N
   c) If $IG(X) - IG(Y) > \epsilon$ return X as alternative attribute for splitting at node N

22.8 Creating Alternate Nodes

When a node N is identified as 'suspect', one possible action would be to convert it back to a leaf, throwing away its descendant subtree, and rely on the normal process of growing/forgetting as new records arrive to evolve a new subtree structure as time passes. The problem with doing this is that while it is going on, there is likely to be a substantial drop in the predictive accuracy of the tree for unseen records, especially if the node concerned is close to the root.

Instead we create an 'alternate node' for any suspect node N with initially a one-level subtree hanging from it formed by splitting on the 'alternative splitting attribute' X. We will assume that this alternate node is numbered $N1$. Node $N1$ is given the same *currentAtts*, *hitcount*, *classtotals* and *acvCounts* arrays as node N but its splitting attribute (the value of array element *splitAtt[N1]*) is different. It has the value X.

Next we create a branch from node $N1$ to a new node for each value of the new splitting attribute.

Node $N1$ and its substructure are not part of our classification tree but we can consider nodes N and $N1$ being linked by a dotted line as in Figure 22.5, where N and $N1$ are 2 and 10 respectively. Node 10 is an *alternate node* for node 2 in the main tree.

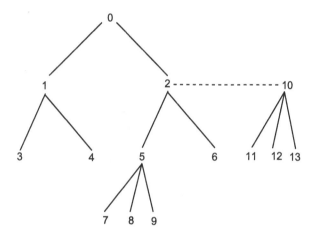

Figure 22.5 A CDH-Tree with an Alternate Node

As time goes by more than one alternate node and its substructure can be associated with a suspect node. As the grow/forget process continues the substructure below each alternate node may also evolve.

At some later time (see Section 22.10) a decision will be made whether or not to replace each of the suspect internal nodes by one of its alternate nodes, and if there is more than one of them which one. At that time Figure 22.5 may have evolved to look like this (Figure 22.6).

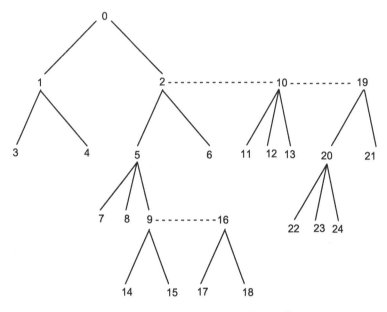

Figure 22.6 CDH-Tree at a Later Stage

To record the link between nodes in the main tree and their alternate nodes in array form we use a seventh array: *altTreeList*. This is a two-dimensional array. For Figure 22.6 *altTreeList*[2] is the array $\{10, 19\}$. The *altTreeList* array is only applicable to nodes in the main tree, not alternate nodes or any other nodes in the substructure hanging from them[3].

We can now replace the words in italics in pseudocode fragment 6:

---

[3]This is a restriction imposed by the CDH-Tree algorithm. It would be possible to allow nodes in an alternate tree to have their own alternate nodes but at the risk of creating and needing to maintain an increasingly unwieldy structure, most of which will never form part of the main tree. It is only the current main tree that is used for prediction.

Pseudocode 6: Review Node N and all its Descendants that are Internal Nodes
(version 2)

1. If N is a leaf node stop
   else
   a) Examine internal node N (see pseudocode 7)
   b) If node N is suspect with alternative attribute X
      i. set *newnode* to *nextnode*
      ii. increase *nextnode* by 1
      iii. add *newnode* to the array at *altTreeList*[N]
      iv. copy arrays *hitcount, classtotals, acvCounts* and *currentAtts* from node N to node *newnode*
      v. split at node *newnode* using attribute X (see pseudocode 2)
   c) Set A to *splitAtt*[N]
   d) For each value V of attribute A
      i. set $N1$ to *branch*[N][A][V]
      ii. review node $N1$ and all its descendants that are internal nodes

---

Replacing node 2 in Figure 22.6 by its (second) alternate node 19 would give this new tree structure (Figure 22.7).

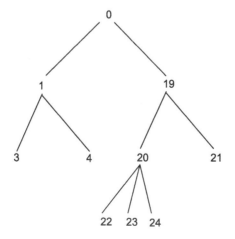

Figure 22.7 CDH-Tree after Node 2 Replaced by Alternate Node

Once a decision is made to replace, say node 2 by its alternate node 19, implementing the change is straightforward. Node 2 is a direct descendant of node 0. Let us say that the branch in question is for attribute *att7* with value *val72*. Then the element of the *branch* array that links nodes 0 and 2 is *branch*[0][*att7*][*val72*]. All we have to do is to change the value of this array element from 2 to 19.

The aim of this cautious approach to 'resplitting' a node on a different attribute from before is to ensure a smooth changeover to the new tree, which will enable it to maintain a high level of predictive accuracy throughout.

Using the 'alternate node' approach would be pointless for stationary data (as the data used with the algorithm developed in Chapter 21 is assumed to be), as it is unlikely that any would ever be created and, if they were, it is unlikely that they would ever replace the original nodes. In the case of time-dependent data it is hoped that using alternate nodes will give a smooth and appropriately cautious way of re-splitting the decision tree at one or more nodes as concept drift occurs.

22.9 Growing/Forgetting an Alternate Node and its Descendants

After any alternate nodes have been created the usual process of growing and forgetting as new records are read continues with the crucial difference that the increases/decreases in the counts are also applied to the alternate nodes and the nodes in the subtrees hanging from them. (In doing this each alternate node is treated as if it were the root of a separate tree.) Leaf nodes in these alternate trees can also be split whenever the Hoeffding Bound requirement is met. To do all this requires a further change to pseudocode fragment 3.

Pseudocode 3: Process Record R with Classification C (version 4)

1. Set N to the number of the root node
2. Set Continue to 'yes'
3. While (Continue = 'yes')
   a) Update arrays at node N
      i. Increase $hitcount[N]$ by 1
      ii. For each attribute Att in the current attributes array for node N
          - set Val to the value that the attribute has in record R
          - increase $acvCounts[N][Att][C][Val]$ by 1
   b) **If $altTreeList[N]$ is not empty, for each node number $nextalt$ in the array, treating node $nextalt$ as the root**
      - **process record R with classification C (*)**
   c) If $splitAtt[N]$ = 'none' set Continue to 'no'
      else
      i. Set A to $splitAtt[N]$
      ii. Set V to value of attribute A in record R
      iii. Set N to $branch[N][A][V]$
4. Set $L = N$
5. Increase $classtotals[L][C]$ by 1
6. **If $L >$ the $idMax$ value of the newest record R in the window, replace it by L**
7. If $hitcount[L]$ is a multiple of G and the classifications of the records sorted to node L are not all the same and $currentAtts[L]$ is not empty
   a) determine whether to split on an attribute at node L (see pseudocode 4)
   b) if answer is 'yes', with splitting attribute A, split at node L, using attribute A (see pseudocode 2)

The notation (*) indicates a recursive call to the same pseudocode fragment.

Pseudocode 5 also needs to be changed to enable forgetting to take place in alternate trees (if applicable) not only the main tree.

Pseudocode 5: Forget Record R_{old} with Classification C_{old} (version 3)

1. Set N to the number of the root node
2. If $N \leq idMax_{old}$
   a) Set Continue to 'yes'
   b) While (Continue = 'yes')
      i. Update arrays at node N
         - decrease $hitcount[N]$ by 1
         - for each attribute Att in the current attributes array for node N
            - set Val to the value that the attribute has in record R
            - decrease $acvCounts[N][Att][C_{old}][Val]$ by 1
      ii. **If $altTreeList[N]$ is not empty, for each node number $nextalt$ in the array, treating node $nextalt$ as the root, forget record R_{old} with classification C_{old} (*)**
      iii. Set N_{last} to N
      iv. If $splitAtt[N]$ = 'none' set Continue to 'no'
         else
         - Set A to $splitAtt[N]$
         - Set V to value of attribute A in record R_{old}
         - Set N to $branch[N][A][V]$
         - If $N > idMax_{old}$ set Continue to 'no'
   c) Decrease $classtotals[N_{last}][C_{old}]$ by 1

22.10 Replacing an Internal Node by One of its Alternate Nodes

All that remains to be added to the algorithm is a mechanism for determining whether and when to replace an internal node by one of its alternate nodes and, if it has more than one alternate node, how to decide which one to choose.

In order to do this, after each T records (say 10,000) are processed the system enters into a testing phase. The next M records (say 500) are used for testing the predictive accuracy of the tree. They do not affect the contents of the window or any of the $acvCounts$, $classtotals$ and $hitcount$ arrays and do not cause any splitting at leaf nodes to occur.

Instead each record processed is sorted to the corresponding leaf node in the main tree and also in any alternate tree linked to any of the internal nodes through which it passes.

To illustrate this Figure 22.8 shows a possible state of the tree at the start of a testing phase. Node 4 has alternate nodes 8 and 14; node 19 has alternate node 23 and node 7 has alternate node 26.

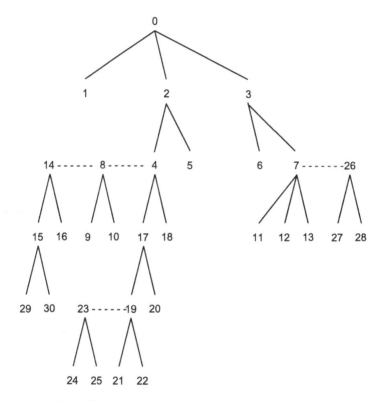

Figure 22.8 Tree Structure at Start of Testing Phase (Including Alternate Trees)

Suppose that a test record is sorted to leaf node 22 following the path 0 → 2 → 4 → 17 → 19 → 22. As the record 'passes through' internal node 4 (on its way to the leaf node) it is automatically copied and passed to the alternate trees hanging from the alternate nodes for node 4, i.e. 8 and 14. This may lead to it also being sorted to leaf nodes 9 and 29. As the record goes on and passes through node 19 it is also automatically copied and passed to that node's alternate, node 23, and from there may be sorted to leaf node 24. Thus a single record is sorted to four different leaf nodes.

We can now make a prediction of the classification at each of the four nodes and compare it with the true classification for the record. We do this using the contents of the *classtotals* array for each of the nodes on the path from the root to the leaf node (including the root and the leaf itself).

To predict the classification at node 22 in the main tree we use the contents of the *classtotals* arrays at nodes 0, 2, 4, 17, 19 and 22. If there are three possible classifications c1, c2 and c3, the array *classtotals*[2], say, will contain three values such as {50, 23, 42}. These correspond to the number of records with each classification that were sorted to that node when it was still a leaf node, i.e. before splitting on an attribute occurred there. We add together the contents of the *classtotals* arrays at nodes 0, 2, 4, 17, 19 and 22, element by element, into a combined array *testTotals* which might then contain values such as {312, 246, 385}. The class with the largest value in the *testTotals* array in our example is c3 and so this is taken to be the class predicted for leaf node 22.

We compare the prediction with the true classification, which in this case we will assume is c3, so in this case the predicted and the true classification are the same.

The same method is used for prediction if a record is sorted to a leaf node in an alternate tree, e.g. node 29. In this case we would combine the contents of the *classtotals* arrays at nodes 0, 2, 14, 15 and 29.

As more records are processed during the testing phase we accumulate a count for each leaf node (in both the main tree and the alternate trees) of the total number of records sorted to it and the number of those records for which the classification is correctly predicted. We store these values for each node in the two-dimensional array *testcounts*. At node 22, say, array elements *testcounts*[22][0] and *testcounts*[22][1] give the number of records so far sorted to that node during the testing stage and the number correctly classified respectively.

At the end of the testing phase we will have a *testcounts* array with contents such as the following for each of the 19 leaf nodes in our tree (Figure 22.9).

We can now fill in the table with *testcounts* array values for each of the internal nodes too, calculated by adding together the values of each of its immediate successors, working upwards from the leaf nodes.

Ignoring at present the possible existence of alternate nodes, the procedure is straightforward. Taking the part of the tree shown in Figure 22.10, the *testcounts* array for node 19 is the sum of those for nodes 21 and 22, i.e. {25, 18} and {5, 3} making a total of {30, 21}. Adding the *testcounts* values for leaf node 20 to this gives the array for internal node 17 as {40, 29}. Proceeding in this way the values at the leaf nodes are propagated up the tree right up to the root.

Leaf Node N	Number of Records $testcounts[N][0]$	Number of Correct Classifications $testcounts[N][1]$
1	25	16
5	6	3
6	5	3
9	20	14
10	24	16
11	10	7
12	5	3
13	5	3
16	14	12
18	4	3
20	10	8
21	25	18
22	5	3
24	15	13
25	15	6
27	10	6
28	10	4
29	20	13
30	10	10

Figure 22.9 Contents of *testcounts* Array at End of Testing Phase

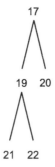

Figure 22.10 Extract from Figure 22.8 – Tree Structure at Start of Testing Phase

However there is an important complication that arises when a node such
as 19 is reached which has an alternate node, in this case 23. We will reinstate
this and the alternate tree hanging from it to give the extract shown in Figure
22.11.

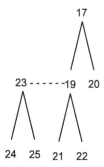

Figure 22.11 Figure 22.10 Augmented with Alternate Node 23 and its
Subtree

Before passing the values from node 19 up to its parent node 17, we first
consider the alternate tree rooted at node 23. The *testcounts* array at node 23
is the combination of those at its successor nodes 24 and 25 (both leaf nodes)
giving $\{30, 19\}$.

We now compare the scores at nodes 19 and 23: $\{30, 21\}$ versus $\{30, 19\}$.
The first elements are identical as they must always be, since the same records
pass through each of them in the testing phase. However the descendants of
node 19 correctly predicted the classifications of 21 records, compared with
only 19 for the descendants of alternate node 23. Node 19 is not replaced by its
alternate node and remains unchanged in the tree, as also does alternate node
23.

When we get to node 4 the performance at that node needs to be compared
with that of the alternate trees rooted at its two alternate nodes, 8 and 14. The
testcounts values are as follows.

Node 4: $\{44, 32\}$
Node 8: $\{44, 30\}$
Node 14: $\{44, 35\}$

This time the alternate tree rooted at node 14 has the best performance,
so node 4 is replaced by alternate node 14.

The tree now looks like this (Figure 22.12)[4].

---

[4] Although nodes 14, 15, 16, 29 and 30 were previously parts of an alternate tree
they are now in the main tree and so potentially can have alternate tree structures
attached to them.

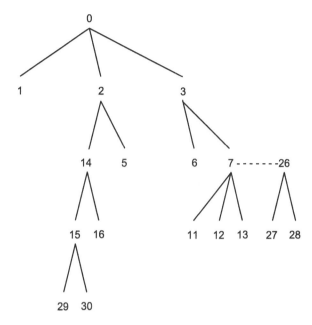

Figure 22.12 Tree Structure Following Replacement of Node 4 by Alternate Node 14

Note that the value of the *testcounts* array for node 2 is now the combination of those for nodes 14 and 5, i.e. {50, 38}.

Finally we come to the decision whether to replace node 7 by its alternate node 26. The *testcounts* arrays are {20, 13} for node 7 and {20, 10} for node 26. Node 7 has the better performance so both nodes remain unchanged in the tree.

This completes the investigation of the tree at the end of the testing phase. Part of the structure has changed but there is still one suspect node, 7, with an alternate, 26. The possibility of replacing the suspect node will be considered again at the end of the next testing phase, by which time new alternate nodes and their subtrees may have been created[5].

The above method requires a final change to the pseudocode for the main CDH-Tree algorithm plus two additional pseudocode fragments 8 and 9.

---

[5]Nodes 4 and 8 in Figure 22.8 and the subtrees hanging from them are not part of the revised structure and are no longer accessible. It may be possible for a practical implementation to reuse the memory they occupy but we will not pursue this here.

Outline of CDH-Tree Algorithm (version 5)

1. Set values of G, *Prob* and W, D, T and M
   Set *testmode* to 'no'
   Set *recordnum* to zero
2. Initialise root node (see pseudocode 1)
3. For each record R with classification C that arrives to be processed
   a) **if *testmode* = 'yes' sort record R and its classification C to leaf node(s) and predict classification(s) (see pseudocode 8) else**
      i. if the number of records in the window $< W$ add R to the window
         else
         - take a copy of the oldest record in the window: R_{old} with classification C_{old}
         - set $idMax_{old}$ to the $idMax$ value of record R_{old}
         - replace R_{old} by R
         - 'forget' record R_{old} with classification C_{old} (see pseudocode 5)
      ii. process record R with classification C (see pseudocode 3)
   b) increase *recordnum* by 1
   c) **if *recordnum* is a multiple of T set *testmode* to 'yes'**
      else if *testmode* = 'yes' and *recordnum* is a multiple of T plus M
      i. **set *testmode* to 'no'**
      ii. **check internal nodes for possible replacement, starting with root node, returning array *tcounts* (see pseudocode 9)**
   d) if *recordnum* is a multiple of D review node 'root' and all its descendants that are internal nodes (see pseudocode 6)

(The array *tcounts* returned by step 3(c)(ii) is not used here, but is important to the recursive definition of pseudocode 9 given below.)

Pseudocode 8: Sort Record R and its Classification C to Leaf Node(s) and Predict Classification(s)

1. Set N to the number of the root node
2. Set elements of *testTotals* array to zero (one for each class)
3. Set Continue to 'yes'
4. While (Continue = 'yes')
   a) Increase elements of *testTotals* array by corresponding elements of *classtotals*[N]
   b) If *splitAtt*[N] != 'none'
      i. If *altTreeList*[N] is not empty
         for each node number $N1$ in the array, treating node $N1$ as the root
         • sort record R and its classification C to leaf node(s) and predict classification(s) (*)
      ii. Set A to *splitAtt*[N]
      iii. Set V to value of attribute A in record R
      iv. Set N to *branch*[N][A][V]
5. Set $L = N$
6. Set predicted class to the class with the largest value in the *testTotals* array
7. Increase first element of array *testcounts*[N] by 1
8. If (predicted class = C) Increase second element of array *testcounts*[N] by 1

Pseudocode 9: Check Internal Nodes for Possible Replacement, Starting with Node *N*, Returning Array *tcounts*

1. If *splitAtt*[*N*] = 'none' Set array *tcounts* (two elements) to be the same as *testcounts*[*N*]

   else

   a) Set array *tcounts* to zero (two elements)

   b) For each immediate descendant node *N1* of node *N*

      i. Check internal nodes for possible replacement, starting with node *N1*, returning array *tcounts1* (*)

      ii. Increase elements of *tcounts* by the corresponding values of array *tcounts1*

   c) If array *altTreeList*[*N*] is not empty

      i. for each alternate node number *alt* in the array

         • check internal nodes for possible replacement, starting with node *alt*, returning array *tcountalt* (*)

      ii. Find alternate node *alt_{best}* with largest value of second element of *tcountalt*

      iii. If that value is larger than the second element of *tcounts*

         • set array *tcounts* to array *tcountalt*

         • replace node *N* in the main tree by alternate node *alt_{best}*

2. Return array *tcounts*

22.11 Experiment: Tracking Concept Drift

The CDH-Tree algorithm is a complex one, at least compared with other classification algorithms described elsewhere in this book. To illustrate how it works with time-dependent data, i.e. in the presence of concept drift, it is probably better to use synthetic data with concept drift introduced in a controlled way rather than real-world data, where it would be very hard to develop any feel for what the classification tree ought to be like at each stage.

As in Chapter 21 we will construct an experiment with an extremely small (but very useful) dataset: *lens24*, an ophthalmological dataset which was described in Chapter 5. It has a mere 24 records, with four attributes: *age*, *specRx*, *astig* and *tears*. Attribute *age* has three values: 1, 2 and 3. The other three attributes have two values: 1 and 2. There are three classes: 1, 2 and 3.

If all 24 records are input to CDH-Tree (in the same order) a large number of times, so the total number of records input is say 2,400, 24,000 or 24,000,000, we can examine the trees produced and compare them with those produced by the tree-generation algorithm TDIDT described in Chapters 4–6. For any exact multiple of the original data records TDIDT will give the same result as if it had only been processed once. In Section 21.8.1 it was shown that at some point between processing 7200 records and processing 9600 records the H-Tree constructed from this data had already produced the same tree as TDIDT and hence the same rules.

After 9600 records (i.e. 400 repetitions of the *lens24* data records in the same order each time) had been processed the decision tree looked like this (Figure 22.13)[6].

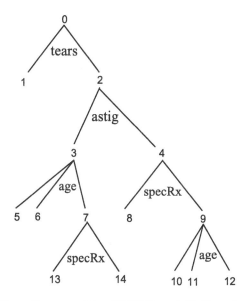

Figure 22.13   Tree Generated by TDIDT and H-Tree for 9,600 Records of *lens24* Data

We can extract rules from such a tree branch by branch, each rule corresponding to the path from the root node to a leaf node, working from left to right.

---

[6]We will adopt the convention that the branches at each internal node correspond to attribute values 1 and 2 (or 1, 2 and 3 in the case of *age*) in that order, working from left to right. So, for example, node 6 corresponds to a rule with left-hand side IF *tears* = 2 AND *astig* = 1 AND *age* = 2. (The corresponding classifications on the right-hand side are not shown.)

In this case there are nine rules generated by both TDIDT and H-Tree (Figure 22.14). All the leaf nodes have a single classification.

---

1. IF *tears* = 1 THEN Class = 3
2. IF *tears* = 2 AND *astig* = 1 AND *age* = 1 THEN Class = 2
3. IF *tears* = 2 AND *astig* = 1 AND *age* = 2 THEN Class = 2
4. IF *tears* = 2 AND *astig* = 1 AND *age* = 3 AND *specRx* = 1 THEN Class = 3
5. IF *tears* = 2 AND *astig* = 1 AND *age* = 3 AND *specRx* = 2 THEN Class = 2
6. IF *tears* = 2 AND *astig* = 2 AND *specRx* = 1 THEN *Class* = 1
7. IF *tears* = 2 AND *astig* = 2 AND *specRx* = 2 AND *age* = 1 THEN Class = 1
8. IF *tears* = 2 AND *astig* = 2 AND *specRx* = 2 AND *age* = 2 THEN Class = 3
9. IF *tears* = 2 AND *astig* = 2 AND *specRx* = 2 AND *age* = 3 THEN Class = 3

Figure 22.14 Rules Extracted from Decision Tree for *lens24* Data (9,600 Records)

Using the same data with the CDH-Tree algorithm, with W set to 9600, will produce exactly the same result[7]. We now need to find a way to introduce concept drift into the stream of data coming into CDH-Tree.

22.11.1 *lens24* Data: Alternative Mode

We start by introducing an alternative way of interpreting the *lens24* data records. Each record comprises four attribute values plus a classification. Normally the first, second, third and fourth attribute values are assigned to attributes *age*, *specRx*, *astig* and *tears* respectively. We will refer to this as the 'standard mode' of the data. If instead the four attribute values are assigned to attributes *age*, *tears*, *specRx* and *astig* in that order we will say the data is in 'alternative mode'[8].

If we run TDIDT, H-Tree or CDH-Tree (with W = 9600) on the *lens24* data in alternative mode for 9,600 records we will obtain exactly the same tree and corresponding nine rules as before except that every occurrence of *specRx*, *astig* and *tears* will be replaced by *tears*, *specRx* and *astig*, respectively.

---

[7]Up to the point where the sliding window is full, and provided D is greater than W, CDH-Tree is effectively the same algorithm as H-Tree.

[8]We have left attribute *age* unchanged to avoid irrelevant complications. It has three attribute values whereas the other attributes all have only two.

The decision tree will now look like this (Figure 22.15).

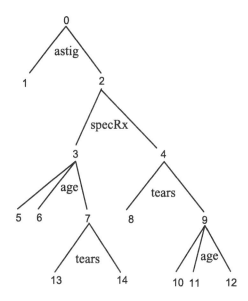

Figure 22.15 Tree Generated by TDIDT and H-Tree for 9,600 Records of *lens24* Alternative Mode

The rules extracted from the tree are now these (Figure 22.16).

1. IF $astig = 1$ THEN $Class = 3$
2. IF $astig = 2$ AND $specRx = 1$ AND $age = 1$ THEN Class = 2
3. IF $astig = 2$ AND $specRx = 1$ AND $age = 2$ THEN Class = 2
4. IF $astig = 2$ AND $specRx = 1$ AND $age = 3$ AND $tears = 1$ THEN Class = 3
5. IF $astig = 2$ AND $specRx = 1$ AND $age = 3$ AND $tears = 2$ THEN Class = 2
6. IF $astig = 2$ AND $specRx = 2$ AND $tears = 1$ THEN Class = 1
7. IF $astig = 2$ AND $specRx = 2$ AND $tears = 2$ AND $age = 1$ THEN Class = 1
8. IF $astig = 2$ AND $specRx = 2$ AND $tears = 2$ AND $age = 2$ THEN Class = 3
9. IF $astig = 2$ AND $specRx = 2$ AND $tears = 2$ AND $age = 3$ THEN Class = 3

Figure 22.16 Rules Extracted from Decision Tree for *lens24* Data – Alternative Mode

22.11.2 Introducing Concept Drift

We are now in a position to introduce concept drift into our stream of data. We will interpret the data as standard mode for the first 19,200 records, then switch to alternative mode for the next 19,200 records and so on indefinitely, alternating between the two modes. Figure 22.17 shows the mode applicable to the part of the infinite stream of records that we will use for our experiment.

Records	*lens24* Mode
0–19,199	Standard
19,200–38,399	Alternative
38,400–57,599	Standard
57,600–76,799	Alternative

Figure 22.17 Modes for Concept Drift Experiment

22.11.3 An Experiment with Alternating *lens24* Data

The following is a description of the behaviour of our implementation of the
CDH-Tree algorithm when applied to the alternating *lens24* data, with the
following variable settings:

Prob = 0.999
G = 500
W = 9600
D = 14000
T = 18000
M = 1200

Every D (i.e. 14,000) records the system checks for possible concept drift
by checking that each internal node of the tree is split in the way that it would
be split if the decision were made with the current contents of the sliding
window. If not, it considers creating alternate nodes for some of the nodes in
the main tree. Any internal node for which an alternate node is created can be
considered 'suspect'. Initially each such alternate node has a one-level subtree
hanging from it, split on the now preferred attribute.

Every T (i.e. 18,000) records the system goes into a testing phase. It uses the
next M (i.e. 1,200) records not to develop the tree but to test the performance
of each of the suspect internal nodes against the performance of each of its
alternate nodes. The performance of a node is measured by the number of the
M records that are correctly classified by the subtree hanging from it. At the
end of the testing phase any internal node that is outperformed by one or more
of its alternates is replaced by the best one.

The results shown below are a series of 'snapshots' of the state of the tree
as more and more records are processed.

9600 Records
The data is in standard mode.

The sliding window is now complete for the first time (W = 9600). The
tree and corresponding rules are those shown in Figures 22.13 and 22.14,
respectively.

14,000 Records
The first check for concept drift is made (D = 14000). No nodes are found
to be suspect. This is unsurprising as the standard data mode is still being
used.

18,000 Records
The first testing phase begins (T = 18000). There are no alternate nodes,
so this is certain to have no effect.

19,200 Records

The first testing phase ends (T = 18000, M = 1200). With no alternate nodes, no changes to the tree are possible. The tree predicts perfectly the classification of all 1,200 records.

Next the alternative data mode begins.

28,000 Records

The second check for concept drift is made (D = 14000). The split on attribute *tears* at node 0 is found no longer to be the best choice. An alternate node 15 is created with a one-level subtree split on attribute *astig*. No other suspect nodes are found.

The tree now looks like this (Figure 22.18). It is in transition from Figure 22.13 (standard mode of *lens24* data) towards Figure 22.15 (alternative mode of the data).

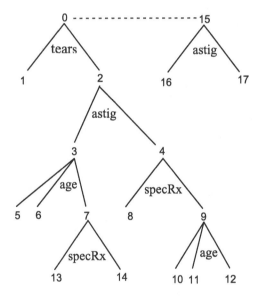

Figure 22.18   Tree After 28,000 Records Showing Alternate Node

The corresponding rules are now (Figure 22.19):

---

1. IF $tears = 14$ THEN Class $= \{1100, 734, 2966\}$
2. IF $tears = 2$ AND $astig = 1$ AND $age = 1$ THEN Class $= \{0, 66, 734\}$
3. IF $tears = 2$ AND $astig = 1$ AND $age = 2$ THEN Class $= \{0, 66, 734\}$
4. IF $tears = 2$ AND $astig = 1$ AND $age = 3$ AND $specRx = 1$ THEN
   Class $= 3$
5. IF $tears = 2$ AND $astig = 1$ AND $age = 3$ AND $specRx = 2$ THEN
   Class $= \{0, 34, 366\}$
6. IF $tears = 2$ AND $astig = 2$ AND $specRx = 1$ THEN Class $= \{100, 1100, 0\}$
7. IF $tears = 2$ AND $astig = 2$ AND $specRx = 2$ AND $age = 1$ THEN
   Class $= 1$
8. IF $tears = 2$ AND $astig = 2$ AND $specRx = 2$ AND $age = 2$ THEN
   Class $= 3$
9. IF $tears = 2$ AND $astig = 2$ AND $specRx = 2$ AND $age = 3$ THEN
   Class $= 3$

Figure 22.19 Rules After 28,000 Records

The arrays shown for several of the rules give the classcounts for the three classes (1, 2 and 3) in order.

The concept drift between one mode of the *lens24* data and another is clearly having an effect on the predictions that would be made about the classification of records sorted to the different leaf nodes.

36,000 Records

The tree now looks like this (Figure 22.20):

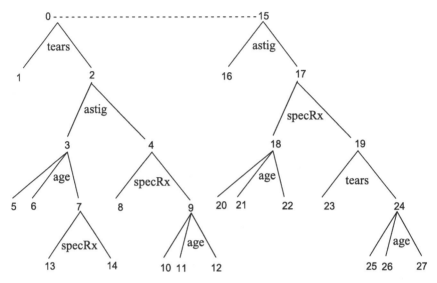

Figure 22.20 Tree after 36,000 Records

The alternate tree hanging from alternate node 15 is the same as Figure 22.15 (with the node numbers from 15 onwards rather than 0 onwards but in the same order) except that node 22 has not yet been split on attribute *tears*.

The corresponding rules are shown in Figure 22.21.

---

1. IF *tears* = 1 THEN Class = {1200, 800, 2800}
2. IF *tears* = 2 AND *astig* = 1 AND *age* = 1 THEN Class = 3
3. IF *tears* = 2 AND *astig* = 1 AND *age* = 2 THEN Class = 3
4. IF *tears* = 2 AND *astig* = 1 AND *age* = 3 AND *specRx* = 1 THEN Class = 3
5. IF *tears* = 2 AND *astig* = 1 AND *age* = 3 AND *specRx* = 2 THEN Class = 3
6. IF *tears* = 2 AND *astig* = 2 AND *specRx* = 1 THEN *Class* = 2
7. IF *tears* = 2 AND *astig* = 2 AND *specRx* = 2 AND *age* = 1 THEN Class = 1
8. IF *tears* = 2 AND *astig* = 2 AND *specRx* = 2 AND *age* = 2 THEN Class = 3
9. IF *tears* = 2 AND *astig* = 2 AND *specRx* = 2 AND *age* = 3 THEN Class = 3

Figure 22.21 Rules Corresponding to Figure 22.20

The second testing phase now begins (T = 18000).

37,200 Records

The second testing phase ends (T = 18000, M = 1200)

The results show that alternative node 15 has out-performed node 0. Out of the 1200 examples it made the correct prediction for 1,050 of them whereas node 0 correctly predicted only 950 of them. Thus node 15 replaces node 0, in this case as the root node of the tree.

The new tree now looks like this (Figure 22.22).

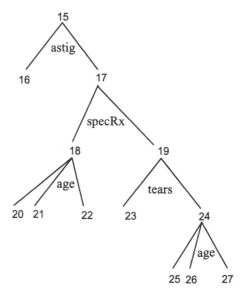

Figure 22.22 Tree After Substitution of Alternate Node 15 for Root Node

38,182 Records

Attribute 22 is split on attribute *tears*, giving new nodes 28 and 29. The tree is now identical to Figure 22.15.

38,400 Records

The data returns to standard mode.

At this point the rules corresponding to the nodes in the tree are identical to those shown in Figure 22.16.

40,198 Records

Attribute 23 is split on attribute *age*, giving new nodes 30, 31 and 32. The tree is starting its journey back towards Figure 22.13, i.e. the shape it had after 9,600 records.

<u>42,000 Records</u>
The third check for concept drift is made (D = 42000). Now nodes 18
and 19 are found to be 'suspect'. Node 18 is given an alternate node 33, from
which hangs a one-level tree split on attribute *tears* (nodes 34 and 35). Node
19 is given an alternate node 36 from which hangs a one-level subtree split on
attribute *age* (nodes 37, 38 and 39).

The tree now looks like Figure 22.23.

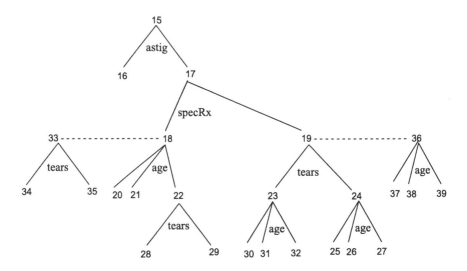

Figure 22.23 Tree After 42,000 Records

<u>47,984 Records</u>
Node 37 is split on attribute *tears* (giving new nodes 40 and 41).

<u>48,000 Records</u>
The rules corresponding to the tree are now as shown in Figure 22.24:

<u>54,000 Records</u>
The third testing phase begins (T = 18000)

<u>55,200 Records</u>
The third testing phase ends (T = 18000, M = 1200). Node 18 is replaced
by alternative node 33.

1. IF $astig = 1$ THEN Class $= \{0, 2000, 2800\}$
2. IF $astig = 2$ AND $specRx = 1$ AND $age = 1$ THEN Class $= \{400, 0, 400\}$
3. IF $astig = 2$ AND $specRx = 1$ AND $age = 2$ THEN Class $= \{400, 0, 400\}$
4. IF $astig = 2$ AND $specRx = 1$ AND $age = 3$ AND $tears = 1$ THEN
   Class $= 3$
5. IF $astig = 2$ AND $specRx = 1$ AND $age = 3$ AND $tears = 2$ THEN
   Class $= 1$
6. IF $astig = 2$ AND $specRx = 2$ AND $tears = 1$ AND $age = 1$ THEN
   Class $= 3$
7. IF $astig = 2$ AND $specRx = 2$ AND $tears = 1$ AND $age = 2$ THEN
   Class $= 3$
8. IF $astig = 2$ AND $specRx = 2$ AND $tears = 1$ AND $age = 3$ THEN
   Class $= 3$
9. IF $astig = 2$ AND $specRx = 2$ AND $tears = 2$ AND $age = 1$ THEN
   Class $= 1$
10. IF $astig = 2$ AND $specRx = 2$ AND $tears = 2$ AND $age = 2$ THEN
    Class $= 3$
11. IF $astig = 2$ AND $specRx = 2$ AND $tears = 2$ AND $age = 3$ THEN
    Class $= 3$

Figure 22.24 Rules After 48,000 Records

56,000 Records

The fourth check for concept drift is made (D $=$ 14000). Node 17 is considered suspect and is replaced by node 42 which has a one-level descendant subtree split on attribute *tears* (new nodes 43 and 44). The state of the tree is now as shown in Figure 22.25.

It seems to be much harder for the tree to get back to the shape it had in Figure 22.13 than it was to get from there to Figure 22.15. The prevalence of splits on attribute *tears* appears to be a partial substitute for splitting on that attribute at the root node.

57,600 Records

The rules corresponding to the classification tree are now as shown in Figure 22.26.

The alternative data mode begins.

57,996 Records

Node 43 is split on attribute *specRx* (giving new nodes 45 and 46).

58,000 Records

Node 44 is split on attribute *specRx* (giving new nodes 47 and 48).

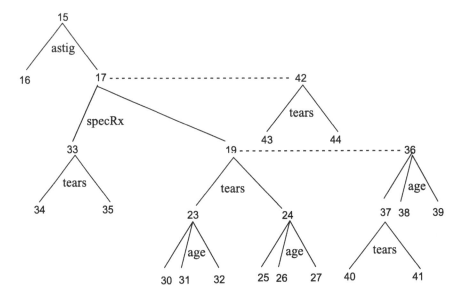

Figure 22.25 Tree After 56,000 Records

1. IF $astig = 1$ THEN Class $= \{0, 2000, 2800\}$
2. IF $astig = 2$ AND $specRx = 1$ AND $tears = 1$ THEN Class $= 3$
3. IF $astig = 2$ AND $specRx = 1$ AND $tears = 2$ THEN Class $= 1$
4. IF $astig = 2$ AND $specRx = 2$ AND $tears = 1$ AND $age = 1$ THEN Class $= 3$
5. IF $astig = 2$ AND $specRx = 2$ AND $tears = 1$ AND $age = 2$ THEN Class $= 3$
6. IF $astig = 2$ AND $specRx = 2$ AND $tears = 1$ AND $age = 3$ THEN Class $= 3$
7. IF $astig = 2$ AND $specRx = 2$ AND $tears = 2$ AND $age = 1$ THEN Class $= 1$
8. IF $astig = 2$ AND $specRx = 2$ AND $tears = 2$ AND $age = 2$ THEN Class $= 3$
9. IF $astig = 2$ AND $specRx = 2$ AND $tears = 2$ AND $age = 3$ THEN Class $= 3$

Figure 22.26 Rules After 57,600 Records

60,000 Records

We will leave the continuing story here. The tree now has nine corresponding rules, shown in Figure 22.27.

---

1. IF $astig = 1$ THEN Class = $\{0, 1500, 3300\}$
2. IF $astig = 2$ AND $specRx = 1$ AND $tears = 1$ THEN
   Class = $\{0, 200, 1000\}$
3. IF $astig = 2$ AND $specRx = 1$ AND $tears = 2$ THEN
   Class = $\{900, 300, 0\}$
4. IF $astig = 2$ AND $specRx = 2$ AND $tears = 1$ AND $age = 1$ THEN
   Class = $\{100, 0, 300\}$
5. IF $astig = 2$ AND $specRx = 2$ AND $tears = 1$ AND $age = 2$ THEN
   Class = $\{100, 0, 300\}$
6. IF $astig = 2$ AND $specRx = 2$ AND $tears = 1$ AND $age = 3$ THEN
   Class = $\{100, 0, 300\}$
7. IF $astig = 2$ AND $specRx = 2$ AND $tears = 2$ AND $age = 1$ THEN
   Class = 1
8. IF $astig = 2$ AND $specRx = 2$ AND $tears = 2$ AND $age = 2$ THEN
   Class = 3
9. IF $astig = 2$ AND $specRx = 2$ AND $tears = 2$ AND $age = 3$ THEN
   Class = 3

Figure 22.27 Rules After 60,000 Records

Following all the changes caused by the concept drift introduced into the stream of input records, the tree now misclassifies five of each batch of 24 records.

22.11.4 Comments on Experiment

Starting from Figure 22.13 with the data in standard mode after 9,600 records, the tree evolved very satisfactorily into Figure 22.15[9] with the data then in alternative mode. However this depended crucially on a suitable choice of variables W, D, T and M.

---

[9]Strictly, the nodes were numbered differently from Figure 22.15, but in the same order.

After a total of 60,000 records the tree still showed little sign of evolving back to Figure 22.13. The third check for concept drift, after 42,000 records, led to alternate nodes being associated with nodes 18 and 19 (Figure 22.23) but unfortunately not with the new root node 15. This in turn led to a drop in the predictive accuracy of the tree.

The algorithm appears to be very sensitive to the choice of variables, especially D and T. Their sizes relative to each other and to W may well be critical to the success of the algorithm on real-world data

22.12 Chapter Summary

This chapter builds on the description in Chapter 21 of the H-Tree algorithm for classifying *streaming data*, i.e. data which arrives (generally in large quantities) from some automatic process over a period of days, months, years or potentially forever. Chapter 21 was concerned with stationary data generated from a fixed causal model; Chapter 22 is concerned with data that is time-dependent, where the underlying model can change from time to time, perhaps seasonally. This phenomenon is known as *concept drift*.

The algorithm given here, *CDH-Tree*, is a variant of the popular CVFDT algorithm which generates a type of decision tree called a *Hoeffding Tree*. The algorithm is described and explained in detail with accompanying pseudocode for the benefit of readers who may be interested in developing their own implementations. A detailed example using synthetic data is given to illustrate the way in which the classification tree evolves as more and more records are processed in the presence of concept drift.

22.13 Self-assessment Exercises for Chapter 22

1. Under what circumstances would entering a testing phase not be appropriate? How can it be avoided?
2. Why would it not be appropriate to use the *hitcount* or *acvCounts* arrays when predicting the classification of a test record or a record with an unknown classification?

References

[1] Domingos, P., & Hulten, G. (2000). Mining high-speed data streams. In *Proceedings of the sixth ACM SIGKDD international conference on knowledge discovery and data mining* (pp. 71–80). New York: ACM.

[2] Hulten, G., Spencer, L., & Domingos, P. (2001). Mining time-changing data streams. In *Proceedings of the seventh ACM SIGKDD international conference on knowledge discovery and data mining* (pp. 97–106). New York: ACM.

$$23$$

An Introduction to Neural Networks

23.1 Introduction

Artificial Neural Networks, generally abbreviated to just *Neural Networks* or *Neural Nets* are computing systems inspired by the neurons in the brain and the connections between them. Neural Nets have proved successful in several areas of Artificial Intelligence including object recognition, natural language processing, numerical prediction and classification. It is this last topic that is of particular interest for this book.

In this introductory chapter we can only scratch the surface of a large topic that would justify a book (or possibly several books) of its own. We will explain the basic principles and some widely-used techniques, aiming particularly at the use of Neural Nets for classification tasks of the type studied elsewhere in the book and finishing with examples where a Neural Network is used for classification with the *iris* and *seeds* datasets.

A neural net comprises a set of nodes, known as *neurons*, arranged into an ordered sequence of at least three groups known as *layers*. The first layer in the sequence is called the *input layer*; the last is called the *output layer*; the others are known as *hidden layers*. The best choice of the number of layers in a neural network and the number of nodes in each layer is task-dependent and knowing what to choose is a matter of judgement and experience. For relatively simple neural nets there is only one hidden layer, but more complex nets can have several.

© Springer-Verlag London Ltd., part of Springer Nature 2020   427
M. Bramer, *Principles of Data Mining*, Undergraduate Topics
in Computer Science, DOI 10.1007/978-1-4471-7493-6_23

As we shall see, in a Neural Net data values are propagated from the input layer through the hidden layers to the output layer, one layer at a time. In the figures in this book we will show the layers arranged vertically from left (input) to right (output). The order in which the nodes are positioned in each layer is arbitrary.

Figure 23.1 is a simplified example of a basic neural network. It shows three interconnected collections of nodes. The two on the left of the figure comprise the *input layer*, the two in the middle form the *hidden layer* and those on the right comprise the *output layer*. In this example each layer comprises just two nodes.[1] Adjacent layers are *fully connected*, i.e. each node in a layer is connected to every node in the previous layer (if there is one) and the next layer (if there is one) by a link.[2] There are no links between nodes that are in the same layer or more than one layer apart.

The choice of the number of hidden layers and the number of nodes in each layer determines the basic *architecture* of the neural net. (There are some other design decisions to make, which we will come to as we go along.) The architecture of a neural network determines how it transforms its inputs into its outputs.

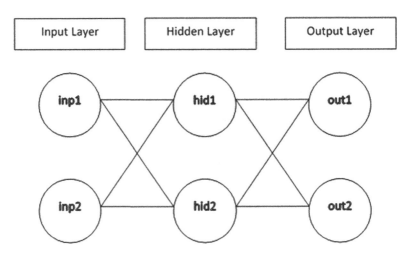

Figure 23.1 Neural Net for Example 1

The link between each pair of nodes has an associated numerical value called its *weight*, which can be either positive or negative. The first task when using

---

[1] To avoid possible confusion, there is no reason why all the layers should have the same number of nodes. Also, a layer with just a single node is permitted.

[2] In the neural network literature, the links between nodes are often described as the connections between neurons.

a neural net is to initialise the weight of each link to a random value: a small positive or negative number. (Restricting the initial weights to the range -0.5 to 0.5 is often advised.) The nodes in the network have no initial values.

A neural net can be looked at as a machine (made of software) that takes in numerical values via the input nodes on the left-hand side and repeatedly propagates them to the next layer to the right, using the values of the nodes and the weights of the links to the nodes in the next layer, one layer at a time until the final layer (output nodes) is reached. For each combination of input values there is a set of target output values. The instances in a training set are presented to the network one by one, over and over again, usually many times and the aim is to adjust the weights by trial and error so that eventually the outputs are as close to the target values as possible for all the training instances.[3] We can say that the machine approximates a mapping that takes each set of input values in the training data to its corresponding target output values. How close an approximation can be achieved depends on a number of factors, including the number of hidden layers and the initial choice of weights.

In its original form a neural net had only an input layer and an output layer and was known as a *Perceptron*. Perceptrons proved very effective for approximating some standard mathematical functions (i.e. mappings where there is only one output value), such as the logical AND and OR functions but inadequate for others such as Exclusive-OR. The addition of hidden layers overcame many of the limitations of the early Perceptrons. In this book we will only consider the case of a single hidden layer. In general, the more hidden layers there are, the more complex the tasks that can be tackled using the net, but at the cost of a substantial increase in processing time as each additional layer is added.

The interconnected structure of nodes in a neural net is reminiscent of the interconnections between the neurons in the brain and that interpretation has driven much of the development and also the terminology of neural nets. It has also led some writers and enthusiasts into making statements that are wildly over the top, such as 'this is how the brain works' or even 'this must be the best method for solving a problem because it is how the brain does it'. Neural nets are a powerful computational device that do not need this type of hype. We will avoid that kind of exaggeration and will generally call the nodes in a neural net by that name, rather than 'neurons' and will avoid unnecessary biological terminology.

---

[3] The training data used with Neural Networks can have any number of output values, not just the single value (the class value) included in the training data used for classification tasks elsewhere in this book. The use of a neural net for classification is discussed in Section 23.6.

23.2 Neural Nets Example 1

Returning now to Figure 23.1, we will illustrate the operation of a basic neural network.

Deciding on the basic architecture of the network is a matter of experience rather than an exact science. Having done so and generated the initial values of weights by some random process, the instances in a training set are now presented to the network one by one. Each instance comprises a value to be given to each input node and the target value to be obtained for each output node for those inputs. As each instance is processed, the values of the nodes in a layer and the weights of the links to the next layer are used to calculate the values to assign to the nodes in the next layer. This process continues layer by layer until the nodes in the output layer have been assigned values. This process is called *forward propagation* and this type of neural network is accordingly called a *feed-forward neural network*.

It is almost certain that the calculated output values will not match the target values precisely, in which case the errors in the output nodes (i.e. the discrepancies between the target and the calculated values) are used to work backwards through the network layer by layer to calculate adjustments to make to each of the weights. This process is called *backpropagation*.

Backpropagation is a supervised learning method that is widely used with feed-forward neural networks to train the weights. It can be used for either classification or numerical prediction, but here we will focus on classification. Backpropagation applied to large multi-layer feed-forward neural networks is often described as *deep learning*.

The processing of one instance through the network (forward propagation followed by backpropagation) is called a *pass*. After a pass has been completed, the next instance is presented to the network and the next pass begins. The processing of all the instances in a training set one-by-one is called an *epoch*.

The process continues epoch by epoch, with the weights changing slowly until an acceptable level of accuracy is reached. This may take many epochs to achieve, frequently tens or hundreds of thousands or even more.

In its final form the network is considered *trained*, i.e. propagating the input values through the network will give close approximations to the target output values for all the training instances.

Values propagate forward through the network layer by layer in a two-stage process. To illustrate this, we will assume that we have the values given in Figure 23.2 for the weights of the links between nodes in the layers shown in Figure 23.1.

For our example instance we will take the values for inp1 and inp2 to be 6 and -4 respectively.

From Node	To Node	Weight
inp1	hid1	-0.2
inp1	hid2	0.3
inp2	hid1	0.1
inp2	hid2	-0.2
hid1	out1	0.01
hid1	out2	0.3
hid2	out1	0.5
hid2	out2	-0.5

Figure 23.2 Weights for the Links Between the Layers in Figure 23.1

We start by considering each hidden node in turn. We will look at hid1 and then hid2. For each hidden node we calculate the weighted sum of the values of the nodes that feed into it, i.e. inp1 and inp2. The weightings to use are of course the weights of the links.

Figure 23.3 shows the links between the input layer and the hidden layer plus the values for the two input nodes.

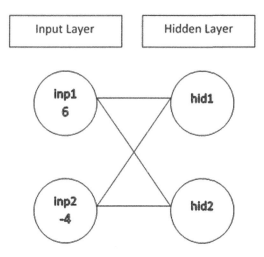

Figure 23.3 Links Between the Input and Hidden Layers in Figure 23.1

We calculate:
hid1 = 6*(-0.2)+(-4)*0.1 = -1.6
hid2 = 6*0.3+(-4)*(-0.2) = 2.6

That completes the first stage of the processing of the hidden layer, called the *neural activation stage*. The current values of hid1 and hid2 are usually called their *activation values*, but we will use the more self-explanatory term *weighted sum values*. If there were no second stage, we would now use these values to calculate the values for the output nodes in the same way.

Figure 23.4 shows the links between the hidden and the output layers plus the values so far calculated for hid1 and hid2.

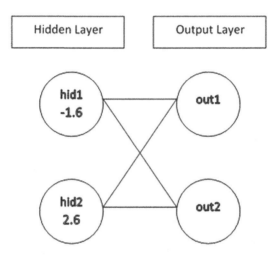

Figure 23.4 Links Between the Hidden and Output Layers in Figure 23.1

If there were no second stage when calculating hid1 and hid2, we would now calculate

out1 = (-1.6)*0.01+2.6*0.5 = 1.284
out2 = (-1.6)*0.3+2.6*(-0.5) = -1.78

The need for a second stage of processing at each node arises from the requirement in many application areas, including classification, to constrain the values generated as each layer is processed. In particular, we often wish the values to be constrained to a small range, especially from zero to one, or even just to the two values zero and one themselves. We can think of zero and one as corresponding to false and true, respectively, and so might take, say, 0.8 to mean 'probable' and 0.1 to mean 'very unlikely'. The significance of this for classification will be explained in Section 23.6.

In order to adjust the values generated we take each weighted sum value and give it to a function called a *transfer function* or an *activation function* which converts it to a new numerical value which we will call its *transformed value.* This is called the *neuron transfer stage.* It is then the transformed value that is passed on to the next layer.

One commonly used transfer function is the *step function* which converts any value X to zero if X≤0 and 1 if X>0. However, this function is too crude for many purposes as it means that a small negative value such as -0.0001 is treated in a completely different way from a small positive value such as 0.0001.

An alternative transfer function which increases smoothly as the value of X increases is the *sigmoid function,* also called the *logistic function.* The function converts a value X to sigmoid(X), which is defined by the formula

$$\textbf{sigmoid}\,(\textbf{X}) = \frac{1}{1+e^{-X}}$$

Figure 23.5 shows the shape of the sigmoid function.

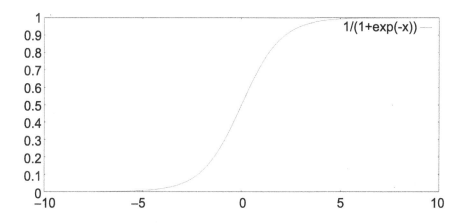

Figure 23.5 The Sigmoid Function

We can see that – as is generally desirable – a small change in the value of X leads to a small change in the function value, which varies smoothly from zero to one as X increases. This is the transfer function that we will use in the remainder of this chapter.

Returning now to the point where we have just calculated the weighted sum values of hid1 and hid2 (values -1.6 and 2.6 respectively), we next calculate their transformed values. The value of hid1 becomes sigmoid(-1.6) = 0.1680 and hid2 becomes sigmoid(2.6) = 0.9309.

These transformed values are now used in the calculation of the weighted sum values of out1 and out2:

out1 = 0.1680*0.01+0.9309*0.5 = 0.4671

out2 = 0.1680*0.3+0.9309*(-0.5) = -0.4151

Finally, the sigmoid transfer function is applied to the weighted sum values of out1 and out2: out1 becomes sigmoid(0.4671) = 0.6147 and out2 becomes sigmoid(-0.4151) = 0.3977.

These values of out1 and out2 are compared with the target values for those nodes and the errors (the target values minus the calculated values) are backpropagated through the network to give the first set of adjustments to the weights. We will defer a description of the backpropagation process for adjusting the weights until Section 23.4.

We will now examine a more complex (but still small scale) network, explain the forward propagation process in more detail and derive the formulae needed to calculate the weighted sum and transformed values of each hidden and output node.

23.3 Neural Nets Example 2

Figure 23.6 shows a small neural net with two input nodes, three hidden nodes and two output nodes. It also shows an optional feature of a neural net not described previously, i.e. the use of nodes of a special type called *bias nodes* with links to the hidden and output layers.

To make this figure easier to interpret, Figure 23.7 shows just the nodes linked to hidden node hid1.

Two of the links are from input nodes inp1 and inp2 as we would expect. The third is from a node which contains the fixed value 1. We will call this the *bias node* for the hidden layer. Bias nodes are not part of any of the layers. Unlike other nodes, they have no links coming into them from the left and they have an initial value of 1, which never changes.

The link from the bias node to hid1 has a weight, like all other links, and this value is called the *hidden layer bias weight.*

Like other weights, the bias weight will be adjusted by the backpropagation process. However, unlike other weights, the value of the bias weight is always the same for every node in a given layer.[4]

A bias node can be associated with every layer except the input one. Initially the bias weights are set randomly to small positive or negative numbers, in the same way as for the other weights.

---

[4] As a variation, a different bias weight can be associated with each hidden and output node. In this book we will assume that every node in a layer always has the same value of the bias weight.

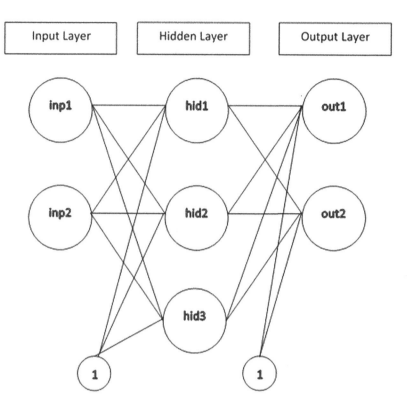

Figure 23.6 Neural Net for Example 2

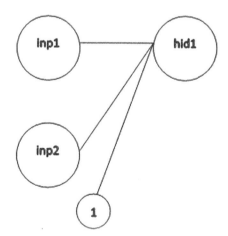

Figure 23.7 Nodes Linked to Hidden Node hid1

We will now go through the forward propagation process again in more detail, taking into account the bias nodes and weights. It will be helpful initially to think of each node in Figure 23.6 (except the two bias nodes) as holding the value of a variable with the same name as the node, which starts by being uninitialized.

To illustrate the method, we will use the neural net shown in Figure 23.6 and the initial values of the weights shown in Figure 23.8. We will consider

WEIGHTS		
Link from node	Link to node	Weight
inp1	hid1	0.2
inp1	hid2	-0.4
inp1	hid3	0.5
inp2	hid1	0.3
inp2	hid2	0.2
inp2	hid3	-0.1
hid1	out1	-0.3
hid1	out2	-0.4
hid2	out1	0.2
hid2	out2	0.4
hid3	out1	-0.1
hid3	out2	0.5

BIAS WEIGHTS		
	Layer	
	hidden	-0.3
	output	0.1

Figure 23.8   Initial Weights Associated with Figure 23.1

a single training instance, shown in Figure 23.9, which we can imagine as a training set with just one instance. (We will look at larger training sets in Section 23.5.)

Input values		Target values	
inp1	inp2	out1	out2
2	-1	0.6	-0.2

Figure 23.9   Initial Training Instance

23.3.1 Forward Propagating the Values of the Input Nodes

We are going to derive the general formulae for forward propagation (and later for backpropagation) in a neural network with three layers. We will start by defining some notation in Figure 23.10.

Notation	Meaning
inpi	The value of the ith input node
Whidj	The weighted sum value of the jth hidden node
Thidj	The transformed value of the jth hidden node
Woutk	The weighted sum value of the kth output node
Toutk	The transformed value of the kth output node
targk	The target value for the kth output node
biasH	The bias weight associated with the hidden layer
biasO	The bias weight associated with the output layer
wij	The weight associated with the link between input node inpi and hidden node hidj. (Note the initial lower-case letter w.)
Wjk	The weight associated with the link between hidden node hidj and output node outk. (Note the initial capital letter W.)
E	The overall error (sum squared error) at the end of the forward propagation stage

Figure 23.10 Neural Network Notation

There are some important changes from the notation used in the last section.

- For a hidden node hidj the weighted sum value is denoted by Whidj and the transformed value is denoted by Thidj.

- For an output node outk the weighted sum value is denoted by Woutk and the transformed value is denoted by Toutk.

    We can now think of a hidden node hidj as containing the values of two variables: Whidj and Thidj. Similarly, output node outk contains the values of variables Woutk and Toutk.

- In the interests of keeping the notation (relatively) uncluttered we now also distinguish the weights of the links between the input and hidden layers from those of the links between the hidden and output layers. Thus:

    – w12 (with an initial lower-case letter) represents the weight of the link between inp1 and hid2

    – W12 (with an initial capital letter) represents the weight of the link between hid1 and out2.

We are going to derive the formulae needed for forward propagation. We already have the formula for the sigmoid transfer function, which will be used in the following description. It is:

$$sigmoid\,(X) = \frac{1}{1+e^{-X}}\ [1]$$

The values of the nodes in the hidden and output layers are calculated in two steps, layer by layer.

1. Hidden Layer

Step 1
For each node in the hidden layer, a weighted sum is formed to which each node in the input layer contributes its value multiplied by the weight of the link between the two nodes. If there is a bias node associated with the hidden layer, the bias weight is then added to the total for the node to give its weighted sum value Whidj. We can represent this by the formula

$$Whidj = \sum_i (inpi \ * \ wij) + biasH\ [2]$$

for all hidden nodes hidj.

Working through the nodes in the hidden layer in turn, the inputs to node hid1 are shown in Figure 23.11. The input nodes inp1 and inp2 are linked to hid1 with weights 0.2 and 0.3, respectively and the hidden layer bias weight, biasH, is -0.3.

We calculate the weighted sum of the values of the input nodes as: 2*0.2+(-1)*0.3 = 0.1 and add to this the value of the bias weight, i.e. -0.3, making a total value for Whid1 of -0.2.

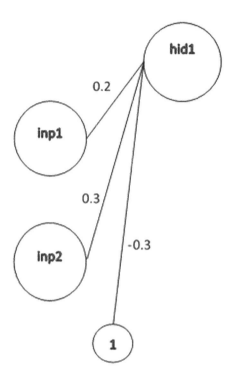

Figure 23.11   Inputs to Node hid1 (With Weights Shown)

We can calculate the weighted sum values of hid2 and hid3 in the same way, i.e.

Whid2 = 2*(-0.4)+(-1)*0.2-0.3 = -1.3
Whid3 = 2*0.5+(-1)*(- 0.1)-0.3 = 0.8

Step 2
The second stage is to take each of the weighted sum values in turn and transform it using the sigmoid transfer function. The relationship between the weighted sum value Whidj at the jth hidden node and its transformed value Thidj is

$$Thidj = sigmoid\,(Whidj) = \frac{1}{1 + e^{-Whidj}} \;\; [3]$$

for all hidden nodes hidj.

For the network shown in Figure 23.6, with the weights given, the calculated values of each of the hidden nodes are as follows:
Hidden node hid1
Weighted value Whid1 = -0.2

Transformed value Thid1 = sigmoid(-0.2) = 0.4502[5]
Hidden node hid2
Weighted value Whid2 = -1.3
Transformed value Thid2 = sigmoid(-1.3) = 0.2142
Hidden node hid3
Weighted value Whid3 = 0.8
Transformed value Thid3 = sigmoid(0.8) = 0.6900

Having applied this two-step process to the hidden layer we can now use the same approach to propagate the values of the hidden nodes through to the output layer.

2. Output Layer

The procedure for the output layer is very similar to that for the hidden layer. For each node in the output layer, a weighted sum is formed to which each node in the hidden layer contributes its (transformed) value multiplied by the weight of the link between the two nodes. If there is a bias node associated with the output layer, the bias weight is then added to the total for the node. For each output node outk

$$Woutk = \sum_{j} (Thidj * Wjk) + biasO \text{ [4]}$$

After the weighted value Woutk is calculated it is then transformed using the sigmoid function, so

$$Toutk = sigmoid(Woutk) = \frac{1}{1 + e^{-Woutk}} \text{ [5]}$$

for all output nodes outk.

For output node out1 we have
Weighted value Wout1 = 0.4502*(-0.3)+0.2142*0.2+0.6900*(-0.1)+0.1
= -0.0612
Transformed value Tout1 = sigmoid(-0.0612) = 0.4847
For output node out2 we have
Weighted value Wout2 = 0.4502*(-0.4)+0.2142*0.4+0.6900*0.5+0.1
= 0.3506
Transformed value Tout2 = sigmoid(0.3506) = 0.5868
The values of the complete set of nodes are now as shown in Figure 23.12. (The transformed values of the nodes in the hidden and output layers are given.)

---

[5] Numbers are generally displayed to four decimal places but full accuracy is retained in future calculations.

inp1	inp2	hid1	hid2	hid3	out1	out2
2	-1	0.4502	0.2142	0.6900	0.4847	0.5868

Figure 23.12 Result of Forward Propagation Applied to the Network

Next, we calculate the error value for each output node, i.e. its target value minus its calculated (transformed) value.

For node out1 this is 0.6-0.4847 = 0.1153 and for out2 it is -0.2-0.5868 = -0.7868.

From these error values we calculate the overall error, called the *Sum Squared Error*. This is defined as half the sum of the squares of the error values for the output nodes,[6] i.e.

$$E = 0.5 \: * \: \sum_k (targk - Toutk)^2 \quad [6]$$

For our example network, E = $0.5*((0.1153)^2+(-0.7868)^2)$ = 0.31614246 to eight decimal places. The Sum Squared Error is a long way from our desired error value of zero, so the system now works backwards layer-by-layer from the output layer, via the hidden layer, to the input layer, calculating new values for the weights associated with the links from each layer to the one before and also the two bias weights. This process is known as *backpropagation*. It will be explained in detail in Section 23.4.

After backpropagation the weights associated with the links in our network are now as shown in Figure 23.13. They are not very different from the initial values.

This process then continues with the instances in the training set processed one by one in turn for many epochs, with the weights adjusted – often very slightly – as it goes along. (Exactly when the weights are adjusted when a training set consists of more than one instance will be discussed in Section 23.5.) This continues until the error value drops below a required level, perhaps 0.0001, or we stop trying to reduce it any further, in which case we consider the network as *trained*. The trained network gives the required output for the instances in the training set (to some level of error) and so can be used to predict the output values for previously unseen values of the inputs.

The aim is that repeatedly revising the weights leads to a steady (although often slight) reduction in the value of the sum squared error. However, this cannot be guaranteed. To train even a simple network can require the processing of many thousands of epochs.

---

[6] A factor of 0.5 is included to make some of the mathematical calculations at a later stage easier. It makes very little practical difference.

WEIGHTS		
Link from node	Link to node	Weight
inp1	hid1	0.2033
inp1	hid2	-0.4024
inp1	hid3	0.4958
inp2	hid1	0.2983
inp2	hid2	0.2012
inp2	hid3	-0.0979
hid1	out1	-0.2987
hid1	out2	-0.4086
hid2	out1	0.2006
hid2	out2	0.3959
hid3	out1	-0.0980
hid3	out2	0.4868
BIAS WEIGHTS		
	Layer	
	hidden	-0.3016
	output	0.0838

Figure 23.13 Revised Weights After One Pass Through the Network

23.3.2 Forward Propagation: Summary of Formulae

$$sigmoid\,(X) = \frac{1}{1+e^{-X}}\ [1]$$

For all hidden nodes hidj

$$Whidj = \sum_i (inpi\ *\ wij) + biasH\ [2]$$

$$Thidj = sigmoid\,(Whidj) = \frac{1}{1+e^{-Whidj}}\ [3]$$

For all output nodes outk (formulae [4] and [5] only

$$Woutk = \sum_j (Thidj\ *\ Wjk) + biasO\ [4]$$

$$Toutk = sigmoid\,(Woutk) = \frac{1}{1+e^{-Woutk}}\ [5]$$

$$E = 0.5\ *\ \sum_k (targk - Toutk)^2\ [6]$$

23.4 Backpropagation

Backpropagation is the process of determining adjustments (often very small ones) to be made to the values of the weights (including bias weights), using the current values of the various nodes plus the target values of the output nodes.

Explaining the basic backpropagation method is harder than explaining forward propagation and parts of the method used are difficult to justify to anyone who is not familiar with the basics of differential calculus.[7]

As many (perhaps most) of the readers of this book are likely to be in this category, we will explain the method and simply ask for some of the justification to be taken on trust. This should not prevent readers from being able to use the method described.

23.4.1 Stochastic Gradient Descent

The most commonly used method of backpropagation is called *stochastic gradient descent*. The first word simply indicates that the weights are initially assigned at random. The gradient descent method is applied at the end of each forward pass through the network. The key idea is to consider the Sum Squared Error, E, as a function of the values of the nodes in the hidden and output layers, plus the weights, the values given to the input nodes and the target values of the output nodes.

Most (all?) of us cannot visualise functions of so many variables so we will just consider a single variable, a weight which we will call W. If we plotted a graph showing values of E (on the vertical axis) against values of W (on the horizontal axis), keeping all the other variables fixed, it might look like Figure 23.14 with the current position on the graph marked as A. We would of course like to be at the minimum point, which is marked as M.

The gradient descent method is to calculate the slope or *gradient* of the curve at point A and then reduce the value of W by a proportion of that value.

Roughly speaking the gradient of any variable y which depends on the value of another variable x corresponds to the amount that y would increase/decrease if we made a small increase/decrease in the value of x, assuming that all other variables that affect the value of y remain constant. In calculus textbooks this quantity is called 'the partial derivative of y with respect to x' and is often

---

[7] Differential calculus is a branch of mathematics concerned with the rate of change of one variable with respect to another. For example, velocity is the rate of change of distance from a fixed point 'with respect to time', i.e. as time changes. Acceleration is the rate of change of velocity with respect to time.

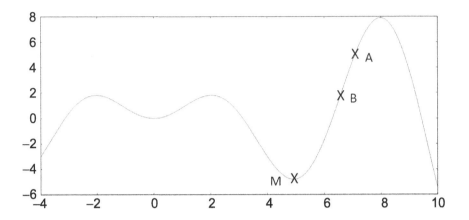

Figure 23.14 Plot of E Against an Arbitrary Weight W

written as dy/dx or $\partial y/\partial x$ (pronounced 'dee-why by dee-ex' or 'dee-why over dee-ex'). However here we will use the simpler notation g(y,x) and refer to 'the gradient of y with respect to x'. We wish to estimate the gradient of E with respect to each of the weights, including the bias weights.

Having found the gradient of E with respect to a weight such as w12, i.e. g(E,w12), we reduce the value of the weight by a proportion of that value.[8] The proportion used is the same for all the weights and is called the *learning factor*. We will represent it by the name *alpha*.

The aim is that after the value of the weight is adjusted, it will be lower down the curve, e.g. at point B in Figure 23.14 and so closer to the minimum point M.

The choice of learning factor alpha can be significant. Using a small value for alpha – a cautious learning approach – may mean that the learning takes an unnecessarily large number of epochs to reach or get close to point M. However, the opposite approach may also lead to problems. This can be illustrated by Figure 23.15 which is an augmented version of Figure 23.14.

A fairly cautious choice of alpha may bring us from point A to point B, whereas by choosing a larger value we might have got much closer to M at point C. On the other hand, if alpha is too large, after the next adjustment we might move from C to point D, on the other side of the minimum M, *en route* to the next minimum M2, which is appreciably higher than M.

For the purpose of this example we will use the cautious value of 0.1 for alpha.

---

[8] The effect of this approach is that if the gradient is positive, the weight is reduced; if it is negative, the weight is increased.

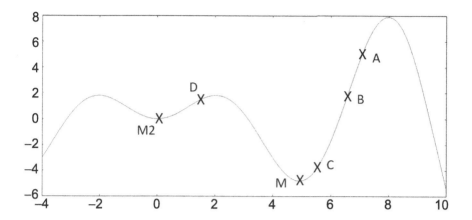

Figure 23.15 Plot of E Against an Arbitrary Weight W (Augmented)

23.4.2 Finding the Gradients

In order to adjust the weights, we need to find the gradient of E with respect
to each one, i.e.

- g(E,wij) for all input nodes inpi and hidden nodes hidj

- g(E,Wjk) for all hidden nodes hidj and output nodes outk

- g(E,biasH)

- g(E,biasO)

We have no way of measuring these values directly but we can calculate
them indirectly by combining other gradient values such as g(E,Toutk) and
g(Toutk,Woutk) using a technique known as the *chain rule*.

Fortunately, we have a technique for finding these other gradient values.
Differential calculus tells us how to take a formula defining, say, Woutk and
use it to find a formula for gradients such as g(Woutk,Wjk). The process of
doing so is known as *differentiating* variable Woutk with respect to variable
Wjk.

As many readers of this book may not be familiar with calculus, all the
results that rely on it have been gathered together for reference in Figure
23.16. We start with the formulae numbered 2 to 5 derived in Section 23.3 and
from them obtain eight new formulae for gradients of different kinds. If you do
not understand how these formulae are derived, it should not be an obstacle to
using them in what follows.

Incidentally, it was to obtain the tidy result given as formula [H] that the
factor of 0.5 was used in the definition of sum squared error.

Results from Calculus

From Formulae 2-6 in Section 23.3 we can obtain eight formulae for gradients.

- From Formula 2: $Whidj = \sum_i (inpi * wij) + biasH$
  Differentiating with respect to variables wij and biasH, respectively, we have the formulae

  For all input nodes inpi and hidden nodes hidj
  g(Whidj,wij) = inpi [A]
  For all hidden nodes hidj
  g(Whidj,biasH) = 1 [B]

- From Formula 3: $Thidj = sigmoid(Whidj) = \frac{1}{(1+e^{-Whidj})}$
  Differentiating by Whidj we can show that

  For all hidden nodes hidj
  g(Thidj,Whidj) = Thidj*(1-Thidj) [C]

- From Formula 4: $Woutk = \sum_j (Thidj * Wjk) + biasO$
  by differentiating with respect to variables Wjk, Thidj and biasO, respectively we obtain the three formulae:

  For all hidden nodes hidj and output nodes outk
  g(Woutk,Wjk) = Thidj [D]
  g(Woutk,Thidj) = Wjk [E]
  For all output nodes outk
  g(Woutk,biasO) = 1 [F]

- From Formula 5: $Toutk = sigmoid(Woutk) = \frac{1}{(1+e^{-Woutk})}$
  Differentiating by Woutk we can show that

  For all output nodes outk
  g(Toutk,Woutk) = Toutk*(1-Toutk) [G]

- From Formula 6: $E = 0.5 * \sum_k (targk - Toutk)^2$
  by differentiating with respect to variable Toutk, we obtain the formula

  For all output nodes outk
  g(E,Toutk) = Toutk-targk [H]

Figure 23.16 Results from Calculus

Having established these results, we can now look at the Backpropagation process in two stages, first working backwards from the output layer to the hidden layer and then working back further from the hidden layer to the input layer.

23.4.3 Working backwards from the output layer to the hidden layer

At this stage we wish to find the value of g(E,Wjk) for all pairs of hidden and output nodes and also the value of g(E,biasO).

Before going on, it will be helpful to extend Figure 23.6 to include an extra node labelled E (the error node), to the right of the output layer and linked to the two output nodes out1 and out2. This gives us Figure 23.17.

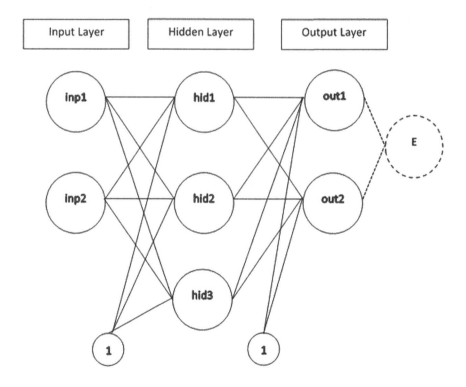

Figure 23.17 Figure 23.6 Extended with Error Node

The error node is not part of the neural net itself and the links from it to the output nodes have no weights and are ignored in what follows. Dashed lines are used to indicate this. The value of augmenting Figure 23.6 in this way is to make it easier to see the paths that will be described subsequently.

In order to calculate g(E,Wjk) we need to find the path from the error node back to the link between hidden node hidj and output node outk, which has weight Wjk. This is shown in Figure 23.18, in which the outk node has been enlarged to show the two variables Woutk and Toutk 'contained in' the outk node. The weight Wjk of the link from hidden node hidj to output node outk is also shown.

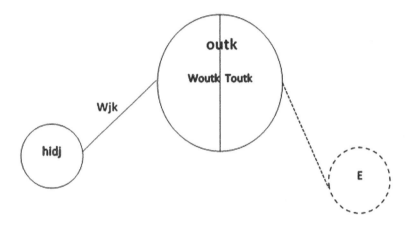

Figure 23.18   The Path from Error Node E to Weight Wjk

From Figure 23.18 we can see that the path (right to left) from E to Wjk starts by going from E to Toutk, then goes on to Woutk and finally arrives at Wjk, i.e. it is E → Toutk → Woutk → Wjk.

We can now use the *chain rule*, an extremely useful relationship amongst gradient values that can be justified using calculus. In this case the formula is:

g(E,Wjk) = g(E,Toutk)*g(Toutk,Woutk)*g(Woutk,Wjk)

The sequence of terms on the right-hand side of the formula corresponds to the path from E to Wjk. Chain rule formulae have an intuitive appeal: the second argument of every term on the right-hand side (except the last) appears to be somehow 'cancelled out' by the first argument of the term that follows.

In this case we already have formulae H, G and D, which we can use for each of the three components of the product on the right-hand, respectively.

Substituting we have:

g(E,Wjk) = (Toutk-targk)*Toutk*(1-Toutk)*Thidj [I]

for all hidden nodes hidj and output nodes outk

For our network, using the values given in Figures 23.9 and 23.12, this gives

g(E,W11) = (0.4847-0.6)*0.4847*0.5153*0.4502 = -0.0130
g(E,W12) = (0.5868+0.2)*0.5868*0.4132*0.4502 = 0.0859
g(E,W21) = (0.4847-0.6)*0.4847*0.5153*0.2142 = -0.0062
g(E,W22) = (0.5868+0.2)*0.5868*0.4132*0.2142 = 0.0409
g(E,W31) = (0.4847-0.6)*0.4847*0.5153*0.6900 = -0.0199
g(E,W32) = (0.5868+0.2)*0.5868*0.4132*0.6900 = 0.1316

The gradient of E with respect to biasO is more complex. Again, we need to identify the path from error node E to the link with weight biasO. The complication here is that there is one path for each output node outk, i.e. E→Toutk→Woutk→biasO. When there are multiple paths, we need to add together the values obtained from each one.

Using the chain rule, we obtain the formula

$$g\left(E, biasO\right) = \sum_k g\left(E, Toutk\right) * g\left(Toutk, Woutk\right) * g(Woutk, biasO)$$

Simplifying the right-hand side using formulae H, G and F gives

$g\left(E, biasO\right) = \sum_k \left(Toutk-targk\right) * Toutk * \left(1-Toutk\right)$ [J]

For our network g(E,biasO) = (0.4847-0.6)*0.4847*0.5153
    +(0.5868+0.2)*0.5868*0.4132 = 0.1620.

This gives a partly completed set of gradient values (Figure 23.19), which we will later use to increment the weights of the links between the hidden nodes and the output nodes, plus the output layer bias weight.

The formulae used for calculating gradients during the first stage of back-propagation are given for ease of reference in Figure 23.20.
It remains to carry out the final part of the backpropagation, this time moving from the hidden layer to the input layer.

23.4.4 Working backwards from the hidden layer to the input layer

In a similar way to the previous stage we wish to find the value of g(E,wij) for all pairs of input and hidden nodes and also the value of g(E,biasH). However, we need to use a different set of formulae.

We will start by establishing a formula for g(E,Thidj). To calculate this, we note that there is a separate path from E to hidden node hidj via every output node outk, i.e. E → Toutk → Woutk → Thidj.

Unlike our previous uses of the chain rule, when there was only one path to consider, in this case we add the result for each of the paths together, so

$$g\left(E, Thidj\right) = \sum_k g\left(E, Toutk\right) * g\left(Toutk, Woutk\right) * g(Woutk, Thidj)$$

Link from node	Link to node	Gradient
inp1	hid1	
inp1	hid2	
inp1	hid3	
inp2	hid1	
inp2	hid2	
inp2	hid3	
hid1	out1	-0.0130
hid1	out2	0.0859
hid2	out1	-0.0062
hid2	out2	0.0409
hid3	out1	-0.0199
hid3	out2	0.1316
	Layer	**(Bias)**
	hidden	
	output	0.1620

Figure 23.19 Gradient Values (partial list)

Formulae for Calculating Gradients During First Stage of Back-propagation

For all hidden nodes hidj and output nodes outk
g(E,Wjk) = (Toutk-targk)*Toutk*(1-Toutk)*Thidj [I]

$g\left(E, \text{biasO}\right) = \sum_{k} \left(\text{Toutk} - \text{targk}\right) * \text{Toutk} * \left(1 - \text{Toutk}\right)$ [J]

Figure 23.20 Formulae for Calculating Gradients During First Stage of Back-propagation

Using formulae H, G and E we can rewrite this as:
For all hidden nodes hidj
$\mathbf{g\left(E, Thidj\right) = \sum_{k} \left(Toutk - targk\right) * Toutk * \left(1 - Toutk\right) * Wjk}$ **[K]**

Next, we note that the path from error node E to weight wij via Thidj is:
E → Thidj → Whidj → wij.

Using the chain rule, we have the formula:
g(E,wij) = g(E,Thidj)*g(Thidj,Whidj)*g(Whidj,wij)

We can replace the second and third terms on the right-hand side using Formulae C and A, giving

For all input nodes inpi and hidden nodes hidj
g(E,wij) = g(E,Thidj)*Thidj*(1-Thidj)*inpi [L]

For our network
$\qquad$(Tout1-targ1)*Tout1*(1-Tout1) = -0.0288
$\qquad$(Tout2-targ2)*Tout2*(1-Tout2) = 0.1908
$\qquad$Thid1*(1-Thid1) = 0.2475
$\qquad$Thid2*(1-Thid2) = 0.1683
$\qquad$Thid3*(1-Thid3) = 0.2139

We first calculate, using the values given above:
g(E,Thid1) =
$\qquad$(Tout1-targ1)*Tout1*(1-Tout1)*W11+(Tout2-targ2)*Tout2*(1-Tout2)
$\qquad$*W12 = -0.0288*(-0.3)+0.1908*(-0.4) = -0.0677
g(E,Thid2) =
$\qquad$(Tout1-targ1)*Tout1*(1-Tout1)*W21 +(Tout2-targ2)*Tout2*(1-Tout2)
$\qquad$*W22 = -0.0288*0.2+0.1908*0.4 = 0.0705
g(E,Thid3) =
$\qquad$(Tout1-targ1)*Tout1*(1-Tout1)*W31+(Tout2-targ2)*Tout2*(1-Tout2)
$\qquad$*W32 = -0.0288*(-0.1)+0.1908*0.5 = 0.0983

We can now calculate the required gradients for E with respect to the weights.
g(E,w11) = g(E,Thid1)*Thid1*(1-Thid1)*inp1 = -0.0677*0.2475*2
$\qquad$= -0.0335
g(E,w12) = g(E,Thid2)*Thid2*(1-Thid2)*inp1 = 0.0705*0.1683*2 = 0.0237
g(E,w13) = g(E,Thid3)*Thid3*(1-Thid3)*inp1 = 0.0983*0.2139*2 = 0.0420
g(E,w21) = g(E,Thid1)*Thid1*(1-Thid1)*inp2 = -0.0677*0.2475*(-1) = 0.0167
g(E,w22) = g(E,Thid2)*Thid2*(1-Thid2)*inp2 = 0.0705*0.1683*(-1) = -0.0119
g(E,w23) = g(E,Thid3)*Thid3*(1-Thid3)*inp2 = 0.0983*0.2139*(-1) = -0.0210

The final gradient to calculate is g(E,biasH). This is fairly straightforward given that we already know the formula for g(E,Thidj) for each hidden node.
$\qquad$There is a route from E to biasH via every hidden node hidj, i.e.
E→Thidj→Whidj→biasH.
As there is more than one route, we need to add the values calculated for each route together. The chain rule gives

$$g\,(E, biasH) = \sum_j g(E, Thidj) * g(Thidj, Whidj) * g(Whidj, biasH)$$

$\qquad$Substituting for the second and third terms of the product on the right-hand side using Formulae C and B gives:

$$g\,(\mathbf{E}, \mathbf{biasH}) = \sum_j g\,(\mathbf{E}, \mathbf{Thidj}) * \mathbf{Thidj} * (1 - \mathbf{Thidj})\ [\mathbf{M}]$$

For our network:

g(E,biasH)

    = g(E,Thid1)*Thid1*(1-Thid1)+g(E,Thid2)*Thid2*(1-Thid2)

    +g(E,Thid3)*Thid3*(1-Thid3)

    = -0.0677*0.2475+0.0705*0.1683+0.0983*0.2139 = 0.0161.

This finally gives us the complete set of gradient values to use to increment the weights in the neural network (Figure 23.21).

Link from node	Link to node	Gradient
inp1	hid1	-0.0335
inp1	hid2	0.0237
inp1	hid3	0.0420
inp2	hid1	0.0167
inp2	hid2	-0.0119
inp2	hid3	-0.0210
hid1	out1	-0.0130
hid1	out2	0.0859
hid2	out1	-0.0062
hid2	out2	0.0409
hid3	out1	-0.0199
hid3	out2	0.1316
	Layer	**(Bias)**
	hidden	0.0161
	output	0.1620

Figure 23.21 Gradient Values After First Pass Through Network

The formulae used for calculating gradients during the second stage of back-propagation are given for ease of reference in Figure 23.22.

23.4.5 Updating the Weights

We have found the value of the gradient for all the weights, i.e. the gradient of the Sum Squared Error E with respect to each one. The next step is to reduce the value of each weight (including the bias weights) by a proportion between zero and one of its gradient value. The proportion used is the learning factor alpha, which was introduced earlier in this section.

Formulae for Calculating Gradients During Second Stage of Backpropagation

For all hidden nodes hidj
$g(E, Thidj) = \sum_k (Toutk - targk) *Toutk* (1 - Toutk) *Wjk$ [K]

For all input nodes inpi and hidden nodes hidj
$g(E,wij) = g(E,Thidj)*Thidj*(1-Thidj)*inpi$ [L]

$g(E, biasH) = \sum_j g(E, Thidj) *Thidj * (1 - Thidj)$ [M]

Figure 23.22 Formulae for Calculating Gradients During Second Stage of Backpropagation

The learning factor is used to (try to) reduce the risk of over-adjusting some of the weights. Too high a value of alpha can sometimes result in the overall error going up rather than steadily being reduced as the number of epochs increases. Too low a value of alpha can result in an unnecessarily large number of epochs being needed to reduce the error to a low value.

Here we will use the value 0.1 for alpha. This gives a revised set of weights at the end of the first pass, or equivalently the first epoch (as there is only one instance in our training set), which is shown in Figure 23.23 below. (The values are the same as in Figure 23.13.)

If we now make a second pass through the network with the same single instance and the revised weights, we will obtain a revised overall error value of E = 0.31038952. This is lower that the value for the first pass (0.31614246), but still probably much higher than we would like. By making repeated passes through the network with the same training instance we can see how rapidly the error decreases. Note that as there is only one training instance, each pass through the network, forwards and then backwards, constitutes a whole epoch.

Figure 23.24 shows the value of E after different numbers of epochs from one up to a million. In all cases alpha = 0.1.

For this example, it does not seem possible to reduce the overall error below about 0.02. Whether or not this is good enough depends on the purpose for which the network is to be used.

This example demonstrates that it is often necessary to run training data through a neural net multiple times to obtain a satisfactory error level, but it also shows that beyond a certain point adding additional runs is likely to achieve little or nothing. We could try specifying the termination condition 'continue until a value of E is obtained that is less than 0.0001', say, for our

WEIGHTS		
Link from node	Link to node	Weight
inp1	hid1	0.2033
inp1	hid2	-0.4024
inp1	hid3	0.4958
inp2	hid1	0.2983
inp2	hid2	0.2012
inp2	hid3	-0.0979
hid1	out1	-0.2987
hid1	out2	-0.4086
hid2	out1	0.2006
hid2	out2	0.3959
hid3	out1	-0.0980
hid3	out2	0.4868
BIAS WEIGHTS		
	Layer	
	hidden	-0.3016
	output	0.0838

Figure 23.23 Revised Weights After One Pass Through the Network

Epochs	alpha = 0.1
1	0.31614246
10	0.26831552
100	0.09770540
1,000	0.02384615
10,000	0.02033106
100,000	0.02002914
1,000,000	0.02000272

Figure 23.24 Values of E for Varying Numbers of Epochs with alpha = 0.1

net, but unfortunately there is no guarantee that this can be achieved.

Figure 23.25 shows the effect of varying the training rate alpha from 0.1 up to 0.5 and again up to its maximum value of 1.0.

For this example, choosing a training rate less than 1.0 just resulted in it taking longer to reach a low value of E, for no benefit, but that would not always be the case.

The learning rate is an example of a *hyperparameter* or *tuning parameter*. These are ones set by the user as opposed to being calculated from the data

Epochs	alpha = 0.1	alpha = 0.5	alpha = 1.0
1	0.31614246	0.31614246	0.31614246
10	0.26831552	0.15764040	0.10471755
100	0.09770540	0.02867036	0.02384230
1,000	0.02384615	0.02068691	0.02033149
10,000	0.02033106	0.02006048	0.02002921
100,000	0.02002914	0.02000551	0.02000272
1,000,000	0.02000272	0.02000054	0.02000027

Figure 23.25 Values of E for Varying Numbers of Epochs and Values of Training Rate alpha

itself. Making a good choice of hyperparameters is a skill that comes from a combination of experience and trial and error experiment.

23.5 Processing a Multi-instance Training Set

Up to now we have only considered a training set with a single instance. To be of practical use we need to be able to process training sets with many instances – realistically possibly many thousands of instances or more – and the method described so far can easily be adjusted for this purpose. Processing all the instances in the training set constitutes one epoch. There are two important decisions to make.

1. **When should the weights be adjusted?**

   There are two main options:

   (i) Adjusting the weights after each pass through the neural net (i.e. after each instance is processed forwards and backwards). This is called *stochastic training* or *online training*.

   (ii) Accumulating the adjustments for all the instances and then making them at the end of each epoch. This is called *batch training*.

   A middle option is to divide the training set into a number of equally-sized parts called *mini-batches*. The adjustments are accumulated and then made at the end of each mini-batch. This is called *mini-batch training*.

   In the examples in the following sections we will use the online training option, i.e. we will adjust the weights after each instance has been processed.

2. **When should tests for the error being below a required threshold value be made?**

Applying the test after, say, the first or the last pass in an epoch (or mini-batch) is too vulnerable to a chance result to be a good approach. The best way is probably to add together the values of E for an entire epoch (or mini-batch) to give a Total Error value, and then compare the Total Error with the required threshold value, say 0.0001, multiplied by the number of instances in the training set (or mini-batch).

23.6 Using a Neural Net for Classification: the *iris* Dataset

For classification tasks we first need to decide how the classifications of the instances should be represented in the training set.

A good approach for a classification task with N possible classifications is to have an output layer with N nodes, and use what is known as *one hot encoding*. For each instance one output node is given the target value 1, representing 'on' and the others are all given the target value zero, representing 'off'.

For example, if there are three classifications a, b and c, they can be represented by the target values 1, 0, 0 for a, 0, 1, 0 for b and 0, 0, 1 for c.

When the network has been trained, it can be used to predict the classification for unseen instances. For each one, the output node with the largest value (a number in the range zero to one) is identified. That node is given the value 1 and the other output nodes are given the value zero. Reversing the one hot encoding then gives the predicted classification.

We will illustrate the process using the *iris* dataset for iris plant classification from the UCI Repository. This is one of the best-known classification datasets. It was first analysed by the British statistician and biologist Sir Ronald Fisher back in 1936 and has been cited many times in the pattern recognition and data mining research literature. The aim is to classify iris plants into one of three classes: Iris-setosa, Iris-versicolor and Iris-virginica, on the basis of four continuous attributes: sepal length, sepal width, petal length and petal width (all measured in centimetres). There are 150 instances in the iris dataset: 50 for each classification.

The first step in processing the *iris* dataset for an experiment using a feedforward neural network with backpropagation for training is to separate the data into training and test instances.

The 150 instances in the *iris* dataset are arranged with the fifty that are classified as Iris-setosa first, followed by the fifty classified as Iris-vericolor and then finally the fifty classified as Iris-virginica. To create a training set the data was considered as comprising fifty groups of three instances. The first and

second members of each group were used for training and the third member of
each group was used for testing. That gave a training set of 100 instances and
a test set of 50 instances, of which 16, 17 and 17 were classified as Iris-setosa,
Iris-versicolor and Iris-virginica, respectively.

We next need to decide on the overall architecture for our neural network.
As there are four continuous attributes in the training data, our neural net will
have a training layer with four input nodes, inp1, inp2, inp3 and inp4. We will
(fairly arbitrarily) have a hidden layer which also has four nodes, hid1, hid2,
hid3 and hid4. Finally, as there are three possible classifications, we will have
an output layer with three nodes, out1, out2 and out3.

The next step is to convert the classifications to a one hot encoding. We will
set the target values of the three output nodes out1, out2 and out3 to be 1,0
and 0 respectively to denote Iris-setosa, with the combination 0, 1, 0 denoting
Iris-versicolor and the combination 0, 0, 1 denoting Iris-virginica.

Figure 23.26 shows three of the one hundred instances in the original *iris*
training set (chosen at random for this example).

sepal length	sepal width	petal length	petal width	Class
5.1	3.5	1.4	0.2	Iris-setosa
6.4	3.2	4.5	1.5	Iris-versicolor
6.3	3.3	6.0	2.5	Iris-virginica

Figure 23.26 Three Instances Extracted from the *iris* Dataset

The corresponding instances in the training set used with the neural net
are shown in Figure 23.27. Each one has the values of the four input nodes and
the target values of the three output nodes.

Input Values				Target Values		
inp1	inp2	inp3	inp4	out1	out2	out3
5.1	3.5	1.4	0.2	1	0	0
6.4	3.2	4.5	1.5	0	1	0
6.3	3.3	6.0	2.5	0	0	1

Figure 23.27 Instances for Neural Net Classifier Corresponding to those in
Table 23.26

All one hundred instances in the training set will be processed repeatedly
by the neural net.

There are two remaining steps. The first is to choose a value for the learning rate alpha. Here we will use a value of 0.1.

The final step is to set the initial weights, including the bias weights. In principle this should be done by choosing values at random from a small range, typically -0.5 to +0.5. In this case, the initial values were chosen (arbitrarily) by the author. They are shown in Figure 23.28.

Initial weights	hid1	hid2	hid3	hid4	Initial weights	out1	out2	out3
inp1	0.2	-0.4	0.5	0.1	hid1	-0.3	-0.4	0.4
inp2	0.3	0.2	-0.1	-0.2	hid2	0.2	0.4	0.3
inp3	0.05	-0.02	0.03	-0.04	hid3	-0.1	0.5	0.2
inp4	0.1	0.2	-0.1	-0.3	hid4	0.2	-0.1	0.25
biasH	-0.3				biasO	0.1		

Figure 23.28 Initial Weights (*iris* Data)

After 1,000 epochs the values of the weights had changed considerably, as is shown (to two decimal places) in Figure 23.29.

Initial weights	hid1	hid2	hid3	hid4	Initial weights	out1	out2	out3
inp1	0.20	-0.32	-1.01	3.55	hid1	1.25	-6.98	2.64
inp2	0.70	1.10	-2.75	11.73	hid2	2.10	-2.93	-0.15
inp3	-0.39	-2.12	3.00	-9.20	hid3	-6.71	5.97	4.30
inp4	0.24	-0.63	1.33	-10.30	hid4	3.88	8.51	-9.43
biasH	4.65				biasO	-2.79		

Figure 23.29 Final Weights after 1,000 Epochs (*iris* Data)

After one epoch the total of the 100 error values (one for each training instance) was 34.595490778744. By the end of the 1,000th epoch this had fallen to 1.0683857439195, so this appeared to be a suitable time to terminate the training process.

We can now regard the neural net as trained and use it to predict the classifications of the 50 instances in the test set. The first of these instances is shown in Figure 23.30 in 'converted' form.

For this testing stage we need only apply the forward propagation algorithm to each instance. Backpropagation does not take place, as the weights will not change, and the target values of the output nodes are not used. After forward

Input Values				Target Values		
inp1	inp2	inp3	inp4	out1	out2	out3
4.7	3.2	1.3	0.2	1	0	0

Figure 23.30 Test Instance for the *iris* Dataset (Input and Target Values)

propagation is applied to the test instance shown in Figure 23.30, we obtain the following values for the three output nodes (Figure 23.31).

Calculated Values			Target Values		
out1	out2	out3	out1	out2	out3
0.98700	0.01670	0.00006	1	0	0

Figure 23.31 Test Instance for the *iris* Dataset (Output and Target Values)

We now identify the output node with the largest calculated value, which in this case is out1. This indicates that the calculated, i.e. predicted, class value is Iris-setosa. The pattern of target values shows that the actual class of the instance is also Iris-setosa.

Working in this way for each test instance, we can construct a confusion matrix tabulating the number of test instances for each class that are classified as each predicted class. The result is shown in Figure 23.32.

	Classified as		
Correct classification	Iris-setosa	Iris-versicolor	Iris-virginica
Iris-setosa	16	0	0
Iris-versicolor	0	15	2
Iris-virginica	0	0	17

Figure 23.32 Confusion Matrix for Test Set (*iris* Data)

Two instances have been misclassified out of 50, i.e. the predictive accuracy is 96%. This is a good result.

Figure 23.33 below shows how the total of the 100 error values changes as the number of epochs rises from 1 to 1,000. Starting at approximately 34.5955 it drops quite rapidly to about 1 and then continues at a low level.

However, the scale of the graph conceals quite a lot of variation after the

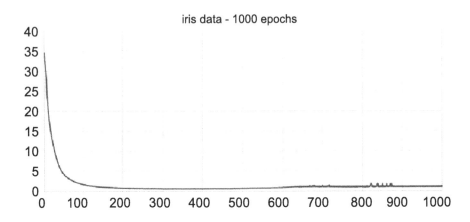

Figure 23.33   Total Error Value – Epochs 1 to 1,000 (iris Data)

early drop in the total value. Figure 23.34 shows the part from epoch 400 to epoch 1,000 drawn to a larger scale.

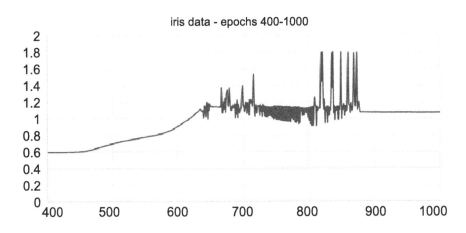

Figure 23.34   Total Error Value – Epochs 400 to 1,000 (iris Data)

A closer examination shows that the total error declines for the first 404 epochs, reaching a minimum value of 0.5935 and then starts increasing. Between epochs 640 and 880, the value fluctuates up and down several times, reaching a maximum value of 1.7959 at the 837th epoch. After the 880th epoch it declines slowly to an eventual low point after 1,000 epochs of 1.0684. This confirms the statement made earlier that the stochastic gradient decent technique used by backpropagation for adjusting weights does not guarantee that the error value will always go down.

The lowest total error value also does not guarantee the greatest predictive accuracy. For this example and with this initial choice of weights, stopping the processing after 404 epochs (when the total error value was at its lowest, i.e. 0.5935) would have given three misclassifications, i.e. 94% accuracy, rather than the two misclassifications obtained after 1,000 epochs (total error 1.0684). The alternative of terminating the process after 10,000 epochs (with a total error value 0.9146) would have given just one misclassification out of 50, i.e. 98% accuracy. Running the network for more epochs is likely to improve the classification accuracy, but this also cannot be guaranteed. In practice, knowing when to stop a neural network adjusting weights is largely a matter of judgement (and how much computing power is available).

23.7 Using a Neural Net for Classification: the *seeds* Dataset

The final example in this chapter uses a backpropagation feed-forward neural network to classify the data in the *seeds* dataset, which is one of those often used in data mining experiments. It can be downloaded from the UCI Machine Learning Repository at `https://archive.ics.uci.edu/ml/datasets/seeds`.

The dataset contains measurements of the geometrical properties of kernels belonging to three different varieties of wheat: Kama, Rosa and Canadian. There are 210 records, 70 with each classification, linking seven numerical features to one of the three classifications.

The data was collected from combine harvested wheat grain originating from experimental fields, explored at the Institute of Agrophysics of the Polish Academy of Sciences in Lublin, Poland. High quality visualization of the internal structure of each kernel was carried out using a soft X-ray technique. The continuous attributes are measurements of seven geometric parameters of wheat kernels:

- Area A

- Perimeter P

- Compactness C $= 4*\Pi*\mathrm{A}/\mathrm{P}^2$

- Length of kernel

- Width of kernel

- Asymmetry coefficient

- Length of kernel groove

To construct a classifier for this data, we first need to choose a neural network architecture. As there are seven input values (as well as the classification), we will have seven nodes in the input layer. We will (fairly arbitrarily) also have a hidden layer with seven nodes.

As this is a classification problem with three possible classifications, we will have three nodes in our output layer and use a one hot encoding:

- Classification *Kama* is represented by the values 1, 0, 0 for out1, out2 and out3 respectively

- Classification *Rosa* is represented by the values 0, 1, 0 for out1, out2 and out3 respectively

- Classification *Canadian* is represented by the values 0, 0, 1 for out1, out2 and out3 respectively

Much of the methodology is the same as for the *iris* dataset, as described in Section 23.6. The 210 instances in the *seeds* dataset are arranged with the seventy classified as Kama first, followed by the seventy classified as Rosa and then finally the seventy classified as Canadian. To create separate training and test sets the data was considered as comprising seventy groups of three instances. The first and second members of each group were used for training and the third member of each group was used for testing. That gave a training set of 140 instances and a test set of 70 instances, of which 23, 23 and 24 were classified as Kama, Rosa and Canadian, respectively.

There are two remaining steps. The first is to choose a value for the learning rate alpha. As for the *iris* data, we will use a value of 0.1.

The final step is to set the initial weights, including bias weights. These were chosen (arbitrarily) by the author. They are shown in Figure 23.35.

As before we will use the 'online training' option, i.e. we will adjust the weights after each instance has been processed.

For this training set it takes considerably more epochs to obtain a satisfactory trained net than for the *iris* data. After 1,000 epochs the trained net classifies every one of the test instances as Canadian!

However, if we continue up to 4,980 epochs the result is much better. At this point the weights are as shown in Figure 23.36 (to two decimal places).

If we take this version of the trained net and run it against the test data, in the same way as in Section 23.6, we obtain the following confusion matrix (Figure 23.37).

There are six wrongly classified instances out of 70, giving a predictive accuracy of 91.4%.

The behaviour of the Total Error value, i.e. the sum of the error values for all 140 instances in each epoch, is somewhat strange for this choice of architecture and – perhaps more importantly – this initial choice of weights. After one epoch

Initial weights	hid1	hid2	hid3	hid4	hid5	hid6	hid7
inp1	0.2	-0.1	0.3	0.4	0.1	-0.4	0.5
inp2	-0.05	0.02	-0.35	0.5	0.45	0.1	-0.2
inp3	0.1	0.2	0.3	0.4	0.5	0.6	0.7
inp4	0.4	-0.25	0.31	0.26	-0.5	-0.25	0.3
inp5	0.1	-0.2	0.3	-0.4	0.5	-0.6	0.7
inp6	0.05	-0.1	0.15	-0.2	0.25	-0.25	0.3
inp7	0.4	-0.35	0.41	-0.38	0.43	-0.24	0.5
biasH	0.23						

Initial weights	out1	out2	out3
hid1	-0.1	-0.4	-0.5
hid2	0.25	-0.25	0.4
hid3	0.4	0.1	0.2
hid4	-0.2	0.5	0.4
hid5	-0.1	-0.4	-0.3
hid6	0.2	0.36	0.45
hid7	-0.1	-0.26	0.4
biasO	0.4		

Figure 23.35   Initial Weights (*seeds* Data)

it has its initial value of 36.50. Unexpectedly (and very undesirably) this rises steadily up to Epoch 2130, when it reaches a value of 46.23. It then comes down (with fluctuations) until it reaches a value of 9.98 at Epoch 4980. Using either Total Error or the number of epochs as a stopping criterion is clearly not always reliable.

23.8 Neural Nets: A Note of Caution

Neural networks are powerful computational devices that have been used successfully for many tasks, including classification. The term deep learning has become widely used to describe large neural nets with multiple hidden layers and in recent years deep learning has become regarded as one of the great success stories of Artificial Intelligence. However, using neural nets can bring with it some serious problems and it is important that potential developers and

Initial weights	hid1	hid2	hid3	hid4	hid5	hid6	hid7
inp1	-0.31	-0.36	-0.13	-22.87	-27.30	-0.64	0.52
inp2	-0.84	-0.36	-1.07	9.11	25.52	-0.09	-0.18
inp3	0.04	0.17	0.25	1.80	6.48	0.59	0.70
inp4	0.07	-0.40	0.01	5.89	14.16	-0.33	0.31
inp5	-0.05	-0.27	0.16	-2.11	11.25	-0.64	0.70
inp6	-0.39	-0.29	-0.21	6.37	-5.40	-0.28	0.31
inp7	0.06	-0.51	0.13	22.85	-14.46	-0.31	0.51
biasH	8.28						

Initial weights	out1	out2	out3
hid1	-0.69	0.18	-0.80
hid2	-0.11	0.53	-0.13
hid3	-0.36	0.46	-0.06
hid4	-4.25	-5.40	5.30
hid5	4.65	-5.13	1.20
hid6	0.18	0.40	0.09
hid7	-1.80	3.53	-3.02
biasO	-0.93		

Figure 23.36 Weights after 4,980 Epochs (*seeds* Data)

	Classified as		
Correct classification	Kama	Rosa	Canadian
Kama	17	4	2
Rosa	0	23	0
Canadian	0	0	24

Figure 23.37 Confusion Matrix for Test Set (*seeds* Data)

users are aware of them.

- Using a neural net can be computationally expensive, especially when there are a large number of nodes in a layer or more than one hidden layer. Even in fairly simple cases, there is often a need to run the application for tens or hundreds of thousands of epochs to obtain a reasonable level of accuracy.

- Building a neural net involves making a lot of design decisions such as the number of nodes in each layer, the number of hidden layers, the learning rate etc., and these are difficult to make in a principled way. The random choice of initial values for the weights adds a large additional arbitrary element. Different decision choices or initial choices of weights may lead to entirely different performance. In addition, as the examples in this chapter have shown, judging when a neural network should stop processing more epochs can be difficult to do.

- The most frequent criticism of neural nets is that they are fundamentally inscrutable. It is difficult to justify a predicted classification except by saying that the 'neural net said so'. The same is true for numerical predictions such as future stock market prices or the rainfall tomorrow. It can no more be justified than we can explain why the eighth digit after the decimal point in the expansion of the mathematical constant pi (3.141592653589....) is 5. That is the answer simply because if you do all the calculations it turns out to be the answer. This probably does not matter if the application is, for example, to play chess against a top grandmaster, but what if the application is to give a medical diagnosis, decide who to offer a loan or a job or who is a likely suspect for a crime? Is it really satisfactory to make such decisions without being able to give any human-understandable explanation?

- Closely related to the above is the risk of building bias into the decisions made by a neural net. For example, it may be that some types of people have been most successful as company executives, heads of universities or Supreme Court judges in the past, whilst others may have been the most likely to commit certain types of crime, but that does not imply that this must, should or will always remain so. Building in bias is a risk for any application that makes decisions or offers recommendations based on historical data but it is most dangerous when the reasons for the system's conclusions cannot realistically be explained in human terms.

23.9 Chapter Summary

This chapter gives an introduction to the important topic of neural networks, computing systems based loosely on the connections between the neurons in the brain, which are increasingly widely used in data mining as well as other areas. A feed-forward neural network with backpropagation is described and its operation explained in detail. It is shown how such a network can be used for classification tasks and experimental results with two well-known datasets are presented. The chapter ends with some cautionary remarks about the drawbacks involved in using a neural net, relating mainly to inscrutability and the risk of inadvertently building bias into the system's conclusions.

23.10 Self-assessment Exercises for Chapter 23

1. Assuming that we have the neural net and initial weights shown in Section 23.3 and that for a different input instance the transformed values of nodes hid1, hid2 and hid3 are 0.9, 0.65 and 0.1, respectively, what are the weighted sum value and the transformed value of output node out2? What is the largest value that Tout1 can take?

2. Are the calculated values shown for the test instance (from the *iris* test set) given in Section 23.6 probabilities? If not, what are they?

A
Essential Mathematics

This appendix gives a basic description of the main mathematical notation and techniques used in this book. It has four sections, which deal with, in order:

- the subscript notation for variables and the Σ (or 'sigma') notation for summation (these are used throughout the book, particularly in Chapters 4, 5, 6 and 23)

- tree structures used to represent data items and the processes applied to them (these are used particularly in Chapters 4, 5 and 9)

- the mathematical function $\log_2 X$ (used particularly in Chapters 5, 6 and 10)

- set theory (which is used in Chapter 17).

If you are already familiar with this material, or can follow it fairly easily, you should have no trouble reading this book. Everything else will be explained as we come to it. If you have difficulty following the notation in some parts of the book, you can usually safely ignore it, just concentrating on the results and the detailed examples given.

A.1 Subscript Notation

This section introduces the subscript notation for variables and the Σ (or 'sigma') notation for summation which are used throughout the book, particularly in Chapters 4, 5, 6 and 23.

© Springer-Verlag London Ltd., part of Springer Nature 2020
M. Bramer, *Principles of Data Mining*, Undergraduate Topics
in Computer Science, DOI 10.1007/978-1-4471-7493-6

It is common practice to use variables to represent numerical values. For example, if we have six values we can represent them by a, b, c, d, e and f, although any other six variables would be equally valid. Their sum is $a + b + c + d + e + f$ and their average is $(a + b + c + d + e + f)/6$.

This is fine as long as there are only a small number of values, but what if there were 1,000 or 10,000 or a number that varied from one occasion to another? In that case we could not realistically use a different variable for each value.

The situation is analogous to the naming of houses. This is reasonable for a small road of 6 houses, but what about a long road with 200 or so? In the latter case, it is greatly more convenient to use a numbering system such as 1 High Street, 2 High Street, 3 High Street etc.

The mathematical equivalent of numbering houses is to use a *subscript notation* for variables. We can call the first value a_1, the second a_2 and so on, with the numbers 1, 2 etc. written slightly 'below the line' as subscripts. (We pronounce a_1 in the obvious way as the letter 'a' followed by the digit 'one'.) Incidentally, there is no need for the first value to be a_1. Subscripts beginning with zero are sometimes used, and in principle the first subscript can be any number, as long as they then increase in steps of one.

If we have 100 variables from a_1 up to a_{100}, we can write them as $a_1, a_2, \ldots, a_{100}$. The three dots, called an *ellipsis*, indicate that the intermediate values a_3 up to a_{99} have been omitted.

In the general case where the number of variables is unknown or can vary from one occasion to another, we often use a letter near the middle of the alphabet (such as n) to represent the number of values and write them as $a_1, a_2, \ldots, a_n$.

A.1.1 Sigma Notation for Summation

If we wish to indicate the sum of the values $a_1, a_2, \ldots, a_n$ we can write it as $a_1 + a_2 + \cdots + a_n$. However there is a more compact and often very useful notation which uses the Greek letter Σ ('sigma'). Sigma is the Greek equivalent of the letter 's', which is the first letter of the word 'sum'.

We can write a 'typical' value from the sequence $a_1, a_2, \ldots, a_n$ as a_i. Here i is called a *dummy variable*. We can use other variables instead of i, of course, but traditionally letters such as i, j and k are used. We can now write the sum $a_1 + a_2 + \cdots + a_n$ as

$$\sum_{i=1}^{i=n} a_i$$

(This is read as 'the sum of a_i for i equals 1 to n' or 'sigma a_i for $i = 1$ to n'.) The notation is often simplified to

$$\sum_{i=1}^{n} a_i$$

The dummy variable i is called the *index of summation*. The *lower* and *upper bounds of summation* are 1 and n, respectively.

The values summed are not restricted to just a_i. There can be any formula, for example

$$\sum_{i=1}^{i=n} a_i^2 \text{ or } \sum_{i=1}^{i=n} (i.a_i).$$

The choice of dummy variable makes no difference of course, so

$$\sum_{i=1}^{i=n} a_i = \sum_{j=1}^{j=n} a_j$$

Some other useful results are

$$\sum_{i=1}^{i=n} k.a_i = k. \sum_{i=1}^{i=n} a_i \text{ (where } k \text{ is a constant)}$$

and

$$\sum_{i=1}^{i=n} (a_i + b_i) = \sum_{i=1}^{i=n} a_i + \sum_{i=1}^{i=n} b_i$$

A.1.2 Double Subscript Notation

In some situations a single subscript is not enough and we find it helpful to use two (or occasionally even more). This is analogous to saying 'the fifth house on the third street' or similar.

We can think of a variable with two subscripts, e.g. a_{11}, a_{46}, or in general a_{ij} as representing the cells of a table. The figure below shows the standard way of referring to the cells of a table with 5 rows and 6 columns. For example, in a_{45} the first subscript refers to the fourth row and the second subscript refers to the fifth column. (By convention tables are labelled with the row numbers increasing from 1 as we move downwards and column numbers increasing from 1 as we move from left to right.) The subscripts can be separated by a comma if it is necessary to avoid ambiguity.

a_{11}	a_{12}	a_{13}	a_{14}	a_{15}	a_{16}
a_{21}	a_{22}	a_{23}	a_{24}	a_{25}	a_{26}
a_{31}	a_{32}	a_{33}	a_{34}	a_{35}	a_{36}
a_{41}	a_{42}	a_{43}	a_{44}	a_{45}	a_{46}
a_{51}	a_{52}	a_{53}	a_{54}	a_{55}	a_{56}

We can write a typical value as a_{ij}, using two dummy variables i and j.

If we have a table with m rows and n columns, the second row of the table is $a_{21}, a_{22}, \ldots, a_{2n}$ and the sum of the values in the second row is

$a_{21} + a_{22} + \cdots + a_{2n}$, i.e.

$$\sum_{j=1}^{j=n} a_{2j}$$

In general the sum of the values in the ith row is

$$\sum_{j=1}^{j=n} a_{ij}$$

To find the total value of all the cells we need to add the sums of all m rows together, which gives

$$\sum_{i=1}^{i=m} \sum_{j=1}^{j=n} a_{ij}$$

(This formula, with two 'sigma' symbols, is called a 'double summation'.)

Alternatively we can form the sum of the m values in the jth column, which is

$$\sum_{i=1}^{i=m} a_{ij}$$

and then form the total of the sums for all n columns, giving

$$\sum_{j=1}^{j=n} \sum_{i=1}^{i=m} a_{ij}$$

It does not matter which of these two ways we use to find the overall total. Whichever way we calculate it, the result must be the same, so we have the useful result

$$\sum_{i=1}^{i=m} \sum_{j=1}^{j=n} a_{ij} = \sum_{j=1}^{j=n} \sum_{i=1}^{i=m} a_{ij}.$$

A.1.3 Other Uses of Subscripts

Finally, we need to point out that subscripts are not always used in the way shown previously in this appendix. In Chapters 5, 6 and 10 we illustrate the calculation of two values of a variable E, essentially the 'before' and 'after' values. We call the original value E_{start} and the second value E_{new}. This is just a convenient way of labelling two values of the same variable. There is no meaningful way of using an index of summation.

A.2 Trees

Computer Scientists and Mathematicians often use a structure called a *tree* to represent data items and the processes applied to them.

Trees are used extensively in the first half of this book, especially in Chapters 4, 5 and 9.

Figure A.1 is an example of a tree. The letters A to M are labels added for ease of reference and are not part of the tree itself.

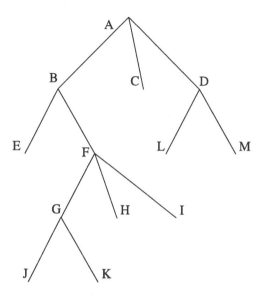

Figure A.1 A Tree with 13 Nodes

A.2.1 Terminology

In general a tree consists of a collection of points, called *nodes*, joined by straight lines, called *links*. Each link has a single node at each end. This is an example of a link joining two nodes G and J.

Figure A.1 comprises 13 nodes, labelled from A to M, joined by a total of 12 links.

The node at the top of the tree is called the *root* of the tree, or the *root node* or just the *root*. (In Computer Science, trees grow downwards from their roots.)

There is an implicit notion of movement down the tree, i.e. it is possible to go from the root node A to node D, or from node F to node H via a link. There is also a *path* from node A to node H via the 'chain' of links A to B, B to F, F to H and a path from node F to node K via links F to G then G to K. There is no way of going from B to A or from G to B, as we cannot go 'backwards' up the tree.

There are a number of conditions that must be satisfied to make a structure such as Figure A.1 a tree:

1. There must be a single node, the root, with no links 'flowing into' it from above.

2. There must be a path from the root node A to every other node in the tree (so the structure is connected).

3. There must be only *one path* from the root to each of the other nodes. If we added a link from F to L to Figure A.1 it would no longer be a tree, as there would be two paths from the root to node L: A to B, B to F, F to L and A to D, D to L.

Nodes such as C, E, H, I, J, K, L and M that have no other nodes below them in the tree are called *leaf nodes* or just *leaves*. Nodes such as B, D, F and G that are neither the root nor a leaf node are called *internal nodes*. Thus Figure A.1 has one root node, eight leaf nodes and four internal nodes.

The path from the root node of a tree to any of its leaf nodes is called a *branch*. Thus for Figure A.1 one of the branches is A to B, B to F, F to G, G to K. A tree has as many branches as it has leaf nodes.

A.2.2 Interpretation

A tree structure is one with which many people are familiar from family trees, flowcharts etc. We might say that the root node A of Figure A.1 represents the most senior person in a family tree, say John. His children are represented by nodes B, C and D, their children are E, F, L and M and so on. Finally John's great-great-grandchildren are represented by nodes J and K.

For the trees used in this book a different kind of interpretation is more helpful.

Figure A.2 is Figure A.1 augmented by numbers placed in parentheses at each of the nodes. We can think of 100 units placed at the root and flowing down to the leaves like water flowing down a mountainside from a single source (the root) to a number of pools (the leaves). There are 100 units at A. They flow down to form 60 at B, 30 at C and 10 at D. The 60 at B flow down to E (10 units) and F (50 units), and so on. We can think of the tree as a means of distributing the original 100 units from the root step-by-step to a number

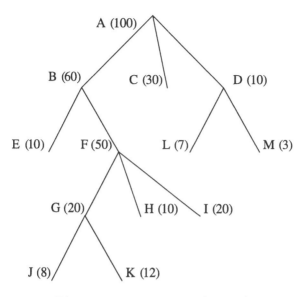

Figure A.2 Figure A.1 (revised)

of leaves. The relevance of this to using decision trees for classification will become clear in Chapter 4.

A.2.3 Subtrees

If we consider the part of Figure A.1 that hangs below node F, there are six nodes (including F itself) and five links which form a tree in their own right (see Figure A.3). We call this a *subtree* of the original tree. It is the subtree 'descending from' (or 'hanging from') node F. A subtree has all the characteristics of a tree in its own right, including its own root (node F).

Sometimes we wish to 'prune' a tree by removing the subtree which descends from a node such as F (leaving the node F itself intact), to give a simpler tree, such as Figure A.4. Pruning trees in this way is dealt with in Chapter 9.

A.3 The Logarithm Function $\log_2 X$

The mathematical function $\log_2 X$, pronounced 'log to base 2 of X', 'log 2 of X' or just 'log X' is widely used in scientific applications. It plays an important

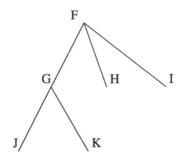

Figure A.3 Subtree Descending From Node F

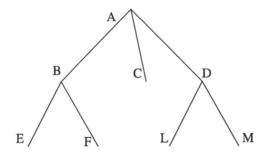

Figure A.4 Pruned Version of Figure A.1

part in this book, especially in connection with classification in Chapters 5 and 6 and in Chapter 10.

$\log_2 X = Y$ means that $2^Y = X$.

So for example $\log_2 8 = 3$ because $2^3 = 8$.

The 2 is always written as a subscript. In $\log_2 X$ the value of X is called the 'argument' of the $\log_2$ function. The argument is often written in parentheses, e.g. $\log_2(X)$ but we will usually omit the parentheses in the interests of simplicity when no ambiguity is possible, e.g. $\log_2 4$.

The value of the function is only defined for values of X greater than zero. Its graph is shown in Figure A.5. (The horizontal and vertical axes correspond to values of X and $\log_2 X$, respectively.)

Some important properties of the logarithm function are given in Figure A.6.

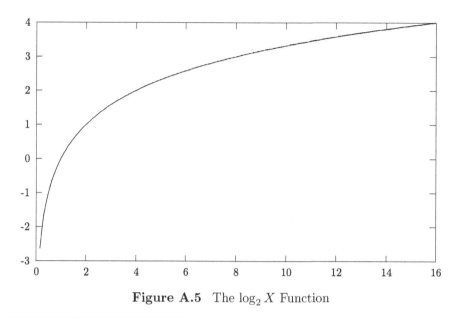

Figure A.5 The $\log_2 X$ Function

The value of $\log_2 X$ is

-- negative when $X < 1$

-- zero when $X = 1$

-- positive when $X > 1$

Figure A.6 Properties of the Logarithm Function

Some useful values of the function are given below.

$$
\begin{aligned}
\log_2(1/8) &= -3 \\
\log_2(1/4) &= -2 \\
\log_2(1/2) &= -1 \\
\log_2 1 &= 0 \\
\log_2 2 &= 1 \\
\log_2 4 &= 2 \\
\log_2 8 &= 3 \\
\log_2 16 &= 4 \\
\log_2 32 &= 5
\end{aligned}
$$

The $\log_2$ function has some unusual (and very helpful) properties that greatly assist calculations using it. These are given in Figure A.7.

$$\log_2(a \times b) = \log_2 a + \log_2 b$$
$$\log_2(a/b) = \log_2 a - \log_2 b$$
$$\log_2(a^n) = n \times \log_2 a$$
$$\log_2(1/a) = -\log_2 a$$

Figure A.7   More Properties of the Logarithm Function

So, for example,

$$\log_2 96 = \log_2(32 \times 3) = \log_2 32 + \log_2 3 = 5 + \log_2 3$$
$$\log_2(q/32) = \log_2 q - \log_2 32 = \log_2 q - 5$$
$$\log_2(6 \times p) = \log_2 6 + \log_2 p$$

The logarithm function can have other bases as well as 2. In fact any positive number can be a base. All the properties given in Figures A.6 and A.7 apply for any base.

Another commonly used base is base 10. $\log_{10} X = Y$ means $10^Y = X$, so $\log_{10} 100 = 2$, $\log_{10} 1000 = 3$ etc.

Perhaps the most widely used base of all is the 'mathematical constant' with the very innocuous name of e. The value of e is approximately 2.71828. Logarithms to base e are of such importance that instead of $\log_e X$ we often write $\ln X$ and speak of the 'natural logarithm', but explaining the importance of this constant is considerably outside the scope of this book.

Few calculators have a $\log_2$ function, but many have a $\log_{10}$, $\log_e$ or $\ln$ function. To calculate $\log_2 X$ from the other bases use $\log_2 X = \log_e X/0.6931$ or $\log_{10} X/0.3010$ or $\ln X/0.6931$.

A.3.1 The Function $-X \log_2 X$

The only base of logarithms used in this book is base 2. However the $\log_2$ function also appears in the formula $-X \log_2 X$ in the discussion of entropy in Chapters 5 and 10. The value of this function is also only defined for values of X greater than zero. However the function is only of importance when X is between 0 and 1. The graph of the important part of this function is given in Figure A.8.

The initial minus sign is included to make the value of the function positive (or zero) for all X between 0 and 1.

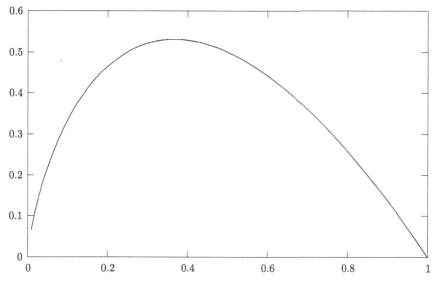

Figure A.8 The function $-X \log_2 X$

It can be proved that the function $-X \log_2 X$ has its maximum value when $X = 1/e = 0.3679$ (e is the 'mathematical constant' mentioned above). When X takes the value $1/e$, the value of the function is approximately 0.5307.

Values of X from 0 to 1 can sometimes usefully be thought of as probabilities (from $0 =$ impossible to $1 =$ certain), so we may write the function as $-p \log_2(p)$. The variable used is of course irrelevant as long as we are consistent. Using the fourth property in Figure A.7, the function can equivalently be written as $p \log_2(1/p)$. This is the form in which it mainly appears in Chapters 5 and 10.

A.4 Introduction to Set Theory

Set theory plays an important part in Chapter 17: Association Rule Mining II.

A set is a sequence of items, called *set elements* or *members*, separated by commas and enclosed in braces, i.e. the characters { and }. Two examples of sets are $\{a, 6.4, -2, dog, alpha\}$ and $\{z, y, x, 27\}$. Set elements can be numeric, non-numeric or a combination of the two.

A set can have another set as a member, so $\{a, b, \{a, b, c\}, d, e\}$ is a valid set, with five members. Note that the third element of the set, i.e. $\{a, b, c\}$ is counted as a single member.

No element may appear in a set more than once, so $\{a, b, c, b\}$ is not a valid set. The order in which the elements of a set are listed is not significant, so $\{a, b, c\}$ and $\{c, b, a\}$ are the same set.

The *cardinality* of a set is the number of elements it contains, so $\{\text{dog}, \text{cat}, \text{mouse}\}$ has cardinality three and $\{a, b, \{a, b, c\}, d, e\}$ has cardinality five. The set with no elements $\{\}$ is called the empty set and is written as $\emptyset$.

We usually think of the members of a set being drawn from some 'universe of discourse', such as all the people who belong to a certain club. Let us assume that set A contains all those who are aged under 25 and set B contains all those who are married.

We call the set containing all the elements that occur in either A or B or both the *union* of the two sets A and B. It is written as $A \cup B$. If A is the set $\{\text{John}, \text{Mary}, \text{Henry}\}$ and B is the set $\{\text{Paul}, \text{John}, \text{Mary}, \text{Sarah}\}$ then $A \cup B$ is the set $\{\text{John}, \text{Mary}, \text{Henry}, \text{Paul}, \text{Sarah}\}$, the set of people who are either under 25 or married or both. Figure A.9 shows two overlapping sets. The shaded area is their union.

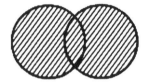

Figure A.9   Union of Two Overlapping Sets

We call the set containing all the elements (if there are any) that occur in both A and B the *intersection* of the two sets A and B. It is written $A \cap B$. If A is the set $\{\text{John}, \text{Mary}, \text{Henry}\}$ and B is the set $\{\text{Paul}, \text{John}, \text{Mary}, \text{Sarah}\}$ as before, then $A \cap B$ is the set $\{\text{John}, \text{Mary}\}$, the set of people who are both under 25 and married. Figure A.10 shows two overlapping sets. In this case, the shaded area is their intersection.

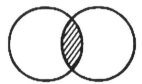

Figure A.10   Intersection of Two Overlapping Sets

Two sets are called *disjoint* if they have no elements in common, for example $A = \{\text{Max}, \text{Dawn}\}$ and $B = \{\text{Frances}, \text{Bryony}, \text{Gavin}\}$. In this case their intersection $A \cap B$ is the set with no elements, which we call the empty set and represent by {} or (more often) by $\emptyset$. Figure A.11 shows this case.

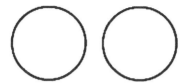

Figure A.11   Intersection of Two Disjoint Sets

If two sets are disjoint their union is the set comprising all the elements in the first set and all those in the second set.

There is no reason to be restricted to two sets. It is meaningful to refer to the union of any number of sets (the set comprising those elements that appear in any one or more of the sets) and the intersection of any number of sets (the set comprising those elements that appear in all the sets). Figure A.12 shows three sets, say A, B and C. The shaded area is their intersection $A \cap B \cap C$.

Figure A.12   Intersection of Three Sets

A.4.1 Subsets

A set A is called a *subset* of another set B if every element in A also occurs in B. We can illustrate this by Figure A.13, which shows a set B (the outer circle) with a set A (the inner circle) completely inside it. The implication is that B includes A, i.e. every element in A is also in B and there may also be one or more other elements in B. For example B and A may be $\{p, q, r, s, t\}$ and $\{q, t\}$ respectively.

We indicate that A is a subset of B by the notation $A \subseteq B$. So $\{q, t\} \subseteq \{p, r, s, q, t\}$. The empty set is a subset of every set and every set is a subset of itself.

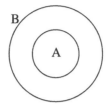

Figure A.13 A is a Subset of B

We sometimes want to specify that a subset A of set B must have fewer elements than B itself, in order to rule out the possibility of treating B as one of its own subsets. In this case we say that A is a *strict subset* of B, written $A \subset B$. So $\{q, t\}$ is a strict subset of $\{p, r, s, q, t\}$ but $\{t, s, r, q, p\}$ is not a strict subset of $\{p, r, s, q, t\}$, as it is the same set. (The order in which the elements are written is irrelevant.)

If A is a subset of B, we say that B is a *superset* of A, written as $B \supseteq A$.

If A is a strict subset of B we say that B is a *strict superset* of A, written as $B \supset A$.

A set with three elements such as $\{a, b, c\}$ has eight subsets, including the empty set and itself. They are $\emptyset$, $\{a\}$, $\{b\}$, $\{c\}$, $\{a, b\}$, $\{a, c\}$, $\{b, c\}$ and $\{a, b, c\}$.

In general a set with n elements has 2^n subsets, including the empty set and the set itself. Each member of the set can be included or not included in a subset. The number of possible subsets is therefore the same as the total number of possible include/do not include choices, which is 2 multiplied by itself n times, i.e. 2^n.

The set containing all the subsets of A is called the *power set* of A. Thus the power set of $\{a, b, c\}$ is $\{\emptyset, \{a\}, \{b\}, \{c\}, \{a, b\}, \{a, c\}, \{b, c\}, \{a, b, c\}\}$.

If set A has n elements its power set contains 2^n elements.

A.4.2 Summary of Set Notation

$\{\}$	The 'brace' characters that enclose the elements of a set, e.g. {apples, oranges, bananas}
$\emptyset$	The empty set. Also written as $\{\}$
$A \cup B$	The union of sets A and B. The set that contains all the elements that occur either in A or B or both.
$A \cap B$	The intersection of two sets A and B. The set that includes all the elements (if there are any) that occur in both A and B.
$A \subseteq B$	A is a subset of B, i.e. every element in A also occurs in B.
$A \subset B$	A is a strict subset of B, i.e. A is a subset of B and A contains fewer elements than B.
$A \supseteq B$	A is a superset of B. True if and only if B is a subset of A.
$A \supset B$	A is a strict superset of B. True if and only if B is a strict subset of A.

B
Datasets

The methods described in this book are illustrated by tests on a number of datasets, with a range of sizes and characteristics. Basic information about each dataset is summarised in Figure B.1.

Dataset	Description	classes*	attributes**		instances	
			categ	cts	training set	test set
anonymous	Football/ Netball Data (anonymised)	2 (58%)	4		12	
bcst96	Text Classi- fication Dataset	2		13430 !	1186	509
chess	Chess Endgame	2 (95%)	7		647	
contact_ lenses	Contact Lenses	3 (88%)	5		108	
crx	Credit Card Applica- tions	2 (56%)	9	6	690 (37)	200 (12)
degrees	Degree Class	2 (77%)	5		26	

© Springer-Verlag London Ltd., part of Springer Nature 2020
M. Bramer, *Principles of Data Mining*, Undergraduate Topics
in Computer Science, DOI 10.1007/978-1-4471-7493-6

football/ netball	Sports Club Preference	2 (58%)	4		12	
genetics	DNA Sequences	3 (52%)	60		3190	
glass	Glass Identification Database	7 (36%)		9 !!	214	
golf	Decision Whether to Play	2 (64%)	2	2	14	
hepatitis	Hepatitis Data	2 (79%)	13	6	155 (75)	
hypo	Hypothyroid Disorders	5 (92%)	22	7	2514 (2514)	1258 (371)
iris	Iris Plant Classification	3 (33.3%)		4	150	
labor-ne	Labor Negotiations	2 (65%)	8	8	40 (39)	17 (17)
lens24	Contact Lenses (reduced version)	3 (63%)	4		24	
monk1	Monk's Problem 1	2 (50%)	6		124	432
monk2	Monk's Problem 2	2 (62%)	6		169	432
monk3	Monk's Problem 3	2 (51%)	6		122	432
pima-indians	Prevalence of Diabetes in Pima Indian Women	2 (65%)		8	768	
seeds	Classification of Varieties of Wheat	3 (33%)		7	210	

sick-euthyroid	Thyroid Disease Data	2 (91%)	18	7	3163	
train	Train Punctuality	4 (70%)	4		20	
vote	Voting in US Congress	2 (61%)	16		300	135
wake_vortex	Air Traffic Control	2 (50%)	3	1	1714	
wake_vortex2	Air Traffic Control	2 (50%)	19	32	1714	

* % size of largest class in training set is given in parentheses.

** 'categ' and 'cts' stand for Categorical and Continuous, respectively.
If there are instances with missing values the number is shown in parentheses.

! Including 1749 with only a single value for instances in the training set.

!! Plus one 'ignore' attribute.

Figure B.1 Basic Information About Datasets

The *degrees*, *train*, *football/netball* and *anonymous* datasets were created by the author for illustrative purposes only. The *bcst96*, *wake_vortex* and *wake_vortex2* datasets are not generally available. Details of the other datasets are given on the following pages. In each case the class with the largest number of corresponding instances in the training set is shown in **bold**.

Datasets shown as 'Source: UCI Repository' can be downloaded (sometimes with slight differences) from the World Wide Web at
https://archive.ics.uci.edu/ml/.

Dataset *chess*

Description

This dataset was used for one of a well-known series of experiments by the Australian researcher Ross Quinlan, taking as an experimental testbed the Chess endgame with White king and rook versus Black king and knight. This endgame served as the basis for several studies of Machine Learning and other Artificial Intelligence techniques in the 1970s and 1980s.

The task is to classify positions (all with Black to move) as either 'safe' or 'lost', using attributes that correspond to configurations of the pieces. The classification 'lost' implies that whatever move Black makes, White will immediately be able to give checkmate or alternatively will be able to capture the Knight without giving stalemate or leaving his Rook vulnerable to immediate capture. Generally this is not possible, in which case the position is 'safe'. This task is trivial for human experts but has proved remarkably difficult to automate in a satisfactory way. In this experiment (Quinlan's 'third problem'), the simplifying assumption is made that the board is of infinite size. Despite this, the classification task remains a hard one. Further information is given in [1].

Source: Reconstructed by the author from description given in [1].

Classes
safe, lost

Attributes and Attribute Values

The first four attributes represent the distance between pairs of pieces (wk and wr: White King and Rook, bk and bn: Black King and Knight). They all have values 1, 2 and 3 (3 denoting any value greater than 2).

dist_bk_bn
dist_bk_wr
dist_wk_bn
dist_wk_wr

The other three attributes all have values 1 (denoting true) and 2 (denoting false).

inline (Black King and Knight and White Rook in line)
wr_bears_bk (White Rook bears on the Black King)
wr_bears_bn (White Rook bears on the Black Knight)

Instances
Training set: 647 instances
No separate test set

Dataset *contact_lenses*

Description
Data from ophthalmic optics relating clinical data about a patient to a decision as to whether he/she should be fitted with hard contact lenses, soft contact lenses or none at all.

Source: Reconstructed by the author from data given in [2].

Classes
hard lenses: The patient should be fitted with hard contact lenses
soft lenses: The patient should be fitted with soft contact lenses
no lenses: The patient should not be fitted with contact lenses

Attributes and Attribute Values
age: 1 (young), 2 (pre-presbyopic), 3 (presbyopic)

specRx (Spectacle Prescription): 1 (myopia), 2 (high hypermetropia), 3 (low hypermetropia)

astig (Whether Astigmatic): 1 (no), 2 (yes)

tears (Tear Production Rate): 1 (reduced), 2 (normal)

tbu (Tear Break-up Time): 1 (less than or equal to 5 seconds), 2 (greater than 5 seconds and less than or equal to 10 seconds), 3 (greater than 10 seconds)

Instances
Training set: 108 instances
No separate test set

Dataset *crx*

Description

This dataset concerns credit card applications. The data is genuine but the attribute names and values have been changed to meaningless symbols to protect confidentiality of the data.

Source: UCI Repository

Classes

+ and − denoting a successful application and an unsuccessful application, respectively (largest class for the training data is −)

Attributes and Attribute Values

A1: b, a
A2: continuous
A3: continuous
A4: u, y, l, t
A5: g, p, gg
A6: c, d, cc, i, j, k, m, r, q, w, x, e, aa, ff
A7: v, h, bb, j, n, z, dd, ff, o
A8: continuous
A9: t, f
A10: t, f
A11: continuous
A12: t, f
A13: g, p, s
A14: continuous
A15: continuous

Instances

Training set: 690 instances (including 37 with missing values)
Test set: 200 instances (including 12 with missing values)

Dataset *genetics*

Description
Each instance comprises the values of a sequence of 60 DNA elements classified into one of three possible categories. For further information see [3].

Source: UCI Repository

Classes
EI, IE and **N**

Attributes and Attribute Values
There are 60 attributes, named A0 to A59, all of which are categorical. Each attribute has eight possible values: A, T, G, C, N, D, S and R.

Instances
Training set: 3190 instances
No separate test set

Dataset *glass*

Description
This dataset is concerned with the classification of glass left at the scene
of a crime into one of six types (such as 'tableware', 'headlamp' or 'build-
ing_windows_float_processed'), for purposes of criminological investigation.
The classification is made on the basis of nine continuous attributes (plus
an identification number, which is ignored).

Source: UCI Repository

Classes
1, **2**, 3, 5, 6, 7
Type of glass:
1 building_windows_float_processed
2 building_windows_non_float_processed
3 vehicle_windows_float_processed
4 vehicle_windows_non_float_processed (none in this dataset)
5 container
6 tableware
7 headlamp

Attributes and Attribute Values
Id number: 1 to 214 (an 'ignore' attribute)
plus nine continuous attributes
RI: refractive index
Na: Sodium (unit measurement: weight percent in corresponding oxide, as
are the attributes that follow)
Mg: Magnesium
Al: Aluminum
Si: Silicon
K: Potassium
Ca: Calcium
Ba: Barium
Fe: Iron

Instances
Training set: 214 instances
No separate test set

Dataset *golf*

Description
A synthetic dataset relating a decision on whether or not to play golf to
weather observations.

Source: UCI Repository

Classes
Play, Don't Play

Attributes and Attribute Values
outlook: sunny, overcast, rain
temperature: continuous
humidity: continuous
windy: true, false

Instances
Training set: 14 instances
No separate test set

Dataset *hepatitis*

Description
The aim is to classify patients into one of two classes, representing 'will live' or 'will die', on the basis of 13 categorical and 9 continuous attributes.

Source: UCI Repository

Classes
1 and **2** representing 'will die' and 'will live' respectively

Attributes and Attribute Values
Age: continuous.
Sex: 1, 2 (representing male, female)
Steroid: 1, 2 (representing no, yes)
Antivirals: 1, 2 (representing no, yes)
Fatigue: 1, 2 (representing no, yes)
Malaise: 1, 2 (representing no, yes)
Anorexia: 1, 2 (representing no, yes)
Liver Big: 1, 2 (representing no, yes)
Liver Firm: 1, 2 (representing no, yes)
Spleen Palpable: 1, 2 (representing no, yes)
Spiders: 1, 2 (representing no, yes)
Ascites: 1, 2 (representing no, yes)
Varices: 1, 2 (representing no, yes)
Bilirubin: continuous
Alk Phosphate: continuous
SGOT: continuous
Albumin: continuous
Protime: continuous
Histology: 1, 2 (representing no, yes)

Instances
Training set: 155 instances (including 75 with missing values)
No separate test set

Dataset *hypo*

Description
This is a dataset on Hypothyroid disorders collected by the Garvan Institute in Australia. Subjects are divided into five classes based on the values of 29 attributes (22 categorical and 7 continuous).

Source: UCI Repository

Classes
hyperthyroid, primary hypothyroid, compensated hypothyroid, secondary hypothyroid, **negative**

Attributes and Attribute Values
age: continuous
sex: M, F
on thyroxine, query on thyroxine, on antithyroid medication, sick, pregnant, thyroid surgery, I131 treatment, query hypothyroid, query hyperthyroid, lithium, goitre, tumor, hypopituitary, psych, TSH measured **ALL** f, t
TSH: continuous
T3 measured: f, t
T3: continuous
TT4 measured: f, t
TT4: continuous
T4U measured: f, t
T4U: continuous
FTI measured: f, t
FTI: continuous
TBG measured: f, t
TBG: continuous
referral source: WEST, STMW, SVHC, SVI, SVHD, other

Instances
Training set: 2514 instances (all with missing values)
Test set: 1258 instances (371 with missing values)

Dataset *iris*

Description
Iris Plant Classification. This is one of the best known classification datasets, which is widely referenced in the technical literature. The aim is to classify iris plants into one of three classes on the basis of the values of four continuous attributes.

Source: UCI Repository

Classes
Iris-setosa, Iris-versicolor, Iris-virginica (there are 50 instances in the dataset for each classification)

Attributes and Attribute Values
Four continuous attributes: sepal length, sepal width, petal length and petal width.

Instances
Training set: 150 instances
No separate test set

Dataset *labor-ne*

Description
This is a small dataset, created by *Collective Bargaining Review* (a monthly publication). It gives details of the final settlements in labor negotiations in Canadian industry in 1987 and the first quarter of 1988. The data includes all collective agreements reached in the business and personal services sector for local organisations with at least 500 members (teachers, nurses, university staff, police, etc).

Source: UCI Repository

Classes
good, bad

Attributes and Attribute Values
duration: continuous [1..7] *
wage increase first year: continuous [2.0..7.0]
wage increase second year: continuous [2.0..7.0]
wage increase third year: continuous [2.0..7.0]
cost of living adjustment: none, tcf, tc
working hours: continuous [35..40]
pension: none, ret_allw, empl_contr (employer contributions to pension plan)
standby pay: continuous [2..25]
shift differential: continuous [1..25] (supplement for work on II and III shift)
education allowance: yes, no
statutory holidays: continuous [9..15] (number of statutory holidays)
vacation: below average, average, generous (number of paid vacation days)
longterm disability assistance: yes, no
contribution to dental plan: none, half, full
bereavement assistance: yes, no (employer's financial contribution towards covering the costs of bereavement)
contribution to health plan: none, half, full

Instances
Training set: 40 instances (39 with missing values)
Test set: 17 instances (all with missing values)

* The notation [1..7] denotes a value in the range from 1 to 7 inclusive

Dataset *lens24*

Description
A reduced and simplified version of *contact_lenses* with only 24 instances.

Source: Reconstructed by the author from data given in [2].

Classes
1, 2, **3**

Attributes and Attribute Values
age: 1, 2, 3
specRx: 1, 2
astig: 1, 2
tears: 1, 2

Instances
Training set: 24 instances
No separate test set

Dataset *monk1*

Description
Monk's Problem 1. The 'Monk's Problems' are a set of three artificial problems with the same set of six categorical attributes. They have been used to test a wide range of classification algorithms, originally at the second European Summer School on Machine Learning, held in Belgium during summer 1991. There are $3 \times 3 \times 2 \times 3 \times 4 \times 2 = 432$ possible instances. All of them are included in the test set for each problem, which therefore includes the training set in each case.
The 'true' concept underlying Monk's Problem 1 is: *if (attribute#1 = attribute#2) or (attribute#5 = 1) then class = 1 else class = 0*

Source: UCI Repository

Classes
0, 1 (62 instances for each classification)

Attributes and Attribute Values
attribute#1: 1, 2, 3
attribute#2: 1, 2, 3
attribute#3: 1, 2
attribute#4: 1, 2, 3
attribute#5: 1, 2, 3, 4
attribute#6: 1, 2

Instances
Training set: 124 instances
Test set: 432 instances

Dataset *monk2*

Description

Monk's Problem 2. See *monk1* for general information about the Monk's Problems. The 'true' concept underlying Monk's problem 2 is: *if (attribute#n = 1) for exactly two choices of n (from 1 to 6) then class = 1 else class = 0*

Source: UCI Repository.

Classes

0, 1

Attributes and Attribute Values

attribute#1: 1, 2, 3
attribute#2: 1, 2, 3
attribute#3: 1, 2
attribute#4: 1, 2, 3
attribute#5: 1, 2, 3, 4
attribute#6: 1, 2

Instances

Training set: 169 instances
Test set: 432 instances

Dataset *monk3*

Description
Monk's Problem 3. See *monk1* for general information about the Monk's Problems. The 'true' concept underlying Monk's Problem 3 is:
if (attribute#5 = 3 and attribute#4 = 1) or (attribute#5 ≠ 4 and attribute#2 ≠ 3) then class = 1 else class = 0
This dataset has 5% noise (misclassifications) in the training set.

Source: UCI Repository

Classes
0, 1

Attributes and Attribute Values
attribute#1: 1, 2, 3
attribute#2: 1, 2, 3
attribute#3: 1, 2
attribute#4: 1, 2, 3
attribute#5: 1, 2, 3, 4
attribute#6: 1, 2

Instances
Training set: 122 instances
Test set: 432 instances

Dataset *pima-indians*

Description

The dataset concerns the prevalence of diabetes in Pima Indian women. It is considered to be a difficult dataset to classify.

The dataset was created by the (United States) National Institute of Diabetes and Digestive and Kidney Diseases and is the result of a study on 768 adult female Pima Indians living near Phoenix. The goal is to predict the presence of diabetes using seven health-related attributes, such as 'Number of times pregnant' and 'Diastolic blood pressure', together with age.

Source: UCI Repository

Classes

0 ('tested negative for diabetes') and 1 ('tested positive for diabetes')

Attributes and Attribute Values

Eight attributes, all continuous: Number of times pregnant, Plasma glucose concentration, Diastolic blood pressure, Triceps skin fold thickness, 2-Hour serum insulin, Body mass index, Diabetes pedigree function, Age (in years).

Instances

Training set: 768 instances

No separate test set

Dataset *seeds*

Description
Classification of different varieties of wheat using measurements of geometrical properties of kernels. The data was collected from combine harvested wheat grain originating from experimental fields, explored at the Institute of Agrophysics of the Polish Academy of Sciences in Lublin, Poland. High quality visualization of the internal structure of each kernel was carried out using a soft X-ray technique. The continuous attributes are measurements of seven geometric parameters of wheat kernels.

Source: UCI Repository

Classes
Kama, Rosa and Canadian (70 instances each)

Attributes (seven, all continuous)
Area
Perimeter
Compactness
Length of kernel
Width of kernel
Asymmetry coefficient
Length of kernel groove

Instances
Training set: 210 instances
No separate test set

Dataset *sick-euthyroid*

Description Thyroid Disease data.

Source: UCI Repository

Classes
sick-euthyroid and **negative**

Attributes and Attribute Values
age: continuous
sex: M, F
on_thyroxine: f, t
query_on_thyroxine: f, t
on_antithyroid_medication: f, t
thyroid_surgery: f, t
query_hypothyroid: f, t
query_hyperthyroid: f, t
pregnant: f, t
sick: f, t
tumor: f, t
lithium: f, t
goitre: f, t
TSH_measured: y, n
TSH: continuous
T3_measured: y, n
T3: continuous
TT4_measured: y, n
TT4: continuous
T4U_measured: y, n
T4U: continuous.
FTI_measured: y, n
FTI: continuous
TBG_measured: y, n
TBG: continuous

Instances
Training set: 3163 instances
No separate test set

•

Dataset *vote*

Description
Voting records drawn from the Congressional Quarterly Almanac, 98th Congress, 2nd session 1984, Volume XL: Congressional Quarterly Inc. Washington, DC, 1985.

This dataset includes votes for each of the US House of Representatives Congressmen on the 16 key votes identified by the CQA. The CQA lists nine different types of vote: voted for, paired for, and announced for (these three simplified to yea), voted against, paired against, and announced against (these three simplified to nay), voted present, voted present to avoid conflict of interest, and did not vote or otherwise make a position known (these three simplified to an unknown disposition).

The instances are classified according to the party to which the voter belonged, either Democrat or Republican. The aim is to predict the voter's party on the basis of 16 categorical attributes recording the votes on topics such as handicapped infants, aid to the Nicaraguan Contras, immigration, a physician fee freeze and aid to El Salvador.

Source: UCI Repository

Classes
democrat, republican

Attributes and Attribute Values
Sixteen categorical attributes, all with values y, n and u (standing for 'yea', 'nay' and 'unknown disposition', respectively): handicapped infants, water project cost sharing, adoption of the budget resolution, physician fee freeze, el salvador aid, religious groups in schools, anti satellite test ban, aid to nicaraguan contras, mx missile, immigration, synfuels corporation cutback, education spending, superfund right to sue, crime, duty free exports, export administration act south africa.

Instances
Training set: 300 instances
Test set: 135 instances

References

[1] Quinlan, J. R. (1979). Discovering rules by induction from large collections
     of examples. In D. Michie (Ed.), *Expert systems in the micro-electronic age*
     (pp. 168–201). Edinburgh: Edinburgh University Press.

[2] Cendrowska, J. (1990). *Knowledge acquisition for expert systems: inducing
     modular rules from examples*. PhD Thesis, The Open University.

[3] Noordewier, M. O., Towell, G. G., & Shavlik, J. W. (1991). Training knowl-
     edge-based neural networks to recognize genes in DNA sequences. In *Ad-
     vances in neural information processing systems* (Vol. 3). San Mateo: Mor-
     gan Kaufmann.

C
Sources of Further Information

Websites

There is a great deal of information about all aspects of data mining available on the World Wide Web. A good place to start looking is the 'Knowledge Discovery Nuggets' site at `http://www.kdnuggets.com`, which has links to information on software, products, companies, datasets, other websites, courses, conferences etc.

Another very useful source of information is The Data Mine at `http://www.the-data-mine.com`.

The Natural Computing Applications Forum (NCAF) is an active British-based group specialising in Predictive Analytics, Data Mining and related technologies. Their website is at `http://www.ncaf.org.uk`.

Books

There are many books on Data Mining. Some popular ones are listed below.

1. **Data Mining: Concepts and Techniques (third edition)** by J. Han, M. Kamber and J. Pei. Morgan Kaufmann, 2012. ISBN: 978-0-12-381479-1.

© Springer-Verlag London Ltd., part of Springer Nature 2020
M. Bramer, *Principles of Data Mining*, Undergraduate Topics in Computer Science, DOI 10.1007/978-1-4471-7493-6

2. **The Elements of Statistical Learning: Data Mining, Inference and Prediction (second edition)** by T. Hastie, R. Tibshirani and J. Friedman. Springer-Verlag, 2009. ISBN: 0-38784-857-6.

3. **Data Mining: Practical Machine Learning Tools and Techniques (fourth edition)** by I.H. Witten, E. Frank, M. Hall and C. Pal. Morgan Kaufmann, 2017. ISBN: 978-0-12-804291-5.

   This book is based around *Weka*, a collection of open source machine learning algorithms for data mining tasks that can either be applied directly to a dataset or called from the user's own Java code. Full details are available at `http://www.cs.waikato.ac.nz/ml/weka/`.

4. **C4.5: Programs for Machine Learning** by Ross Quinlan. Morgan Kaufmann, 1993. ISBN: 1-55860-238-0.

   This book gives a detailed account of the author's celebrated tree induction system C4.5, together with a machine-readable version of the software and some sample datasets.

5. **Machine Learning** by Tom Mitchell. McGraw-Hill, 1997. ISBN: 0-07-115467-1.

6. **Text Mining: Applications and Theory** by Michael Berry and Jacob Kogan. Wiley, 2010. ISBN: 0-47-074982-2.

7. **Introduction to Data Mining** by P.-N. Tan, M. Steinbach, A. Karpatne and V. Kumar. Pearson, 2018. ISBN: 0-13-312890-3.

8. **Neural Networks for Pattern Recognition** by Chris Bishop. Clarendon Press: Oxford, 2004. ISBN: 978-0-19-853864-6.

9. **Pattern Recognition and Neural Networks** by Brian Ripley. Cambridge University Press, 2007. ISBN: 978-0-521-71770-0.

10. **Neural Networks and Deep Learning** by C. Aggarwal. Springer, 2018. ISBN: 3-31-994462-2.

Conferences

There are many conferences and workshops on Data Mining every year. Two of the most important regular series are:

The annual KDD-20xx series of conferences organised by SIGKDD (the ACM Special Interest Group on Knowledge Discovery and Data Mining) in locations around the world. For details see `http://www.kdd.org`.

The annual IEEE ICDM (International Conferences on Data Mining) series. These move around the world, with usually every second year in the United States or Canada. For details see the ICDM website at `http://icdm.bigke.org`.

Information About Association Rule Mining

A valuable source of information is the repository established by two international workshops known as *FIMI* (Frequent Itemset Mining Implementations), which were run as part of the annual International Conference on Data Mining organised by the Institution of Electrical and Electronic Engineering. The FIMI website at `http://fimi.ua.ac.be` holds not only a collection of research papers but also downloadable implementations of many of them and a collection of standard datasets that researchers can use to test their own algorithms.

D
Glossary and Notation

$a < b$	a is less than b
$a \leq b$	a is less than or equal to b
$a > b$	a is greater than b
$a \geq b$	a is greater than or equal to b
a_i	i is a *subscript*. Subscript notation is explained in Appendix A
$\sum_{i=1}^{N} a_i$	The sum $a_1 + a_2 + a_3 + \cdots + a_N$
$\sum_{i=1}^{N} \sum_{j=1}^{M} a_{ij}$	The sum $a_{11} + a_{12} + \cdots + a_{1M} + a_{21} + a_{22} + \cdots + a_{2M} + \cdots + a_{N1} + a_{N2} + \cdots + a_{NM}$
$\prod_{j=1}^{M} b_j$	The product $b_1 \times b_2 \times b_3 \times \cdots \times b_M$
$P(E)$	The **probability of event** E occurring (a number from 0 to 1 inclusive)
$P(E \mid x = a)$	The **probability of event** E occurring *given that* variable x has value a (a **conditional probability**)
$\log_2 X$	Logarithm to base 2 of X. Logarithms are explained in Appendix A
$dist(X, Y)$	The distance between two points X and Y
Z_{CL}	In Chapter 7, the number of **standard errors** needed for a **confidence level** of CL

© Springer-Verlag London Ltd., part of Springer Nature 2020
M. Bramer, *Principles of Data Mining*, Undergraduate Topics
in Computer Science, DOI 10.1007/978-1-4471-7493-6

$a \pm b$	Generally 'a plus or minus b', e.g. 6 ± 2 denotes a number from 4 to 8 inclusive. In Chapter 7, $a \pm b$ is used to indicate that a **classifier** has a **predictive accuracy** of a with **standard error** b
N_{LEFT}	The number of **instances** matching the left-hand side of a rule
N_{RIGHT}	The number of **instances** matching the right-hand side of a rule
N_{BOTH}	The number of **instances** matching both sides of a rule
N_{TOTAL}	The total number of **instances** in a dataset
$\{\}$	The 'brace' characters that enclose the elements of a set, e.g. $\{$apples, oranges, bananas$\}$
$\emptyset$	The **empty set**. Also written as $\{\}$
$A \cup B$	The **union** of sets A and B. The set that contains all the elements that occur either in A or B or both
$A \cap B$	The **intersection** of two sets A and B. The set that includes all the elements (if there are any) that occur in both A and B
$A \subseteq B$	A is a **subset** of B, i.e. every element in A also occurs in B
$A \subset B$	A is a **strict subset** of B, i.e. A is a **subset** of B and A contains fewer elements than B
$A \supseteq B$	A is a **superset** of B. True if and only if B is a **subset** of A
$A \supset B$	A is a **strict superset** of B. True if and only if B is a **strict subset** of A
$\mathrm{count}(S)$	The **support count** of **itemset** S. See Chapter 17
$\mathrm{support}(S)$	The **support** of **itemset** S. See Chapter 17
$cd \rightarrow e$	In **Association Rule Mining** used to denote the rule 'if we know that items c and d were bought, predict that item e was also bought'. See Chapter 17
L_k	The set containing all **supported itemsets** with **cardinality** k. See Chapter 17
C_k	A **candidate set** containing **itemsets** of **cardinality** k. See Chapter 17
$L \rightarrow R$	Denotes a rule with **antecedent** L and **consequent** R
$\mathrm{confidence}(L \rightarrow R)$	The **confidence** of the rule $L \rightarrow R$
${}_kC_i$	Represents the value $\frac{k!}{(k-i)!i!}$ (The number of ways of selecting i values from k, when the order in which they are selected is unimportant)

A posteriori probability Another name for **posterior probability**

A priori probability Another name for **prior probability**

Abduction A type of reasoning. See Section 4.3

Activation Function A function used during the **forward propagation** of values from one **layer** of a **Neural Net** to the next. It converts each value calculated during the **neural activation stage** of **forward propagation** to a new numerical value called its **transformed value**

Activation Value See **Weighted Sum Value**

Adequacy Condition (for **TDIDT** algorithm) The condition that no two **instances** with the same values of all the **attributes** may belong to different **classes**

Agglomerative Hierarchical Clustering A widely used method of **clustering**

Alternate Node In the context of the **CDH-Tree algorithm** refers to a potential replacement **node** associated with a **node** in the main **tree** under development

Antecedent of a Rule The 'if' part (left-hand side) of an *IF... THEN* rule

Apriori Algorithm An algorithm for **Association Rule Mining**. See Chapter 17

Architecture of a Neural Network A specification of the defining characteristics of a **Neural Net**, such as the number of **layers**, the number of **nodes** in each **layer** and the **activation function**

Artificial Neural Network See **Neural Net**

Association Rule A rule representing a relationship amongst the values of **variables**. A general form of rule, where a conjunction of *attribute = value* terms can occur on both the left- and the right-hand side

Association Rule Mining (ARM) The process of extracting **association rules** from a given **dataset**

Attribute An alternative name for **variable**, used in some areas of **data mining**

Attribute Selection In this book, generally used to mean the selection of an **attribute** for splitting on when generating a **decision tree**

Attribute Selection Strategy An algorithm for **attribute selection**

Automatic Rule Induction Another term for **Rule Induction**

Average-link Clustering For **hierarchical clustering**, a method of calculating the distance between two **clusters** using the average distance from any member of one cluster to any member of the other

Backed-up Error Rate Estimate (at a **node** in a **decision tree**) An estimate based on the estimated **error rates** of the nodes below it in the tree

Backpropagation The processing of error values through the **layers** in a **Neural Net**, one by one, starting with the **output layer**, until the **input layer** is reached

Backward Pruning Another name for **post-pruning**

Bag-of-Words Representation A word-based representation of a text document

Bagging A technique for constructing multiple **training sets** used in **ensemble classification**

Base Classifier An individual **classifier** in an **Ensemble of Classifiers**

Batch Learner A learning algorithm, such as **TDIDT**, which begins with all the data collected together in some suitable file store

Batch Mode A mode of processing data which uses a **batch learner**, such as **TDIDT**

Batch Training A form of training used in a **feed-forward neural network** with **backpropagation**, where the **weights** are adjusted after each **epoch**

Bias Node A **node** with a fixed value of one which is linked to all the **nodes** in one of the **layers** of a **Neural Net**

Bigram A combination of two consecutive characters in a text document

Binary Variable A type of **variable**. See Section 2.2

Bit (short for 'binary digit') The basic unit of information. It corresponds to a switch being open or closed or an electric current flowing or not flowing

Blackboard See **Blackboard Architecture**

Blackboard Architecture An architecture for solving a problem analogous to a group of experts all working together on the problem, communicating with each other by writing to or reading from a common storage area known as a **blackboard**

Body of a Rule Another name for rule **antecedent**

Bootstrap Aggregating See **Bagging**

Branch (of a **decision tree**) The path from the **root node** of a **tree** to any of its **leaf nodes**

Candidate Set A set containing **itemsets** of **cardinality** k that includes all the **supported itemsets** of that cardinality and possibly also some non-supported ones

Cardinality of a Set The number of members of the **set**

Categorical Attribute An **attribute** that can only take one of a number of distinct values, such as 'red', 'blue', 'green'

CDH-Tree Algorithm An algorithm for constructing a **Hoeffding Tree** for **time-dependent data** based on the **CVFDT algorithm**

CDM See **Cooperating Data Mining**

Centroid of a Cluster The 'centre' of a **cluster**

Chain Rule A technique that gives an indirect means of calculating **gradients** as part of the **stochastic gradient descent** method of **backpropagation** in a **Neural Net**

Chi Square Attribute Selection Criterion A measure used for **attribute selection** for the **TDIDT algorithm**. See Chapter 6

Chi Square Test A statistical test used as part of the **ChiMerge algorithm**

ChiMerge An algorithm for **global discretisation**. See Section 8.4

City Block Distance. Another name for **Manhattan distance**

Clash (in a **training set**) A situation where two or more of the **instances** in a training set have identical **attribute** values but different **classifications**

Clash Set A set of **instances** in a **training set** associated with a **clash**

Clash Threshold A middle approach between the 'delete branch' and the 'majority voting' strategies for dealing with **clashes** when generating a **decision tree**. See Chapter 9

Class One of a number of mutually **exclusive and exhaustive categories** to which **objects** are assigned by a **classification** process or algorithm

Classification

1. A process of dividing up **objects** so that each object is assigned to one of a number of **mutually exclusive and exhaustive categories** known as **classes**

2. For **labelled data** the classification is the value of a specially designated **categorical attribute**. The aim is frequently to predict the classification for one or more **unseen instances**

3. **Supervised learning** where the designated attribute has **categorical** values

Classification Rules A set of **rules** that can be used to predict the **classification** of an **unseen instance**

Classification Tree A way of representing a set of **classification rules**

Classifier Any algorithm that assigns a **classification** to **unseen instances**

Cluster A group of **objects** that are similar to one another and (relatively) dissimilar to those in other clusters

Clustering Grouping together **objects** (e.g. **instances** in a **dataset**) that are similar to each other and (relatively) dissimilar to the objects belonging to other **clusters**

Community Experiments Effect The undesirable effect caused when many people share a small repository of datasets and repeatedly use those datasets for experiments. See Chapter 15

Complete-link Clustering For **hierarchical clustering**, a method of calculating the distance between two **clusters** using the longest distance from any member of one cluster to any member of the other

Completeness A **rule interestingness measure**

Concept Drift Refers to the situation where the **underlying causal model** being modelled by a learning algorithm changes because of data that is **time-dependent**

Conditional FP-tree An abbreviation for Conditional Frequent Pattern Tree. A tree structure developed when executing the **FP-Growth** algorithm

Conditional Probability The probability of an event occurring given that we have additional information (as well as its observed frequency in a series of trials)

Confidence Interval A range of values within which it is estimated that a unknown value of interest lies. See Chapter 15

Confidence Level The probability with which we know (or wish to know) the interval in which the **predictive accuracy** of a **classifier** lies

Confidence of a Rule The **predictive accuracy** of a rule (a **rule interestingness measure**)

Confident Itemset An **itemset** on the right-hand side of an **association rule** for which the value of **confidence** is greater than or equal to a minimum threshold value

Conflict Resolution Strategy A strategy for deciding which **rule** or rules to give priority when two or more **rules fire** for a given **instance**

Confusion Matrix A tabular way of illustrating the performance of a classifier. The table shows the number of times each combination of predicted and actual **classifications** occurred for a given **dataset**

Connections Between Neurons Another term for links between **nodes** in a **Neural Net**

Consequent of a Rule The 'then' part (right-hand side) of an *IF... THEN* rule

Continuous Attribute An **attribute** that takes numerical values

Cooperating Data Mining A model for **distributed data mining.** See Chapter 13

Count of an Itemset Another name for **support count of an itemset**

Cross-entropy An alternative name for *j***-measure**

Cut Point An end point of one of a number of non-overlapping ranges into which the values of a **continuous attribute** are split

Cut Value Another name for **cut point**

CVFDT Algorithm An algorithm for classifying **streaming data** that is **time-dependent**

Data Compression Converting the data in a **dataset** to a more compact form such as a **decision tree**

Data Mining The central data processing stage of **Knowledge Discovery.** See Introduction

Dataset The complete set of data available for an application. Datasets are divided into **instances** or **records**. A dataset is often represented by a table, with each row representing an **instance** and each column containing the values of one of the **variables** (**attributes**) for each of the instances

Decision Rule Another term for **classification rule**

Decision Tree Another name for a **classification tree**

Decision Tree Induction Another term for **tree induction**

Deduction A type of reasoning. See Section 4.3

Deep Learning A term often used to describe the processing of data by a **Neural Net** with multiple **layers**

Dendrogram A graphical representation of **agglomerative hierarchical clustering**

Depth Cutoff A possible criterion for **pre-pruning** a **decision tree**

Descendant Subtree A **tree** structure which hangs below a specified **node** in a larger **tree** structure

Dictionary (for **text classification**) See **Local Dictionary** and **Global Dictionary**

Differential Calculus A branch of Mathematics concerned with the rate of change of one **variable** with respect to another

Dimension The number of **attributes** recorded for each **instance**

Dimension Reduction An alternative term for **feature reduction**

Discretisation The conversion of a continuous attribute to one with a discrete set of values, i.e. a **categorical attribute**

Discriminability A **rule interestingness measure**

Disjoint Sets Sets with no common members

Disjunct One of a set of rules in **disjunctive normal form**

Disjunctive Normal Form (DNF) A rule is in disjunctive normal form if it comprises a number of terms of the form *variable = value* (or *variable $\neq$ value*) joined by the logical 'and' operator. For example the rule *IF x = 1 AND y = 'yes' AND z = 'good' THEN class = 6* is in DNF

Distance-based Clustering Algorithm A method of **clustering** that makes use of a measure of the distance between two **instances**

Distance Measure A means of measuring the similarity between two **instances**. The smaller the value, the greater the similarity

Distributed Data Mining System A form of **data mining** that makes use of more than one processor. See Chapter 13

Dot Product (of two **unit vectors**) The sum of the products of the corresponding pairs of component values

Downward Closure Property of Itemsets The property that if an **itemset** is **supported**, all its (non-empty) subsets are also supported

Eager Learning For **classification** tasks, a form of learning where the **training data** is generalised into a representation (or model) such as a table of probabilities, a **decision tree** or a neural net without waiting for an **unseen instance** to be presented for classification. See **Lazy Learning**

Empty set A **set** with no elements, written as $\emptyset$ or $\{\}$

Ensemble Classification A technique for improving the accuracy of **classification** by using a set of **classifiers** to make **predictions** rather than just one. See Chapter 14

Ensemble Learning A technique where a set of models is learnt that collectively can be applied to solving a problem. See **Ensemble Classification**

Ensemble of Classifiers A set of **classifiers** used for **ensemble classification**

Entropy An information-theoretic measure of the 'uncertainty' of a **training set**, due to the presence of more than one **classification**. See Chapters 5 and 10

Entropy Method of Attribute Selection (when constructing a **decision tree**) Choosing to split on the **attribute** that gives the greatest value of **Information Gain**. See Chapter 5

Entropy Reduction Equivalent to **information gain**

Epoch The processing of all the instances in a **training set** through a **Neural Net** one-by-one

Equal Frequency Intervals Method A method of **discretising** a **continuous attribute**

Equal Width Intervals Method A method of **discretising** a **continuous attribute**

Error Node An additional **node** added to a **Neural Net** in this book to make it easier to visualise uses of the **chain rule** during **backpropagation**

Error Rate The 'reverse' of the **predictive accuracy** of a **classifier**. A predictive accuracy of 0.8 (i.e. 80%) implies an error rate of 0.2 (i.e. 20%)

Euclidean Distance Between Two Points A widely used measure of the distance between two points

Exact Rule One for which the value of **confidence** is 1

Exclusive Clustering Algorithm A **clustering** algorithm that places each **object** in precisely one of a set of **clusters**

Expandable Leaf Node A **leaf node** which has one or more **attributes** available for **splitting**

Expanding a Leaf Node Splitting a **leaf node** on an **attribute**, i.e. creating a one-level **descendant subtree** for the **node** with one **branch** for each value of the **attribute**

F1 Score A performance measure for a **classifier**

False Alarm Rate Another name for **false positive rate**

False Negative Classification The classification of an **unseen instance** as negative, when it is actually positive

False Negative Rate of a Classifier The proportion of positive instances that are classified as negative

False Positive Classification The classification of an **unseen instance** as positive, when it is actually negative

False Positive Rate of a Classifier The proportion of negative instances that are classified as positive

Feature Another name for **attribute**

Feature Reduction The reduction of the number of **features** (i.e. **attributes** or **variables**) for each **instance** in a **dataset**. The discarding of relatively unimportant **attributes**

Feature Space For **text classification**, the set of words included in the **dictionary**

Feed-forward Neural Network A widely used type of **Neural Net** which learns to perform a task by repeatedly processing a given set of examples

Forgetting a Record In the context of the **CDH-Tree algorithm** the process of restoring the array values at the **nodes** that were previously affected by **sorting a record** to the values that they would have had if the **record** had never been processed

Forward Propagation The processing of input values through the **layers** in a **Neural Net**, one by one, starting with the **input layer** until the **output layer** is reached

Forward Pruning Another name for **pre-pruning**

FP-Growth An abbreviation for Frequent Pattern Growth. An algorithm for **Association Rule Mining**. See Chapter 18

FP-tree An abbreviation for Frequent Pattern Tree. A tree structure developed when executing the **FP-Growth** algorithm

Frequency Table A table used for **attribute selection** for the **TDIDT algorithm**. It gives the number of occurrences of each **classification** for each value of an **attribute**. See Chapter 6. (The term is used in a more general sense in Chapter 11.)

Frequent Itemset Another name for **supported itemset**

Gain Ratio A measure used for **attribute selection** for the **TDIDT algorithm**. See Chapter 6

Generalised Rule Induction (GRI) Another name for **Association Rule Mining**

Generalising a Rule Making a rule apply to more **instances** by deleting one or more of its **terms**

Gini Index of Diversity A measure used for **attribute selection** for the **TDIDT Algorithm**. See Chapter 6

Global Dictionary In **text classification** a dictionary that contains all the words that occur at least once in any of the documents under consideration. See **Local Dictionary**

Global Discretisation A form of **discretisation** where each **continuous attribute** is converted to a **categorical attribute** once and for all before any **data mining** algorithm is applied

Grace Period For the **H-Tree algorithm** and the **CDH-Tree algorithm** refers to the number of incoming **records** that need to arrive at a **leaf node** before the **node** is considered as a candidate for **splitting on an attribute**

Gradient of a Curve A measurement used as part of the **stochastic gradient descent** method of **backpropagation** in a **Neural Net**

H-Tree Algorithm An algorithm for constructing a **Hoeffding Tree** for **stationary data** based on the **VFDT algorithm**

Head of a Rule Another name for rule **consequent**

Heterogeneous Ensemble An **ensemble** in which the **classifiers** are of different kinds

Hidden Layer One of the **layers** in a **Neural Net**

Hidden Layer Bias Weight The **weight** of the links from the **nodes** in a **hidden layer** of a **Neural Net** to the corresponding **bias node**

Hidden Node A node in a **hidden layer** of a **Neural Net**

Hierarchical Clustering In this book, another name for **Agglomerative Hierarchical Clustering**

Hit Rate Another name for **true positive rate**

Hits on a Leaf Node For the **H-Tree algorithm** and the **CDH-Tree algorithm** the number of times that an incoming **record** has been **sorted** to the **node**

Hoeffding Bound A value used in the construction of a **Hoeffding Tree**

Hoeffding Tree A type of **classification tree** where **splitting on an attribute** only takes place if the difference between the best choice of **attribute** and the second best exceeds a value called the **Hoeffding Bound**

Homogeneous Ensemble An **ensemble** in which all the **classifiers** are of the same kind (e.g. **decision trees**)

Horizontal Partitioning of Data A method of dividing up a **dataset** amongst a number of processors by giving a subset of the **instances** to each one

Hyperparameter For a **Neural Net**, one set by the user as opposed to being calculated from the data

Hypertext Categorisation The automatic classification of web documents into predefined categories

Hypertext Classification Another name for **hypertext categorisation**

Ignore Attribute An **attribute** that is of no significance for a given application

Incremental Classification Algorithm A type of **classification** algorithm used when the data is not all available at the start of the process. The **classifier** is created and then changed as further **instances** are collected (usually in batches)

Induction A type of reasoning. See Section 4.3

Inductive Bias A preference for one algorithm, formula etc. over another that is not determined by the data itself. Inductive bias is unavoidable in any inductive learning system

Information Gain When constructing a **decision tree** by **splitting on attributes**, information gain is the difference between the **entropy** of a node and the weighted average of the entropies of its immediate descendants. It can be shown that the value of information gain is always positive or zero

Input Layer One of the **layers** in a **Neural Net**

Input Node A **node** in the **input layer** of a **Neural Net**

Instance One of the stored examples in a **dataset**. Each **instance** comprises the values of a number of **variables**, which in **data mining** are often called **attributes**

Integer Variable A type of **variable**. See Section 2.2

Internal Node (of a **tree**) A **node** of a tree that is neither a **root node** nor a **leaf node**

Intersection (of two **sets**) The intersection of two sets A and B, written as $A \cap B$, is the set that includes all the elements (if there are any) that occur in both of the sets

Interval-scaled Variable A type of **variable**. See Section 2.2

Invalid Value An **attribute** value that is invalid for a given dataset. See **Noise**

Item For **Market Basket Analysis**, each item corresponds to one of the purchases made by a customer, e.g. bread or milk. We are not usually concerned with items that were not purchased

Itemset For **Market Basket Analysis**, a set of **items** purchased by a customer, effectively the same as a **transaction**. Itemsets are generally written in list notation, e.g. {fish, cheese, milk}

J-Measure A **rule interestingness measure** that quantifies the information content of a rule

j-Measure A value used in calculating the **J-measure** of a rule

Jack-knifing Another name for **N-fold cross-validation**

k-fold Cross-validation A strategy for estimating the performance of a **classifier**

k-Means Clustering A widely used method of **clustering**

k-Nearest Neighbour Classification A method of classifying an **unseen instance** using the **classification** of the **instance** or instances closest to it (see Chapter 3)

Knowledge Discovery The non-trivial extraction of implicit, previously unknown and potentially useful information from data. See Introduction

Labelled Data Data where each **instance** has a specially designated **attribute** which can be either **categorical** or **continuous**. The aim is generally to predict its value. See **Unlabelled Data**

Landscape-style Dataset A **dataset** for which there are far more **attributes** than **instances**

Large Itemset Another name for **Supported Itemset**

Layer (for Neural Net) A group of **nodes** in a **Neural Net**. Layers are arranged into an ordered sequence. Each **node** in a layer is connected to all those **nodes** in the adjacent layer(s) and no other **nodes**

Lazy Learning For **classification** tasks, a form of learning where the **training data** is left unchanged until an **unseen instance** is presented for classification. See **Eager Learning**

Leaf Node A **node** of a **tree** which has no other **nodes** descending from it

Learning Factor A user-specified value used as part of the **stochastic gradient descent** method of **backpropagation** in a **Neural Net**

Leave-one-out Cross-validation Another name for N**-fold cross-validation**

Length of a Vector The square root of the sum of the squares of its component values. See **Unit Vector**

Leverage A rule interestingness measure

Lift A rule interestingness measure

Local Dictionary In **text classification** a dictionary that contains only those words that occur in the documents under consideration that are classified as being in a specific category. See **Global Dictionary**

Local Discretisation A form of **discretisation** where each **continuous attribute** is converted to a **categorical attribute** at each stage of the **data mining** process

Logarithm Function See Appendix A

Logistic Function See **Sigmoid Function**

Majority Voting A method for combining the **predictions** of the individual **classifiers** in an **ensemble**

Manhattan Distance A measure of the distance between two points

Market Basket Analysis A special form of **Association Rule Mining**. See Chapter 17

Matches An **itemset** matches a **transaction** if all the items in the former are also in the latter

Maximum Dimension Distance A measure of the distance between two points

Mini-batch One of a number of equally-sized parts into which a **training set** is sometimes divided when training a **Feed-forward Neural Network**

Mini-batch Training A form of training used in a **feed-forward neural network** with **backpropagation**, where the **weights** are adjusted after each **mini-batch** has been processed

Missing Branches An effect that can occur during the generation of a **decision tree** that makes the tree unable to classify certain **unseen instances**. See Section 6.7

Missing Value An **attribute** value that is not recorded

Model-based Classification Algorithm One that gives an explicit representation of the **training data** (in the form of a **decision tree**, **set of rules** etc.) that can be used to classify **unseen instances** without reference to the training data itself

Mutually Exclusive and Exhaustive Categories A set of categories chosen so that each **object** of interest belongs to precisely one of the categories

Mutually Exclusive and Exhaustive Events A set of events, one and only one of which must always occur

n-dimensional Space A point in n-dimensional space is a graphical way of representing an **instance** with n **attribute** values

N-dimensional Vector In **text classification**, a way of representing a **labelled instance** with N **attributes** by its N attribute values (or other values derived from them), enclosed in parentheses and separated by commas, e.g. (2, yes, 7, 4, no). The **classification** is not generally included

N-fold Cross-validation A strategy for estimating the performance of a **classifier**

Naïve Bayes Algorithm A means of combining **prior and conditional probabilities** to calculate the probability of alternative **classifications**. See Chapter 3

Naïve Bayes Classification A method of classification that uses Mathematical probability theory to find the most likely classification for an **unseen instance**

Nearest Neighbour Classification See *k*-**Nearest Neighbour Classification**

Neural Activation Stage The first part of the **forward propagation** of values from one **layer** of a **Neural Net** to the next. See Section 23.2

Neural Net An interconnected set of **nodes**, inspired by the connections in the human brain, which learns to perform a task by repeatedly processing a given set of examples

Neural Network See **Neural Net**

Neuron An alternative name for a **node** in a **Neural Net**

Neuron Transfer Stage The second part of the **forward propagation** of values from one **layer** of a **Neural Net** to the next. See Section 23.2

Node (in a Neural Net) One of a collection of points not joined in a tree structure but grouped together into a number of interconnected **layers**

Node (of a **decision tree**) A **tree** consists of a collection of points, called **nodes**, joined by straight lines, called *links*. See Appendix A.2

Noise An **attribute** value that is valid for a given dataset, but is incorrectly recorded. See **Invalid Value**

Nominal Variable A type of **variable**. See Section 2.2

Non-expandable Leaf Node A **leaf node** with no **attributes** still available for **splitting**

Normalisation (of an **Attribute**) Adjustment of the values of an **attribute**, generally to make them fall in a specified range such as 0 to 1

Normalised Vector Space Model A **vector space model** where the components of a **vector** are adjusted so that the **length** of each vector is 1

Null Hypothesis A default assumption, e.g. that the performance of two **classifiers** *A* and *B* is effectively the same

Numerical Prediction Supervised learning where the designated **attribute** has a numerical value. Also called *regression*

Object One of a **universe of objects**. It is described by the values of a number of **variables** that correspond to its properties

Objective Function For **clustering**, a measure of the quality of a set of **clusters**

Online Training A form of training used in a **feed-forward neural network** with **backpropagation**, where the **weights** are adjusted after each **pass** through the network

Opportunity Sampling A method of **sampling**. See Chapter 15

Order of a Rule The number of terms in the **antecedent** of a rule in **disjunctive normal form**

Ordinal Variable A type of **variable**. See Section 2.2

Output Layer One of the **layers** in a **Neural Net**

Output Layer Bias Weight The **weight** of the links from the **nodes** in the **output layer** of a **Neural Net** to the corresponding **bias node**

Output Node A **node** in the **output layer** of a **Neural Net**

Overfitting A **classification** algorithm is said to overfit to the **training data** if it generates a **decision tree**, set of **classification rules** or any other representation of the data that depends too much on irrelevant features of the training instances, with the result that it performs well on the training data but relatively poorly on **unseen instances**. See Chapter 9

Paired t-test A statistical test used in comparing **classification** algorithms. See Chapter 15

Pass Through a Neural Net The processing of a single instance through the net, i.e. **forward propagation** followed by **backpropagation**

Perceptron An early form of **Neural Net** without any **Hidden Layers**

Piatetsky-Shapiro Criteria Criteria that it has been proposed should be met by any **rule interestingness measure**

Portrait-style Dataset A **dataset** for which there are far more **instances** than **attributes**

Positive Predictive Value Another name for **precision**

Post-pruning a Decision Tree Removing parts of a **decision tree** that has already been generated, with the aim of reducing **overfitting**

Posterior Probability The probability of an event occurring given additional information that we have

Pre-pruning a Decision Tree Generating a **decision tree** with fewer **branches** than would otherwise be the case, with the aim of reducing **overfitting**

Precision A performance measure for a **classifier**

Prediction Using the data in a **training set** to predict (as far as this book is concerned) the **classification** for one or more previously **unseen instances**

Predictive Accuracy For **classification** applications, the proportion of a set of **unseen instances** for which the correct **classification** is predicted. A **rule interestingness** measure, also known as **confidence**

Prior Probability The probability of an event occurring based solely on its observed frequency in a series of trials, without any additional information

Prism An algorithm for inducing **classification rules** directly, without using the intermediate representation of a **decision tree**

Probability of an Event The proportion of times we would expect an event to occur over a long series of trials

Pruned Tree A **tree** to which **pre-pruning** or **post-pruning** has been applied

Pruning Set Part of a **dataset** used during **post-pruning** of a **decision tree**

Pseudo-attribute A test on the value of a **continuous attribute**, e.g. $A < 35$. This is effectively the same as a **categorical attribute** that has only two values: true and false

Pseudocode An informal notation used for communicating algorithms

Random Decision Forests A method of ensemble classification

Random Forests A method of ensemble classification

Ratio-scaled Variable A type of **variable**. See Section 2.2

Recall Another name for **true positive rate**

Receiver Operating Characteristics Graph The full name for **ROC Graph**

Record Another term for **instance**

Recursive Partitioning Generating a **decision tree** by repeatedly **splitting on the values of attributes**

Reliability A **rule interestingness** measure. Another name for **confidence**

Respltting at a Node In the context of the **CDH-Tree algorithm** refers to changing the **attribute** on which an **internal node** was previously split by replacing the **node** by an **alternate node** split on a different **attribute**

RI Measure A rule interestingness measure

ROC Curve A **ROC Graph** on which related points are joined together to form a curve

ROC Graph A diagrammatic way of representing the **true positive rate** and **false positive rate** of one or more **classifiers**

Root Node The top-most **node** of a **tree**. The starting node for every **branch**

Rule The statement of a relationship between a condition, known as the **antecedent**, and a conclusion, known as the **consequent**. If the condition is satisfied, the conclusion follows

Rule Fires The **antecedent** of the rule is satisfied for a given **instance**

Rule Induction The automatic generation of rules from examples

Rule Interestingness Measure A measure of the importance of a rule

Ruleset A collection of rules

Sample Standard Deviation A statistical measure of the 'spread' of the numbers in a sample. The square root of the **sample variance**

Sample Variance A statistical measure of the 'spread' of the numbers in a sample. The square of the **sample standard deviation**

Sampling The selection of a subset of the members of a **dataset** (or other collection of objects, people etc.) that it is hoped will accurately represent the characteristics of the whole population

Sampling with Replacement A form of **sampling** where the whole population of objects is available for selection at each stage (implying that the sample may include an object two or more times)

Scale-up of a Distributed Data Mining System A measure of the performance of a distributed data mining system

Search Space In Chapter 16, the set of possible rules of interest

Search Strategy A method of examining the contents of a **search space** (usually in an efficient order)

Sensitivity Another name for **true positive rate**

Set An unordered collection of items, known as *elements*. See Appendix A. The elements of a set are often written between 'brace' characters and separated by commas, e.g. {apples, oranges, bananas}

Sigmoid Function A type of **activation function** frequently used with **feed-forward neural networks**

Significance Test A test applied to estimate the probability that an apparent relationship between two variables is (or is not) a chance occurrence

Simple Majority Voting See **Majority Voting**

Single-link Clustering For **hierarchical clustering**, a method of calculating the distance between two **clusters** using the shortest distance from any member of one cluster to any member of the other

Size Cutoff A possible criterion for **pre-pruning** a **decision tree**

Size-up of a Distributed Data Mining System A measure of the performance of a distributed data mining system

Sliding Window Method In the context of the **CDH-Tree algorithm**, a method for ensuring that an evolving **classification tree** is based only on the most recent W **records** processed, where W is called the **window size**

Slope of a Curve See **Gradient of a Curve**

Sorting a Record In the context of the **CDH-Tree algorithm** refers to the (notional) moving of an input **record** from the **root** of the **classification tree** to the **leaf node** that corresponds to the values of its **attributes**

Specialising a Rule Making a rule apply to fewer **instances** by adding one or more additional **terms**

Specificity Another name for **true negative rate**

Speed-up Factor of a Distributed Data Mining System A measure of the performance of a distributed data mining system

Speed-up of a Distributed Data Mining System A measure of the performance of a distributed data mining system

Split Information A value used in the calculation of **Gain Ratio**. See Chapter 6

Split Value A value used in connection with **continuous attributes** when **splitting on an attribute** to construct a **decision tree**. The test is normally whether the value is 'less than or equal to' or 'greater than' the split value

Splitting on an Attribute (while constructing a **decision tree**) Testing the value of an **attribute** and then creating a branch for each of its possible values

Standard Deviation of a Sample See **Sample Standard Deviation**

Standard Error (associated with a value) A statistical estimate of the reliability of the value. See Section 7.2.1

Static Error Rate Estimate (at a **node** in a **decision tree**) An estimate based on the **instances** corresponding to the node, as opposed to a **backed-up estimate**

Stationary Data Data arising from an underlying process that is fixed

Stemming Converting a word to its linguistic root (e.g. 'computing', 'computer' and 'computation' to 'comput')

Step Function A type of **activation function** that converts any value to either zero or one

Stochastic Gradient Descent A commonly used method of **backpropagation** in a **Neural Net**

Stochastic Training See **Online Training**

Stop Words Common words that are unlikely to be useful for **text classification**

Stratified Sampling A method of **sampling**. See Chapter 15

Streaming Data Data transferred in real-time as effectively an infinite continuous stream, for an application such as CCTV

Strict Subset A **set** A is a strict subset of a set B, written as $A \subset B$, if A is a subset of B and A contains fewer elements than B

Strict Superset A **set** A is a strict superset of a set B, written as $A \supset B$, if and only if B is a **strict subset** of A

Subset A **set** A is a subset of a set B, written as $A \subseteq B$, if every element in A also occurs in B

Subtree The part of a **tree** that descends from (or 'hangs from') one of its **nodes** A (including node A itself). A subtree is a tree in its own right, with its own **root node** (A) etc. See Appendix A.2

Sum Squared Error An error value calculated at the end of the **forward propagation** stage of processing a training instance through a **Neural Net**

Superset A **set** A is a superset of a set B, written as $A \supseteq B$, if and only if B is a **subset** of A

Supervised Learning A form of **Data Mining** using **labelled data**

Support Count of an Itemset For **Market Basket Analysis**, the number of **transactions** in the database matched by the **itemset**

Support of a Rule The proportion of the database to which the rule successfully applies (a **rule interestingness measure**)

Support of an Itemset The proportion of **transactions** in the database that are matched by the **itemset**

Supported Itemset An **itemset** for which the **support** value is greater than or equal to a minimum threshold value

Suspect Node In the context of the **CDH-Tree algorithm**, a **node** at which it is considered possible that a splitting decision that has previously been made will later need to be changed, resulting in an **alternate node** (plus **descendant subtree**) being attached to the main **tree** under development

Symmetry condition (for a **distance measure**) The distance from point A to point B is the same as the distance from point B to point A

TDIDT An abbreviation for *Top-Down Induction of Decision Trees*. See Chapter 4

Term In this book, a component of a rule. A term takes the form *variable = value*. See **Disjunctive Normal Form**

Term Frequency In **text classification**, the number of occurrences of a term in a given document

Test of Significance See **Significance Test**

Test Set A collection of **unseen instances**

Text Classification A particular type of **classification**, where the **objects** are text documents such as articles in newspapers, scientific papers etc. See also **Hypertext Categorisation**

TFIDF (**Term Frequency Inverse Document Frequency**) In **text classification**, a measure combining the frequency of a term with its rarity in a set of documents

Time-dependent Data Data arising from an underlying process that varies over time (e.g. seasonally)

Top Down Induction of Decision Trees A widely-used algorithm for **classification**. See Chapter 4

Total Error Value The total of the **sum squared errors** for an entire **epoch** or **mini-batch** when training a **feed-forward neural network**

Track Record Voting A method for combining the **predictions** of the individual **classifiers** in an **ensemble**

Train and Test A strategy for estimating the performance of a **classifier**

Trained Neural Net A **Neural Net** for which repeated training of the **weights** has terminated on the basis of some criterion set by the user

Training Data Another name for **training set**

Training Set A **dataset** or part of a dataset that is used for purposes of **classification**

Training Weights Adjusting the **Weights** of the links in a **Neural Net** by repeated processing of a **training set**

Transaction Another name for **record** or **instance**, generally used when the application is **Market Basket Analysis**. A transaction generally represents a set of **items** bought by a customer

Transfer Function See **Activation Function**

Transformed Value of a Node The output from the **neuron transfer stage** of the **forward propagation** of values from one **layer** of a **Neural Net** to the next

Tree A structure used to represent data items and the processes applied to them. See Appendix A.2

Tree Induction Generating **decision rules** in the implicit form of a **decision tree**

Triangle Inequality (for a **distance measure**) A condition corresponding to the idea that 'the shortest distance between any two points is a straight line'

Trigram A combination of three consecutive characters in a text document

True Negative Classification The correct classification of an **unseen instance** as negative

True Negative Rate of a Classifier The proportion of negative instances that are classified as negative

True Positive Classification The correct classification of an **unseen instance** as positive

True Positive Rate of a Classifier The proportion of positive instances that are classified as positive

Tuning Parameter See **Hyperparameter**

Two-dimensional Space See n-**dimensional Space**

Two-tailed Significance Test A **significance test** in which a given **null hypothesis** will be rejected when a calculated value is either sufficiently small or sufficiently large. See Chapter 15

Type 1 Error Another name for **false positive classification**

Type 2 Error Another name for **false negative classification**

UCI Repository The library of datasets maintained by the University of California at Irvine. See Section 2.6

Unconfident Itemset An **itemset** which is not **confident**

Underlying Causal Model The underlying process that determines the classification in a given domain of interest

Union of Two Sets The set of items that occur in either or both of the sets

Unit Vector A **vector** of length 1

Universe of Objects See Section 2.1

Unlabelled Data Data where each instance has no specially designated **attribute**. See **Labelled Data**

Unseen Instance An instance that does not occur in a **training set**. We frequently want to predict the **classification** of one or more unseen instances. See also **Test Set**

Unseen Test Set Another term for **test set**

Unsupervised Learning A form of **Data Mining** using **unlabelled data**

Validation Dataset A dataset used by some **classification** algorithms to assist in the development of a **classifier**, as opposed to a **test set**, which is used to estimate a **classifier's** accuracy once it is constructed

Variable One of the properties of an **object** in a **universe of objects**

Variance of a Sample See **Sample Variance**

Vector In **text classification**, another name for N-**dimensional vector**

Vector Space Model (VSM) The complete set of **vectors** corresponding to a set of documents under consideration. See N-**dimensional vector**

Vertical Partitioning of Data A method of dividing up a **dataset** amongst a number of processors by giving a subset of the **attributes** (for all the **instances**) to each one

VFDT Algorithm An algorithm for classifying streaming data that is not time-dependent

Weight of a Link A numerical value associated with each link between nodes in a **Neural Net**, which is used for **forward propagation** and **backpropagation** of values through the net

Weighted Majority Voting A method for combining the **predictions** of the individual **classifiers** in an **ensemble**

Weighted Sum Value The value calculated for a **node** in a **Neural Net** during the **neural activation stage** of **forward propagation**

Window Size The maximum number of **records** that can be stored at any one time when using the **CDH-Tree** algorithm

Self-assessment Exercise 2

Question 1

Labelled data has a specially designated attribute. The aim is to use the data given to predict the value of that attribute for instances that have not yet been seen. Data that does not have any specially designated attribute is called unlabelled.

Question 2

Name: Nominal
Date of Birth: Ordinal
Sex: Binary
Weight: Ratio-scaled
Height: Ratio-scaled
Marital Status: Nominal (assuming that there are more than two values, e.g. single, married, widowed, divorced)
Number of Children: Integer

Question 3

- Discard all instances where there is at least one missing value and use the remainder.

- Estimate missing values of each categorical attribute by its most frequently occurring value in the training set and estimate missing values of each continuous attribute by the average of its values for the training set.

© Springer-Verlag London Ltd., part of Springer Nature 2020   535
M. Bramer, *Principles of Data Mining*, Undergraduate Topics
in Computer Science, DOI 10.1007/978-1-4471-7493-6

Self-assessment Exercise 3

Question 1

Using the values in Figure 3.2, the probability of each class for the unseen instance

weekday	summer	high	heavy	????

is as follows.

class = on time
$0.70 \times 0.64 \times 0.43 \times 0.29 \times 0.07 = 0.0039$

class = late
$0.10 \times 0.5 \times 0 \times 0.5 \times 0.5 = 0$

class = very late
$0.15 \times 1 \times 0 \times 0.33 \times 0.67 = 0$

class = cancelled
$0.05 \times 0 \times 0 \times 1 \times 1 = 0$

The largest value is for class = on time
The probability of each class for the unseen instance

sunday	summer	normal	slight	????

is as follows.

class = on time
$0.70 \times 0.07 \times 0.43 \times 0.36 \times 0.57 = 0.0043$

class = late
$0.10 \times 0 \times 0 \times 0.5 \times 0 = 0$

class = very late
$0.15 \times 0 \times 0 \times 0.67 \times 0 = 0$

class = cancelled
$0.05 \times 0 \times 0 \times 0 \times 0 = 0$

The largest value is for class = on time

Question 2

The distance of the first instance in Figure 3.5 from the unseen instance is the square root of $(0.8 - 9.1)^2 + (6.3 - 11.0)^2$, i.e. 9.538.

The distances for the 20 instances are given in the table below.

Attribute 1	Attribute 2	Distance	
0.8	6.3	9.538	
1.4	8.1	8.228	

2.1	7.4	7.871	
2.6	14.3	7.290	
6.8	12.6	2.802	*
8.8	9.8	1.237	*
9.2	11.6	0.608	*
10.8	9.6	2.202	*
11.8	9.9	2.915	*
12.4	6.5	5.580	
12.8	1.1	10.569	
14.0	19.9	10.160	
14.2	18.5	9.070	
15.6	17.4	9.122	
15.8	12.2	6.807	
16.6	6.7	8.645	
17.4	4.5	10.542	
18.2	6.9	9.981	
19.0	3.4	12.481	
19.6	11.1	10.500	

The five nearest neighbours are marked with asterisks in the rightmost column.

Self-assessment Exercise 4

Question 1

No two instances with the same values of all the attributes may belong to different classes.

Question 2

The most likely cause is probably noise or missing values in the training set.

Question 3

Provided the adequacy condition is satisfied the TDIDT algorithm is guaranteed to terminate and give a decision tree corresponding to the training set.

Question 4

A situation will be reached where a branch has been generated to the maximum length possible, i.e. with a term for each of the attributes, but the corresponding subset of the training set still has more than one classification.

| Self-assessment Exercise 5 |

Question 1

(a) The proportions of instances with each of the two classifications are 6/26 and 20/26. So $E_{start} = -(6/26) \log_2(6/26) - (20/26) \log_2(20/26) = 0.7793$.

(b) The following shows the calculations.

Splitting on SoftEng
SoftEng = A
Proportions of each class: FIRST 6/14, SECOND 8/14
Entropy $= -(6/14) \log_2(6/14) - (8/14) \log_2(8/14) = 0.9852$
SoftEng = B
Proportions of each class: FIRST 0/12, SECOND 12/12
Entropy $= 0$ [all the instances have the same classification]
Weighted average entropy $E_{new} = (14/26) \times 0.9852 + (12/26) \times 0 = 0.5305$
Information Gain $= 0.7793 - 0.5305 = 0.2488$

Splitting on ARIN
ARIN = A
Proportions of each class: FIRST 4/12, SECOND 8/12
Entropy $= 0.9183$
ARIN = B
Proportions of each class: FIRST 2/14, SECOND 12/14
Entropy $= 0.5917$
Weighted average entropy $E_{new} = (12/26) \times 0.9183 + 14/26 \times 0.5917 = 0.7424$
Information Gain $= 0.7793 - 0.7424 = 0.0369$

Splitting on HCI
HCI = A
Proportions of each class: FIRST 1/9, SECOND 8/9
Entropy $= 0.5033$
HCI = B
Proportions of each class: FIRST 5/17, SECOND 12/17
Entropy $= 0.8740$
Weighted average entropy $E_{new} = (9/26) \times 0.5033 + (17/26) \times 0.8740 = 0.7457$
Information Gain $= 0.7793 - 0.7457 = 0.0337$

Splitting on CSA
CSA = A
Proportions of each class: FIRST 3/7, SECOND 4/7
Entropy $= 0.9852$
CSA = B

Proportions of each class: FIRST 3/19, SECOND 16/19
Entropy $= 0.6292$
Weighted average entropy $E_{new} = (7/26) \times 0.9852 + (19/26) \times 0.6292 = 0.7251$
Information Gain $= 0.7793 - 0.7251 = 0.0543$

Splitting on Project

Project $=$ A
Proportions of each class: FIRST 5/9, SECOND 4/9
Entropy $= 0.9911$
Project $=$ B
Proportions of each class: FIRST 1/17, SECOND 16/17
Entropy $= 0.3228$
Weighted average entropy $E_{new} = (9/26) \times 0.9911 + (17/26) \times 0.3228 = 0.5541$
Information Gain $= 0.7793 - 0.5541 = 0.2253$
The maximum value of information gain is for attribute SoftEng.

Question 2

The TDIDT algorithm inevitably leads to a decision tree where all nodes have entropy zero. Reducing the average entropy as much as possible at each step would seem like an efficient way of achieving this in a relatively small number of steps. The use of entropy minimisation (or information gain maximisation) appears generally to lead to a small decision tree compared with other attribute selection criteria. The *Occam's Razor* principle suggests that small trees are most likely to be the best, i.e. to have the greatest predictive power.

Self-assessment Exercise 6

Question 1

The frequency table for splitting on attribute SoftEng is as follows.

| | Attribute value | |
Class	A	B
FIRST	6	0
SECOND	8	12
Total	14	12

Using the method of calculating entropy given in Chapter 6, the value is:
$-(6/26) \log_2(6/26) - (8/26) \log_2(8/26) - (12/26) \log_2(12/26)$
$+ (14/26) \log_2(14/26) + (12/26) \log_2(12/26)$
$= 0.5305$

This is the same value as was obtained using the original method for Self-assessment Exercise 1 for Chapter 5. Similar results apply for the other attributes.

Question 2

It was shown previously that the entropy of the chess dataset is: 0.7793.
The value of Gini Index is $1 - (6/26)^2 - (20/26)^2 = 0.3550$.

Splitting on attribute SoftEng

	Attribute value	
Class	A	B
FIRST	6	0
SECOND	8	12
Total	14	12

The entropy is:
$-(6/26)\log_2(6/26) - (8/26)\log_2(8/26) - (12/26)\log_2(12/26)$
$+ (14/26)\log_2(14/26) + (12/26)\log_2(12/26)$
$= 0.5305$
The value of split information is $-(14/26)\log_2(14/26) - (12/26)\log_2(12/26)$
$= 0.9957$
The information gain is $0.7793 - 0.5305 = 0.2488$
Gain ratio is $0.2488/0.9957 = 0.2499$

Gini Index Calculation
Contribution for 'SoftEng = A' is $(6^2 + 8^2)/14 = 7.1429$
Contribution for 'SoftEng = B' is $(0^2 + 12^2)/12 = 12$
New value of Gini Index $= 1 - (7.1429 + 12)/26 = 0.2637$

Splitting on attribute ARIN

	Attribute value	
Class	A	B
FIRST	4	2
SECOND	8	12
Total	12	14

The value of entropy is 0.7424
The value of split information is 0.9957
So the information gain is $0.7793 - 0.7424 = 0.0369$
and the gain ratio is $0.0369/0.9957 = 0.0371$
New value of Gini Index $= 0.3370$

Splitting on attribute HCI

	Attribute value	
Class	A	B
FIRST	1	5
SECOND	8	12
Total	9	17

The value of entropy is 0.7457
The value is split information is 0.9306
So the information gain is $0.7793 - 0.7457 = 0.0337$
and the gain ratio is $0.0336/0.9306 = 0.0362$
New value of Gini Index $= 0.3399$

Splitting on attribute CSA

	Attribute value	
Class	A	B
FIRST	3	3
SECOND	4	16
Total	7	19

The value of entropy is 0.7251
The value is split information is 0.8404
So the information gain is $0.7793 - 0.7251 = 0.0543$
and the gain ratio is $0.0542/0.8404 = 0.0646$
New value of Gini Index $= 0.3262$

Splitting on attribute Project

	Attribute value	
Class	A	B
FIRST	5	1
SECOND	4	16
Total	9	17

The value of entropy is 0.5541
The value of split information is 0.9306
So the information gain is $0.7793 - 0.5541 = 0.2253$
and the gain ratio is $0.2252/0.9306 = 0.2421$
New value of Gini Index $= 0.2433$
The largest value of Gain Ratio is when the attribute is SoftEng.

The largest value of Gini Index reduction is for attribute Project. The reduction is $0.3550 - 0.2433 = 0.1117$.

Question 3

Any dataset for which there is an attribute with a large number of values is a possible answer, e.g. one that contains a 'nationality' attribute or a 'job title' attribute. Using Gain Ratio will probably ensure that such attributes are not chosen.

Self-assessment Exercise 7

Question 1

vote Dataset, Figure 7.14

The number of correct predictions is 127 and the total number of instances is 135.

We have $p = 127/135 = 0.9407$, $N = 135$, so the standard error is $\sqrt{p \times (1-p)/N} = \sqrt{0.9407 \times 0.0593/135} = 0.0203$.

The value of the predictive accuracy can be expected to lie in the following ranges:

probability 0.90: from $0.9407 - 1.64 \times 0.0203$ to $0.9407 + 1.64 \times 0.0203$, i.e. from 0.9074 to 0.9741

probability 0.95: from $0.9407 - 1.96 \times 0.0203$ to $0.9407 + 1.96 \times 0.0203$, i.e. from 0.9009 to 0.9806

probability 0.99: from $0.9407 - 2.58 \times 0.0203$ to $0.9407 + 2.58 \times 0.0203$, i.e. from 0.8883 to 0.9932

glass Dataset, Figure 7.15

The number of correct predictions is 149 and the total number of instances is 214.

We have $p = 149/214 = 0.6963$, $N = 214$, so the standard error is $\sqrt{p \times (1-p)/N} = \sqrt{0.6963 \times 0.3037/214} = 0.0314$.

The value of the predictive accuracy can be expected to lie in the following ranges:

probability 0.90: from $0.6963 - 1.64 \times 0.0314$ to $0.6963 + 1.64 \times 0.0314$, i.e. from 0.6447 to 0.7478

probability 0.95: from $0.6963 - 1.96 \times 0.0314$ to $0.6963 + 1.96 \times 0.0314$, i.e. from 0.6346 to 0.7579

probability 0.99: from $0.6963 - 2.58 \times 0.0314$ to $0.6963 + 2.58 \times 0.0314$, i.e. from 0.6152 to 0.7774

Question 2

False positive classifications would be undesirable in applications such as the prediction of equipment that will fail in the near future, which may lead to expensive and unnecessary preventative maintenance. False classifications of individuals as likely criminals or terrorists can have very serious repercussions for the wrongly accused.

False negative classifications would be undesirable in applications such as medical screening, e.g. for patients who may have a major illness requiring treatment, or prediction of catastrophic events such as hurricanes or earthquakes.

Decisions about the proportion of false negative (positive) classifications that would be acceptable to reduce the proportion of false positives (negatives) to zero is a matter of personal taste. There is no general answer.

Self-assessment Exercise 8

Question 1

Sorting the values of *humidity* into ascending numerical order gives the following table.

Humidity (%)	Class
65	play
70	play
70	play
70	don't play
75	play
78	play
80	don't play
80	play
80	play
85	don't play
90	don't play
90	play
95	don't play
96	play

The amended rule for selecting cut points given in Section 8.3.2 is: 'only include attribute values for which the class value is different from that for the previous attribute value, together with any attribute which occurs more than once and the attribute immediately following it'.

This rule gives the cut points for the *humidity* attribute as all the values in the above table except 65 and 78.

Question 2

Figure 8.12(c) is reproduced below.

Value of A	Frequency for class			Total	Value of χ^2
	$c1$	$c2$	$c3$		
1.3	1	0	4	5	3.74
1.4	1	2	1	4	5.14
2.4	6	0	2	8	3.62
6.5	3	2	4	9	4.62
8.7	6	0	1	7	1.89
12.1	7	2	3	12	1.73
29.4	0	0	1	1	3.20
56.2	2	4	0	6	6.67
87.1	0	1	3	4	1.20
89.0	1	1	2	4	
Total	27	12	21	60	

After the 87.1 and 89.0 rows are merged, the figure looks like this.

Value of A	Frequency for class			Total	Value of χ^2
	$c1$	$c2$	$c3$		
1.3	1	0	4	5	3.74
1.4	1	2	1	4	5.14
2.4	6	0	2	8	3.62
6.5	3	2	4	9	4.62
8.7	6	0	1	7	1.89
12.1	7	2	3	12	1.73
29.4	0	0	1	1	3.20
56.2	2	4	0	6	**6.67**
87.1	1	2	5	8	
Total	27	12	21	60	

The previous values of χ^2 are shown in the rightmost column. Only the one given in bold can have been changed by the merging process, so this value needs to be recalculated.

For the adjacent intervals labelled 56.2 and 87.1 the values of O and E are as follows.

Value of A	Frequency for class						Total
	c1		c2		c3		observed
	O	E	O	E	O	E	
56.2	2	1.29	4	2.57	0	2.14	6
87.1	1	1.71	2	3.43	5	2.86	8
Total	3		6		5		14

The O (observed) values are taken from the previous figure. The E (expected) values are calculated from the row and column sums. Thus for row 56.2 and class c1, the expected value E is $3 \times 6/14 = 1.29$.

The next step is to calculate the value of $(O - E)^2/E$ for each of the six combinations. These are shown in the Val columns in the figure below.

Value of A	Frequency for class									Total observed
	c1			c2			c3			
	O	E	Val	O	E	Val	O	E	Val	
56.2	2	1.29	0.40	4	2.57	0.79	0	2.14	2.14	6
87.1	1	1.71	0.30	2	3.43	0.60	5	2.86	1.61	8
Total	3			6			5			14

The value of χ^2 is then the sum of the six values of $(O - E)^2/E$. For the pair of rows shown the value of χ^2 is 5.83.

This gives a revised version of the frequency table as follows.

Value of A	Frequency for class			Total	Value of χ^2
	c1	c2	c3		
1.3	1	0	4	5	3.74
1.4	1	2	1	4	5.14
2.4	6	0	2	8	3.62
6.5	3	2	4	9	4.62
8.7	6	0	1	7	1.89
12.1	7	2	3	12	1.73
29.4	0	0	1	1	3.20
56.2	2	4	0	6	5.83
87.1	1	2	5	8	
Total	27	12	21	60	

The smallest value of χ^2 is now 1.73, in the row labelled 12.1. This value is less than the threshold value of 4.61, so the rows (intervals) labelled 12.1 and 29.4 are merged.

Self-assessment Exercise 9

The decision tree shown in Figure 9.8 is reproduced below for ease of reference.

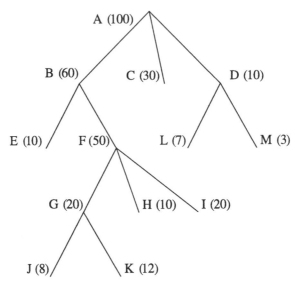

The table of error rates specified in the question is as follows.

Node	Estimated error rate
A	0.2
B	0.35
C	0.1
D	0.2
E	0.01
F	0.25
G	0.05
H	0.1
I	0.2
J	0.15
K	0.2
L	0.1
M	0.1

The post-pruning process starts by considering the possibility of pruning at
node G.

The backed-up error rate at that node is $(8/20) \times 0.15 + (12/20) \times 0.2 = 0.18$. This is more than the static error rate, which is only 0.05. This means that splitting at node G increases the error rate at that node so we prune the subtree descending from G, giving the following figure [which is the same as Figure 9.11].

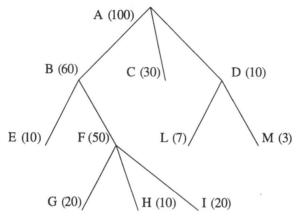

We now consider pruning at node F. The backed-up error rate is $(20/50) \times 0.05 + (10/50) \times 0.1 + (20/50) \times 0.2 = 0.12$. This is less than the static error rate. Splitting at node F reduces the average error rate so we do not prune.

The method given in Chapter 9 specifies that we only consider pruning at nodes that have a descendant subtree of depth one (i.e. all the nodes one level down are leaf nodes).

The only remaining candidate is node D. For this node the backed-up error rate is $(7/10) \times 0.1 + (3/10) \times 0.1 = 0.1$. This is less than the static error rate at the node, so we do not prune.

There are no further candidates for pruning, so the process terminates.

Self-assessment Exercise 10

Question 1

The entropy of a training set depends only on the relative proportions of the classifications, not on the number of instances it contains. Thus for both training sets the answer is the same.

$$\text{Entropy} = -0.2 \times \log_2 0.2 - 0.3 \times \log_2 0.3 - 0.25 \times \log_2 0.25 - 0.25 \times \log_2 0.25$$
$$= 1.985$$

Question 2

It is best to ask any question that divides the people into two approximately equal halves. An obvious question would be 'Is the person male?'. This might well be appropriate in a restaurant, a theatre etc. but would not be suitable for a group where there is a large predominance of one sex, e.g. a football match. In such a case a question such as 'Does he or she have brown eyes?' might be better, or even 'Does he or she live in a house or flat with an odd number?'

Self-assessment Exercise 11

The *degrees* dataset given in Figure 4.3 is reproduced below for ease of reference.

SoftEng	ARIN	HCI	CSA	Project	Class
A	B	A	B	B	SECOND
A	B	B	B	A	FIRST
A	A	A	B	B	SECOND
B	A	A	B	B	SECOND
A	A	B	B	A	FIRST
B	A	A	B	B	SECOND
A	B	B	B	B	SECOND
A	B	B	B	B	SECOND
A	A	A	A	A	FIRST
B	A	A	B	B	SECOND
B	A	A	B	B	SECOND
A	B	B	A	B	SECOND
B	B	B	B	A	SECOND
A	A	B	A	B	FIRST
B	B	B	B	A	SECOND
A	A	B	B	B	SECOND
B	B	B	B	B	SECOND
A	A	B	A	A	FIRST
B	B	B	A	A	SECOND
B	B	A	A	B	SECOND
B	B	B	B	A	SECOND
B	A	B	A	B	SECOND
A	B	B	B	A	FIRST
A	B	A	B	B	SECOND
B	A	B	B	B	SECOND
A	B	B	B	B	SECOND

The Prism algorithm starts by constructing a table showing the probability of class = FIRST occurring for each attribute/value pair over the whole training set of 26 instances.

Attribute/value pair	Frequency for class = FIRST	Total frequency (out of 26 instances)	Probability
SoftEng = A	6	14	0.429
SoftEng = B	0	12	0
ARIN = A	4	12	0.333
ARIN = B	2	14	0.143
HCI = A	1	9	0.111
HCI = B	5	17	0.294
CSA = A	3	7	0.429
CSA = B	3	19	0.158
Project = A	5	9	0.556
Project = B	1	17	0.059

The maximum probability is when Project = A
Incomplete rule induced so far:

IF Project = A THEN class = FIRST

The subset of the training set covered by this incomplete rule is:

SoftEng	ARIN	HCI	CSA	Project	Class
A	B	B	B	A	FIRST
A	A	B	B	A	FIRST
A	A	A	A	A	FIRST
B	B	B	B	A	SECOND
B	B	B	B	A	SECOND
A	A	B	A	A	FIRST
B	B	B	A	A	SECOND
B	B	B	B	A	SECOND
A	B	B	B	A	FIRST

The next table shows the probability of class = FIRST occurring for each attribute/value pair (not involving attribute Project) for this subset.

Attribute/value pair	Frequency for class = FIRST	Total frequency (out of 9 instances)	Probability
SoftEng = A	5	5	1.0
SoftEng = B	0	4	0
ARIN = A	3	3	1.0

ARIN = B	2	6	0.333
HCI = A	1	1	1.0
HCI = B	4	8	0.5
CSA = A	2	3	0.667
CSA = B	3	6	0.5

Three attribute/value combinations give a probability of 1.0. Of these Soft-Eng = A is based on most instances, so will probably be selected by tie-breaking.

Incomplete rule induced so far:

IF Project = A AND SoftEng = A THEN class = FIRST

The subset of the training set covered by this incomplete rule is:

SoftEng	ARIN	HCI	CSA	Project	Class
A	B	B	B	A	FIRST
A	A	B	B	A	FIRST
A	A	A	A	A	FIRST
A	A	B	A	A	FIRST
A	B	B	B	A	FIRST

This subset contains instances with only one classification, so the rule is complete.

The final induced rule is therefore:

IF Project = A AND SoftEng = A THEN class = FIRST

Self-assessment Exercise 12

The true positive rate is the number of instances that are correctly predicted as positive divided by the number of instances that are actually positive.

The false positive rate is the number of instances that are wrongly predicted as positive divided by the number of instances that are actually negative.

		Predicted class	
		+	−
Actual class	+	50	10
	−	10	30

For the table above the values are:

True positive rate: 50/60 = 0.833

False positive rate: 10/40 = 0.25

The Euclidean distance is defined as: $Euc = \sqrt{fprate^2 + (1 - tprate)^2}$

For this table $Euc = \sqrt{(0.25)^2 + (1 - 0.833)^2} = 0.300$.

For the other three tables specified in the Exercise the values are as follows.

Second table

> True positive rate: $55/60 = 0.917$
> False positive rate: $5/40 = 0.125$
> $Euc = 0.150$

Third table

> True positive rate: $40/60 = 0.667$
> False positive rate: $1/40 = 0.025$
> $Euc = 0.334$

Fourth table

> True positive rate: $60/60 = 1.0$
> False positive rate: $20/40 = 0.5$
> $Euc = 0.500$

The following ROC graph shows the four classifiers as well as the four hypothetical ones at $(0,0)$, $(1,0)$, $(0,1)$ and $(1,1)$.

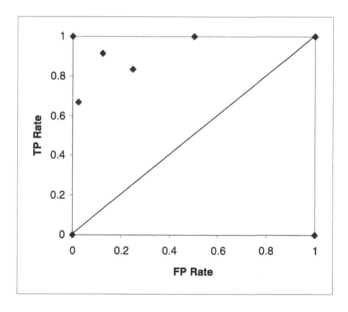

If we were equally concerned about avoiding false positive and false negative classifications we should choose the one given in the second table in the Exercise, which has true positive rate 0.917 and false positive rate 0.125. This is the one closest to $(0,1)$ the perfect classifier in the ROC graph.

Self-assessment Exercise 13

Question 1

The frequency tables for the four attributes are given below, followed by the class frequency table. The attribute values needed for part (2) are shown in bold.

Attribute	class			
day	on time	late	very late	cancelled
weekday	**12**	**2**	**5**	**1**
saturday	3	1	0	1
sunday	2	0	0	0
holiday	3	0	0	0

Attribute	class			
season	on time	late	very late	cancelled
spring	4	0	0	1
summer	**10**	**1**	**1**	**1**
autumn	2	0	1	0
winter	4	2	3	0

Attribute	class			
wind	on time	late	very late	cancelled
none	8	0	0	1
high	**5**	**2**	**2**	**1**
normal	7	1	3	0

Attribute	class			
rain	on time	late	very late	cancelled
none	9	1	1	1
slight	10	0	1	0
heavy	**1**	**2**	**3**	**1**

	class			
	on time	late	very late	cancelled
TOTAL	20	3	5	2

Question 2

For convenience we can put the rows shown in bold in the four attribute frequency tables together in a single table, augmented by the corresponding class frequencies and probabilities.

	class			
	on time	late	very late	cancelled
weekday	$12/20 = 0.60$	$2/3 = 0.67$	$5/5 = 1.0$	$1/2 = 0.50$
summer	$10/20 = 0.50$	$1/3 = 0.33$	$1/5 = 0.20$	$1/2 = 0.50$
high	$5/20 = 0.25$	$2/3 = 0.67$	$2/5 = 0.40$	$1/2 = 0.50$
heavy	$1/20 = 0.05$	$2/3 = 0.67$	$3/5 = 0.60$	$1/2 = 0.50$

We can also construct a table of prior probabilities from the class frequency table, using the total frequency (30) as the denominator.

	class			
	on time	late	very late	cancelled
Prior Probability	$20/30 = 0.67$	$3/30 = 0.10$	$5/30 = 0.17$	$2/30 = 0.07$

We can now calculate a score for each possible classification as follows:

class = on time $0.67 * 0.60 * 0.50 * 0.25 * 0.05 = 0.0025$
class = late $0.10 * 0.67 * 0.33 * 0.67 * 0.67 = 0.0099$
class = very late $0.17 * 1.0 * 0.20 * 0.40 * 0.60 = 0.0082$
class = cancelled $0.07 * 0.50 * 0.50 * 0.50 * 0.50 = 0.0044$

The class with the largest score is selected, in this case class = *late*.

Self-assessment Exercise 14

Question 1

Setting a threshold of 0.5 has the effect of eliminating classifiers 4 and 5, leaving a reduced table as follows.

Classifier	Predicted Class	Vote for Class			Total
		A	B	C	
1	A	0.80	0.05	0.15	1.0
2	B	0.10	0.80	0.10	1.0
3	A	0.75	0.20	0.05	1.0
6	C	0.05	0.05	0.90	1.0
7	C	0.10	0.10	0.80	1.0
8	A	0.75	0.20	0.05	1.0
9	C	0.10	0.00	0.90	1.0
10	B	0.10	0.80	0.10	1.0
Total		2.75	2.20	3.05	8.0

The winning class is C.

Question 2

Increasing the threshold to 0.8 has the further effect of eliminating classifiers 3 and 8, leaving a further reduced table.

Classifier	Predicted Class	Vote for Class			Total
		A	B	C	
1	A	0.80	0.05	0.15	1.0
2	B	0.10	0.80	0.10	1.0
6	C	0.05	0.05	0.90	1.0
7	C	0.10	0.10	0.80	1.0
9	C	0.10	0.00	0.90	1.0
10	B	0.10	0.80	0.10	1.0
Total		1.25	1.80	2.95	6.0

The winning class is again C, this time by a much larger margin.

Self-assessment Exercise 15

Question 1

The average value of $B - A$ is 2.8.

Question 2

The standard error is 1.237 and the t value is 2.264.

Question 3

The t value is larger than the value in the 0.05 column of Figure 4 for 19 degrees of freedom, i.e. 2.093, so we can say that the performance of classifier B is significantly different from that of classifier A at the 5% level. As the answer to Question 1 is a positive value we can say that classifier B is significantly better than classifier A at the 5% level.

Question 4

The 95% confidence interval for the improvement offered by classifier B over classifier A is $2.8 \pm (2.093 * 1.237) = 2.8 \pm 2.589$, i.e. we can be 95% certain that the true average improvement in predictive accuracy lies between 0.211% and 5.389%.

Self-assessment Exercise 16

Question 1

Using the formulae for Confidence, Completeness, Support, Discriminability and RI given in Chapter 16, the values for the five rules are as follows.

Rule	Confid.	Complete	Support	Discrim.	RI
1	0.972	0.875	0.7	0.9	124.0
2	0.933	0.215	0.157	0.958	30.4
3	1.0	0.5	0.415	1.0	170.8
4	0.5	0.8	0.289	0.548	55.5
5	0.983	0.421	0.361	0.957	38.0

Question 2

Let us assume that the attribute w has the three values w_1, w_2 and w_3 and similarly for attributes x, y and z.

If we arbitrarily choose attribute w to be on the right-hand side of each rule, there are three possible types of rule:

IF ... THEN $w = w_1$
IF ... THEN $w = w_2$
IF ... THEN $w = w_3$

Let us choose one of these, say the first, and calculate how many possible left-hand sides there are for such rules.

The number of 'attribute = value' terms on the left-hand side can be one, two or three. We consider each case separately.

One term on left-hand side

There are three possible terms: x, y and z. Each has three possible values, so there are $3 \times 3 = 9$ possible left-hand sides, e.g.

IF $x = x_1$

Two terms on left-hand side

There are three ways in which a combination of two attributes may appear on the left-hand side (the order in which they appear is irrelevant): x and y, x and z, and y and z. Each attribute has three values, so for each pair of attributes there are $3 \times 3 = 9$ possible left-hand sides, e.g.

IF $x = x_1$ AND $y = y_1$

There are three possible pairs of attributes, so the total number of possible left-hand sides is $3 \times 9 = 27$.

Three terms on left-hand side

All three attributes x, y and z must be on the left-hand side (the order in which they appear is irrelevant). Each has three values, so there are $3 \times 3 \times 3 = 27$ possible left-hand sides, ignoring the order in which the attributes appear, e.g.

IF $x = x_1$ AND $y = y_1$ AND $z = z_1$

So for each of the three possible '$w = $ value' terms on the right-hand side, the total number of left-hand sides with one, two or three terms is $9 + 27 + 27 = 63$. Thus there are $3 \times 63 = 189$ possible rules with attribute w on the right-hand side.

The attribute on the right-hand side could be any of four possibilities (w, x, y and z) not just w. So the total possible number of rules is $4 \times 189 = 756$.

Self-assessment Exercise 17

Question 1

At the join step of the *Apriori-gen* algorithm, each member (set) is compared with every other member. If all the elements of the two members are identical except the right-most ones (i.e. if the first two elements are identical in the case of the sets of three elements specified in the Exercise), the union of the two sets is placed into C_4.

For the members of L_3 given the following sets of four elements are placed into C_4: $\{a, b, c, d\}$, $\{b, c, d, w\}$, $\{b, c, d, x\}$, $\{b, c, w, x\}$, $\{p, q, r, s\}$, $\{p, q, r, t\}$ and $\{p, q, s, t\}$.

At the prune step of the algorithm, each member of C_4 is checked to see whether all its subsets of 3 elements are members of L_3.

The results in this case are as follows.

Itemset in C_4	Subsets all in L_3?
$\{a, b, c, d\}$	Yes
$\{b, c, d, w\}$	No. $\{b, d, w\}$ and $\{c, d, w\}$ are not members of L_3
$\{b, c, d, x\}$	No. $\{b, d, x\}$ and $\{c, d, x\}$ are not members of L_3
$\{b, c, w, x\}$	No. $\{b, w, x\}$ and $\{c, w, x\}$ are not members of L_3
$\{p, q, r, s\}$	Yes
$\{p, q, r, t\}$	No. $\{p, r, t\}$ and $\{q, r, t\}$ are not members of L_3
$\{p, q, s, t\}$	No. $\{p, s, t\}$ and $\{q, s, t\}$ are not members of L_3

So $\{b, c, d, w\}$, $\{b, c, d, x\}$, $\{b, c, w, x\}$, $\{p, q, r, t\}$ and $\{p, q, s, t\}$ are removed by the prune step, leaving C_4 as $\{\{a, b, c, d\}, \{p, q, r, s\}\}$.

Question 2

The relevant formulae for support, confidence, lift and leverage for a database of 5000 transactions are:

support$(L \rightarrow R) =$ support$(L \cup R) =$ count$(L \cup R)/5000 = 3000/5000 = 0.6$

confidence$(L \rightarrow R) =$ count$(L \cup R)/$count$(L) = 3000/3400 = 0.882$

lift$(L \rightarrow R.) = 5000 \times$ confidence$(L \rightarrow R)/$count$(R) = 5000 \times 0.882/4000 = 1.103$

leverage$(L \rightarrow R) =$ support$(L \cup R) -$ support$(L) \times$ support(R)
$=$ count$(L \cup R)/5000 - ($count$(L)/5000) \times ($count$(R)/5000) = 0.056$

Self-assessment Exercise 18

Question 1

The conditional FP-tree for itemset $\{c\}$ is shown below.

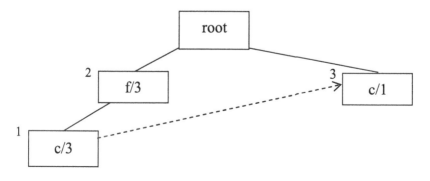

Question 2

The support count can be determined by following the link joining the two c nodes and adding the support counts associated with each of the nodes together. The total support count is $3 + 1 = 4$.

Question 3

As the support count is greater than or equal to 3, itemset $\{c\}$ is frequent.

Question 4

The contents of the four arrays corresponding to the conditional FP-tree for itemset c are given below.

$index$	$item$ $name$	$count$	$linkto$	$parent$		$oldindex$
1	c	3	3	2		1
2	f	3				2
3	c	1				9

$nodes2$ array

$oldindex$

$index$	$startlink2$	$lastlink$
p		
m		
a		
c	1	3
f	2	2
b		

link arrays

Self-assessment Exercise 19

Question 1

We begin by choosing three of the instances to form the initial centroids. We can do this in many possible ways, but it seems reasonable to select three instances that are fairly far apart. One possible choice is as follows.

	Initial	
	x	y
Centroid 1	2.3	8.4
Centroid 2	8.4	12.6
Centroid 3	17.1	17.2

In the following table the columns headed $d1$, $d2$ and $d3$ show the Euclidean distance of each of the 16 points from the three centroids. The column headed 'cluster' indicates the centroid closest to each point and thus the cluster to which it should be assigned.

	x	y	$d1$	$d2$	$d3$	cluster
1	10.9	12.6	9.6	2.5	7.7	2
2	2.3	8.4	0.0	7.4	17.2	1
3	8.4	12.6	7.4	0.0	9.8	2
4	12.1	16.2	12.5	5.2	5.1	3
5	7.3	8.9	5.0	3.9	12.8	2
6	23.4	11.3	21.3	15.1	8.6	3
7	19.7	18.5	20.1	12.7	2.9	3
8	17.1	17.2	17.2	9.8	0.0	3
9	3.2	3.4	5.1	10.6	19.6	1
10	1.3	22.8	14.4	12.4	16.8	2
11	2.4	6.9	1.5	8.3	17.9	1
12	2.4	7.1	1.3	8.1	17.8	1
13	3.1	8.3	0.8	6.8	16.6	1
14	2.9	6.9	1.6	7.9	17.5	1
15	11.2	4.4	9.8	8.7	14.1	2
16	8.3	8.7	6.0	3.9	12.2	2

We now reassign all the objects to the cluster to which they are closest and recalculate the centroid of each cluster. The new centroids are shown below.

	After first iteration	
	x	y
Centroid 1	2.717	6.833
Centroid 2	7.9	11.667
Centroid 3	18.075	15.8

We now calculate the distance of each object from the three new centroids. As before the column headed 'cluster' indicates the centroid closest to each point and thus the cluster to which it should be assigned.

x	y	$d1$	$d2$	$d3$	cluster
10.9	12.6	10.0	3.1	7.9	2
2.3	8.4	1.6	6.5	17.4	1
8.4	12.6	8.1	1.1	10.2	2
12.1	16.2	13.3	6.2	6.0	3
7.3	8.9	5.0	2.8	12.8	2

23.4	11.3	21.2	15.5	7.0	3
19.7	18.5	20.6	13.6	3.2	3
17.1	17.2	17.7	10.7	1.7	3
3.2	3.4	3.5	9.5	19.4	1
1.3	22.8	16.0	12.9	18.2	2
2.4	6.9	0.3	7.3	18.0	1
2.4	7.1	0.4	7.1	17.9	1
3.1	8.3	1.5	5.9	16.7	1
2.9	6.9	0.2	6.9	17.6	1
11.2	4.4	8.8	8.0	13.3	2
8.3	8.7	5.9	3.0	12.1	2

We now again reassign all the objects to the cluster to which they are closest and recalculate the centroid of each cluster. The new centroids are shown below.

	After second iteration	
	x	y
Centroid 1	2.717	6.833
Centroid 2	7.9	11.667
Centroid 3	18.075	15.8

These are unchanged from the first iteration, so the process terminates. The objects in the final three clusters are as follows.

Cluster 1: 2, 9, 11, 12, 13, 14

Cluster 2: 1, 3, 5, 10, 15, 16

Cluster 3: 4, 6, 7, 8

Question 2

In Section 19.3.1 the initial distance matrix between the six objects a, b, c, d, e and f is the following.

	a	b	c	d	e	f
a	0	12	6	3	25	4
b	12	0	19	8	14	15
c	6	19	0	12	5	18
d	3	8	12	0	11	9
e	25	14	5	11	0	7
f	4	15	18	9	7	0

The closest objects are those with the smallest non-zero distance value in the table. These are objects a and d which have a distance value of 3. We combine these into a single cluster of two objects which we call ad. We can now rewrite the distance matrix with rows a and d replaced by a single row ad and similarly for the columns.

As in Section 5.3.1, the entries in the matrix for the various distances between b, c, e and f obviously remain the same, but how should we calculate the entries in row and column ad?

	ad	b	c	e	f
ad	0	?	?	?	?
b	?	0	19	14	15
c	?	19	0	5	18
e	?	14	5	0	7
f	?	15	18	7	0

The question specifies that complete link clustering should be used. For this method the distance between two clusters is taken to be the longest distance from any member of one cluster to any member of the other cluster. On this basis the distance from ad to b is 12, the longer of the distance from a to b (12) and the distance from d to b (8) in the original distance matrix. The distance from ad to c is also 12, the longer of the distance from a to c (6) and the distance from d to c (12) in the original distance matrix. The complete distance matrix after the first merger is now as follows.

	ad	b	c	e	f
ad	0	12	12	25	9
b	12	0	19	14	15
c	12	19	0	5	18
e	25	14	5	0	7
f	9	15	18	7	0

The smallest non-zero value in this table is now 5, so we merge c and e giving ce.

The distance matrix now becomes:

	ad	b	ce	f
ad	0	12	25	9
b	12	0	19	15
ce	25	19	0	18
f	9	15	18	0

The distance from ad to ce is 25, the longer of the distance from c to ad (12) and the distance from e to ad (25) in the previous distance matrix. Other values are calculated in the same way.

The smallest non-zero in this distance matrix is now 9, so ad and f are merged giving adf. The distance matrix after this third merger is given below.

	adf	b	ce
adf	0	15	25
b	15	0	19
ce	25	19	0

Self-assessment Exercise 20

Question 1

The value of TFIDF is the product of two values, t_j and $\log_2(n/n_j)$, where t_j is the frequency of the term in the current document, n_j is the number of documents containing the term and n is the total number of documents.

For term 'dog' the value of TFIDF is $2 \times \log_2(1000/800) = 0.64$

For term 'cat' the value of TFIDF is $10 \times \log_2(1000/700) = 5.15$

For term 'man' the value of TFIDF is $50 \times \log_2(1000/2) = 448.29$

For term 'woman' the value of TFIDF is $6 \times \log_2(1000/30) = 30.35$

The small number of documents containing the term 'man' accounts for the high TFIDF value.

Question 2

To normalise a vector, each element needs to be divided by its length, which is the square root of the sum of the squares of all the elements. For vector $(20, 10, 8, 12, 56)$ the length is the square root of $20^2 + 10^2 + 8^2 + 12^2 + 56^2 = \sqrt{3844} = 62$. So the normalised vector is $(20/62, 10/62, 8/62, 12/62, 56/62)$, i.e. $(0.323, 0.161, 0.129, 0.194, 0.903)$.

For vector $(0, 15, 12, 8, 0)$ the length is $\sqrt{433} = 20.809$. The normalised form is $(0, 0.721, 0.577, 0.384, 0)$.

The distance between the two normalised vectors can be calculated using the dot product formula as the sum of the products of the corresponding pairs of values, i.e. $0.323 \times 0 + 0.161 \times 0.721 + 0.129 \times 0.577 + 0.194 \times 0.384 + 0.903 \times 0 = 0.265$.

Self-assessment Exercise 21

Question 1

The TDIDT algorithm relies on having all the data available for repeated use as the decision tree is built. As each node is split on an attribute it is necessary to re-scan the data in order to construct the frequency tables for each of the descendant nodes.

Question 2

The use of a Hoeffding Bound is intended to make the algorithm make more cautious decisions about splitting on an attribute. Once a node has been split on an attribute it cannot be unsplit or resplit, so it is important to avoid making bad decisions about splitting, even at the risk of occasionally not making a good one.

Question 3

After splitting on an attribute at a node the algorithm creates an empty frequency table for each attribute in the current attributes array for each of the descendant nodes as it has no means of re-scanning the data to construct tables with the correct values (see solution to Question 1). If there is a large amount of data – and assuming that the underlying model does not change – newly-arriving records should accumulate values in the frequency tables that are in approximately the same proportions as those of the frequency tables that would have been produced if all the data had been stored.

Question 4

The candidate attribute for splitting is *att3* as it has the largest value of Information Gain. The difference between this value and the second largest (which corresponds to attribute *att4*) is $1.3286 - 1.0213 = 0.3073$.

The formula for the Hoeffding Bound is given in Section 21.5 as:

$$R * \sqrt{\frac{\ln(1/\delta)}{2 * nrec}}$$

In this formula *nrec* is the number of records sorted to the given node, which is the sum of the values in the *classtotals*[Z] array, i.e. 100.

The Greek letter δ is used to represent the value of 1-*Prob*. From Figure 21.12 we can see that the value of $\ln(1/\delta)$ is 6.9078.

The value R corresponds to the range of values that Information Gain can take at node Z, which we are assuming is the same as the 'initial entropy' at the node. We can calculate this using the values in the *classtotals* array. These are in the same proportions as the values in the example in Section 21.4 and so give the same result, i.e. 1.4855 (to 4 decimal places).

Putting these values into the formula for the Hoeffding Bound we obtain the value $1.4855 * \sqrt{6.9078/200} = 0.2761$. The difference between IG(*att3*) and IG(*att4*) is 0.3073, which is larger than the value of the Hoeffding Bound so we will decide to split on attribute *att3* at node Z.

Self-assessment Exercise 22

Question 1

The aim of the testing phase is to determine whether any of the internal nodes in the main tree can be replaced by one of its alternate nodes, so if none of the internal nodes has an alternate a testing phase is certain to have no effect. This does no harm apart from testing records unnecessarily. The system can avoid it by maintaining a count of the number of alternate nodes assigned to internal nodes in the main tree and only entering a testing phase if the count is positive. When an internal node is substituted by one of its alternates, the count needs to be reduced by the total number of alternates for that node which may be greater than one.

Question 2

The *hitcount* and *acvCounts* arrays are incremented at each of the nodes through which each incoming record passes on its path from the root to a leaf node, so there is multiple counting of records. By contrast the *classtotals* array has precisely one entry for each record in the current sliding window, at the leaf node to which it was sorted when it was processed (which may since have been split on an attribute and become an internal node).

Self-assessment Exercise 23

Question 1

The links to output node out2 from hidden nodes hid1, hid2 and hid3 have weights -0.4, 0.4 and 0.5 respectively. The link from the output bias node has weight 0.1. So, the weighted sum value of out2 is given by the formula

Wout2 $= 0.9 \times (-0.4) + 0.65 \times 0.4 + 0.1 \times 0.5 + 0.1 = 0.05$.

The transformed value, Tout2, is sigmoid(0.05) $= 0.5125$ (to 4 decimal places).

The transformed value Tout1 is calculated as sigmoid(Wout1). Without knowing any more about the values of the input nodes, we have no way of knowing what the value of Wout1 is, but whatever it is, the sigmoid function will transform it into a value in the range from 0 to 1.

Question 2

The values are not probabilities and do not necessarily add up to one. It is probably best to regard the calculated transformed value for an output node just as an estimate that the classification is the one corresponding to that node, under the one hot encoding system. The largest value will determine the predicted classification.

Index

© Springer-Verlag London Ltd., part of Springer Nature 2020
M. Bramer, *Principles of Data Mining*, Undergraduate Topics
in Computer Science, DOI 10.1007/978-1-4471-7493-6

Printed in the United States
By Bookmasters